Combating Weapons of Mass Destruction

STUDIES IN SECURITY AND INTERNATIONAL AFFAIRS

Combating Weapons of Mass Destruction

The Future of International Nonproliferation Policy

EDITED BY *Nathan E. Busch and Daniel H. Joyner*

The University of Georgia Press | *Athens and London*

© 2009 by the University of Georgia Press
Athens, Georgia 30602
www.ugapress.org
All rights reserved
Set in Electra by Graphic Composition, Inc.

Printed digitally in the United States of America

Library of Congress Cataloging-in-Publication Data

Combating weapons of mass destruction : the future
of international nonproliferation policy / edited by
Nathan E. Busch and Daniel H. Joyner.
    p. cm.
Includes bibliographical references and index.
ISBN-13: 978-0-8203-3010-5 (hardcover)
ISBN-10: 0-8203-3010-8 (hardcover)
ISBN-13: 978-0-8203-3221-5 (pbk.)
ISBN-10: 0-8203-3221-6 (pbk.)
1. Nuclear nonproliferation. I. Busch, Nathan E.,
1971– II. Joyner, Daniel.
JZ5675.C65 2008
327.1'747—dc22   2008035443

British Library Cataloging-in-Publication Data available

Contents

Foreword

Mitchell B. Reiss

International nonproliferation regimes do not lack for challenges, as the collection of essays in this volume attests. Broadly construed as interlocking networks of bilateral and multilateral alliances, security assurances, treaties, agreements, regulations, voluntary controls, and norms, these regimes have been painstakingly constructed over more than six decades. Historically, they have withstood both the skeptics who predicted that proliferation was inevitable, and those episodic failures that seemed to prove, albeit temporarily, that the skeptics might be right. Yet, on the whole, these regimes have consistently proved more potent, resilient, and flexible than anticipated.

Nonetheless, we appear to be experiencing another periodic eruption of skepticism over whether the regimes can adapt, survive, and perhaps even prosper in the prevailing conditions of the twenty-first century. Distressingly, this time the skeptics may have the better argument. They marshal numerous examples—institutional and structural, regional and local—to support their claims that the regime is under fresh assault. A short list would include the following:

- ongoing political and technical hurdles to corralling and safeguarding the nuclear materials and weapons of the former Soviet Union;
- concerns over the safety and security of Pakistan's nuclear arsenal;
- anxieties over the spread of increasingly sophisticated, dual-use biotechnology capabilities;
- spread of medium- and long-range missiles around the world;
- fears over the possible acquisition of nuclear weapons or radioactive materials by terrorist groups; and
- variegated challenges to the Nuclear Nonproliferation Treaty (NPT), International Atomic Energy Agency (IAEA) inspections system, and regional security by the nuclear ambitions of North Korea and Iran.

These developments have led some observers to adopt what Scott Sagan has decried as a "creeping fatalism" about the ability of the United States and other members of the international community to prevent future proliferation.[1]

Fueling this fatalism is the sense that the regimes' institutions and arrangements are no longer adequate. If progress has been made in the past fifteen years, as Sharon Squassoni argues, "to tighten loopholes, build up political consensus, and enhance technical capabilities to detect noncompliance," the shortfall must lie elsewhere. It does: with enforcement.

During the past twenty years, enforcing compliance with the regimes' agreements, regulations, and norms has lagged. North Korea and Iran have flagrantly defied their IAEA safeguard agreements and hindered inspections, while India was allowed an exceptional, privileged arrangement that will require amending nuclear supplier guidelines and U.S. nonproliferation laws. The Soviet Union and now Russia have failed to comply with the Biological and Toxin Weapons Convention. These actions have come at a high cost—the loss of confidence across the entire nonproliferation agenda.

To be sure, recent innovative accomplishments have strengthened enforcement. The Proliferation Security Initiative (PSI) is a noteworthy contribution to global efforts to deter the trade in weapons of mass destruction (WMD) technology and advertise the concept of inflicting real penalties on proliferators, even though it is not yet responsible for successfully interdicting a single vessel. Its lesser-known cousin, the Illicit Activities Initiative (IAI), has had far more success in freezing financial assets and disrupting distribution networks; it has literally raised the price of doing this type of business for both state and nonstate actors. The U.S. Treasury Department has identified key sources of funding for proliferation activities and moved swiftly to sanction those financial institutions and threaten others that may want to do business with them. And in Resolution 1540, the UN Security Council made the proliferation of all weapons of mass destruction by and to nonstate actors a violation of international law, called on states to maintain appropriate accounting and physical protection measures of WMD-related items, and requested the creation of "effective" export control laws, even if it then relied on states to self-enforce its provisions. These measures are welcome and long overdue.

On the whole, however, recent negative trends in enforcement have outweighed the positive ones. Regrettably, the problem of enforcement is likely to get worse before it gets better.

Enforcement Deficiencies: An Old Story . . .

Social scientists have long studied the dilemmas involved with collective action, negative spillovers, externalities, and socially optimal outcomes. Among their observations, they have realized that "For players to believe that cheating is not beneficial from a long-term perspective, cheating should be detected quickly and the punishment that follows . . . should be sufficiently swift, sure and painful."[2]

Consequently, enforcing compliance with nonproliferation agreements, pledges, codes, rules, and regulations has been a longstanding challenge, even as it has been recognized that it is essential to the long-term success of the regimes. The reasons are not hard to find. Countries sometimes have different assessments over allegations that a state is cheating on its nonproliferation commitments, perhaps not trusting the evidence presented.[3] Or countries may share the same assessment but believe that the cheating is not an urgent problem, that the cheater is not proximate and is therefore less threatening, or that the cheating is not substantial enough to rise to the level of a material breach. Or countries may share the same assessment but have competing interests or other priorities that mitigate against their banding together to enforce a group punishment. The social science literature here is instructive. "The inflicting of punishment is itself a collective action game and suffers from the same temptation to 'shirk'; that is, not participate in the punishment."[4] In this case, countries do not want to pay the price of absorbing particular, tangible, short-term pain (the loss of trading partners and market share, for example) for the sake of a collective, more abstract, and longer-term gain.

Many of these scenarios encompass elements of what has been termed the free rider problem. Again, from social science: "In large group games, diffusion of responsibility can lead to behavior in which individual persons wait for others to take action and free ride off the benefits of that action. If help is needed, it is less likely to be given at all as the size of the group available to provide it grows."[5]

The implications are stark for nonproliferation efforts. Even where there is widespread agreement that a country is cheating, that the cheating is substantial, and that the threat is both urgent and proximate, there is a structural incentive to free ride and allow other countries, or a single country, to act and assume both the risks and the consequences.

. . . but with New and Worse Variations

In many cases, that single country is the United States. Unfortunately, new factors and recent trends promise to make it even more difficult in the future than in the past for the United States to redress the free rider problem and assemble collective action to enforce compliance with nonproliferation commitments.

Trust is essential to forging and leading a collective enforcement effort. Yet America's standing around the world has rarely been lower than it is at the moment, as confirmed by the Pew Global Attitudes Project, the Transatlantic Trends by the German Marshall Fund, and other polls. This negative image has real foreign policy implications because the success of U.S. foreign policy depends, at least partially, on Washington's ability to persuade friends, allies, and even adversaries to trust our judgment and support, or at least not oppose, our preferences. In short, credibility matters.

With respect to enforcement, America's diminished stature makes other countries more reluctant to accept U.S. leadership. Other countries must have confidence that the evidence is accurate, the breach serious, and the threat urgent. Here the shortcomings of the American intelligence assessment of Iraq's WMD program gravely damaged trust in American judgment, competence, and credibility; it has cast a long shadow. This shadow was lengthened in November 2007 with the release of the National Intelligence Estimate (NIE) on Iran's nuclear intentions and capabilities. The NIE contradicted key judgments from its May 2005 assessment, claiming new information, and downplayed the threat posed by Iran's nuclear weapons program, an impression that the national security advisor and President George W. Bush tried to counter during subsequent press briefings. Many observers were left confused. None believed that the administration enhanced its credibility or reputation for competence.

Devaluing U.S. credibility further has been loose rhetoric from senior Bush administration officials. Numerous intemperate, ill-considered, or overstated comments on the Iraq war during the past few years have eroded public trust in the United States and abroad. On the nuclear side, the administration has expressly staked out hard-line positions with respect to North Korea, only to backtrack after Pyongyang launched ballistic missiles and tested a nuclear device. Its handling of the Banco Delta Asia case perhaps best illustrates the dangers of loose rhetoric. In September 2005, the Bush administration initially froze bank accounts that contained proceeds allegedly from illicit activities and announced it would not release them. Over the ensuing twelve months, the administration's position evolved from not releasing any of the proceeds to releasing some of the proceeds to pleading with Pyongyang to take all the proceeds in the accounts so that it would return to the Six Party Talks. This record is not one to instill confidence in America's judgment or competence.

Enforcement is also complicated, in at least two ways, by globalization. First, the forces of globalization make it easier for anyone, ranging from sovereign states to "super-empowered individuals," to use Thomas Friedman's phrase, to acquire nuclear technology. There are no nuclear secrets anymore, at least none that presents insuperable obstacles for would-be nuclear aspirants. (Recall that as far back as 1964, the *Los Alamos Primer* revealed many of the technical details of atomic weapons design; the November 1979 and January 1980 editions of the *Progressive* did the same for hydrogen weapons.) Precision-guided machine tools and specialized technologies are available, both licitly and illicitly, all over the world. To cite but one example, a decade ago who would have thought that Malaysia would be an important source of technology for the A. Q. Khan network? As Scott Jones, Michael Beck, and Seema Gahlaut write in their chapter on strategic trade controls and international security, "there are now several dozen international suppliers of high-technology items." More suppliers make it more difficult to shut down supply lines, especially if they cooperate with one another to undermine or avoid export controls.

Second, globalization hinders enforcement efforts because states increasingly have far-flung economic interests that may slow, or prevent entirely, their willingness to sign on to enforcement measures. The trading relationships that China (oil), Russia (nuclear technology, military hardware), and Europe (across the board) have with Iran have complicated American efforts to adopt tougher sanctions in the UN Security Council.

Enforcement may also be more difficult in the coming years because the scope of the challenge may be greater. Over the coming decades, the world will see an increasing global demand for energy, a demand that is expected to be 50 percent higher in 2030 than today.[6] Most of this growth will come from the developing world, driven by the projected economic rise of China and India, as well as newcomers such as Brazil. Environmental concerns are likely to cause a reduction in reliance on fossil fuels and the promotion of energy sources that do not contribute to global warming.[7] One response to this increased energy demand and heightened environmental sensitivity will be a greater reliance on nuclear power. There are already signs that the debate about "energy futures" has changed in recent years, and it is likely that an increasing number of countries will see nuclear power as part of their national energy portfolio. Some of these countries will want to ensure their energy independence by mastering indigenously all aspects of the nuclear fuel cycle, including enrichment and reprocessing. And at least some of these countries can be expected to hedge or openly renege on their nuclear nonproliferation commitments, thereby threatening the regime unless enforcement can be "sufficiently swift, sure and painful."[8]

Ameliorative Steps

Without a sea change in the way the international community conducts its nonproliferation policies, a traditional disincentive to WMD acquisition—fear of penalties and retribution—will continue to wither, and with it the international nonproliferation regimes.

To be sure, there are some ameliorative steps the United States and other leading members of these regimes could take. Senior American officials, especially the president, need to be more careful with public statements and declaratory policy. The United States could also work more diligently to build consensus for enforcement, demonstrating a decent respect for the opinions of others. In addition, policymakers need to think through more carefully the consequences of policy choices that seek to enforce nonproliferation commitments. In October 2002, for example, the Bush administration confronted North Korea over its uranium enrichment activities. Pyongyang immediately moved to withdraw from the NPT, boot out IAEA inspectors, and resume reprocessing its spent fuel to separate plutonium for additional nuclear devices. Because even weak adversaries have options, "first, do no harm" should be a useful maxim to guide nonproliferation as well as caregivers.

Practically speaking, it is unclear how faithfully any American administration can heed this advice or how much more effective international enforcement would become even if it did so. But if we are entering a period of weaker enforcement mechanisms for regime offenders, there are three main policy implications.

First, where there are fewer sticks, there will need to be juicier carrots to prevent proliferation. If unable or unwilling to inflict penalties on cheaters, the United States and the international community will have to offer much greater incentives—economic, financial, diplomatic, and security—for countries to abandon their nuclear ambitions. Yet in certain contexts, this type of behavior could be characterized by domestic critics in highly charged terms, such as "bribery" or "appeasement." This, in turn, will make it more difficult for democratic governments to deliver on this policy.

Second, if sufficient inducements are not possible for domestic or other reasons, then the United States would be left with few options. One remaining option would be unilateral enforcement: the use of U.S. military force to eliminate the WMD program in the target state. This option presumes that Washington has high confidence about the location of the proscribed activities, that it has the operational capability and munitions to destroy them, and that it can manage the collateral damage, within the state, the region, and to America's interests and image around the world.

Third, if the international community is unwilling to enforce compliance with nonproliferation agreements, rules, and norms, and the United States recoils from preemptive military strikes, the policy consequences then become straightforward: the world will see more states with weapons of mass destruction.

The Current Volume

This volume of essays, compiled and contributed to by Professors Nathan Busch and Daniel Joyner, is a significant contribution to scholarly consideration of all aspects of WMD proliferation. Its authors include some of the world's leading specialists in their sub-fields of study, and the composite result of their work is an authoritative and highly useful consideration of the challenges facing national and international nonproliferation policies and regimes, including some novel proposals for strengthening their soundness and effectiveness. This volume will be an important and influential reference work for all those interested in strengthening international efforts in combating the proliferation of weapons of mass destruction.

Notes

1. See Scott Sagan, "How to Keep the Bomb from Iran," *Foreign Affairs* 85, no. 5 (September/October 2006): 45.

2. Avinash K. Dixit and Susan Skeath, *Games of Strategy*, 2nd ed. (New York: W. W. Norton, 1999), 396.

3. There is also the problem that much information is classified and is only selectively released to allies, the IAEA, or the public.

4. Dixit and Skeath, *Games of Strategy*, 397.

5. Ibid., 419.

6. See International Energy Agency, *World Energy Outlook 2006* (Paris: International Energy Agency, 2006); Fatih Birol, "World Energy Prospects and Challenges," *Australian Economic Review* 39, no. 2 (June 2006): 190–95; and Energy Information Administration, *International Energy Outlook 2007* (Washington, DC: Department of Energy, 2007), http://www.eia.doe.gov/oiaf/ieo/ieorefcase.html.

7. See John M. Deutsch and Ernest J. Moniz, "The Nuclear Option," *Scientific American* 295, no. 3 (September 2006): 76; Max Schulz, "Nuclear Power Is the Future," *Wilson Quarterly* 30, no. 4 (Autumn 2006): 59–63; and W. Conrad Holton, "Power Surge: Renewed Interest in Nuclear Energy," *Environmental Health Perspectives* 113, no. 11 (November 2005): A742–A749.

8. There is a potential paradox here. Without sufficient enforcement actions, the regime collapses. With too many enforcement actions, the regime risks suffering from enforcement "fatigue."

Combating Weapons of Mass Destruction

Nonproliferation at a Crossroads

Nathan E. Busch

and Daniel H. Joyner

The spread of WMD (weapons of mass destruction) technologies poses one of the greatest threats to international peace and security in the modern era. Since the detonation of the first atomic bomb in Hiroshima in 1945, and its evidence of the destructive capabilities of nonconventional weaponry, the international community has been concerned about the spread and threat of the use of nuclear, chemical, and biological weapons by both states and nonstate actors.

In order to combat this threat, states have constructed policies, and both political and legal normative frameworks, at the national and international levels aimed at regulating the production and stockpiling of WMD-sensitive materials within states, as well as their spread through the increasingly globalized channels of international trade to other states and to nonstate actors.

The character and orientation of these nonproliferation policies have undergone development and significant change, however, due to changing world political and economic circumstances. The ending of the Cold War brought about a realignment of state interests and alliances, and forced a restructuring of the nonproliferation policies and laws of many states and to the structure of international organizations and treaty regimes. In this new strategic environment, some states perceived the interest and the opportunity to acquire the capabilities to produce weapons of mass destruction.

The dangers of proliferation have increased in subsequent years. States recognized as nuclear weapons states (NWS) under the 1968 Nuclear Nonproliferation Treaty (NPT) seem determined not to move toward complete disarmament, per their obligations under Article VI of the NPT. Additionally, a number of states not recognized as NWS under the NPT, including India, Pakistan, North Korea, Israel, and Iran, have continued to acquire technologies that would allow them to produce nuclear weapons and in a number of cases have in fact joined the club of de facto nuclear weapons–possessing states.

In addition to the potential destabilization produced by nuclear proliferation to these states themselves, as horizontal proliferation continues to new regions of the globe there is an additional danger that such proliferation could create incentives for yet more states to begin acquiring such weapons technologies. As George Tenet, the director of Central Intelligence at the time, put it, "The desire for nuclear weapons is on the upsurge. Additional countries may decide to seek nuclear weapons as it becomes clear their neighbors and regional rivals are already doing so. The 'domino theory' of the 21st century may well be nuclear."[1]

In addition to the specter of nuclear proliferation, there are also increasing concerns regarding the spread of chemical and biological weapons. These weapons, while not as devastating as nuclear weapons, could nevertheless cause severe casualties, undermine troop morale, and create public hysteria in the event of their use. Despite the clear importance of preventing the proliferation of these weapons, however, the regimes that have been created for this end, particularly the Biological and Toxin Weapons Convention (BWC) and the Chemical Weapons Convention (CWC), have significant shortcomings with their verification and enforcement mechanisms. Moreover, given the dual-use nature of many of the technologies that could be used to produce chemical and biological weapons, it is increasingly difficult to identify covert programs.

The threats posed by WMD proliferation were further driven home on September 11, 2001, when the terrorist attacks by al Qaeda raised concerns that international terrorist groups with radical ideologies might be interested in using WMD to carry out mass casualty attacks. Osama bin Laden has stated that he considers acquiring WMD to be a religious duty, and terrorist groups have reportedly attempted to acquire WMD technologies on several occasions.[2] John Negroponte, the U.S. director of National Intelligence, summarized these threats in 2006: "Al-Qa'ida remains interested in acquiring chemical, biological, radiological, and nuclear materials or weapons to attack the United States, U.S. troops, and U.S. interests worldwide."[3]

The ability of the international community to stem the tide of proliferation has been further constrained by a number of troubling trends. Since the end of the Cold War, there have been increasing opportunities for aspiring states and terrorist groups to acquire WMD technologies. States in the former Soviet Union have had significant difficulties in maintaining control over their nuclear, biological, and chemical weapons technologies, as the security systems that protected these technologies have eroded.[4] Moreover, revelations in early 2004 of a long-standing clandestine smuggling ring in nuclear materials and related dual-use goods, headed by the father of Pakistan's nuclear programs, Dr. Abdul Qadeer

Khan, have made states increasingly aware of the effects of globalized markets in facilitating the spread of WMD-related technologies.[5]

As John Negroponte has explained:

> Our adversaries have more access to acquire and more opportunities to deliver such weapons than in the past. Technologies, often dual-use, move freely in our globalized economy, as do the scientific personnel who design them. So it is more difficult for us to track efforts to acquire those components and production technologies that are so widely available. The potential dangers of proliferation are so grave that we must do everything possible to discover and disrupt attempts by those who seek to acquire materials and weapons.[6]

These and other more recent challenges to traditional nonproliferation policies and regimes have been added to long-standing problems, which have consistently bedeviled efforts to effectively coordinate national nonproliferation policies. These problems include the nonuniversality of the nonproliferation regimes system and the problem of secondary proliferation, or proliferation by states and other actors outside of the established international normative frameworks.

As the United States and the international community attempt to address these issues, a number of critical questions arise. What are the capabilities of international terrorists to acquire these weapons? What steps can the international community take to prevent the acquisition of these weapons technologies by states and nonstate actors of concern? How can the international community maintain or strengthen the existing international nonproliferation regimes to improve verification techniques and to ensure universal compliance with the regimes? What further steps should be taken to assist Russia in controlling its nuclear weapons and related technologies? What steps can, or should, be taken to persuade proliferating states such as North Korea to renounce their WMD programs? To what extent and under what circumstances should states be willing to use force to prevent states from acquiring WMD?

This book tackles some of these major questions by gathering together the thoughts of some of the world's leading scholars and policymakers on WMD nonproliferation. These contributors identify obstacles to the effectiveness of nonproliferation policies across a range of issue areas and regional particularities and propose future directions for policy and lawmaking to strengthen existing nonproliferation regimes and meet the challenges these regimes face.

The first section of this book focuses on framing the primary threats posed by WMD proliferation and WMD terrorism. In chapters 1 and 2, Joseph F. Pilat and Charles D. Ferguson provide comprehensive examinations of the threat to international security posed by the proliferation of nuclear, biological, and chemical weapons to aspiring states and terrorist groups. Arguing that we must correctly identify the risks before calibrating an appropriate response, Pilat provides an initial threat assessment by examining the general dangers posed by WMD proliferation, obstacles in nonproliferation regimes, and the primary political issues that will need to be tackled if these threats are to be addressed. Ferguson explains the primary concerns associated with WMD terrorism, including the different types of weapons and methods that terrorists might attempt to employ, the capabilities of terrorists in carrying out such attacks, and the potential consequences of these types of terrorist attacks.

In the second part of the book, John Simpson, Julian Perry Robinson, John Hart and Vitaly Fedchenko, and Scott A. Jones, Michael D. Beck, and Seema Gahlaut analyze the challenges facing existing nonproliferation treaties and other normative regimes, including the NPT, the CWC, the BWC and related inspection and verification regimes, and multilateral strategic trade control regimes. These regimes comprise the central institutional elements of traditional nonproliferation efforts which have been pursued by the international community. However, each has encountered profound difficulties in implementation and enforcement. These chapters assess the strengths and shortcomings of these regimes and recommend steps that might be taken in order to address the challenges to effectiveness they face.

The third part of the book provides an analysis of the steps that some states have taken to respond to the challenges faced by the traditional system of nonproliferation law and policy, by shifting emphasis within their national policies away from nonproliferation treaties and regimes and toward more forceful, proactive, and sometimes unilateral policies of counterproliferation. James R. Holmes and Andrew C. Winner examine the Proliferation Security Initiative, which coordinates efforts to search and seize suspect shipments of WMD-related materials and technologies. M. Elaine Bunn examines the role that force and the threat of force will continue to play in U.S. and international counterproliferation policies, particularly to preempt WMD proliferation. Daniel H. Joyner examines this trend toward counterproliferation approaches in light of the rules of international law.

Finally, a number of chapters in the volume are devoted to consideration of specific case studies presenting some of the most critical current challenges to international nonproliferation policy. Ian Anthony, Seema Gahlaut, Bates Gill, Jonathan D. Pollack, Sharon Squassoni, Elizabeth Turpen and Brian Finlay, and Nathan E. Busch and James R. Holmes examine, respectively, the European perspective on nonproliferation and counterproliferation, proliferation concerns in East and South Asia, the North Korean and Iranian nuclear crises, and the challenges posed by weaknesses in Russia's ability to prevent theft of its nuclear weapons and related materials.

As the world enters the twenty-first century, understanding the problems of WMD proliferation currently facing states and the international community as a whole is of the greatest importance. The present and future direction of policy-making and lawmaking both at the national and international level in the area of WMD proliferation will have profound implications for the future of international security. It is the hope of the editors of this volume that the chapters herein will assist policymakers in identifying the most pressing challenges to nonproliferation efforts and in pointing the way forward for the pursuit of enlightened nonproliferation policy in the future.

Notes

1. George Tenet, "The Worldwide Threat in 2003: Evolving Dangers in a Complex World," testimony before the Senate Select Committee on Intelligence, February 11, 2003, https://www.cia.gov/news-information/speeches-testimony/2003/dci_speech_02112003.html.

2. Benjamin Weiser, "Bin Laden Tried to Develop Nuclear Weapons, U.S. Says," *New York Times*, September 26, 1998; Michael Grunwald and Vernon Loeb, "Charges Filed against Bin Laden," *Washington Post*, November 5, 1998, A17.

3. John Negroponte, "Threat Assessment of the Director of National Intelligence for the Senate Armed Services Committee," February 28, 2006, http://www.dni.gov/testimonies/20060228_testimony.htm.

4. Matthew Bunn and Anthony Wier, *Securing the Bomb 2006: The New Global Imperatives* (Cambridge, MA: Belfer Center, Harvard University, and Washington, DC: Nuclear Threat Initiative, July 2006; Nathan Busch, "Russian Roulette: The Continuing Relevance of Russia to the Nuclear Proliferation Debate," *Security Studies* 11, no. 3 (Spring 2002): 44–90.

5. See, for example, David Albright and Corey Hinderstein, "Unraveling the A. Q. Khan and Future Proliferation Networks," *Washington Quarterly* 28, no. 2 (Spring 2005): 111–28.

6. Negroponte, "Threat Assessment."

PART ONE

Framing the Issues

CHAPTER ONE

Dealing with Proliferation and Terrorism Involving WMD

Joseph F. Pilat

At the end of the Cold War, there was a prediction concerning the end of history.[1] History never disappeared, but any belief that it had was dissolved as history reasserted itself in bloody post–Cold War struggles in the former Yugoslavia, Rwanda, and elsewhere in the 1990s.[2]

At the same time, based in part on the end of Eastern Bloc state support and a brief decline in the number of attacks as seen in the statistics compiled by the U.S. Department of State, some observers speculated that international terrorism was ending as well.[3] Long before the brutal terrorist attacks of September 11, 2001, bombings in Nairobi, Dar es Salaam, Omagh, and Moscow belied this naïve belief.[4]

The proliferation of weapons of mass destruction (WMD) did not appear to be coming to an end at this time. Iraqi development and use of chemical weapons and the post–Gulf War revelations of extensive Iraqi nuclear and biological weapons programs, along with North Korea's nuclear program and the persistent problems of the three Nuclear Nonproliferation Treaty (NPT) holdout states—India, Israel, and Pakistan—illustrated the difficult proliferation cases confronting the world. But a series of developments—the disarmament of Iraq under the United Nations Special Commission on Iraq (UNSCOM), the conclusion of the Chemical Weapons Convention (CWC), the denuclearization of South Africa, Belarus, Kazakhstan, and Ukraine, and the indefinite extension of the NPT in 1995—led some to think the problem was waning, especially in the nuclear realm.[5] This perception shifted dramatically in 1998, following the nuclear tests in South Asia, and was later reinforced by intelligence reports on Iraq, revelations about North Korean and Iranian noncompliance, the discovery of the A. Q. Khan network, the North Korean nuclear test, and the like.[6]

The collapse of the Soviet Union and the Warsaw Pact also led to speculations about the changing role of nuclear weapons. It was held by many that these weapons, which had dominated military and strategic thinking during the Cold War, would become a diminishing element of the backdrop, or background, of international relations, with their role limited exclusively to deterring nuclear weapon use.[7] The belief they might be abolished altogether—in an end of nuclear history—grew at this time in some quarters.[8]

There have been significant, successful efforts over the last fifteen years to reduce the number and roles of nuclear weapons through arms accords and unilateral actions, to rethink deterrence in light of transformed U.S.-Russian relations, and to diminish the nuclear dimension of great power competition. But, in this area as in others, the world of the early twenty-first century is not what was predicted by many in the 1990s.

Predictions today look very different from those of fifteen years ago. In the context of rising regional instability and conflict, along with increased incidents of global terrorism, in a dynamic, uncertain security environment, emerging nuclear and other WMD threats—both proliferation and terrorism—are seen as growing dangers giving rise to increasing global insecurity.

Many believe today that additional states as well as nonstate actors will obtain a nuclear-weapon capability or nuclear weapons, and that these weapons are more likely to be used than in the past. It has been argued that at least the terrorists are undeterrable: "If they have them, they'll use them."[9]

Assessing the Threats: A Worst-Case Scenario

One scenario—retro to the 1940s and 1950s—invokes the notion of nuclear anarchy or a "nuclear-armed crowd," that is, a vast nuclear-armed group of nations due to an anticipated action-reaction phenomena extending from the United States and Soviet Union to Swaziland. What would this scenario look like today, expanding the scenario to other WMD and taking into account the developments of the last fifty years?

The most striking feature of this world is a climate of pervasive insecurity marked by widespread WMD proliferation and acts of terrorism. To survive amid the insecurity, all states that can do so engage in the development of latent WMD capabilities as a hedge. But for many states this approach will not be viewed as sufficient. These states will move to develop and deploy nuclear and other weapons of mass destruction. As more and more states take this path, there is a reversal of nuclear arms reductions and the emergence of new nuclear arms races in troubled regions. More widely, the hopes of eliminating biological and chemical weapons will disappear as states increasingly see them as "poor man's" counters to nuclear arms. In conjunction with the proliferation of offensive weapons, there will be a rise in the numbers and in the significance of defenses, both active and passive.

The world depicted here will witness the collapse of the global nonproliferation regimes, including the NPT, the International Atomic Energy Agency (IAEA), the CWC, and other treaties and institutions or, more likely, their increasing irrelevance. As the regimes fade as a result of spiraling proliferation, their decline will exacerbate the proliferation problem. As well, the loss of these pillars of world order will result in the diminishment and ultimate disappearance of the normative value invested in them, along with questions raised about the authority and legitimacy of ad hoc, self-help actions including acts of interdiction, preemption, and prevention. Commerce in the biological and chemical areas will be seen as increasingly dangerous and deeply constrained with horrific human costs. Even more, there will be growing concerns about the dangers of utilizing nuclear energy, except under the most extraordinary security; this perception will end all talk of a nuclear renaissance and have grave economic, environmental, and other consequences.

The developments and trend lines from which the scenario is extrapolated are familiar, and certainly worrisome. The proliferation problem today is serious. There have been growing concerns about increasing proliferation dangers, including rogue states and terrorists. The prospects for WMD terrorism are seen to be rising—concern over a proliferation/terrorism nexus after 9/11 has never been higher. But, the threat is not new, even though perceptions have shifted during the last decades.

Shifting Perceptions of the Threat

Concern over nuclear proliferation is as old as the nuclear age. For the past sixty years, and especially since the 1970s, the proliferation of nuclear weapons has been seen as a serious concern in the United States and other states. Yet, unlike the threat of the Soviet Union's strategic nuclear forces during the Cold War, little attention was devoted to the military and strategic aspects of this threat. The legacy of the Baruch Plan and Eisenhower's Atoms-for-Peace program—early U.S. -led efforts to control nuclear power—was to see proliferation primarily as a misuse of peaceful nuclear energy activities, which were promoted as an incentive designed to forestall military nuclear programs.[10] From this largely technical-legal perspective on the problem, the literature on nuclear proliferation treated the issue primarily as a fuel cycle problem, and analyses were focused on the nuclear energy infrastructures of so-called problem countries, perhaps with a political section that proclaimed the country at issue would be interested in weapons because of its desire for prestige or for security. The policy debate was between prevention and management in the context of a global treaty and safeguards system. The growing interest in nuclear power around the globe, as exemplified in the Bush administration's Global Nuclear Energy Partnership (GNEP), has revived old fuel cycle debates and has the potential to force the debate back to the future.

Many of the academic and other open literature analyses of the strategic (and even the military) aspects of the threat, which would be germane to thinking about military responses, have been limited to whether proliferants are deterrable, whether nuclear weapons could prevent regional power projection by coalitions of the willing, and the like.[11] Such issues are important, but they have often been addressed in limited fashion and in abstract terms, as is apparent when one compares the Cold War literature on deterrence with that of recent vintage. Moreover, equally important issues are being ignored today. Understanding the reverberations of, and effectively responding to, events like the recent North Korean test have not fully been addressed in the post–Cold War nonproliferation debates. Such issues are being discussed, of course, but the discussion suggests that they are largely viewed as they would have been had they occurred decades ago in a very different geopolitical and geostrategic context.

Since the 1980s and until the South Asian tests in 1998, chemical, biological, and missile proliferation was largely the focus of attention in the United States, especially on the part of the U.S. military. However, the nuclear threat was not forgotten. Even before the South Asian developments, Cooperative Threat Reduction (CTR) programs—the high-level bilateral effort to control nuclear security in the former Soviet Union—reflected and reflect serious concerns about nuclear proliferation.[12] Nonetheless, during this period, there was more attention to military aspects of the chemical-biological threat, primarily due to Iraqi chemical usage in the 1980s and the threat of Iraqi use of these weapons in the Gulf War. The threats posed by these weapons are quite different from each other, as well as those posed by nuclear weapons, and we may expect that the potential strategic impact of these threats reflects this fact. However, the threats as portrayed do not always appear credible. In particular, while there is clear evidence that many states are pursuing biological weapons, little is known about how these weapons would be used.[13] The preferred approach to controlling both types of weapons has been disarmament via global treaty and export controls. This approach faces a greater challenge since the end of the Cold War, in a climate of global trading and technology transfer where governments have ever less control over dual-use technologies, materials, and equipment.

Missiles have also been given attention, primarily because they are a WMD delivery means. But the open literature is limited and largely focuses either on export controls or missile defenses. There have been a number of decent military studies of missiles, but a comprehensive, credible assessment of their strategic impact in the current environment has not been undertaken.

Given these shifts in the perceived threat of WMD proliferation over the last fifty years, it should not be surprising that the current level of proliferation is less severe than many believed or imagined.[14] States of concern have not changed much in the last two or three decades. Indeed, in the nuclear arena, there are actually fewer nuclear suspected or open proliferants today than in the 1970s, a previous period of heightened proliferation concern. South Africa, Argentina, and Brazil are among states that have halted nuclear weapons programs, and a new threat was avoided when Ukraine, Belarus, and Kazakhstan agreed to return old Soviet weapons to Russia. Most states remain unlikely at present to develop nuclear weapons. Nonproliferation and the regime that promotes it are in their interests and are seen to be so. Their national security is a key, but not the only consideration, in this assessment. However, a relatively small number of states are still seeking nuclear weapons for security, status, domestic political advantage, etc. Technology is an important factor in, but is unlikely to be a driver of, a nuclear-weapon program.

In any event, under any realistic scenario we are living in a dangerous world. From where do current proliferation concerns stem? Areas of concern include Iran's suspicious and extensive WMD programs, especially its nuclear and missile activities. The discovery of the large enrichment facility at Natanz as well as other clandestine activities revealed two decades of Iranian noncompliance with its international obligations.[15] North Korea's nuclear test and its diplomatic brinkmanship highlight the increasing dangers of its long-standing nuclear and missile programs and missile exports. South Asia has also become a primary area of concern following the Indian and Pakistani nuclear and missile tests in the late 1990s. The specter of dangerous nuclear arms and missile races exists on the subcontinent, along with the prospect of battlefield and strategic use. Finally, there are continuing concerns (at very different levels) about the WMD, and especially nuclear weapon intentions and capabilities, of Syria.[16]

The growing reality of cooperation among rogue states is especially troubling. The WMD and missile cooperation between North Korea, Pakistan, and Iran has been examined in the open literature. The question is whether that cooperation was limited to these or a few other states or provides a blueprint for the future. Clearly, there are a growing number of states that now possess or are developing WMD- and missile-related technological capabilities and expertise. Will these capabilities be shared, and under what if any constraints? Will they wind up in black markets? In either case, they will erode export control efforts like the Nuclear Suppliers Group (NSG).[17]

To these country concerns may be added the following concerns:

- technology diffusion via the Internet as well as through loose nukes, materials leakage, and brain drain in the former Soviet Union, Pakistan, and other states and through nonstate actors like the A. Q. Khan network;
- Chinese and Russian nonproliferation commitments and behavior, including continuing issues involving nuclear and missile export behavior and whether both states hope to use nonproliferation to leverage (equalize) or even counter perceived U.S. "hegemony";
- the security of WMD/missile technology, materials, and expertise in Russia and the other Soviet successor states, as well as in such states as South Africa, Argentina, and Brazil; and
- the possibility of catastrophic WMD terrorism.

Beyond today's concerns, there is a second tier of states that, it was argued, might consider nuclear or other weapons of mass destruction in the future, including Algeria, Taiwan, South Korea, Ukraine, Kazakhstan, Nigeria, Egypt, Turkey, Japan, and Indonesia. Surprises may also occur with respect to proliferation and terrorism. The conditions under which one could envision widespread proliferation in the longer term depends on such factors as globalization, technology diffusion, regional and international security environments (particularly changes in Russia and China), and the like.

Ameliorating Factors in the Threat Calculus

Given these concerns, a serious deterioration is possible, but the worst-case scenario outlined above is not the only—and not the most likely—outcome. New developments, actions, and measures are not fully factored into the worst-case analysis, including, among others, the impacts of successful threat reduction and rollback cases over the last fifteen years, including South African and Libyan disarmament and the termination of weapons programs in Argentina and Brazil.

Another factor not addressed in this calculus is the war on terrorism and its still undetermined impact on terrorist operations and possible state supporters of terrorism. If successful, this counterterrorism effort should have deterrent and dissuasive effects on those seeking weapons of mass destruction. The impacts of CTR programs, the Proliferation Security Initiative (PSI), the Global Threat Reduction Initiative (GTRI), and other new initiatives, as well as proposed nonproliferation strengthening measures, are also largely ignored in worst-case analyses of the evolution of the threat.

In similar fashion, the effects of growing concerns about the threat in the international community, including the growing realization that this is an issue of international peace and security, are largely ignored, even though they could be significant in shaping the future. And the potential leverage in combating proliferation and terrorism that may come with new monitoring and verification as well as other technologies has not been fully considered.

Finally, the worst-case scenario also fails to fully take into account a number of other factors. Unanticipated developments—"shocks"—could change this picture for better or worse. Among the shocks we could experience include geopolitical changes, positive and negative as well as technological changes, particularly new ways to produce designer "bugs" and nuclear-weapon materials. Shocks may also be direct WMD proliferation or terrorism events, such as withdrawals from nonproliferation treaties, nuclear tests, sales of weapons of mass destruction, especially nuclear weapons and materials, interdictions, and further WMD use by states or terrorists.

Addressing the Proliferation and Terrorism Threats

Faced with the prospect of nuclear proliferation and terrorism threats, what is to be done? From a U.S. perspective, proliferation has been seen from the beginning as a global problem. Responses to the threat in the nuclear realm have been primarily global in nature, including the Baruch Plan (based upon the Acheson-Lilienthal report), which was a failure; the Atoms-for-Peace initiative, a modest proposal that traded off access to civil nuclear technology for restraints on military applications; the IAEA, envisioned in the Atoms for Peace proposal; and the NPT.

Global treaties and institutions are supported by export controls, national laws and regulations, economic and security assurances, sanctions, and regional arrangements of various types, including nuclear-free zones.

As noted, biological, chemical, and missile proliferation did not attain the priority of nuclear proliferation until the 1980s, especially following the first Gulf War and Iraqi use of chemical weapons against Iran as well as Iraqi Kurds. The United States also saw this reappearance of a chemical-biological problem in global terms, and the response was again primarily global in scope. This response consisted of focusing on international treaties, which led to the negotiation and conclusion of the CWC, a growing attention to verification of the older Biological and Toxin Weapons Convention (BWC), and the creation of supplier regimes, primarily the Australia Group and the Missile Technology Control Regime (MTCR).[18]

Within this context, a decades-long debate has been taking place on the question of whether the nonproliferation regimes have been successful. The global treaty approach has been important for setting norms concerning weapons of mass destruction and missiles, and the treaties have been influential in redefining thinking about the problem. In this context, international interest in strengthening the various global treaty regimes designed to control or eliminate WMD has grown, but the issues have been difficult and the results limited. Efforts to improve international nuclear verification are being undertaken by the IAEA to improve the effectiveness and efficiency of safeguards for NPT parties. While such efforts are widely supported, expectations may be unduly high because of the inherent difficulties of detecting clandestine nuclear facilities and activities. The ratification of the CWC provoked a debate in the United States over the treaty and the effectiveness of the proposed CWC verification regime that led to a number of U.S. reservations. The effort to establish a verification protocol for the BWC, which has no formal verification provisions, produced measures that were ultimately rejected by the Bush administration.

The NPT: A Critical Test Case

While all the nonproliferation regimes face similar, albeit clearly not identical, challenges, the future may be dependent on the fate of the NPT regime, as many have seen the problems encountered at the 2005 NPT Review Conference in New York as a harbinger of the treaty's decline. In this context, let us examine the prospects for the NPT, along with its relevance for current and future efforts to deal with nuclear proliferation and terrorism threats.

The NPT, the centerpiece of the international nuclear nonproliferation regime, is clearly challenged today by the following factors:

- states acquiring weapons, including India and Pakistan, that cannot be accommodated within the treaty as nuclear-weapon states or nonnuclear-weapon states;
- the impact of these states' actions on the views of key states parties to the treaty like Japan and Brazil concerning the NPT's value;
- North Korea's withdrawal from the treaty and the limited international response;
- North Korea's nuclear test;

- serious noncompliance, including Iran, and limited consensus on compliance enforcement;
- growing access of states (and nonstate actors) to sensitive materials and technologies and the rise of virtual or latent weapons programs;
- the issue of the NPT's relevance to activities by nonstate actors, including black marketeers and potential nuclear terrorists;
- the tensions between reemerging commercial interest in the civil nuclear fuel cycle and nonproliferation aims, which are reflected in the emerging Article IV debate; and
- an increasingly divisive debate over the arms control and disarmament provisions of Article VI.

Other elements of the regime are also under pressure. The IAEA is restricted by the limits of its verification mandate and burdened by noncompliance issues, which raise questions about the value and effectiveness of international safeguards. The Additional Protocol (AP), which expanded and strengthened the authority of the agency to conduct NPT safeguards, is an important new tool.[19] Although most states with significant nuclear activities have now brought the AP into force, there remain a large number of states that have not yet ratified the AP, including Iran. The agency and member states are trying to remedy this situation. The effectiveness of the new measures in the AP also remains to be fully demonstrated in the field.

Export control efforts are under pressure, and Nuclear Suppliers Group (NSG) rules need to be reinforced and strengthened. There is reason to be concerned about Russian and other countries' exports. Technology diffusion, black markets, and lateral proliferation also raise questions about the long-term relevance of the NSG, as these developments show nuclear supply is no longer the preserve of a few advanced industrial states.

A review of the UN Security Council (UNSC) reveals limited consensus on regime enforcement. It was paralyzed in Iraq. Until recently, it was also unable to act in Iran and in North Korea. Will it ultimately be effective in dealing with North Korea? Will it be able to implement Iran sanctions and to respond to continuing Iranian defiance of its demands?

The NPT and the international nuclear nonproliferation regime were created in a different time to deal with different threats. All of the problems with, and stresses on, the regime pose real challenges and have been seen in some quarters as portending the regime's collapse or increasing irrelevance. It would be folly to act as if these problems did not exist, or that they could be adequately addressed using exclusively old measures and approaches or resolved merely by muddling through. In the face of these developments, do we need regime change—a change in the NPT-IAEA regime? It seems the calls for regime change, which, at least until recently, have been voiced at a level not heard before, are rational. They are certainly understandable.

Is it possible to create something better, however? There has, for example, been considerable interest in a revived (and revised) Baruch Plan for over a decade, as well as some interest in efforts to apply the full disarmament approach of the CWC and the BWC to the nuclear arena through a Nuclear Weapons Convention (NWC). There is reason to be skeptical of the prospects for such proposals or for any efforts to fundamentally alter the regime. Current institutions and treaties still command significant international support and consensus—such consensus as exists. But consensus is largely limited on tough issues and difficult cases. This suggests little prospect that entirely new institutions would more effectively deal with these issues than the existing regime.

As opposed to putting forward alternatives to the nonproliferation regime, the regime is essential to current and future nonproliferation efforts; it needs to be maintained and strengthened, not replaced. It must be reformed. President Bush's landmark February 11, 2004, nonproliferation speech recognized this need and offered initiatives to, inter alia, take practical steps to limit fuel cycle risks by a ban on new states from developing reprocessing and enrichment technologies; strengthen export controls, especially for sensitive technologies; require the AP as a condition of supply; deal with noncompliance, in part through reforming the IAEA Board of Governors to make it a more effective, less political arbiter of compliance; and build on successful CTR and PSI actions.

The Bush initiatives, along with other proposals to reform the NPT-IAEA regime in the last few years, have reduced calls for a radical restructuring or replacement of the regime. Reflecting in part the problems addressed by the Bush initiatives, there are a number of areas where there is a growing consensus on the need to act, if not also on the best approaches.

Reforming or strengthening the regime requires serious efforts to deal with noncompliance. Enforcement of treaty obligations will be difficult, especially against determined proliferators, as coercive responses are not acceptable to many states.

There is also a need to address the structural problems of the treaty, especially with Articles IV and X. The so-called loophole in Article IV of the NPT, which allows states to develop indigenous nuclear capabilities and virtual weapon capabilities by pursuing uranium enrichment and plutonium reprocessing under the cover of peaceful programs, must be closed by limiting access to sensitive nuclear technology, in particular enrichment and reprocessing, and offering inducements to achieve this goal. The withdrawal provisions in Article X of the treaty need to be revised to prevent noncompliant states from escaping the consequences of their actions.

In addition to strengthening the treaty itself, further strengthening of safeguards including universalizing comprehensive safeguards agreements (CSAs) and APs is important, as is staunching NSG erosion and strengthening export controls (especially on enrichment, reprocessing, and other sensitive nuclear technologies). It is also necessary to expand extra-regime activities/tools, including the CTR (to address real threats and provide a model for future arms control), PSI, and counterproliferation.

Developing and delivering better incentives for nonproliferation, i.e., dealing with the demand side, is also critical. Assured supply has been put forward as an inducement to nonproliferation. Assured fuel supply involves a collective obligation to states. To succeed, it should have front- and back-end features, and the "carrot" value of dealing with disposing of spent fuel might be more attractive than ensuring continued fresh fuel supply. Any credible approach must convince recipients that it can count on supply, and that there will be no introduction of extraneous political factors into a decision to provide the fuel.

Multinational or multilateral ownership has been proposed by IAEA Director-General Mohamed ElBaradei as a means to address this issue. Such approaches have failed before, but there are key differences in the situation today from that of the earlier considerations of various proposals, including a more widespread sense of insecurity; the rise of new, illegitimate sources of supply, including black marketers; evidence of NPT noncompliance and the use of the Article IV loophole; and the prospect of nuclear terrorism. In any event, the viability of current proposals depends ultimately on common interests (commercial, political, industrial, etc.). They cannot be imposed from the top down, nor should they interfere with market mechanisms.

Unless the worst case emerges, a reformed regime is likely to be the critical feature of global efforts to combat nuclear proliferation threats; perhaps more surprisingly, directly or indirectly, it can play a growing, albeit limited, role in preventing nuclear terrorism.

The NPT and Nuclear Terrorism

Efforts to control proliferation, including the NPT, should play a role in preventing nuclear terrorism. To the extent that the NPT works to prevent an increase in the number of states with nuclear weapons, it decreases opportunities for the emergence of new weapon states with possibly inadequate security measures.

The NPT also can play a positive role in preventing terrorism through controls on nuclear materials. The NPT has provided a basis for ongoing efforts to control these materials, and there are proposals from the United States, the IAEA, and others to impose greater controls on sensitive fuel cycle activities—specifically, enrichment and reprocessing.

Moreover, as NPT safeguards involve state systems of accounting and control, safeguards can provide a line of defense against nuclear theft and could offer a degree of early warning of the loss of materials that may be used in an improvised nuclear explosive device.

In this fashion, the NPT, if fully implemented, can function as one of many lines of defense against nuclear terrorism, by reducing access to or the availability of nuclear weapons and materials. This highlights the importance of compliance with the treaty, including the need to address clandestine procurement networks that can be exploited by terrorists. Other elements of the regime and extra-regime activities are also addressing this problem, including IAEA programs, CTR, PSI, GTRI, the Global Initiative to Combat Nuclear Terrorism, UNSC Resolution 1540, amendments to the Convention on the Physical Protection of Nuclear Material, and so on.[20]

It is clear that since 9/11 there has been considerable progress through these and other efforts to improve the security of nuclear and radiological materials, to strengthen controls over these materials, and to expand the norms and measures developed to combat proliferation into the counterterrorist realm.

More needs to be done, however. There is a need—on counterterrorism as well as nonproliferation grounds—to continue to strengthen the NPT by such actions as promoting the universality of Additional Protocol, by tightening export controls, and by addressing noncompliance more vigorously. It is also essential to support the CTR, PSI, GTRI, and other initiatives; this should have not only nonproliferation but also counterterrorism benefits. In addition, states should support IAEA efforts to address nuclear terrorism, as well as promote the effective implementation/enforcement of Resolution 1540.

These efforts are important but, as suggested, they are only a part of the picture—and probably not the most important part of efforts to combat nuclear terrorism. All of these efforts can reinforce—and will be reinforced by—other counterterrorism and counterproliferation efforts, including possible efforts to deter, dissuade, and defend against nuclear terrorism. The normative and legal weight of the regime is important for counterterrorism as well as nonproliferation, but it will not likely directly affect the behavior of terrorists. Preventing terrorists from achieving their objectives if they attempt to pursue nuclear and radiological terrorism may deter and dissuade them, as may a credible prospect of punishment. These possibilities, like the role of the regime, need further study. They may be useful, but we must understand the possibility that they may not be fully realized.

Conclusion

In conclusion, the future of a decades-long effort to prevent the further spread of weapons of mass destruction is at a crossroads today. As suggested, the NPT regime is the cornerstone of efforts to combat nuclear proliferation and an important element of the struggle against nuclear terrorism. In recognition of this reality, there are ongoing and proposed efforts to strengthen the regime and to deal effectively with outstanding problems, particularly noncompliance.

The efforts to reform the NPT regime to address the challenges of today and tomorrow should be viewed as having the highest priority, as the future of nonproliferation approaches in the chemical and biological as well as the nuclear realms depends on their success. The outcome is by no means assured. If these efforts are successful, however, they will point to ways of addressing the problems of other regimes as well because, as suggested, all of the other nonproliferation regimes face difficult challenges similar to those of the NPT regime.

Global approaches will likely continue to be the foundation of any practicable responses. Even in the best case, however, a strengthened NPT regime and similarly strengthened CWC and BWC regimes will not be sufficient. Additional efforts to address WMD and missile threats will be needed. Some long-standing elements of policy, including deterrence, security assurances and assistance, and arms control, will likely have a role in addressing the new and evolving threats. Military options may be critical but probably only in limited contingencies.

An integrated, multitiered response will almost certainly be necessary. However, the roles of weapons of mass destruction and missiles have been changing since the end of the Cold War and the Gulf War. It will be necessary to move ahead within great uncertainties, in a fluid environment, in order to promote nonproliferation and counterterrorism objectives. Yet, without understanding changes and recognizing the political and technological limits to any new initiatives, it will be difficult to craft credible, effective responses and determine where the most fruitful expenditures of scarce resources to achieve them are to be made. The stakes are high.

Notes

1. These remarks are the author's own and not those of the Los Alamos National Laboratory, the National Nuclear Security Administration, the Department of Energy or any other U.S government agency.

2. The most famous formulation of the end of history was presented in Francis Fukuyama, "The End of History?" *National Interest* 16 (Summer 1989): 3–18.

3. For example, the U.S. State Department reported in its annual report *Patterns of Global Terrorism* that 1990 was "one of the few [years] in recent times in which there were no 'spectacular' terrorist incidents resulting in the death or injury of a large number of victims." It further noted that while the threat of terrorism still remains, "the continuing decline in the number of international terrorist incidents during 1990 is encouraging. From a peak of 856 in 1988, the number of incidents decreased to 455 in 1990. Even more encouraging is the increasing counter-terrorist cooperation among governments and our numerous successes in bringing the rule of law to bear on terrorists." See Office of the U.S. Secretary of State, introduction to *Patterns of Global Terrorism: 1990*, released April 30, 1991, http://www.fas.org/irp/threat/terror_90/index.html.

4. Nuclear terrorism was scarcely an issue until the mid-1990s, when concern in the United States rose as a result of Aum Shinrikyo's sarin attack in Tokyo and the Oklahoma City bombing, and it was later reinforced by 9/11.

5. See for example, Leonard S. Spector, "Repentant Nuclear Proliferants," *Foreign Policy*, no. 88 (Fall 1992): 21–37.

6. See, for example, Victor Utgoff, ed. *The Coming Crisis: Nuclear Proliferation, U. S. Interests, and World Order*, BCSIA Studies in International Security (Cambridge, MA: MIT Press, 2000).

7. Carl Kaysen, Robert S. McNamara, and George W. Rathjens, "Nuclear Weapons after the Cold War," *Foreign Affairs* 70, no. 4 (Fall 1991): 95–110; McGeorge Bundy, William J. Crowe Jr., and Sidney D. Drell, "Reducing Nuclear Danger," *Foreign Affairs* 72, no. 2 (Spring 1993): 141–55.

8. See, for example, the essays by Michael MccGwire and Lee Butler in John Baylis and Robert O'Neill, eds., *Alternative Nuclear Futures: The Role of Nuclear Weapons in the Post–Cold War World* (Oxford: Oxford University Press, 2000).

9. See for example, Graham Allison, *Nuclear Terrorism: The Ultimate Preventable Catastrophe* (New York: Times Books, 2004), 120, 130–32.

10. For details on these programs, see Joseph Pilat, ed., *Atoms for Peace: A Future after Fifty Years?* (Baltimore: Johns Hopkins University Press, 2007).

11. See, for example, Kenneth N. Waltz, "More May Be Better," in *The Spread of Nuclear Weapons: A Debate Renewed*, ed. Scott Sagan and Kenneth N. Waltz, 2nd ed. (New York: W. W. Norton, 2003), 3–45; Derek D. Smith, *Deterring America: Rogue States and Weapons of Mass Destruction* (New York: Cambridge University Press, 2006).

12. For discussions of South Asian proliferation and the CTR programs, see chapters 11 and 15 of this volume.

13. For a discussion of states suspected of pursuing biological weapons, see Joseph Cirincione, Jon B. Wolfsthal, and Miriam Rajkumar, *Deadly Arsenals: Tracking Weapons of Mass Destruction* (Washington, DC: Carnegie Endowment for International Peace, June 2002), 45–68.

14. While in widespread use, the phrase "weapons of mass destruction" can be highly misleading, especially in the context of forecasts. Nuclear, biological, and chemical weapons and missiles present widely different security problems. The impact of each category of weapon can vary widely and does not necessarily present an apocalyptic or possibly an even

militarily significant danger. Assessments of future threats differ as well by specific weapon type, with the less capable weapons of mass destruction generally the most likely to spread. As a consequence, overall predictions concerning WMD are almost necessarily distortive and often more alarmist than is warranted.

15. For the IAEA report on Iran's clandestine activities, see Implementation of the NPT Safeguards Agreement in the Islamic Republic of Iran, IAEA Board of Governors document GOV/2004/83, November 29, 2004, http://www.iaea.org/Publications/Documents/Board/2004/gov2004-83.pdf.

16. In January 2004, Pakistani investigators reportedly confirmed an IAEA allegation that the A. Q. Khan nuclear smuggling network offered nuclear technology to Syria. U.S. intelligence agencies are "concerned that expertise or technology could have been transferred." (See the Office of the Director of National Intelligence, *Unclassified Report to Congress on the Acquisition of Technology Relating to Weapons of Mass Destruction and Advanced Conventional Munitions, 1 January through 31 December 2004*, November 2004, 4, http://www.dni.gov/reports/2004_unclass_report_to_NIC_DO_16Nov04.pdf.)

17. For a fuller discussion of second-tier suppliers, see Chaim Braun and Christopher F. Chyba, "Proliferation Rings: New Challenges to the Nuclear Nonproliferation Regime," *International Security* 29, no. 2 (Fall 2004): 5–49.

18. For discussions of these treaties, see chapters 4 and 6 of this volume.

19. For the text and status of the Additional Protocol, see the IAEA Web site: INFCIRC 540 (corrected), http://www.iaea.org/Publications/Documents/Infcircs/1997/infcirc540corrected.pdf; and "Strengthened Safeguards System: Status of Additional Protocols," http://www.iaea.org/OurWork/SV/Safeguards/sg_protocol.html.

20. For explanations of these programs, see chapters 7 and 15 of this volume, as well as the White House, "Fact Sheet: The Global Initiative to Combat Nuclear Terrorism," July 15, 2006, http://www.whitehouse.gov/news/releases/2006/07/20060715-3.html; David Albright and Corey Hinderstein, "The A. Q. Khan Illicit Nuclear Trade Network and Implications for Nonproliferation Efforts," *Strategic Insights* 5, no. 6 (July 2006): 8, http://www.ccc.nps.navy.mil/si/2006/Jul/albrightJul06.pdf; IAEA, "Convention on the Physical Protection of Nuclear Material," adopted October 26, 1979, http://www.iaea.org/Publications/Documents/Conventions/cppnm.html.

CHAPTER TWO

WMD Terrorism

Charles D. Ferguson

In 1933, U.S. president Franklin D. Roosevelt consoled the American people facing the Great Depression with the words "the only thing we have to fear is fear itself." Today, in the early years of the twenty-first century, Americans and other peoples live in an age pervaded by anxiety and fear, exacerbated by terrorism. Terrorism, by its very nature, stimulates the visceral response of fear. Like a chain reaction, catastrophic terrorism that results in massive destruction exponentially increases the fear arising from terrorist acts. Although the terrorist attacks of September 11, 2001, did not employ weapons of mass destruction in the traditional sense of nuclear, biological, or chemical weapons, the damage wrought during 9/11 killed about 3,000 people and scarred the collective psyche of the American public. Because of these horrific effects, 9/11 prompted renewed fears about weapons of mass destruction (WMD) wielded by terrorists.

Instead of consoling Americans, the Bush administration's response to 9/11 has further amplified public concerns. The administration declared war on terror and announced a doctrine that allows for preemptive strikes against nation-states suspected of harboring or sponsoring terrorists, especially those states possessing or trying to develop WMD. Thus, the administration believed that terrorists were most likely to obtain WMD through state sponsors. In contrast to the Roosevelt administration's plan to end the Great Depression as quickly as possible, senior U.S. government officials have described the Global War on Terror as a never-ending fight or a long war and the threat of weapons of mass destruction as an everlasting menace.

A detailed critique of the Global War on Terror is beyond the scope of this chapter. Instead, this analysis focuses on explaining what is known about the threat of terrorists using WMD and how likely it is that a terrorist group will use these weapons. If past experience is prologue for the future threat environment, very few terrorist groups will employ WMD, and only a tiny fraction of terrorist acts will involve WMD. Still, even though it is a low probability event, an act of massive destruction can, by definition, have devastating and far-reaching consequences. Before examining terrorists' motivations to use WMD, it is necessary to define what is meant by WMD. By the end of the chapter, it is hoped and intended that readers' understanding of the threat will grow while their fears will diminish.

Defining Weapons of Mass Destruction

In certain respects, the term "weapons of mass destruction" is a misleading term, especially when linked to terrorist groups, because they are far less capable than nation-states to take chemical, biological, radioactive, and nuclear materials and make weapons that would truly wreak massive destruction. According to the U.S. government's *National Strategy to Combat Weapons of Mass Destruction*, published in December 2002, "Weapons of mass destruction (WMD)—nuclear, biological, and chemical—in the presence of hostile states and terrorists represent one of the greatest security challenges facing the United States." In defining WMD, the U.S. legal code in 18 U.S.C. section 2332a focuses on the unconventional nature of the weapon rather than clearly demarcating how much destruction the weapon should cause before it is considered a WMD. This code, in particular, uses the terms and phrases "poison gas," "any weapon involving a disease organism," and "any weapon that is designed to release radiation to a level dangerous to human life." High explosives are sometimes also considered a form of weapon of mass destruction depending on their explosive energy level. But 18 U.S.C. section 921, which includes conventional explosives in the definition of a "destructive device," does not clearly specify how much damage an explosive would have to cause. Commonly, the term "WMD" is reserved for unconventional weapons.

The United Nations has used the term "WMD" since 1947, and its definition, in contrast to the U.S. legal code, underscores the destructiveness inherent in a real WMD when it describes "atomic explosive weapons, radioactive material weapons, lethal chemical and biological weapons, and any weapons developed in the future which have characteristics comparable in destructive effect to those of the atomic bomb or other weapons mentioned above."

Many analysts have rebelled against the term "WMD." They believe that it is used too flippantly and is brandished by some government officials to stir up fears and blare sirens for preemptive or preventive war. Several of these analysts reserve the concept of weapon of mass destruction exclusively for nuclear weapons.[1] Only the detonation of a nuclear weapon, they reason, is guaranteed to inflict immediate carnage soaring to hundreds of thousands of deaths and injuries if used against a densely populated city.

Chemical or biological weapons, while usually considered WMD, can vary considerably in their destructiveness. While some countries have been able to turn certain chemicals and biological agents into weapons that could kill thousands of people or more, terrorist groups who have coveted chemical or biological arms have struggled to make devastating use of these weapons. Even though radiological weapons are highly unlikely to kill few, if any, people from immediate exposure to ionizing radiation, sometimes these so-called dirty bombs are lumped together with weapons of mass destruction.

From this point onward, this chapter uses the concept of chemical, biological, radiological, and nuclear weapons, also known as CBRN weapons, instead of the more commonly used, but far less accurate, term "WMD." "CBRN" captures the concept of unconventional weapons while stepping away from the hype and hysteria surrounding WMD. Also, the term "CBRN" permits a broadening of the traditional categorization of NBC, or nuclear, biological, and chemical weapons, to include radiological weapons, which are far more accessible to terrorists than nuclear weapons.

Chemical Weapons

A chemical weapon can "deliver poisonous substances into a target population, with the purpose of causing injury, incapacity, or death."[2] Understanding the effects of a chemical weapon requires knowing how likely would use of the weapon lead to death; how would it cause harm to a living body; how fast would the weapon act on a body; how much of the chemical agent would be needed to result in an effect; how long would the chemical linger in the attack area; and how difficult would it be to make the chemical or chemicals into weapons.[3]

Lethality refers to how likely exposure to a chemical weapon would lead to death. An attacker may choose to administer a sublethal dose with the goal of incapacitating rather than killing. Although terrorists inclined toward chemical weapons may be assumed to want to acquire the most lethal chemicals, some may instead choose less lethal chemicals to demonstrate their mastery of unconventional weapons and to show their restraint in employing less lethal forms. Most terrorist groups are not motivated to kill many people.

Mode of action describes how the hazardous chemical would enter and harm a living body such as a human being or an animal. The three main modes are inhalation (through breathing), ingestion (through eating or drinking), and percutaneous (through skin, eyes, or mucus membrane contact). Speed of action measures the delay between exposure to a hazardous chemical and the onset of its effects. The effects can be instantaneous, from seconds to minutes, or can take several hours to manifest themselves. Toxicity refers to the amount of a chemical agent that is needed to produce a specific, deleterious effect. Persistency measures the length of time a chemical agent remains hazardous after its release. Nonpersistent chemicals last from a few minutes to about an hour. Semi-persistent chemicals can stick around from several hours to about a day. Persistent chemicals can remain potent for several days to a few weeks and tend to be thick and oily.

A weapon designer can choose from a large number of chemical agents. These agents form various classes of compounds, including choking agents, blister agents, blood agents, and nerve agents.

Choking agents were some of the first chemicals used in modern warfare. If they are inhaled in sufficient quantities, they can cause pulmonary edema, which means the lungs fill up with fluid. Severe edema could suffocate the victim. In addition, these agents can irritate eyes, nose, and throat. Chlorine, phosgene, diphosgene, and chloropicrin are choking agents that were used in World War I. While chlorine is considered an obsolete battlefield weapon, terrorists could find it attractive because it is readily available in large pressurized tanks near urban environments. Thus, a terrorist group would not have to make chlorine but would want to rupture industrial storage tanks or transport containers, for example, on railcars traveling near or through cities.

Blister agents are also known as vesicants because they cause serious skin irritation including the formation of blisters. In addition, these chemicals can result in temporary or sometimes permanent blindness. Moreover, they can damage the respiratory system, primarily the upper part of the respiratory tract. Like choking agents, blister agents were used during World War I, and they have also been used more recently during the Iran-Iraq War in the 1980s. Blister agents include mustard gas, lewisite, and phosgene oxime.

Blood agents block the use or uptake of oxygen in the blood, thereby causing asphyxiation. Because these agents are highly volatile, they are not particularly useful for chemical warfare. Nonetheless, the lack of persistency has an advantage in that the attacker would not have to wait long for the battlefield to clear of the agent. Hydrogen cyanide, a well-known blood agent, is easy to produce and thus could be attractive for certain terrorist groups.

Nerve agents are the most toxic and lethal chemicals. Varying in their persistence, these chemicals can paralyze respiratory musculature and can cause death in a few minutes. The G-series of nerve agents include GA, or tabun, GB, or sarin, and GD, or soman. The apocalyptic terrorist cult Aum Shinrikyo, for example, used sarin in 1995 during the infamous Tokyo subway attack. Similar to the G-series in chemical form but more lethal, the V-series includes VE, VG, VM, and VX. Aum also made VX, according to the testimony of some of the cult's members.[4]

One of the most important concepts to learn about chemical weapons is that a dangerous or deadly chemical is not by itself considered a chemical weapon. A number of steps are required to turn chemicals into effective weapons. Chemical weapon delivery systems vary in their technical sophistication and effectiveness. Militaries have developed munitions, i.e., warheads that can be fired from rockets or artillery systems or dropped from airplanes as bombs. Designing a warhead that will effectively disperse the chemical agent without destroying or substantially degrading it requires an understanding of how much and what type of conventional explosive is needed. Usually a considerable amount of testing is required to make a warhead that effectively disperses the chemical agent. Terrorist groups would have to surmount this technical challenge.

Sprayers can also be used to disperse chemical agents. Although sprayers appear to pose fewer technical challenges than munitions, effective use of sprayers can trip up terrorists. In particular, creating the one to five micron-sized aerosols for effective chemical agent dispersal is not easily done with sprayers that can be bought at garden supply stores.

Chemical weapon delivery systems can be relatively primitive. For example, in 1995, Aum placed sarin inside polyethylene bags and dispersed the chemical by puncturing holes in the bags with sharpened umbrellas. This ineffective dispersal method and the low concentration of sarin that was used worked against Aum, and fortunately far fewer people (twelve) were killed than could have been (hundreds) had Aum developed a more effective chemical weapon delivery system.

Chemical weapons are sometimes called the poor man's nuclear weapon because they cost less to make than nuclear weapons. Also, chemical weapons production can be easier to hide than the manufacture of nuclear weapons. For a top-end chemical production plant, the necessary equipment would include reactors, agitators, storage tanks, heat exchangers and condensers, distillation and absorption columns, multiwalled and corrosion-resistant piping, and pumps. Aum Shinrikyo built such a plant for about $30 million. In contrast, a low-end plant would not necessarily need corrosion-resistant piping, and a laboratory setup could be sufficient for low-level production. Cost estimates for this type of facility range from a few tens of thousands to a few millions of dollars.

The type of training needed depends significantly on the type of chemical agent and the sophistication of the weapon being made. For nerve agent production, advanced training, most likely at the graduate level or doctorate level, would maximize the chances for successful and safe manufacture. In contrast, only high school–level training would be necessary for making chlorine gas.

In sum, if seeking high lethality, a terrorist group would try to make nerve agents, but these are difficult to manufacture. Blister agents such as mustard are relatively easier to make. Even easier to prepare are choking agents, such as chlorine, but large amounts are needed for a damaging attack. Terrorists who do not want to or cannot manufacture chemical weapons might decide to release already made chemicals stored in industry or transported by rail, ship, or trucks.

Biological Weapons

A biological weapon can use "living organisms or biologically produced toxins to injure or kill humans, animals, or crops."[5] Biological and toxin warfare has often been called "public health in reverse." Toxins are poisons that share many characteristics, especially in health effects, with chemical agents.

While there is some overlap between chemical and biological agents in terms of health effects, there are also distinct differences. For instance, many chemical agents are volatile whereas biological agents are not. Typically milligrams of chemical agents are required to produce toxic effects, but thousand times less, usually micrograms, of biological agents are needed to result in comparable toxicity. Although many chemical agents are dermally active, biological agents generally are not but enter the body through cuts or other breaks in the skin. Concerning latency, chemical agents usually show immediate effects, although some effects can take hours to appear. In comparison, biological agents can require hours to days to manifest their health effects.

Many of the attack methods or weapon delivery systems are similar for chemical and biological agents. That is, both can be disseminated by using commercial backpack sprayers, industrial or military sprayers, crop dusters, munitions, and missiles. With biological agents, there have been instances of contamination of food and water supplies as well as distribution through packages and letters. Moreover, as certain terrorist groups have embraced suicidal terrorism, concerns have arisen that infected individuals could spread contagious biological agents, but such a method faces the significant challenge of controlling the infection rate to ensure the effective spread of the agent. Similar to chemical agents, many biological agents can readily harm humans or animals through inhalation into the respiratory system if made into micron-sized aerosols.

Like chemical weapons, biological weapons are sometimes called the poor man's nuclear bomb. In warfare, biological weapons can force an enemy to don cumbersome protective suits and can increase the "fog of war." Explosives are not needed to disperse biological agents. From a terror perspective, biological agents can instill panic because they are invisible and have not been used much. Thus, potential victims of an attack have more anxiety because they are confronting unseen and relatively unknown substances.

Effective biological warfare agents tend to infect reliably in small doses. They have high virulence without great loss of potency during production, storage, or transport. The incubation period is ideally short. From a military standpoint, an effective biological agent is usually minimally contagious because a military would want to reduce the risk of the contagion spreading to its national population. Terrorist groups may or may not desire a contagious agent. A group that is concerned about infecting its constituency would probably not select a contagious agent. But a group that wants to unleash widespread and indiscriminate damage might gravitate toward a contagious agent. Nevertheless, any military or terrorist group seeking to acquire biological weapons would ideally want an agent that has no widespread immunity in the targeted population. Similarly, an effective agent would be insusceptible to common medical treatment. The agent would preferably have the capability of surviving environmental stresses during dissemination. These are many of the considerations that factor into selecting a biological agent and designing a biological weapon.

Biological agents also vary considerably in infectivity and lethality. Lethal effects could result from as few as tens of organisms to as many as thousands to millions. If the infection is left untreated, fatalities could occur in only a few percent to essentially a hundred percent of the infected population depending on the agent.

Bacterial agents use bacteria to spread infection. (A bacterium is a single-celled organism.) The anthrax bacterium, or *Bacillus anthracis*, the prototypical biowarfare agent, can cause greater than 90 percent fatalities if left untreated. The terrorist anthrax attacks soon after 9/11 used mailed letters to disperse weaponized spores.

Yersinia pestis, the causative bacterial agent for plague, has killed millions of people during the scourge of the Black Death in the fourteenth century and in other historical periods. There are two types of plague: bubonic and pneumonic. Bubonic plague is highly contagious, and victims show the symptoms of buboes (or black hemorrhagic lymph nodes), pneumonia, and internal organ hemorrhage. It can spread through the lymphatic system and then to other parts of the body. The bite of an infected flea, often carried by rats or other rodents, can start the infection. Pneumonic plague, so called because of the onset of pneumonia, is also highly contagious and enters the body via inhalation. Tularemia, which is caused by the bacterial agent *Francisella tularensis*, is moderately lethal; thus it is considered an incapacitating agent. A common bacterial agent, *Vibrio cholerae*, the causative agent for cholera, is moderately lethal. But because of chlorination of most water supplies and other public health protective measures, cholera is not likely to make an effective bioterrorism threat.

While bacteria as one-celled organisms may appear simple in structure, they are quite complex compared to viruses. Reproducing only by hijacking a host, such as a bacterium, plant cell, or animal cell, viruses are very simple structures consisting of RNA genetic code surrounded by a protective coating of protein.

They are very small, usually much less than one micron in size. Viruses have caused the majority of human diseases. By infecting a host, viruses force the host's cells to manufacture new copies of the virus, which can then be released by these cells to infect more host cells.

A formerly very common virus, *Variola major* is the causative agent for smallpox. Person-to-person aerosol contact can spread the disease. The Soviet Union had weaponized smallpox, and Iraq under Saddam Hussein had investigated use of camel pox. In the 1970s, a major public health campaign conquered smallpox, essentially ridding this scourge from the world. However, the United States and Russia maintain heavily guarded samples of *Variola major* in order to help develop defenses against smallpox. With renewed concerns of so-called rogue states and terrorist groups coveting CBRN weapons, fears of smallpox outbreaks have resurfaced.

Hemorrhagic fever viruses include Lassa fever virus and Congo-Crimean fever virus, as well as Ebola and Marburg viruses. They are typically highly lethal. Although few of these viruses have been weaponized, the Soviet Union had done so with the Marburg virus. In contrast, Venezuelan equine encephalitis virus has a low lethality of about a 4 percent fatality rate. A vector such as a mosquito transmits the virus to hosts such as humans and horses. Foot-and-mouth disease results from another viral agent that attacks livestock such as cattle and pigs. If used effectively by an attacker, these animal-targeted agents can cripple agriculture and destabilize the economy.

Biological toxins are poisons produced or derived from organisms. For biological warfare, toxins can offer advantages. Most toxins are exceedingly potent; thus very small amounts can produce deleterious effects. They tend to deteriorate rapidly in the environment, allowing attacking troops to occupy an area quickly. In addition, many toxins are well suited to covert warfare, leaving little or no traces after weeks to months.

However, some disadvantages work against using toxins in warfare or terror weapons. For instance, protein toxins decompose rapidly when exposed to sunlight, air, and heat, but these materials could be used for nighttime attack. Shear forces imposed during aerosolization may inactivate protein toxins. Most toxins do not readily penetrate the skin and do not pose a vapor hazard.

Botulinum toxin is highly lethal and is one of the most poisonous substances known. But weaponized forms tend to lose toxicity. Ricin is a highly lethal toxin derived from castor beans. Some terrorists have shown interest in making ricin because it is a relatively accessible and easy-to-produce agent.

Terrorist groups confront significant technical hurdles to acquisition of biological weapons.[6] While production materials and equipment are dual use and thus available on the commercial market, methods for delivering biological agents with weapons are highly specialized and usually classified. Nonetheless, a state sponsor or former biological weapon scientists might give technical help. Even without such assistance, the technical barriers to large-scale attacks appear to be eroding as knowledge and expertise grow with the increase in biotechnology development. There is an inverse relationship between the probability and scale of potential biological and chemical attacks. Small-scale attacks—for example, the October 2001 anthrax letters—are more likely but will cause limited damage. In contrast, large-scale attacks—for example, a smallpox epidemic—are not very likely but could result in catastrophe with millions dead. With the rapid growth of biotechnology, there may soon come a time when existing microbes can be modified to increase virulence and infectivity, enhance stability in storage or in aerosol form, increase resistance to standard antibiotics, and bioengineer toxins.

Radiological Weapons

Radiological weapons use radioactive materials to disperse or emit ionizing radiation. Ionizing radiation can knock electrons off biological materials in living tissue, potentially harming health.[7] There are two classes of radiological weapons: radiological dispersal devices (RDDs) and radiation emission devices (REDs). A popularly known RDD, "dirty bombs" use conventional explosives to spread radioactive materials. Because of continual and widespread news media use of the term "dirty bomb," many people have developed the misconception that RDDs must employ conventional explosives. Depending on the chemical composition of the radioactive material, nonexplosive methods may result in more effective dispersal than explosive techniques. Some radioactive materials are commercially available in readily dispersible forms. A technically skilled terrorist group could transform other radioactive materials into easily dispersible forms. An RED is considered a stationary RDD in that it does not spread materials that emit radiation, but instead it emits ionizing radiation from radioactive materials inside the radiation emission device. Terrorists might try placing an RED in a crowded location such as a busy train station.

These weapons would not cause massive numbers of dead. In most radiological attack scenarios, few, if any, people would die immediately or shortly after exposure to the ionizing radiation. Nonetheless, depending on the amount of people exposed and the level of exposure, many people could develop cancer several years to decades after the radiological weapon attack. Radiological attack might spur panic and result in high economic costs because of the need for decontamination and possible tearing down and rebuilding of contaminated structures. Thus, radiological weapons are considered weapons of mass disruption.

Radioactive materials include spent nuclear fuel from reactors, nuclear waste, and radioactive sources used in applications such as medicine, food irradiation, research, industrial gauging, and oil prospecting. Because spent nuclear fuel from commercial reactors is usually very highly radioactive, it would appear to offer an ideal type of material for a radiological weapon. However, extremely high radiation levels can serve as a barrier to terrorist acquisition. Without special handling gear, anyone near unshielded spent nuclear fuel can absorb a lethal radiation dose within minutes. In contrast, many research reactors do not "burn up" much of their fuel and thus discharge lightly irradiated spent fuel, which might be relatively safely handled by terrorists without the need for specialized equipment. Nuclear reactors and other nuclear facilities produce other forms of radioactive waste. While much of this radioactive waste is considered very low level in terms of radioactivity content and would result in very little or no readily discernible harm to health if used in an RDD, some types of radioactive waste labeled low level may pose security concerns.

Much of this low-level radioactive waste that could suit terrorists' purposes is derived from disused commercial radioactive sources. These sources represent a substantial category of radioactive materials and are used widely throughout the world. Of the millions of sources, only a small fraction presents inherently high security risks. Still, this fraction contains several thousand sources. A source can be classified as high risk if it has relatively large amounts of radioactivity. In addition, portability can raise the security risk profile of a source. Sources containing significant amounts of readily dispersible materials are inherently high risk.

According to the International Atomic Energy Agency (IAEA), radioactive sources fall into five categories.[8] The IAEA categorization generally follows the safety risk of a source—that is, what harm to health an unshielded source can cause. Security risk in general tends to track the safety risk, but these risk assessments can differ depending on the consideration of other risk factors such as whether a source is portable or whether it is located in a region accessible to terrorists. Category 1 sources could cause permanent injury in a few minutes or death in several minutes to an hour if near an unshielded source. These sources include radioisotope thermoelectric generators, food irradiation sources, research and blood irradiators, and teletherapy machines. Category 2 sources could cause permanent injury in several minutes to an hour or death in few hours to days if near an unshielded source. These sources include industrial gamma radiography devices, high dose–rate brachytherapy sources, and medium dose–rate brachytherapy sources. Category 3 sources could cause permanent injury in days to weeks but are unlikely to be fatal if near an unshielded source. These sources include level gauges, well logging sources, and low dose–rate brachytherapy sources. Finally, categories 4 and 5 sources are extremely unlikely to cause permanent injury or death. These sources include diagnostic medical and medical research sources, smoke detectors, and other detectors such as aerosol and chemical agent detectors.

Terrorist groups could try to steal or buy radioactive sources or find abandoned sources, which are known as "orphan sources." While governmental regulatory agencies have been trying to tighten controls on radioactive sources, many countries still have relatively weak regulatory controls. Even in countries where the controls have been strengthened, there are concerns that terrorists could pose as legitimate users and buy sources using phony licensing documents.

Many security experts have assessed that terrorists could acquire radioactive sources and easily make relatively simple dirty bombs. For instance, in 1995 Chechen rebels demonstrated they had this capability by placing a cesium-137 source strapped to an explosive in a Moscow park. They did not detonate the dirty bomb, but they drew attention to what they could have done by calling a television station to film the device. Still, to date, terrorist groups have not used radiological weapons to release radiation. While the exact reasons they have not are unknown, one reason could be that conventional explosive techniques have served these groups' purposes. Also, creating a radiological weapon that effectively disperses radioactive material is not an easy undertaking. Unless the terrorist group had obtained readily dispersible materials, they would need to know how to chemically transform the materials and build an effective dispersal mechanism. Possibly a major barrier for many terrorists who may have contemplated radiological terrorism is the psychological impediment to working with radioactive materials.

Nuclear Weapons

Terrorists could try to acquire nuclear weapons through two routes: obtain an intact nuclear weapon from a nation-state's arsenal or make their own improvised nuclear device (IND).[9] Terrorists could buy, steal, or be given the weapons or the materials to build weapons.

As of early 2006, there were an estimated 27,000 nuclear warheads in the world. Russia and the United States have all but about 1,000 of these weapons. Britain, China, France, Israel, India, and Pakistan possess the remainder. North Korea, a self-declared nuclear-armed country, may also have upward of about ten nuclear bombs.[10] Although some novels and movies give the impression that terrorists could relatively easily steal nuclear weapons, in reality it appears that nuclear-armed nations strongly guard these weapons.

Nonetheless, concerns have been raised about the security of Russian nuclear weapons, especially the relatively portable tactical nuclear weapons, some of which may not be kept in highly secure central storage depots. In December 2004, the U.S. National Intelligence Council warned, "Russian authorities twice thwarted terrorist efforts to reconnoiter nuclear weapon storage sites in 2002," and that terrorists inside Russia also "showed a suspicious amount of interest in the transportation of nuclear munitions."[11]

But even if terrorists can steal an intact nuclear weapon, they confront other technical hurdles to detonating the weapon. Most modern nuclear weapons are believed to be equipped with integral security features such as permissive action links (PALs). To enable a PAL-equipped nuclear bomb, a special security code must be entered. If there are too many unsuccessful tries in entering the code, the weapon disables itself. These codes are highly protected. However, it is possible that terrorists could bribe or coerce officials to surrender the code to unlock a weapon. Some older Russian tactical nuclear weapons may not employ PALs. Also, it is unknown whether India, Israel, and Pakistan use PALs on their nuclear arms.

Another safety and security mechanism is the safing, arming, firing, and fusing (SAFF) system found on intact nuclear weapons. SAFF procedures require these weapons to undergo a specific set of environmental effects such as changes in altitude and acceleration before the weapons can be detonated. Collusion among or co-option of knowledgeable insiders may allow terrorists to acquire information on SAFF procedures, but as with PAL-protected weapons, a SAFF-equipped weapon, at a minimum, provides another barrier against ease of terrorist access and use of intact nuclear weapons.

Making an IND—a crude, but damaging, nuclear explosive—also confronts formidable barriers. The main and hardest-to-acquire ingredient of an IND is fissile material, which readily fissions and releases tremendous amounts of energy when detonated in an IND. Although there are many types of fissile material, highly enriched uranium (HEU) and plutonium are traditionally the two types of fissile material that have fueled nuclear weapons and are the materials that terrorists would have the greatest opportunity using in an IND.

HEU consists of a mix of uranium isotopes in which the fissile isotope uranium-235 has been increased in concentration to 20 percent or greater. Natural uranium contains only 0.7 percent uranium-235 and 99.2 percent uranium-238 as well as a tiny fraction of uranium-234. The greater the concentration of uranium-235 in HEU the less material is needed to form a supercritical mass to sustain an explosive chain reaction in a nuclear bomb. A critical mass has just enough fissile material to sustain a chain reaction in which a constant amount of fission energy is produced for each future step in the chain. In a supercritical mass, the amount of fissile material exceeds the critical mass, allowing a very rapid exponential growth in the amount of fission energy produced as the chain reaction grows. Weapons-grade uranium has 90 percent or greater concentration of uranium-235.

Global stockpiles of HEU contain enough fissile material to power tens of thousands of nuclear bombs. The estimated total amount of HEU is about 1,850 metric tons.[12] Most of this material resides in military programs, either for bomb production or naval propulsion and power production by fueling the reactors on submarines and other warships. Russia and the United States possess roughly 90 percent of the total amount of HEU. Britain, China, and France, the three other original nuclear-armed countries, have tens of metric tons of HEU. Next in amounts held, South Africa and Pakistan are estimated to have upward of several hundred kilograms, still plenty to build dozens of nuclear weapons. Much smaller amounts of HEU reside in more than 120 research reactors and related facilities in about forty countries. Many of these locations have enough HEU to make at least one IND. Terrorists would have to acquire HEU from these stockpiles because enriching uranium is an expensive and very technically demanding process.

Plutonium, the other fissile material of significant security concern, only exists in trace amounts in nature. Reactors produce plutonium, which is then extracted from spent nuclear fuel using chemical methods called reprocessing. Many countries have employed reprocessing to separate hundreds of metric tons of plutonium from spent fuel. Military stockpiles contain more than 250 metric tons of weapons-grade plutonium. While the United States and Russia own more than 90 percent of this material, Britain, China, France, India, Israel, North Korea, and Pakistan possess the remainder. Britain, Russia, and the United States have declared a small fraction of the total military plutonium as excess to defense needs, but disposing of even this material will require several years.

Civilian plutonium stockpiles are roughly comparable to military stockpiles. The world has more than 230 metric tons of civilian plutonium, which is often termed reactor-grade plutonium. While many countries have stopped producing military plutonium, stockpiles of civilian plutonium are growing at a faster rate than military stockpiles. In recent years, civilian stockpiles are accumulating at the rate of about ten metric tons per year. Reactor-grade plutonium, though not ideal for making bombs, is still bomb-usable. Like uranium enrichment, plutonium production appears to be beyond the capabilities of terrorist groups. Thus, terrorists would have to obtain plutonium from existing military or civilian stockpiles.

Assuming terrorists could acquire enough fissile material for an IND, they would face other technical challenges. They would have to design and build a bomb that would have a decent chance of working. Still, unlike militaries, which demand highly reliable and safe nuclear weapons, terrorist groups would probably be satisfied in building an IND that produces a significant but not necessarily a predictable explosive yield. Relying on weapons technology that has a long and proven track record, nuclear terrorists would likely try to make a first-generation type of nuclear bomb, such as the gun-type or implosion-type device. More advanced designs such as thermonuclear or hydrogen bombs would be too technically challenging for terrorist groups to build unless they had assistance from a nation-state sponsor, and even in that unlikely situation the technical hurdles would be formidable.

The gun-type device is the easiest-to-build nuclear bomb. Like a gun, it simply shoots one subcritical piece of HEU into another subcritical piece of HEU to form a supercritical mass that can rapidly undergo an explosive chain reaction. The first gun-type bomb was used against Hiroshima, Japan, on August 6, 1945. The Manhattan Project weapon designers decided against a full-scale nuclear test prior to the Hiroshima bombing because they were fully confident that this relatively simple bomb would work as designed.

In contrast, the implosion-type device is much more technically complex than the gun-type device. The implosion bomb has to smoothly squeeze a subcritical fissile mass with an imploding shock wave to form a supercritical mass. The fissile material requires precise machining and assembling. Triggering the implosion shock wave so that it proceeds symmetrically poses another daunting technical challenge.

Unlike a gun-type bomb, which can only use HEU to produce a high explosive yield, an implosion-type bomb can use either HEU or plutonium. Another advantage of the implosion bomb is that it needs less fissile material (about 4 to 10 kilograms of plutonium or approximately 25 kilograms of HEU) than the gun bomb (about 55 kilograms of HEU). Weighing the advantages and disadvantages of the two types of first-generation nuclear weapons, terrorists would most likely opt to make a gun-type device because of its relative ease of construction as long as sufficient quantities of HEU were available.

Chain of Causation

The vast majority of terrorists are disinclined to acquire CBRN weapons. Even if so motivated, they would still face high hurdles to carrying out dreadful acts involving CBRN weapons. While CBRN terrorists come to their decision to obtain these weapons through different political and psychological paths, they would have to climb an escalation ladder consisting of the following general steps to use these weapons.

1. The terrorist group must decide to embrace extreme violence to achieve its goals.
2. The group must then choose to acquire CBRN weapons to advance its objectives.
3. The group must then obtain the materials, such as chemicals, biological agents, radioactive sources, or weapons-usable nuclear materials, to make CBRN weapons.
4. Next, the terrorists must acquire the requisite technical skills and knowledge either through learning or buying the services of technical experts.
5. Then the terrorist group must combine the knowledge and skills with the CBRN materials to build effective weapons.
6. The group must next deliver the weapon or weapons to a target such as a populated city or a place associated with political, military, or economic value.
7. The CBRN weapon must then cause sufficient damage to achieve the terrorist group's political, religious, or other motivational goals.

If the terrorist group obtained technical assistance from a state sponsor, it could conceivably skip or find shortcuts through steps 3, 4, and 5. Like criminals, terrorists will not commit a malicious act unless they possess the motives, means, and opportunity. Similarly, like detectives, terrorism analysts should firmly keep in mind these prerequisites when determining if a terrorist group will desire, acquire, and use a CBRN weapon. Because the preceding sections already examined many of the technical constraints faced by CBRN terrorists, the remaining sections analyze the motivations of terrorists and present a realistic view of the CBRN terrorist threat.

Terrorist Motivations and Impediments to Use of CBRN Weapons

Because CBRN weapons have not been used much either by terrorists or nation-states, people tend to fear these weapons more than conventional techniques of attack. The unfamiliar breeds dread. In addition, many people greatly fear weapons they cannot see or hear. For instance, chemical and biological weapons can be unseen or silent killers. Also, chemical, biological, and radiological weapons may not require explosives to disperse the chemicals, biological agents, or radiation. While this feature may appeal to some terrorist groups who want to unleash silent killing and incapacitating devices, others may gravitate more toward CBRN weapons that use explosives in order to attract immediate attention to the attack.

With all of the lethal substances available for CBRN weapons, it might seem amazing that only a tiny fraction of all terrorist attacks have used or attempted to use these unconventional weapons.[13] Several barriers block terrorists from acquiring or even considering acquisition of CBRN weapons.

Arguably, the biggest barrier resides in the mind of a terrorist. As renowned terrorism psychologist Jerrold Post has observed, "We are in the paradoxical position of having a clearer understanding of the interior of the atom than we do of the interior of the mind of the terrorist."[14] According to Post, terrorists confront a motivational paradox. "On the one hand, to be motivated to carry out an act of mass destruction suggests profound psychological distortions usually found only in severely disturbed individuals, such as paranoid psychotics. On the other hand, to implement an act of nuclear terrorism requires not only organizational skills but also the ability to work cooperatively with a small team."[15] A similar paradox holds for terrorists' motivations to do advanced forms of chemical, biological, or radiological terrorism.

Terrorists tend to be conservative in their choice of techniques. They prefer well-proven methods. According to terrorism expert Brian Jenkins, "Six basic tactics have accounted for 95% of all terrorist incidents: bombings, assassinations, arms assaults, kidnappings, hijackings, and barricade and hostage incidents."[16] However, he made this assessment in 1987, which was before the noticeable advent of the "new terrorism." According to many analysts, the 1995 Tokyo subway attack in which Aum Shinrikyo used sarin marked the watershed event for the new breed of terrorists. Now in custody awaiting execution, Shoko Asahara, Aum's leader, had also wanted to spark a nuclear Armageddon.

As early as the 1970s, Jenkins summed up the prevailing view of terrorism when he observed, "Terrorists want a lot of people watching, not a lot of people dead." The new breed wants to kill many and have even more watching in dread. But fortunately this new breed is few in numbers of groups. As noted, Aum Shinrikyo has exemplified this breed. Aum belongs to the apocalyptic type of terrorist group. Leaders of such groups reason that use of weapons of mass destruction can stimulate an apocalypse, thus, in their view, cleansing the world of evil.

Political-religious terrorists, part of the new breed, are religious extremists who embrace political objectives. For example, al Qaeda draws part of its strength from a radical interpretation of Islam and seeks to create a caliphate that would unite the Muslim world under strict religious law. Al Qaeda's interest in CBRN weapons dates back at least to the early 1990s. In 1998, Osama bin Laden proclaimed, "Acquiring weapons for the defense of Muslims is a religious duty. If I have indeed acquired these weapons [of mass destruction], then I thank God for enabling me to do so."[17] Then in May 2003, Shaykh Nasir bin Hamid al-Fahd, a young Saudi cleric, wrote the religious paper "A Treatise on the Legal Status of Using Weapons of Mass Destruction" in an apparent attempt to justify Muslims employing such weapons to defend the Umma, the Islamic community.[18] Moreover, bin Laden has referred to the Hiroshima bombing in some of his speeches "because he wants to do to American foreign policy what the United States did to Japanese imperial surrender policy."[19] While this rhetoric and the religious treatise appear to lay the moral and political groundwork for al Qaeda or affiliated groups to use CBRN weapons, religiously motivated terrorist groups generally have an aversion to such weapons. Religiously motivated terrorists, in particular, fear displeasing their god or supreme being if they fail in their mission. Thus, they tend to avoid overly complicated terror attacks, such as those involving advanced CBRN weapons.

Fear of failure generally serves to motivate many terrorist groups away from unconventional and rarely tried terror techniques. The desire on the part of some apocalyptic and political-religious terrorist groups to obtain CBRN weapons remains more the exception rather than the rule. Most terrorist organizations face substantial psychological and political constraints to CBRN terrorism. For example, earlier the Chechen rebels were mentioned in connection with possible use of radiological weapons. Despite having radioactive sources, the Chechen rebels did not detonate an RDD. Still, if they become more radicalized due to exposure to al Qaeda–affiliated groups, the Chechen rebels may actually use CBRN weapons. However, as long as the Chechen terrorist groups remain strongly connected to the constituency of Chechen civilians desiring independence from Russia, they will shy away from CBRN weapons. In general, national-separatist groups, such as the Chechen rebels, tend to eschew such weapons because of concerns about alienating their constituencies.

Aside from motivational barriers, other constraints can prevent even highly motivated terrorists from using CBRN weapons. These weapons are usually expensive especially as compared to conventional weapons. Even if terrorist groups have significant financial resources, they can still fail to unleash massive destruction. For example, Aum Shinrikyo had in the mid-1990s more than $1 billion in assets, many scientists working for the group, and thousands of members in Russia. But Aum failed to acquire nuclear weapons despite repeated attempts, including approaches to Russian officials to buy these weapons. Although Aum scientists did make biological weapons, their biological attacks failed to cause many casualties. As discussed in earlier sections, several technical problems can derail efforts to make effective CBRN weapons.

Strong desire to acquire CBRN weapons is not enough. Al Qaeda has expressed interest in CBRN weapons for many years but has not used these weapons. This terrorist organization has done preliminary work on anthrax, cyanide, and ricin. Like Aum, al Qaeda has substantial monetary assets, partially through Osama bin Laden's wealth. Al Qaeda operatives had sought to buy enriched uranium, but according to press reporting and court documents, there is at least one known case in which they were duped and instead obtained non-weapons-usable radioactive junk, which may not have been radioactively potent enough to make a powerful RDD.[20] Al Qaeda has also failed at attempts to purchase nuclear weapons. Even with an international network and relatively large financial resources, WMD can remain out of reach. To date, al Qaeda has made more effective use of its financial and organizational power through conventional terror techniques.

Terrorists are not figuratively ten feet tall. They make mistakes. The more barriers that governments can place in front of terrorists desiring CBRN weapons the more likely terrorists will fail or not even try unconventional terrorism.[21] While reading the other chapters of this book, keep in mind how governments can more effectively marshal nonproliferation policy to place better barriers to block terrorists from accessing or making CBRN weapons.

Notes

1. See, for example, Allison MacFarlane, "All Weapons of Mass Destruction Are Not Equal," Audit of the Conventional Wisdom Series, MIT Center for International Studies, July 2005.

2. Eric Croddy with Clarisa Perez-Armendariz and John Hart, *Chemical and Biological Warfare: A Comprehensive Survey for the Concerned Citizen* (New York: Copernicus Books, 2002), 88.

3. For an excellent history on chemical warfare, see Jonathan B. Tucker, *War of Nerves: Chemical Warfare from World War I to al Qaeda* (New York: Pantheon, 2006).

4. "Asahara Trial: Aum Member Explains VX Attack," *Japan Times*, November 2, 1999, http://www.rickross.com/reference/aum/aum155.html (accessed on July 5, 2006).

5. Croddy, *Chemical and Biological Warfare*, 196.

6. Much of the information and analysis in this paragraph is derived from Jonathan B. Tucker, "Case Studies of Bioterrorism," presentation to class in the Johns Hopkins University's Homeland Security Certificate Program, September 29, 2005.

7. For a more detailed exposition of the technical and policy aspects of radiological terrorism, see chapter 6 in Charles D. Ferguson and William C. Potter with Amy Sands, Leonard S. Spector, and Fred L. Wehling, *The Four Faces of Nuclear Terrorism* (New York: Routledge, 2005).

8. International Atomic Energy Agency, "Categorization of Radiation Sources," TECDOC-1344, July 2003.

9. For a more detailed exposition of the technical and policy aspects of nuclear terrorism with INDs and intact nuclear weapons, see chapters 3, 4, and 7 in Ferguson and Potter, *Four Faces of Nuclear Terrorism*. See also, Charles D. Ferguson, *Preventing Catastrophic Nuclear Terrorism*, Council Special Report no. 11, Council on Foreign Relations, March 2006.

10. For the most up-to-date unofficial estimates of nuclear arsenals, see the latest issues of the Natural Resources Defense Council's "Nuclear Notebook" in the *Bulletin of the Atomic Scientists*, available at www.thebulletin.org.

11. National Intelligence Council, "Annual Report to Congress on the Safety and Security of Russian Nuclear Facilities and Military Forces," December 2004, 7–8, http://www.dni .gov/nic/special_russiannuke04.html.

12. For the best unofficial estimates of fissile material stockpiles, see David Albright and Kimberly Kramer, "Fissile Material Stockpiles Still Growing," *Bulletin of the Atomic Scientists* 60, no. 6 (November/December 2004): 14–16. That published estimate is relevant for stockpiles accumulated as of the end of 2003. David Albright et al. publish periodic updates on the Institute for Science and International Security (ISIS) Web site, www.isis-online.org.

13. Personal communication with Dr. Jeffrey Bale, terrorism expert at the Monterey Institute's James Martin Center for Nonproliferation Studies, June 21, 2006.

14. Jerrold M. Post, "Prospects for Nuclear Terrorism: Psychological Motivations and Constraints," in *Preventing Nuclear Terrorism: The Report and Papers of the International Task Force on Prevention of Nuclear Terrorism*, ed. Yonah Alexander and Paul A. Leventhal (Lexington, MA: Lexington Books, 1987), 91.

15. Ibid, 92.

16. Brian Michael Jenkins, "The Future Course of International Terrorism," *Futurist 21*, no. 4 (July/August 1987): 8–13.

17. Osama bin Laden made this statement during a *Time* magazine interview on December 24, 1998. For more information on al Qaeda's interest in WMD, see Kimberly McCloud and Matthew Osborne, "WMD Terrorism and Usama bin Laden," CNS Reports, James Martin Center for Nonproliferation Studies, Monterey Institute for International Studies, November 20, 2001, http://cns.miis.edu/pubs/reports/binladen.htm.

18. Michael Scheur, *Imperial Hubris: Why the West Is Losing the War on Terror* (Washington, DC: Brassey's, 2004), 154–58.

19. Steve Coll, "What Bin Laden Sees in Hiroshima," *Washington Post*, February 6, 2005, B1.

20. Sara Daly, John Parachini, and William Rosenau, *Aum Shinrikyo, Al Qaeda, and the Kinshasa Reactor: Implications of Three Case Studies for Combating Nuclear Terrorism*, documented briefing, RAND, Project Air Force, 2005.

21. Personal communication with Michael A. Levi, May and June 2006; see his *On Nuclear Terrorism* (Cambridge, MA: Harvard University Press, 2007), which makes this argument in the context of nuclear terrorism prevention and response.

PART TWO

Nonproliferation Treaties and Regimes

CHAPTER THREE

The Future of the NPT

John Simpson

Futurology is at best a risky occupation. It usually involves discriminating between those elements of the present (and in some cases the past) which will remain relevant and those which will suddenly or slowly lose salience, as well as identifying new and relevant developments. In the case of the Treaty on the Nonproliferation of Nuclear Weapons (NPT), it is made more difficult because assessments of its future appear to revolve around both the significance of the diplomatic activities associated with it and evolving national and international security threats.

If the starting point for any assessment is to be the past and present, then there can be little doubt that the situation with respect to the proliferation of nuclear weapons today is better than in the 1970s when the NPT came into force. To take just one example, a little-known Hudson Institute study published in 1976 on trends in nuclear proliferation over the period through to 1995 offered a number of proliferation trajectories involving from nine to thirty additional states acquiring nuclear weapons.[1] This did not happen. India and Pakistan declared themselves to be nuclear weapon states (NWS) in 1998; observers confidently claim that Israel has had nuclear weapons for some decades; the Democratic People's Republic of Korea (DPRK) has tested a nuclear device and claims to have a weapon; and Iran is believed by many to have a nuclear weapon program several years away from fruition. All other states which were of proliferation concern in the 1970s (and in several cases are known to have had active nuclear weapon programs) are now nonnuclear weapon state (NNWS) parties to the NPT.

The core issue for the future is thus no longer whether the NPT can be made universal. It is whether the impact on the treaty of the actions of the three states which have never been members, one actual renegade, and one potential renegade can be contained and minimized. At the same time, the treaty has become a victim of both the changed international security environment and its near universality. The threat of nuclear war has been removed from many regions, often accompanied by the creation of nuclear weapon–free zones (NWFZs), thus reducing the apparent and immediate salience of the treaty. The reduction in nuclear stockpiles and 9/11 have stilled the former apocalyptic visions of the end of humankind resulting from interstate and intercontinental nuclear warfare and replaced them by a rise in concerns about individual acts of nuclear terrorism. Thus it is the sense of decreased relevance, if not apathy, toward the NPT which threatens its long-term survival as well as obvious and direct actions by a very few states both inside and outside of the treaty which run counter to its norms.

What Is the NPT?

The Treaty on the Nonproliferation of Nuclear Weapons is just that: *a treaty*. It does not create any administrative structures or integral enforcement mechanisms to support it. Its role is to offer an opportunity for states that do not possess nuclear weapons to make legally binding commitments to remain permanently in that state. They also have to accept International Atomic Energy Agency (IAEA) safeguards over the nuclear materials within their jurisdiction, thus providing assurances to their neighbors that they are not diverting such materials to nondeclared purposes (i.e., nuclear weapons). As no other legal instruments, except those creating regional NWFZ treaties, do this, the NPT is often characterized as the "cornerstone" of the nuclear nonproliferation regime.

This regime is much broader in scope than the NPT and comprises a wide range of legal and political instruments. Its other treaties and arrangements fall into four categories. First there are those treaties which prevent nuclear explosive testing and thus make the development of nuclear weapons by a proliferating state more difficult.[2] Second, there are the NWFZ treaties, which prohibit the development, manufacture, deployment, and stationing of nuclear weapons on the territories of zonal states.[3] Third, there are a series of more informal and exclusive export control guidelines and other arrangements among technology holders aimed at constraining the ability of a proliferating state to make and deliver its own nuclear weapons.[4] Finally, there are the arrangements which together loosely comprise the mechanisms for the global governance of nuclear energy. These center on the IAEA. At their heart is a system to provide assurances that states are not diverting nuclear materials from declared locations. The IAEA also manages mechanisms for monitoring and standard setting in areas such as radiological material and the physical safety and security of nuclear transport and facilities.[5]

Given the wide-ranging and multifaceted nature of the nuclear nonproliferation regime, its relationship to the NPT is both philosophical and practical. The treaty acts as its normative underpinnings and its standard-setting legal instrument. As such it is integral to the regime, as many actions taken through the regime are legitimized by the prohibitions accepted by states through the treaty. In addition, meetings of the NPT parties to review its implementation are arguably the only international forum capable of examining the operations of the regime, identifying its limitations, and discussing methods for strengthening it. Yet many elements of the regime existed prior to the NPT or were not created to implement it. The obvious exception to this is the new form of IAEA safeguards created in 1972 for NNWS party to the NPT.[6]

What then are the core norms on which the NPT is based? What are the rules for international behavior that were negotiated through the text of the treaty? The core norm arises from the proposition that nuclear weapon use is unacceptable to the international community. It followed logically from this that the only future world where nonuse could be guaranteed absolutely was one where nuclear weapons no longer existed. However, when negotiations started in 1966 on the NPT, there was no practical option but to accept that the disarmament of the five existing nuclear weapon states was unlikely in the immediate future. The treaty text was therefore structured around two categories of states with differing commitments: NWS and NNWS. The implicit rules generated by this discriminatory structure were that the NNWS would remain disarmed; no additional states would become NWS; and over an undefined period of time the existing NWS would disarm. Moreover, the armament of others did not justify breaking legal commitments to remain disarmed. Indeed in 1995 the South African government, which in that year played a crucial role in advocating that the NPT should have an indefinite duration, based its position on parallels between human rights norms and nuclear nonproliferation. In both cases, its representatives argued, the absolute norms involved could not be conditioned, time-limited, or bargained over in any way.

A second normative assumption was of a somewhat different nature: that economic development was an "inalienable" right of all states, especially the less well developed ones. It therefore followed that a similar right must exist in the area of peaceful uses of nuclear energy for both parties and nonparties to the treaty. Unfortunately, although technical distinctions could be made between those nuclear materials ideal for making nuclear weapons and those less appropriate for this task, the technology and processes used to produce key weapon materials, namely fuel reprocessing and uranium enrichment, also formed part of peaceful fuel cycles. The NPT solutions were to condition the inalienable rights of those NNWS within the treaty by a voluntary legal commitment not to acquire nuclear weapons, and of those outside by a commitment that all nuclear exports to them from NPT parties should be under IAEA safeguards.[7] A more direct solution was that in 1974 a cartel of existing technology holders was formed, the Nuclear

Suppliers Group (NSG), which agreed informally to deny to other states those capabilities that could be used in weapon production.

Norms represent ideal forms of behavior. Using them as the basis for a treaty runs the risk that when adapting them to existing circumstances, the rules derived from them will contain unanticipated weaknesses. The NPT is no exception, especially as it is a framework treaty. Its most obvious shortcomings are the following:

- the treaty does not allow for the existence of any new NWS;
- there is no specific constraint on one NNWS party assisting another NNWS party to acquire nuclear explosive devices;
- the commitment to disarmament is much more opaque and nonspecific than that relating to nonproliferation (though neither is defined in detail in the treaty);
- the disarmament commitments contain no time frame, and what constitutes progress is also undefined; and
- the boundaries between peaceful and explosive development and use of nuclear energy are also undefined.

These lacunae offer opportunities for political arguments, which in turn reduce the possibilities of sustaining an underlying consensus about the treaty's security value and other virtues. They also form a permanent backdrop to any assessment of the future of the treaty.

Although the treaty text opened its parties to diplomatic frictions, it also resulted in the NPT having an indefinite duration as it offered no means for its members to collectively terminate it. Such an arrangement was discussed during the negotiation of the treaty. What eventually emerged was an arrangement for periodic reviews of the operations of the treaty and a requirement to give three months' notice for the withdrawal of individual states from the treaty.[8] Yet even this latter route is conditioned by the need to specify the "extraordinary events, related to the subject matter of this treaty, [which] have jeopardized the supreme interests of its country." As a consequence, it is difficult to conceive of how the NPT would "collapse" or "implode" in a very visible manner, or how it would ever be removed from the UN list of active treaties, even if some extremely traumatic event were to occur.

Instead, what seems most likely is a path between two extremes. One is that total nuclear disarmament will occur, and it will become universalized, or more probably supplanted by a global nuclear disarmament treaty.[9] The second is that the world will incrementally become a nuclear proliferated one, and the relevance and utility of the norms underlying the treaty and its utility as a yardstick for action will erode, as will the effectiveness of the nuclear nonproliferation regime it underpins.

To explore the drivers which will determine where on a spectrum between these two extremes the future of the NPT will fall, the commitments contained in the NPT and some of the controversies and frictions that have arisen out of the structural weaknesses identified above during its four decades of existence are first examined. The two polar alternatives or "ideal types" of nuclear future and how they might emerge are then discussed. Finally, a view is offered on the characteristics of the development path that now appears most likely.

The Commitments Contained in the NPT

As the basic purpose of the NPT was a discriminatory one—preventing the dissemination and proliferation of nuclear weapons to additional states—it was recognized from the beginning that it was unlikely to be sustained indefinitely unless visible movement occurred toward an end state of nuclear disarmament. As a consequence, the treaty text contained three specific rules:

- the NWS should seek to disarm in the medium to long term (i.e., to give an "unequivocal commitment" to do so)[10];
- all NNWS had the right to engage in the development and use of nuclear energy for peaceful purposes if they accepted IAEA safeguards over all the nuclear materials within their jurisdiction; and
- NWS were prohibited from transferring complete nuclear weapons to any other state, while NNWS were not to attempt to make them or accept assistance from a NWS to do so.

To implement these three rules, the NPT contains a series of legal commitments written in the form of a preamble and eleven short articles. While its structure recognized the existence of NWS, it did not positively legitimize their indefinite existence. However, their numbers were limited legally by defining a NWS in Article IX.3 as "one which has manufactured and exploded a nuclear weapon or other nuclear explosive device prior to 1 January 1967." To have done otherwise would have implied the inevitability of proliferation and undermined any hope of the treaty becoming universal in its membership.

Two types of undertaking were accepted by NWS parties to the treaty. One was not to transfer nuclear weapons or nuclear explosive devices to "any recipient whatsoever," including other NWS and nonstate entities, "directly or indirectly" (Article I). Given its similarity to U.S. domestic legislation, the intention appears to have been that this should be interpreted as covering only complete nuclear weapons, while "indirect" transfer of these weapons meant transfers via third parties.[11] The second type of undertaking was not to "assist, encourage or induce" any NNWS to "manufacture or otherwise acquire" nuclear weapons or explosive devices or acquire "control" over them. However, "assisting" activity remained permissible between NWS (e.g., between the United States and the United Kingdom). Finally, during U.S. legislative hearings on ratification of the treaty, Article I was interpreted by administration officials as permitting NATO states to procure delivery systems intended to carry U.S. nuclear weapons in time of major hostilities, as well as planning for their use, an activity known as "nuclear sharing." The argument was that if such hostilities were to occur, the treaty would no longer be applicable and that it was one where "what was not specifically forbidden was permitted."[12]

Article II prescribed the commitments of NNWS. These parties were not to receive transfers of nuclear weapons or explosive devices from any source; not to seek or receive assistance in manufacturing such weapons or devices; and not to manufacture them indigenously. What the treaty did not specifically address, however, was the case of a NNWS which assisted another NNWS in manufacturing nuclear weapons: at the time it was assumed by most states that this was not possible.

Article III.1 and III.4 committed NNWS parties to accept IAEA "safeguards" and to negotiate and conclude a suitable agreement with the agency to verify "the fulfillment of its obligations assumed under [the NPT] with a view to preventing diversion of nuclear energy from peaceful uses to nuclear weapons or other nuclear explosive devices." The initial safeguards agreement of June 1972 between the IAEA and a state party to the NPT (INFCIRC/153) focused narrowly on diversion of nuclear material from declared facilities and not on the wider task of verifying "the fulfillment of [an NNWS's] obligations under the NPT."

The remaining articles of the treaty applied to all states parties. Article III.2 and III.3 addressed the conditions to be applied by an NPT state party in its nuclear trading activities. The key conditions were that transfers had to be subject to "the safeguards required by this Article" and were to comply with Article IV. Many states believed these safeguards to be NPT or INFCIRC/153 safeguards on all of a state's nuclear materials. A minority held that they should only apply to the artifact or material being transferred. In addition, since 1997 and the advent of the Additional Protocol (AP) to INFCIRC/153 (INFCIRC/540), there have effectively been two versions of NPT safeguards, known as comprehensive (153) and integrated (153 plus 540).

Article IV.1 states that "Nothing in this Treaty shall be interpreted as affecting the inalienable right of all parties to the Treaty to develop research, production and use of nuclear energy for peaceful purposes without discrimination." It then adds the phrase "and in conformity with Articles I and II of this Treaty." This implies that all NNWS parties accept voluntarily that the right is not inalienable nor without discrimination, as it has been conditioned by this last phrase.[13] States parties can therefore refuse to assist others if they believe their assistance with a state's "peaceful" activities would be diverted to military uses.

The final substantive article is Article VI. This commits all parties to "pursue negotiations in good faith on effective measures relating to cessation of the nuclear arms race at an early date and to nuclear disarmament, and on a treaty on general and complete disarmament under strict and effective international control." Three aspects are worthy of note. One is that the article applies to all state parties, not just the NWS. The second is that from the entry into force of the treaty, disagreements have existed over the implications of the positioning of the comma in the sentence, and whether this means that cessation of the nuclear arms race and nuclear disarmament should precede, and be independent of, general and complete disarmament,[14] or occur in parallel to, and be dependent on, it.[15] A third aspect is that in 1996 the commitment to negotiate was interpreted in an advisory opinion of the International Court of Justice (ICJ) as implying that this meant not only engaging in negotiations but also completing them.[16]

Article V, concerning peaceful nuclear explosions, has never been operative. Equally, Article VII is a permissive statement that the treaty does not affect the right of states to make regional NWFZ agreements. The remaining four articles are procedural, though some do have substantive implications.

Article VIII covers two distinct issues. Paragraphs 1 and 2 relate to the procedure for amending the treaty. This has always been regarded as unworkable in practice.[17] Paragraph 3 deals with a completely different issue: the holding of a conference every five years to review the operations of the treaty.[18] Articles IX and XI deal with signature, ratification, deposition, and entry into force. Finally, Article X deals with two separate and distinct issues. Paragraph 1 lays out the process for withdrawal from the treaty, based on the wording found in the PTBT of 1963.[19] Paragraph 2 sets out the process whereby twenty-five years after the entry into force of the treaty (i.e., 1995) a decision could be taken on the further extension of the treaty.[20]

Also noteworthy are several issues not covered by the NPT text. The first is its lack of any mechanism or procedure for addressing noncompliance. It has often been tacitly assumed that for Articles II and III, this will be handled by the UN Security Council (UNSC) via the IAEA safeguards system, the agency's board of governors, and Articles II.B.4 and Article XII of its Statute. Until the early 1990s IAEA safeguards focused narrowly on declared fissile material accountancy and ignored the issue of weaponization. Indeed, the issue of whether it has the authority to address this remains controversial within the Agency, even though this is banned by the NPT.[21] For other articles, there is no specified or obvious route to handle noncompliance.

The second issue is that the treaty has no permanent secretariat or other organizational structure: its only monitoring or deliberating body is a conference of treaty parties to review its operations every five years. The text gives no indication of how these conferences are to be organized and what powers they should have. A third issue is that during the negotiations attempts were made to build into the treaty commitments by the NWS not to use nuclear weapons against NNWS party to the NPT and to assist those who were attacked with such weapons. These commitments were seen as a "halfway house" toward nuclear disarmament. In the end such commitments were omitted from the treaty, though the three depositary states did provide limited commitments of this type through unilateral statements and UNSC resolutions.[22]

Finally, the preamble to the treaty has significance in indicating what the objectives of its architects were. In particular it appears to give priority in disarmament to the "cessation of the nuclear arms race" and the undertaking of "effective measures in the direction of nuclear disarmament." It also recognizes the need to "achieve the discontinuance of all test explosions of nuclear weapons for all time and to continue negotiations to this end." Moreover, it suggests that the "easing of international tension and the strengthening of trust" is necessary in order to pursue a treaty on general and complete disarmament. This process would include measures to halt the manufacturing of nuclear weapons, their stockpiling, and the elimination of nuclear weapons and their means of delivery from national arsenals.

The text of the preamble also has significance in indicating the central role that has been played in discussions at NPT review conferences by the need to achieve a comprehensive test-ban treaty (CTBT) (and the pre-1970 vision that this was the necessary first step toward nuclear disarmament). The preamble also suggests that the end of the nuclear arms race (which in 1968 was clearly interpreted as the U.S.-USSR process of competitive arming) and a process of nuclear disarmament would precede an end state of nuclear disarmament. The latter would encompass manufacture, stocks, and delivery systems and be negotiated in the context of a broader process of WMD and conventional disarmament.

The NPT Review Process as a Guide to the Future of the NPT

The only public forums offering indicators of the successes, failures, and possible futures of the NPT are the NPT review conferences held every five years to assure that "the purposes of the Preamble and the provisions of the Treaty are being realized."[23] However, the way that these conferences have been organized has in itself become an intervening variable for those seeking to use them to make such judgments. The obvious criterion for judging their success, and thus that of the NPT, is a consensus report or Final Document (i.e., one to which no state present objects). Yet this is inherently difficult to achieve: failure is a much more probable outcome. As a result, the strength of any causal link between the visible outcomes of such conferences and the degree of success or failure of the treaty in assuring "the realization of (its) purposes" appears profoundly opaque. This is illustrated by a brief history of these events.

The first NPT review conference in March 1975 divided the articles of the treaty between two main committees for detailed scrutiny. The reports from the committees were to be sent to a drafting committee for consolidation into a single text, called the Final Declaration, to be agreed to by consensus. In practice, consensus through this route proved impossible to achieve, largely because of disagreements over language on a CTBT. The Swedish president of the conference then circulated her own draft and forced it through the final plenary, thus offering the appearance of a successful review.[24]

In 1980 similar disagreements over a CTBT and disarmament occurred, but the Iraqi president was unable to rescue the incomplete report or present an alternative document.[25] In 1985, under an Egyptian president, the structure of the meeting changed, with the number of Main Committees increasing from two to three. This conference did agree to a Final Document by consensus, even though it incorporated differing views in a key passage on a CTBT.[26] In 1990, under a Peruvian president, lack of movement on disarmament and a CTBT could not be circumvented as had happened in 1985, and no Final Declaration emerged.[27]

In 1995, the fifth NPT review conference was merged with the conference "to decide whether the Treaty shall continue in force indefinitely, or shall be extended for an additional fixed period or periods."[28] This choice was narrowed down to an indefinite extension and one for an indefinite number of fixed periods, with the former eventually winning the day. However, a consensus decision on this necessitated the production of three decision documents, followed by the passing of a resolution on the Middle East. The legal implication of this procedure and the linkage, if any, between the three decisions remain open questions.[29] So too does the significance and status of the resolution on the Middle East, without which the consensus decision on the extension might not have been possible politically.[30] This resolution was a procedural first for the NPT review process. It was cosponsored by the United States, and although Israel was not named, the resolution was clearly intended to pressure it to accept IAEA safeguards (and the cosponsorship gave hope to some that the United States would do this).

The 1995 decisions changed the existing NPT review process significantly. The five-yearly conferences were made permanent; ten-day sessions of the Preparatory Committee (PrepCom) of a review conference were to be held in the three years preceding a conference to discuss matters of substance in a systematic manner; and the committee was to make substantive recommendations to its review conference, as well as the more traditional procedural ones.[31] However, the United States was insistent that the annual PrepCom sessions were not meetings of the parties and had no decision-making powers other than to make recommendations to review conferences. The first PrepCom session under the new arrangements was structured similarly to the review conferences, with three sets of "cluster" discussions and an aim of producing some type of rolling text and a compendium of national proposals.[32] These latter exercises collapsed at the end of the 1998 session, and in 1999 no recommendations were sent to the review conference.[33]

The 2000 NPT review conference occurred in what many regarded as a set of very negative internal and external contexts for the treaty: the chances of achieving a consensus outcome appeared near zero. Yet this proved to be the only NPT review conference which produced a genuine "consensus" Final Document out of the work of the main committees. It also appeared to build on, and define in greater detail, the "objectives" set for states parties in 1995. In addition, text was agreed to that removed from the first two annual PrepCom sessions in a cycle the need for a negotiated outcome, with a "factual summary" of the proceedings for transmission to the next session being substituted.[34] As a consequence, the next review cycle started in a relatively harmonious manner.[35] In 2004, however, no substantive recommendations were sent to the review conference, nor was there any agreement on key procedural issues such as its agenda and program of work.

These latter disagreements arose from two interlinked issues: the status and thus significance of the commitments entered into in 1995 and the nonfulfillment of certain of the disarmament pledges made in 2000.[36] The disagreements also raised a more practical question: was the review process "fit for purpose"? Were its specific products supposed to advance those of previous ones in an incremental manner, or was all that could be expected political commitments applicable over the next five years? Some among the NAM (Nonaligned Movement) leadership regarded all future agreements as conditioned by the 1995 extension decision and its linked documents and the 2000 Final Document. In contrast, some of the NWS only accepted that it was the commitments made in 1995 that were indefinite in nature, due to their links to the legally mandated extension decision. Those made in 2000 were seen to have a lesser status, and thus open to change in 2005. The consequence of this and other procedural disagreements was that the conference took more than half of its allotted time to agree on its agenda and program of work, leaving the main committees with no time to complete their tasks—even without the alleged desire of some parties to have a no-consensus outcome.[37]

Outside observers imputed from this situation, and particularly from the lack of a consensus outcome to the conference, that the NPT and the nonproliferation regime were in deep trouble. Indeed some went on to argue that if no Final Document was agreed to at the next review conference in 2010, the demise of the NPT might be at hand. Yet based on its past record and the tasks that have been asked of it, what is usually defined as a "successful" outcome of an NPT review conference is intrinsically unlikely, and the 2000 outcome was probably the result of a unique and unrepeatable set of circumstances.

In the absence of any alternative highly visible internal method of gauging the strength or weakness of the NPT and the nuclear nonproliferation regime, it seems likely the single criterion of the outcome of NPT meetings will continue to be used by the media and those with no direct involvement in the review process as their sole method of evaluating the future of the NPT. Yet while a failure to agree on a Final Document clearly indicates that states parties did not give priority to any common interest in sending a message to the outside world that the "purposes" of the treaty were being assured in 2005, it is at best a problematic indicator of whether international support for the treaty remains strong. But if outcomes of the NPT review process do not offer a clear indicator of the NPT's future, what does?

Alternative Criteria for Assessing the Future of the NPT

Given the opaque and possibly noncausal connections between events in the NPT review process and support for, and engagement with, the treaty, events outside of this process may be where indicators of the NPT's future should be sought, rather than within the treaty's own evaluative mechanism. Four distinct issue areas can be identified here:

- accession of additional states to the treaty, or withdrawal of states from the treaty, and how the treaty mechanisms respond to such withdrawals;
- whether the treaty arrangements can facilitate effective responses to noncompliance with its norms and rules by both member and nonmember states;
- the relevance of the treaty text, and the commitments within it, to evolving perceptions of proliferation threats, particularly after 9/11; and
- explosions of a nuclear weapon or improvised nuclear explosive device.

A. NPT Accessions and Withdrawals

i. Accessions. The NPT is the multilateral arms control treaty with the greatest number of adherents. This has, however, generated perceptions of both strength and weakness. On the one hand, its near universality gives its rules a status similar to customary international law. On the other, the number and significance of recent ratifications or accession can no longer be used as a yardstick of growing support and strength. It is highly unlikely that India, Israel, and Pakistan will join the treaty in the near future. The situation of the remaining possible new entrant, the DPRK, is uncertain. As a consequence, proliferation can now only occur from within the treaty, and logically the only available vector for the treaty appears to be one of it becoming less universal.

When in 1998 first India and then Pakistan engaged in nuclear explosive testing, this resulted in claims that the NPT was no longer relevant, even though both states were not parties to it. In taking this action they destroyed an existing tacit international rule, namely that states outside the treaty would continue to be regarded and treated as NNWS so long as they did not test. This meant that they could evade international sanctions. Before 1993 at least six states fell into this "opaque" category (Argentina, Brazil, India, Israel, Pakistan, and South Africa), but the proliferation situation appeared relatively stable and the NPT effective.

After 1998 this situation changed permanently. The positive impact of the accessions by Argentina, Brazil, and South Africa was overshadowed by the negative effects of the actions of India and Pakistan in testing and declaring themselves to be NWS. There were several reasons for this effect. One was that some foreign ministries had persuaded their governments to agree to become members of the NPT on the grounds that this would prevent further proliferation. A second reason was that the actions of India and Pakistan meant that the text of the NPT could no longer address the situation of these two states. On the one hand, the chances they would enter the NPT as NNWS appeared increasingly remote. On the other, Article IX.3 clearly stated that only states which had exploded a nuclear device prior to the end of 1966 could enter the treaty as NWS. India and Pakistan did not qualify. As in practice the treaty could not be amended, it was impossible for them to engage formally with the NPT in future. Not only did universality of the treaty appear to be out of the question: the consequences of their proliferation could only be handled outside of the treaty context. Thus not only did the NPT appear to have become irrelevant to the situation of these two states, but one of its core rules, nonproliferation, had been ignored by them. Moreover, it had been demonstrated that there existed no treaty mechanism for handling proliferation by nonparties who broke the tacit "nondeclaration" rule.

This situation seems unlikely to improve if states such as the United States, Russia, and China continue to remove nuclear trading constraints imposed on India and Pakistan in 1998 and take actions that gradually recognize their declared nuclear weapon status. The 2005 U.S.-India civil nuclear assistance agreement is a case in point.[38] The situation generates discontent in states within the treaty that see themselves as obtaining no reward for their good behavior, unlike the noncompliant outsiders.

The case of Israel is different, though its effects on the treaty are just as profound. Israel has not declared itself to be a nuclear weapon state and thus does not challenge the basic structure of the NPT. However, the belief among Arab states that Israel has nuclear weapons, and the refusal of the United States to acknowledge this and act on it has both regional and global consequences. The regional consequence is to reduce the relevance and value of the NPT as a nonproliferation mechanism in the eyes of Arab states. It also stimulates them to use the treaty review process as a means of pressuring the United States over Israel's nuclear potential through pressure to implement the 1995 Resolution on the Middle East. The global consequences have been to make the Middle East "regional question" an increasingly significant factor blocking consensus at NPT review conferences. It is a reason also for the Arab states not to engage in chemical and biological disarmament and for internal pressures to arise demanding withdrawal from the NPT.

Overall, the NPT is therefore confronting a structural situation over membership destined to get worse, rather than better, over time. India and Pakistan appear unlikely to roll back their nuclear weapons other than through a global disarmament agreement superseding the NPT. In theory Israel could enter the NPT as a nonnuclear weapon state if it took the route to enter used by South Africa in the early 1990s: disarm first and then accede to the treaty. However, as Israel argues that it will only agree to a regional NWFZ if a political solution is found to the region's frictions, and the Arab states argue equally vehemently that it has to enter a NWFZ before a political solution is possible, its entry appears blocked indefinitely.

ii. Withdrawals. As discussed earlier, while there is no mechanism for collective withdrawal from the NPT, there is one for individual withdrawal. What, then, are the likely forms this would take? It has been suggested that three are available: breaking out, crawling out, and walking out, while the current DPRK case offers a fourth category.[39]

a. Breakouts. In a breakout, a state in good standing has acquired all the necessary capabilities to both make and deliver a nuclear device and has sufficient stockpiled fissile material to move from zero nuclear weapons to tens immediately on reaching the end of its three months' notice period for withdrawal. Having the ability to act in this way has been characterized as being a latent or virtual proliferator. It is unclear how many states are currently in this position. However, advances in the general state of technology, the operation of clandestine state and nonstate procurement networks such as that fashioned by A. Q. Khan, and the projected revival of nuclear power reactor building and operations on a global scale suggest that their numbers will inexorably increase.

Two developments feed into this scenario. The threat of nuclear terrorism is generating a conflict between the commitments contained in the NPT and the knowledge NNWS may regard as essential for creating effective response mechanisms. Where should the line now be drawn between the injunction in Article II to "not otherwise acquire nuclear weapons or other nuclear explosive devices" and such defensive nuclear research? Secondly, many nuclear technologies are inherently dual use in nature, and the inherent technical barriers to nuclear proliferation at the core of the IAEA safeguards mechanisms are degrading. The diffusion of centrifuge enrichment technology for civil purposes is shortening the time between the availability of hard evidence of a state's intention to proliferate and the movement of a proliferating state to an irreversible breakout situation. In some cases, the political "warning time" may now be too short for coercive political (and military?) action to be mobilized to prevent it. Future nonproliferation policies may thus have to be based on noncorroborated intelligence or changes in the rules concerning legitimate and illegitimate fuel cycle activities. This situation is itself closely linked to the second type of withdrawal, crawling out.

b. Crawl-outs. Crawling out implies that states are engaged in a purposeful process to give them an eventual ability to break out from the NPT. The weaponization element of this is likely to be clandestine and difficult to confirm with any certainty due to the dual-use technology involved. Missile or aircraft delivery activities are likely to be more visible but are not subject to international control through an inclusive regime. In addition, nuclear and conventional delivery may be distinguishable only from observation of the flight profiles used in training. Finally, the fissile material needed for weapons might be produced rapidly in bulk by manufacturing safeguarded low-enriched uranium suitable for power reactors and then further enriching it using the same basic technology.

Crawling-out is central to contemporary concerns over Iran's nuclear program. Moreover some in the United States would argue that the situation goes beyond an inability to deal with this specific case. They would argue that what is occurring is "dysfunctional multilateralism."[40] Not only is the NPT unable to prevent proliferation, but it actively assists it by providing a legal umbrella under which proliferators can take shelter while awaiting an opportune moment to proliferate. For over a number of years a "crawl-out state" could position itself to "break out" without being overtly noncompliant with either the NPT or its IAEA safeguards agreements. Only three methods of stopping this from happening appear feasible.

One is to change the rules of global nuclear power activity to ones similar to those envisaged for peaceful nuclear explosives in Article V of the NPT. This would give to a very few states the right to enrich uranium and separate plutonium from used fuel, accompanied by arrangements under which NPT parties would be guaranteed preferential access to nuclear fuel made from these materials. This would alleviate some current proliferation concerns, but it would also create a new form of discrimination and thus be difficult to agree to by consensus.

The second method would be to give the IAEA new powers of intrusive inspection within national territories, including the task of investigating nuclear weaponization in all its aspects. Again this appears unlikely to gain consensus support. Finally there appears to be the option of military action against the key facilities involved once notice of withdrawal from the NPT has been given, something which would be contrary to international law unless the UNSC were to specifically authorize it.

c. Walkouts. In a walkout a state would withdraw from the treaty but would not make any overt attempt to develop a nuclear weapons program. It might be seen symbolically as the ultimate form of protest at the inability of the NPT to address modern proliferation problems. There have been only two cases of walkouts in the history of the NPT—one was that of Taiwan, the province of China which withdrew from the NPT when the PRC took over its seat at the UN. The second was the DPRK, which from 1995 onward ceased to attend NPT meetings on the basis that it had "suspended" its withdrawal from the treaty leading up to the 1994 Framework Agreement and had never returned. Both of these cases were somewhat unique in their circumstances, however.

The type of walkout that might be envisaged is either a tacit or overt one. Tacit walkouts could be defined as situations where states did not participate in any active way in NPT activities. This form of walkout might be evaluated by the number of parties not participating in the NPT review process (although other intervening variables could explain their absence). An overt walkout seems most probable from one of the Arab states as a form of protest against the activities of Israel and the United States. What this might involve is an act of formal withdrawal citing the specific reasons, linked to a request to the IAEA to sustain its NPT safeguards arrangements to provide evidence that it did not intend to acquire nuclear weapons. However, the balance of probability is that few states would act in this way as they would lose the opportunities presented by the NPT review process for direct political action over their concerns.

d. The DPRK case. The activities of the DPRK, and responses to them, have generated a range of negative consequences for the NPT and the nonproliferation regime. It is the only state which has withdrawn from the treaty when in noncompliance; it is also the only one which has then proceeded to explode a nuclear device. It remains to be seen whether this activity was political or security oriented in nature, but it has generated disagreements over whether the DPRK should be treated as a state party in noncompliance with its NPT commitments or a state similar to India and Pakistan which is outside the treaty and has tested.

The situation is further confused by the DPRK not transmitting information on its withdrawal to all the relevant states listed in Article X. Some parties regard it as not having fulfilled the legal conditions for withdrawal and thus remaining a (noncompliant) member of the treaty. Others see it as having been in noncompliance in the past but now being a nonmember. Those taking the latter position appear to have no clear vision of how to respond in the NPT context to the DPRK's actions, other than to negotiate an agreement in the regional six-nation (China, DPRK, Japan, Russia, South Korea, United States) context. In practice, the issue which has driven policies toward the DPRK has been fear of triggering a WMD war on the Korean peninsula rather than any longer-term considerations of the impact of existing and future policies on the nuclear nonproliferation regime and the NPT. Since 1993 this has led negotiations and deal making with the DPRK to take precedence over upholding the NPT rules, first in the shape of the Agreed Framework of October 1994 and more recently the attempts to reach an agreement with the DPRK through the medium of the six-party talks.

It is highly improbable that the eventual outcome of these negotiations will not serve to further reduce the international credibility of the NPT norm and rules. It seems inevitable that it will create new divergences between the overt benefits offered to treaty members and nonmembers. Indeed Iran was not slow to argue in 1994 that even though it was a state in good standing with the NPT, the United States was attempting to prevent it from completing its nuclear power plants while the DPRK was being rewarded for its overt noncompliance with two nuclear reactors and supplies of fuel oil. Now, in similar circumstances, it can again argue that greater rewards are available to the DPRK from leaving the treaty rather than from remaining within it.

e. The Withdrawal Process. The DPRK case has drawn attention to the opaqueness and weaknesses of the existing withdrawal provisions in the treaty. First, Article X.1 allows a state to withdraw by giving three months' notice of its intentions to member states and the UNSC. Second, although the withdrawal clause states that the member has to specify the "extraordinary events" related to the subject matter of the treaty and the "supreme interests" of the withdrawing state that have triggered its action, no process or mechanism is prescribed for questioning such explanations. Indeed the DPRK has never made any attempt to offer a formal explanation on the two occasions it has given notice of withdrawal—and the UNSC has by default acquiesced to this situation.

Moreover, although a withdrawing state has to transmit its notice of withdrawal to all members of the treaty and of the UNSC, the treaty offers no guidance on any responses that might follow. While it is implicit in Article X.1 that the UNSC should act to try to prevent withdrawals, no clear guidance is offered on how this should be done. This was one of the reasons why in the DPRK case, in contrast to that of Iran, action was left to bilateral or six-party negotiations.

A significant number of states have found this situation increasingly unsatisfactory, and the European Union (EU) collectively sought to obtain agreement from the 2005 NPT review conference on a set of guidelines to handle future withdrawal cases.[41] However, Egypt and other states argued this placed additional and unjustified duties on them in the context of the treaty, and no agreement on this course of action was possible. No doubt further attempts will be made to move this matter forward in the 2007–10 review cycle, but it seems likely to continue to generate opposition from NAM states who see themselves as being asked by the developed states to accept added commitments with no apparent reciprocal action in return.

iii. Accessions and Withdrawals: Some Conclusions. If the NPT is to collapse, rather than just degrade in its effectiveness and significance for nuclear nonproliferation, a mass withdrawal of the parties through the Article X.1 route would be required. There are few indications at the moment of this happening. However, in the longer term the only movements related to its universality appear likely to be negative ones: withdrawals and cases of proliferation from within. On the one hand this is an indication of its success in facilitating states accepting its norms and rules. On the other, it suggests that the spotlight will be increasingly focused on the limitations of the NPT and the nuclear nonproliferation regime to address modern proliferation challenges.

One of these limitations is the ability of a state to facilitate proliferation while operating within the NPT and IAEA safeguards contexts or breaching their rules: in short, its dysfunctional multilateralist attributes. Another is its structural inability to address the existence of declared NWS outside the treaty, whose existence impacts negatively on progress in global nuclear disarmament and fulfillment of the treaty's Article VI commitments. It also has a disruptive effect through the "regional issues" such states generate. Finally, problems of recognition hinder effective engagement to persuade the DPRK, India, and Pakistan to accept the NPT rules for technology transfers and thus dissuade them from the types of nuclear-relevant trading activities that have occurred in the past between the DPRK, Pakistan, Iran, and Libya.

One further area of weakness that is now apparent is the lack of clear guidelines for the conditions under which states may withdraw from the treaty. While some want withdrawal to be regarded as unacceptable, others wish it to remain as easy as possible. The latter is in part a product of a move since 1998 from a situation where proliferation was latent and membership of the treaty was moving toward universality to the current situation of almost as many NWS existing outside the treaty as there are within it. In this new postproliferation world, two vectors are discernable: the desire to lock in the accession gains made by the treaty in the past by making withdrawal more difficult and the trend for others to seek to keep options open for the medium term. A similar situation existed in the decade after 1968 as states assessed whether membership of the NPT would gather momentum and nuclear weapon aspirations could safely be abandoned as a result of the belief that it would prove an effective method of preventing proliferation. In the current decade, the tide may again be on the turn, with decreased faith in the treaty leading to a desire on the part of some states to prevent withdrawal becoming more difficult.

B. Noncompliance with the NPT

The issue of noncompliance with the NPT can be approached from either a legal or political perspective. From a legal perspective compliance is an absolute commitment: from a political perspective, equity, reciprocity, and nondiscrimination often color perceptions. Moreover, the commitments in the NPT text differ somewhat in their nature. While Article I, II, and III commitments are absolute, those in Articles IV and VI are more opaque and thus open to different interpretations. While some states view the issue of noncompliance as being almost entirely about the "hard" Article II commitment not to acquire nuclear weapons, others argue that there is a similar commitment contained in Article VI and thus any moves to strengthen noncompliance mechanisms should cover Articles II, IV, and VI equally: nonproliferation, peaceful uses, and disarmament.

i. Article II Noncompliance. Until 1991 and the Iraq case, the issue of dealing with Article II noncompliance was latent. Iraq generated three sets of responses: its nuclear disarmament under far-reaching UNSC resolutions, changes to the scope of IAEA safeguards to facilitate detection of clandestine activities, and the negotiation of the Additional Protocol (AP) to give the agency enhanced investigative powers. This was followed swiftly by the first DPRK crisis. Agreement to implement IAEA safeguards on its territory led to the discovery that its initial declaration was inaccurate. The NPT verification system worked, but the UNSC proved incapable of dealing with the outcome, and the crisis had to be resolved through bilateral negotiations.

One consequence of these two cases was that through to 1991 the NPT Article II rules and norms appeared to have been largely upheld by both participating and nonparticipating states. After that point Iraq's activities demonstrated that sustaining a ban on WMD activities within a sovereign state was going to be extremely difficult. Moreover, even when a disarmament regime was imposed on a state that was more rigorous than the IAEA one, the diverging national interests of the permanent members of the UNSC would make it difficult to enforce. In addition, the rules of procedure of the NPT review system did not debar such a state from participating in decisions and blocking consensus, thus giving it a veto on wording critical of its actions. Indeed the 2000 Final Document was only possible because Iraq and its accusers could read the phrase "the importance of Iraq's full continuous cooperation and compliance with its obligations" as relating to both the past and the future[42] — and the DPRK was absent.

In the period 2002–6 a similar series of contrary trends existed. On the one hand the Iraq issue was resolved by regime change. Arguably this had the positive effect of triggering a decision by Libya to openly declare it had been engaged in nuclear proliferant activities though the A. Q. Khan network and engaging in a process of nuclear and other WMD disarmament.

On the other hand, the DPRK gave notice of its withdrawal from the treaty, reprocessed the fuel rods that had previously been under IAEA observation, and exploded a nuclear device. It was not until February 2007 that the six-party talks led to agreement on a series of step-by-step arrangements holding out some hope of the DPRK retreating to its previous nonnuclear weapon status.

Finally, Iran admitted to a number of clandestine activities dating back to the 1980s. It agreed to freeze its centrifuge enrichment program under arrangements negotiated with France, Germany, and the UK but then reversed that decision. The issue was eventually remitted to the UNSC, which imposed graduated sanctions with time limits for halting its enrichment activities.

All of these cases illuminate the limited ability and willingness of NPT parties to collectively respond to nonproliferation. The treaty has no integral provisions for dealing with noncompliance with Article II. Its review process was not tasked to do this; its text offers no clear or detailed definition of what constitutes noncompliance; and the process of dealing with this issue is external to the treaty. The consequence is that the NPT cannot be directly blamed for the inability of the international community to deal with Article II noncompliance cases, as it offers its parties no means to do so. At the same time it cannot be praised for its handling of those cases where noncompliant behavior has been reversed, except insofar as it has provided a legal basis for action.

ii. Article IV Noncompliance. This article is somewhat contradictory.[43] The consequence is that Iran has argued that the treaty gives it an unrestricted right to the peaceful use of nuclear energy, including enrichment and reprocessing technologies. The United States and many other states have argued that due to the close linkages between civil and military uses of these technologies, their transfer to, and indigenous production in, additional states such as Iran should be discouraged and preferably banned—even though this would be discriminatory.

Until the 1990s, the proliferation of technology was enforced through the informal Nuclear Suppliers Group (NSG). The NSG provided guidelines to adherents on what should and should not be exported. It also required them to exercise "particular caution" (i.e., nontransfer) over the trade in enrichment and reprocessing technology. This system of control was condemned by many NAM states as discriminatory, but justified by exporting states as a means of ensuring that they fulfilled their Article I and II responsibilities. By the mid-1990s, however, the NSG guidelines were being outflanked by the activities of A. Q. Khan's procurement network. Khan's network had been used initially to enable Pakistan to evade the NSG restrictions and was then used to supply enrichment technologies to Libya and Iran on an apparently commercial basis.

One consequence of A. Q. Khan's actions is that export constraints have to be deployed overtly. This has involved instruments such as voluntary freezes of limited duration and UNSC resolutions, as well as making Article IV the subject of considerable public friction and disagreement. Above all, it has changed what was previously a very effective covert method of preventing proliferation of these technologies into a situation where the achievement of this end is now problematic at best, and a near impossibility at worst.

Looking to the future, these issues are likely to become more controversial, rather than less, if global warming and energy shortages lead to a round of ordering of nuclear power plants similar to that which occurred in the first half of the 1970s, a situation which has been described as a "nuclear renaissance." Unless new rules are agreed on that enable this renaissance and national energy security to be based on the offer of "turnkey" contracts to guarantee the supply of fuel and reactors to new entrants and repatriate used fuel, it is difficult to see how a key assumption underpinning the NPT will not become increasingly questioned, namely that civil and military nuclear technologies can be clearly distinguished from each other, and the barriers between them sustained at a high level. Difficulties in sustaining the civil/military distinction may thus degrade belief in the future viability of the NPT norms and rules.

iii. Article VI Noncompliance. Many states parties view the issue of the NWS compliance with Article VI as of equal importance to the nonproliferation and peaceful use pillars of the treaty. Thus in NPT forums, any discussion of noncompliance with the treaty's nonproliferation provisions inevitably opens a discussion on noncompliance with its disarmament ones. At the same time the differing commitments are themselves discriminatory, in that the nonproliferation ones appear absolute, while the disarmament and peaceful uses ones are open to differing interpretations. In the disarmament area, the language addresses negotiations rather than rules and leaves open whether these negotiations are to be about ending the arms race and engaging in nuclear disarmament as isolated acts or as part of negotiations on the 1960s concept of general and complete disarmament. Until 1995, debates in the NPT review process on this issue tended to be accusatory rather than constructive. In 1995 a plan for disarmament action was agreed to, and in 2000 this plan was expanded into the thirteen practical steps. Although some of these steps involved negotiations, many did not, and the listing recognized that disarmament was going to a multifaceted, incremental, and prolonged process and that not all steps were applicable to any individual NWS. However, since not all the steps listed are now possible, it is profoundly unclear how objective judgments should and can be made in the future over compliance or noncompliance with Article VI. Also, it is unclear whether what was agreed to by states was a series of commitments to act or a number of yardsticks to measure progress toward disarmament.

iv. Responses to Noncompliance. The NPT text does not address the issue of how its parties should respond to noncompliance, however defined. In practice, responses have been very ad hoc, with the general rule being that a mixture of sticks and carrots have been employed. The carrots were very noticeable in the Libyan, DPRK, and Iran cases, in the form of economic assistance and a move away from pariah status. In the case of Iraq and Iran, military coercion was also threatened, and in the case of Iraq, it was executed. There seems little likelihood that in future there will be any form of more organized response process. However, responses which involve rewards will tend to lead to questioning by compliant parties if noncompliant behavior is seen to be generating greater rewards than the lesser benefits obtained from compliance.

Some argue that the NPT should have internal provisions to deal with noncompliance. Perceptions of the utility of the treaty are diminished when cases of noncompliance emerge and have to be addressed elsewhere. Evidence for this can be found in the attempts by Canada and other states to fill the "institutional deficit" they believe exists in this area with an executive committee or proposals to summon meetings of the parties to discuss such cases.[44] While it is unclear what advantages in practice such arrangements would have over the UNSC becoming seized of an allegation of noncompliance, the search for new solutions undoubtedly reinforces perceptions of an overall decline in the utility of the treaty. Yet it remains the case that the ability of other international mechanisms to act rests on the NPT's norms and rules.

The debate within NPT forums over what constitutes noncompliance will continue into the future, with every indication that consensus on clear definitions will remain elusive. A particular concern must be that the existing discriminatory mechanisms to deny enrichment and reprocessing technology have now been forced into the open, and it seems likely that proliferation by "crawl-out" will become increasingly difficult to control. Consensus interpretations of the NPT permitting such controls to operate in an overt manner will be difficult, if not impossible, to achieve. Just as worrying are the major difficulties this presents for responding to noncompliance in situations where there is no agreement on what precise actions are to trigger a response, especially if those actions in themselves pose no immediate security threat.

Events and the Relevance of the NPT

One consequence of the post–9/11 international environment for the antiproliferation policies of the United States and its allies has been to radically change the focus of these activities. The issue of nonstate actors stealing weapons, acquiring nuclear materials, and manufacturing nuclear explosive devices is now high on their agenda. Both state and nonstate proliferation activities focus attention on clandestine nuclear procurement networks of the A. Q. Khan type, with the distinction between state and nonstate activities often opaque. In parallel, physical counterproliferation activities not mentioned in the text of the NPT have become more visible and salient: prevention by physical denial is acquiring greater significance in comparison to building international trust to remove the underlying security dilemmas that generate proliferation. Counterproliferation tools and policies now appear to dominate the proliferation scene, with nonproliferation agreements and diplomacy receding into the background.

The impact on the NPT of these changes is difficult to evaluate in any quantitative way, but some indicators of what is occurring can be identified. The most obvious is that while the NPT remains the legal basis for counterproliferation actions and contains the norms which justify them, it was drafted in an age when nonstate nuclear weapon activities were inconceivable. Its focus was, and still is, on interstate activities: it appears to some that it now lacks the flexibility to cover nonstate activities also. One consequence is that almost all the responses to the post–9/11 environment have taken place outside of the ambit of the treaty. This includes the increased authority and status the IAEA has acquired as a flexible global nuclear governance instrument; the UNSC Resolution 1540 mandating effective national nuclear control legislation; the Proliferation Security Initiative (PSI) mechanisms for intercepting clandestine shipments of WMD precursor materials and technology; and homeland security and intelligence exchange arrangements to protect against WMD terrorism.

Moreover, as indicated above, the relevance of the NPT to the three main sets of contemporary state proliferation events—those involving Iraq, Iran, and the DPRK—has been to provide the legal context for action by other mechanisms. States have bypassed the treaty review process in their attempts to deal with these events; hence impressions of its irrelevance have strengthened. At the same time, Iran has used treaty language to defend its own position. Some have therefore seen that the ability for proliferators to defend their actions through the NPT makes it a positive barrier to dealing with the realities of proliferation and thus worse than irrelevant.

Both external changes and its own internal contradictions can thus be seen to have lowered perceptions of the value of the treaty in preventing proliferation. In looking to the future, however, two generic types of proliferation events seem likely to figure large: on the one hand, declaratory statements of nuclear weapon aspirations, possession, and nuclear testing, and, on the other, nuclear weapon use.

A. Declaratory Statements/Nuclear Testing

A precedent now exists for assessing the impact of these sets of events on the treaty: the DPRK. In practice, its withdrawal from the NPT in 2003 and its later declaratory statement of nuclear weapon possession had little discernable effect on the operations of the NPT. Two reasons may account for this. One was the lack of consensus over whether this was a case of withdrawal or of noncompliance. The second was that the regional states decided it should be dealt with as a regional security issue through their six-party forum, rather than a proliferation one. In these circumstances, the UNSC and the NPT parties did not wish to complicate matters further by taking actions which might reduce the chances of a favorable settlement. This was especially so as one objective in these negotiations has been to return the DPRK to full membership of the NPT as a NNWS. The opaqueness over its legal status seems destined to continue so long as the regional negotiations move forward.

The DPRK's nuclear test in 2006 had no precedent in NPT history. While doubts persist over its purpose and success, the same constraints on positive action applied as in the case of its withdrawal from the NPT, namely that making it a major NPT issue might complicate a favorable regional settlement. In this, and probably in any similar future situation, the circumstances of the case are likely to dominate over any other consideration, particularly where an ongoing regional process exists through which the nuclear issues can be resolved through wider negotiations.

B. Nuclear Weapon Use/Terrorist Devices

It is now over sixty years since nuclear weapons were used against Japanese cities. A very significant taboo would be broken if nuclear explosives were to be used in the future by either state or nonstate actors. Much would clearly depend on the circumstances of use and its human consequences: use in a barren and unpopulated area or at sea would clearly generate a different response than use against a city. But in general, two possible responses could result from this situation.

One is that nuclear weapon use would in some respects become legitimized, and additional NNWS would start to think seriously about acquiring nuclear weapons if they did not have convincing nuclear security guarantees from NWS. This would result in withdrawals from the NPT and a further degrading of its credibility as a useful international instrument. The second response is that as in 1945–46, it would stimulate concerted international action to move toward a nonnuclear world. This could lead to the NPT being strengthened in its usefulness and eventually being superseded by a disarmament treaty.

Some Overall Conclusions: Two Scenarios

Logically the only way open to the NPT parties to move forward in a visible manner now is through a combination of the NPT becoming universal and all the NWS giving up their weapons. This makes defining what nuclear disarmament means in practice an important precondition of such a scenario, as well as shaping IAEA safeguards arrangements so they link into any future verification regime for such a disarmament treaty. It is difficult to predict the circumstances in which this long-term goal would become a short-range reality, though nuclear use could be one of them.

The more likely scenario, however, is a continuing loss of saliency for the NPT in the eyes of many of its parties, though the underlying norms and overt legal commitments it contains will continue to shape state and coalition actions. There will not be any sudden collapse or mass defection from the treaty. The problem will be that it, and the regime and the UNSC, have shown themselves incapable of dealing with the various forms of noncompliance with, and withdrawal from, the NPT that have been experienced since 1991 and no doubt will recur in the future. In addition, its review process is just that: it has no executive powers and is open to regional and global political gamesmanship. However, its atmospherics will be considerably enhanced if the CTBT were to be brought into force and a fissile material cut-off treaty (FMCT) agreed to.

The NPT will therefore have to live with the paradox generated by events in 1998: that its success in gaining sufficient accessions to have a near universal membership has been eroded by the existence of declared NWS outside of the treaty. It will also have to live with its lack of precision over issues such as peaceful uses, where any changes to fuel-cycle rules will have to be negotiated outside of the treaty. But the NPT will continue to exist because of what it is: a treaty based on generally agreed-on norms and containing rules for international behavior based on those norms. More positively, there is little doubt that the small number of proliferation "states of concern" today present a much more hopeful prospect for the future than the much larger numbers anticipated by the Dunn and Kahn study in 1976.

Notes

1. Lewis Dunn and Herman Kahn, *Trends in Nuclear Proliferation, 1975–1995*, Prepared for U.S. Arms Control and Disarmament Agency by the Hudson Institute, May 15, 1976, http://stinet.dtic.mil/oai/oai?verb=getRecord&metadataPrefix=html&identifier=ADB011707.

2. These are the Partial Test-Ban Treaty (PTBT) of 1963, which limited explosive testing to underground locations, and the Comprehensive Test-Ban Treaty (CTBT) of 1996, which banned all such testing. The former is in force and has 125 parties; the latter is not yet in force, but all its signatories have observed a moratorium on testing since 1996. Its associated international monitoring system, designed to detect global nuclear testing, does exist and, despite its very low yield, detected and verified the DPRK test in 2006.

3. These treaties go beyond the commitments contained in the NPT in that they include both a prohibition on the stationing of other states' nuclear weapons on national territory and the provision to states within the zone of unconditional negative security assurances by the NPT nuclear weapon states. The areas covered by them are Antarctica; Latin America and the Caribbean (Treaty of Tlatelolco); the South Pacific (Treaty of Rarotonga); South East Asia (Treaty of Bangkok); Africa (Treaty of Pelindaba); and Central Asia. Only the first three of these are fully operative. Other areas suggested for NWFZs include the Middle East and the Gulf Region.

4. The export control arrangements include the Nuclear Suppliers Group (NSG); the Missile Technology Control Regime (MTCR); Hague Code of Conduct (HCoC), which covers missile technology; and the Proliferation Security Initiative (PSI), a mechanism facilitating the interception of clandestine transit of proliferation relevant artifacts and materials.

5. Unlike the NPT, the IAEA has both a secretariat and inspectors based in Vienna, as well as an executive arm, its board of governors, whose sanction powers are limited to the

withdrawal of technical cooperation with a state. If these are judged insufficient, it can report a situation to the UN Security Council (UNSC), which can then use its own powers to act.

6. IAEA safeguards had already been in existence for a decade when the NPT was signed. Its first safeguards system, known as INFCIRC/66, was agreed to in 1965. The NPT system, INFCIRC/153, was not agreed to until 1972.

7. This distinction is based on their isotopic composition. The two materials normally used to make nuclear weapons are uranium or plutonium. They can exist in several forms that differ only in their mass, indicated by a number after their name. The two materials most appropriate for weapons are uranium-235 and plutonium-239.

8. Ben Sanders and George Bunn, "A New View of Review," Programme for Promoting Nuclear Non-proliferation (PPNN), Issue Review, no. 6, September 1996.

9. See Preparatory Committee for the 2010 Review Conference of the Parties to the Treaty on the Non-proliferation of Nuclear Weapons, *Model Nuclear Weapons Convention*, Working Paper submitted by Costa Rica, NPT/CONF.2010/PC.I/WP.17, 1 May 2007, http://www.un.org/NPT2010/offdocs_7_May_onward/NPT_CONF_2010_PC_1_WP_17_E.pdf.

10. The wording is from the Final Document of the 2000 NPT Review Conference.

11. *The Atomic Energy Act of 1954*, August 30, 1954, Public Law 83-703, 68 Stat. 919. The treaty was worded in such a way as to allow continued U.S.-UK collaboration in weapon development by using similar language to that in the U.S. 1958 amendments to its nuclear energy legislation, which prohibited transfer of complete weapons, but not components, materials, and design information.

12. For a detailed discussion to the negotiating background to these issues and the statements in relevant U.S. Senate hearings in 1969, see John Simpson and Jenny Nielsen, *The NPT and Nuclear Sharing*, http://www.mcis.soton.ac.uk.

13. Mohamed I. Shaker, *The Nuclear Non-Proliferation Treaty: Origin and Implementation, 1959–1969*, vol. 1 (London: Oceana, 1980).

14. General and Complete Disarmament was a concept first put forward by the UK in September 1959 at the UN General Assembly and discussed in detail through 1962. Its origins lay in the USSR's perceived preponderance of conventional military armaments in Europe and the belief that U.S. and UK nuclear weapons were offsetting this and thus creating a military balance. Thus any attempt at nuclear disarmament would have to be balanced by a parallel reduction in conventional capabilities. By 1961 a set of guidelines had been agreed to between the U.S. and USSR (the McCloy-Zorin statement), but the parties could not agree on how to implement them, and the exercise eventually produced no concrete results, other than to remain a part of the agenda of successive global disarmament bodies meeting in Geneva. See Jozef Goldblat, *Arms Control: A Guide on Negotiations and Agreements* (London: Sage, published for International Peace Research Institute, Oslo, 1994), 36–38.

15. See Statement by H. E. Mr. François Rivasseau, ambassador, permanent representative of France to the Conference on Disarmament, third session of the Preparatory Committee for the 2005 Review Conference of the Parties to the Treaty on the Non-Proliferation of Nuclear Weapons, cluster I, New York, April 29, 2004.

16. International Court of Justice, *Legality of the Threat or Use of Nuclear Weapons*, advisory opinion, July 8, 1996.

17. While it is feasible that sixty-three states parties could be assembled to trigger an amendment conference, any amendment must then pass over two barriers that appear insuperable. The first is that the amendment must be approved by a majority of the parties to the treaty (i.e., ninety-five states) including the five NWS and all NPT parties that are on the board of the IAEA. If it passes over that barrier, the same conditions apply for its entry into force for those states that have ratified it. In the highly unlikely circumstances where all of these conditions were met, there would then be two treaties extant, the amended and unamended versions, with differing memberships—with those opposed to the amendments in the unamended version of the treaty.

18. See George Bunn and John B. Rhinelander, "NPT Withdrawal: Time for the Security Council to Step In," *Arms Control Today* 35, no. 4 (May 2005): 17–21; and Shaker, *Nuclear Non-Proliferation Treaty*, 885–99.

19. Jenny Nielsen and John Simpson, "The NPT Withdrawal Clause and Its Negotiating History," Mountbatten Centre for International Studies, NPT issue review, July 2004, http://www.mcis.soton.ac.uk/Site_Files/pdf/withdrawal_clause_NPT_nielsen&simpson_2004.pdf.

20. George Bunn, Charles N. van Doren, and David Fischer, "Options and Opportunities: The NPT Extension Conference of 1995," Programme for Promoting Nuclear Non-Proliferation study 2, Mountbatten Centre for International Studies, 1991.

21. James Acton, with Carter Newman, *IAEA Verification of Military Research and Development*, Verification Matters, VERTIC Research Report no. 5, July 2006, http://www.vertic.org/publications/VM5%20(2).pdf.

22. See UN General Assembly resolution 2028 (XX), adopted November 23, 1965, UNSC resolution 255, adopted June 19, 1968, and unilateral statements made in 1978 by the United States and the Soviet Union. For analysis and historical background on security assurances, see George Bunn and Roland M. Timerbaev, "Security Assurances to Non-Nuclear-Weapon States," *Nonproliferation Review* 1, no. 1 (Fall 1993): 11–20; and George Bunn and Roland M. Timerbaev, "Security Assurances to Non-Nuclear-Weapon States: Possible Options for Change," Programme for Promoting Nuclear Non-Proliferation (PPNN) Issue Review no. 7 (September 1996), Mountbatten Centre for International Studies.

23. Article VIII.3.

24. "The Implementation of Agreements Related to Disarmament," in *SIPRI Yearbook 1976: World Armaments and Disarmament* (Cambridge, MA: MIT Press, 1976), 364; and "Appendix 9A: Final Declaration of the Review Conference of the Parties to the Treaty on the Non-Proliferation of Nuclear Weapons, 30 May 1975," in *SIPRI Yearbook 1976*, 403–13.

25. "The Second NPT Review Conference," in *SIPRI Yearbook 1981: World Armaments and Disarmament* (London: Taylor and Francis, 1981), 297–338; and Jozef Goldblat, *Twenty Years of the Non-Proliferation Treaty: Implementation and Prospects* (Oslo: International Peace Research Institute [PRIO], 1990), 50–51.

26. Jozef Goldblat, "The Third Review of the NPT Treaty," in *SIPRI Yearbook 1986: World Armaments and Disarmament* (Oxford: Oxford University Press, 1986), 469–80, and Jozef Goldblat, "Appendix 20A: Final Declaration of the Third Review Conference," in *SIPRI Yearbook 1986: World Armaments and Disarmament*, 481–94.

27. David Fischer and Harald Müller, "The Fourth Review of the Non-Proliferation Treaty," in *SIPRI Yearbook 1991: World Armaments and Disarmament* (Oxford: Oxford University Press, 1991), 555–84, and John Simpson, "The 1990 Review Conference of the Nuclear Non-Proliferation Treaty: Pointer to the Future or Diplomatic Accident," *The Round Table*, no. 318 (April 1991): 139–54.

28. John Simpson, "The Nuclear Non-proliferation Regime after the NPT Review and Extension Conference," in *SIPRI Yearbook 1996: Armaments, Disarmament and International Security* (Oxford University Press: Oxford, 1996), 561–89.

29. In part the uncertainty arises from the procedure used: to agree on the three documents separately, with the extension document last, and then collectively. This process appeared to have been done purposefully to infuse the review conference with both political and legal symbolism, though what it implies remains obscure.

30. NPT/CONF.1995/32/Res.1, May 11, 1995.

31. The wording of paragraph 4 is as follows: "The purpose of the Preparatory Committee meetings would be to consider principles, objectives and ways in order to promote the full implementation of the Treaty, as well as its universality, and to make recommendations thereon to the Review Conference."

32. John Simpson, "The Consequences of the 1997 PrepCom and Their Implications for the Review Process," in *South East Asia: Regional Security and Nuclear Non-Proliferation* (Southampton, UK: Mountbatten Centre for International Studies, Programme for Promoting Nuclear Non-Proliferation, 1997).

33. Tariq Rauf, "The April 1998 NPT PrepCom," *Nonproliferation Review* 5, no. 2 (Winter 1998): 121–31; Tariq Rauf and John Simpson, "The 1999 NPT PrepCom," *Nonproliferation Review* 6, no. 2 (Winter 1999): 121–23; chairman's working paper, NPT/CONF.2000/PC.III/29, May 14, 1999; chairman's revised working paper, NPT/CONF.2000/PC.III/58, May 20, 1999.

34. Rebecca Johnson, "The 2000 NPT Review Conference: A Delicate, Hard-Won Compromise," *Disarmament Diplomacy* 5, no. 46 (May 2000): 4, http://www.acronym.org .uk/dd/dd46/46npt.htm; Tariq Rauf, "An Unequivocal Success? Implications of the NPT Review Conference," *Arms Control Today* 30, no. 6 (July/August 2000): 9–16; Norman A. Wulf, "Observations from the 2000 NPT Review Conference," *Arms Control Today* 30, no. 9 (November 2000): 3–9; John Simpson, "The 2000 NPT Review Conference," *SIPRI Yearbook 2001: Armaments, Disarmament and International Security* (Oxford: Oxford University Press, 2001), 487–502.

35. "Interview: Ambassador Salander on the 2002 NPT Preparatory Committee," conducted by William Potter, Mary Beth Nikitin, and Tariq Rauf, *Nonproliferation Review* 9, no. 2 (Summer 2002): 1–14; Rebecca Johnson, "The NPT PrepCom: Papering Over the Cracks?" *Disarmament Diplomacy*, no. 64 (May/June 2002); Tanya Ogilvie-White and John Simpson, "The NPT and Its 2003 PrepCom Session: A Regime in Need of Intensive Care," *Nonproliferation Review* 10, no. 1 (Spring 2003): 40–58.

36. See Rebecca Johnson, "Report on the 2004 NPT PrepCom," *Disarmament Diplomacy*, no. 77 (May/June 2004); John Simpson and Jenny Nielsen, "Fiddling While Rome

Burns? The 2004 Session of the PrepCom for the 2005 Review Conference," *Nonproliferation Review* 11, no. 2 (Summer 2004): 1–26.

37. See Rebecca Johnson, "Politics and Protection: Why the 2005 NPT Review Conference Failed," *Disarmament Diplomacy*, no. 80 (Autumn 2005); John Simpson and Jenny Nielsen, "The 2005 NPT Review Conference: Mission Impossible?" *Nonproliferation Review* 12, no. 2 (Summer 2005): 271–301.

38. White House, "Joint Statement between President George W. Bush and Prime Minister Manmohan Singh," July 18 2005, http://www.whitehouse.gov/news/releases/2005/07/20050718-6.html. For analysis of the implications of the U.S.-India nuclear deal, see David Albright, testimony before the House Committee on International Relations, Hearing on the U.S.-India "Global Partnership" and Its Impact on Non-Proliferation, October 26, 2005, http://www.isis-online.org/publications/southasia/abrighttestimonyoctober262005usindiadeal.pdf; and Fred McGoldrick, Harold Bengelsdorf, and Lawrence Scheinman "The U.S.-India Nuclear Deal: Taking Stock," *Arms Control Today* 35, no. 8 (October 2005): 6–12.

39. I am grateful to Dr Lewis Dunn for suggesting this useful typology during a recent workshop.

40. See John Simpson, "The Nuclear Landscape in 2004: Past, Present and Future," Weapons of Mass Destruction Commission paper no. 3, 2004, 15–16, http://www.wmdcommission.org/files/No3.pdf.

41. See Preparatory Committee for the 2005 Review Conference of the Parties to the Treaty on the Non-proliferation of Nuclear Weapons, *Withdrawal from the Treaty on the Non-proliferation of Nuclear Weapons: European Union Common Approach*, working paper submitted by Luxembourg on behalf of the European Union, NPT/CONF.2005/WP.32, May 10, 2005, http://www.un.org/events/npt2005/working%20papers.html.

42. See Johnson, "2000 NPT Review Conference"; and Rauf, "Unequivocal Success?"

43. For an extended discussion on these issues see Darryl Howlett and John Simpson, "Nuclear Non-proliferation: How to Ensure an Effective Compliance Mechanism," ch. 1 in *Effective Non-proliferation: The European Union and the 2005 NPT Review Conference*, Chaillot Papers, no. 77, European Union Institute for Security Studies, 11–19, April 2005, http://www.iss.europa.eu/index.php?id=143.

44. See Preparatory Committee for the 2005 Review Conference of the Parties to the Treaty on the Non-proliferation of Nuclear Weapons, *Overcoming the Institutional Deficit of the NPT*, working paper submitted by Canada, NPT/CONF.2005/PC.III/WP.1, April 5, 2004, http://www.dfait.gc.ca/arms/2004npt5-en.asp.

CHAPTER FOUR

Chemical and Biological Weapons

Julian Perry Robinson

This chapter presents a synoptic view of chemical and biological weapons (CBW), their threats to our security, and international efforts to contain them. In preference to "weapons of mass destruction" (WMD), a concept of "governance regime" is used to frame the issues. For while some CBW can properly be treated as WMD, all CBW are WMD only when eccentric meanings are given to these two technical terms. The original 1947–48 United Nations definition of WMD, for example, some of which is followed in present-day U.S. legislation on the subject, embraces only "lethal" chemical and biological weapons, whereas the CBW disarmament treaties of 1972 and 1993 have no such limitation, covering lethal and "nonlethal" CBW alike. This chapter therefore warns that express pursuit of WMD nonproliferation may damage the existing CBW governance regime, which is aimed at suppressing CBW and has proved largely successful in so doing. "Nonproliferation" is itself another technical term that is problematic in its application to CBW, for international law is now either approaching or, depending on one's view, has long since reached the point at which any possession of CBW is illegal. To posit nonproliferation of CBW as a policy objective is therefore to imply that this legal regime is failing. There is no evidence whatsoever for this. Nor, in contrast to nuclear weapons, does any state have license to possess CBW, not even the permanent members of the UN Security Council (UNSC).

So the present chapter does not fit easily into a book about WMD nonproliferation. It starts with an account of what sets CBW apart from other weapons. It then explains its concept of "CBW governance regime" and goes on to consider the challenges facing the regime. It closes with discussion of how the regime might best be strengthened.

The Peculiarities of CBW

CBW are weapons whose intended means for causing harm is either the toxicity of chemicals or the infectivity of disease-causing micro-organisms (including viruses, prions, and other such biological agents that are not, in the strict meaning of the expression, living organisms). There are other categories of biological and chemical that, although highly aggressive in their properties, are not useful in either toxic or infective weapons and which are therefore disregarded in the present chapter: napalm, white phosphorus, smoke agents, malodorants, high explosives, propellants, bacteria that can damage inanimate materials, and many more besides. They all lie beyond the scope, too, of the CBW disarmament treaties just mentioned.[1] Article II of the 1993 Chemical Weapons Convention (CWC) limits the chemicals covered by the treaty to "toxic chemicals and their precursors," qualified by a general purpose criterion (GPC) that reads "except when intended for purposes not prohibited under this Convention, as long as the types and quantities are consistent with such purposes." Article II goes on to define a toxic chemical as "any chemical which through its chemical action on life processes can cause death, temporary incapacitation or permanent harm to humans or animals." The corresponding provision in Article I of the 1972 Biological and Toxin Weapons Convention (BWC) is worded less tightly but also uses a GPC: it extends to all "microbial or other biological agents, or toxins whatever their origin or method of production, of types and in quantities that have no justification for prophylactic, protective or other peaceful purposes."

Readers needing detailed descriptive information about CBW that is reliable and sufficiently extensive to go to the heart of the problems that the weapons present for security—international, national, and human security—are well advised to turn first to three authoritative international texts on CBW—that of the UN secretary-general in 1969, which heralded the BWC negotiation, and those of the World Health Organization (WHO), initially produced as input into the secretary-general's report and later rewritten for the post–Cold War, post–9/11 world.[2] The 2004 WHO volume allows one to understand what makes CBW so peculiar today and why the security and health impacts of CBW armament could be so heavy. Three features in particular stand out from that text.

First and foremost, CBW may resemble other categories of weapon in that they can attack life, killing their victims no less dead than bullets or bayonets, but they may also be targeted to disrupt individual processes that contribute to life, which other weapons cannot do save by accident, not design. The nerve gases, for example, target nerve-signal transmission; the blood gases, cellular respiration. Advances in the life sciences and in those allied technologies that allow the analysis and construction of complex biologically active molecules could eventually make it possible to design a CBW agent that will interfere with *any* life process that can be understood in molecular terms, whether it be the process of development, inheritance, reproduction, locomotion, sensation, cognition, or indeed any other process that keeps us functioning properly, according to expectations. The potential is there, inasmuch as it has not materialized already, for inducing many different forms of malfunction, maybe even ones that discriminate between ethnic groups of human beings. It is this potential for manipulating at will our very humanity, in pursuit of who-knows-what strategy of adversary subjugation, repression, or coercion, that makes CBW especially menacing.[3] Science has a way to go yet before the full horrors can be upon us, but the writing is clearly on the wall. For example, the most obvious motivation that can be imputed to Iraq's program in the 1980s to weaponize aflatoxin is a desire to harm through latent liver cancer a subsequent generation of anticipated adversaries. As one UN Special Committee on Iraq (UNSCOM) commissioner put it, the objective must have been a weapon of delayed genocide.[4] Artillery shells charged with aflatoxin are said to have been used during the suppression of the Shi'ite uprising in March 1991. This has not been confirmed.

The second outstanding characteristic is that, as destroyers of life on a large scale, some CBW are WMD. When first used, on April 22 and 23, 1915, the device that brought chemical warfare out from its prehistory, namely massed cylinders of liquefied chlorine gas that could simultaneously be opened into the wind, reportedly asphyxiated five thousand French and Canadian troops at Ypres in Belgium and harmed a further fifteen thousand. Comparable numbers of people are said to have fallen victim to Iraqi mustard and nerve gas in the Kurdish town of Halabja after chemical air raids during March 16–18, 1988. For biological weapons there has been no similar experience, but during 1964–68 the United States conducted unprecedentedly large field trials over open sea of aircraft germ weapons, each of which was found capable of laying down a cross-wind line source of pathogenic microbial aerosol tens of kilometers long that was able to infect experimental animals at sea level over a distance of several tens of kilometers downwind.[5] That could translate into an infective threat to every person living within an area on the order of thousands, even tens of thousands, of square kilometers. In other words, it appeared from experimental data that some biological weapons would be capable of producing effects comparable in their magnitude to the life-destroying potential of nuclear weapons. Within the North Atlantic Treaty Organization (NATO) at that time, defense scientists were also anticipating a new generation of *chemical* weapons having comparable area effectiveness.[6] Yet the actual historical record of CBW employment is not at all dominated by episodes of mass destruction. Published military doctrine shows that most of the military and other utilities for which user-services have valued possession of CBW have depended on aggressive properties other than mass killing. One may view the available target effects of CBW as lying along spectra that have highly localized, say, or low-casualty effects at one end and large-area or mass-casualty effects at the other. Where along a spectrum a given chemical or biological weapon would manifest its effects is determined by the characteristics of the toxic/infective agent being used (such as the contagiousness of any disease it can cause) and the manner of its use, and by the vulnerability of the threatened population, this reflecting such factors as the health status of the population and degree of preparedness for protecting itself against the disseminated agent. It remains the case today that, in the design of CBW, increasingly severe technological constraints set in as the mass-destruction end of the spectrum is approached: the greater and more assured the area-effectiveness sought for the weapon, the greater the practical difficulties of achieving it. This is why the notion of mass-destruction terrorism using CBW is less plausible than its portrayals have often suggested.

The third outstanding characteristic of CBW is the existence of a uniquely wide array of societal constraints on CBW armament. This array has been building up over time in the law and custom of nations, so that damaging opprobrium is likely to fasten on any future users of CBW. Only nuclear weapons share this feature, but they have not yet attracted anything approaching the proscription of CBW. Some states speak with pride about their nuclear weapons.

From this third characteristic of CBW there stem elements of widely accepted law tending to suppress biological and chemical warfare. This is the "CBW governance regime" referred to earlier: an accretion of norms, rules, and procedures, both national and international, the whole constituting an entity ("regime") that individual states, through their various internal political processes, may judge themselves to be better off inside than outside. Its emergence can be explained in different ways. One of them is in terms of an ancient cross-cultural taboo, evident in different literatures over the millennia, against weapons that exploit disease, whether infectious or noninfectious.[7] One may well imagine this taboo having become transformed into a norm of international behavior, providing a basis for the further development of international law that is uncommonly strong in this peculiar field of armament. Weapons of any type are designed to harm, and there is no obvious reason for regarding one type of weaponized harm as more (or less) reprehensible than another. Is it worse to be the victim of unnatural disease than, say, to be shattered by shell fragments? One may ask this and then be surprised that so strong an obloquy should nevertheless have attached to disease weapons and not to other weapons. There is an irrationality here whose very strength and depth is characteristic of taboo.

The Existing CBW Governance Regime

The more recent milestones in that development of CBW-related law are here identified in turn, the focus being on the major multilateral elements of the regime. The regime has also been extended by developments that have not, in

contrast, rested on wide international consensus, following instead from "plurilateral initiatives" and from a sequence of unilateral renunciations.

The 1925 Geneva Protocol, which is an international treaty whose states parties have agreed among themselves not to use CBW against one another, is the
bedrock of the existing CBW governance regime. More properly known as the
Protocol for the Prohibition of the Use in War of Asphyxiating, Poisonous or
Other Gases, and of Bacteriological Methods of Warfare, it was negotiated during a League of Nations conference in Geneva on the arms trade and was signed
on June 17, 1925. According to a communication in October 2002 from the
Ministry of Foreign Affairs of France, which is the depositary of the treaty, it has
130 states parties (not counting Taiwan) including the five permanent members
of the UNSC and one additional signatory state.[8] The Geneva Protocol builds
on earlier international agreements, such as ones from the 1899 and 1907 peace
conferences in The Hague, and is now widely considered to have entered customary international law, thereby becoming binding on all states whether they
have or have not formally joined the treaty. The fact that the definition of war
crimes in the Rome Statute of the International Criminal Court extends to use of
chemical but not biological weapons is a reflection less of the state of customary
law in 2000 than of a North-South political deal cut during the negotiation on
account of nuclear weapons.

The 1972 Biological Weapons Convention is an international treaty ratified by
155 of the 171 states that, by September 2006, had signed it, thereby renouncing
germ weapons in order to "exclude completely" the possibility of such weapons being used against human beings, other animals, or plants. It reflects the
renunciation of biological weapons by the defeated Axis powers after the Second World War, as in the 1954 revised Brussels Treaty as well as the unilateral
renunciations by the United States in 1969 and France (which did not join the
treaty until 1984) in 1972. The BWC extended the regime of CBW no first use
established by the Geneva Protocol by explicitly outlawing development, production, and stockpiling of biological and toxin weapons, but it has rather few
of the ancillary provisions that are nowadays often thought essential: means of
monitoring, even enforcing, compliance with its prohibitions and prescriptions
of procedure for implementing its other rules, or of international organization for
assisting states parties to discharge their obligations. Opportunities for extending
the regime during the review conferences for which the BWC provides were,
however, soon taken up, as with the institution of a consultative procedure in
the event of problems arising, and also a variety of "confidence-building measures" characterized as "politically binding." But subsequently confirmed reports
of gross violation of the BWC by the USSR, as well as intelligence on Iraqi bio-

logical weapons (BW), promoted the belief that such measures could never in themselves be sufficient. This led, in 1995, to the opening of negotiations for an agreement among the states parties on a legally (as opposed to "politically") binding instrument that would strengthen the treaty by establishing verification or other compliance-promoting procedures. These Compliance Protocol negotiations collapsed in 2001.[9]

The 1977 EnMod Treaty, as the Convention on the Prohibition of Military or Any Other Hostile Use of Environmental Modification Techniques is commonly known, among other things prohibits warfare with chemicals toxic to plants, "having widespread, long-lasting or severe effects." This treaty entered into force in 1978 but is at present subscribed to by less than a majority of the world's states, though among the permanent members of the UNSC only France is a nonparty.

The 1993 Chemical Weapons Convention, like the BWC, originated in intergovernmental talks on CBW that commenced in 1968.[10] It prohibits development, production, and stockpiling of weapons toxic to human beings or other animals, or assistance in acquiring such weapons, and obliges parties to the treaty not only to institute domestic compliance-assuring measures, including penal legislation, but also to participate in a verification system operated by an international agency that the treaty established in The Hague, the Organization for the Prohibition of Chemical Weapons (OPCW). The OPCW includes a trained international inspectorate of 150–200 people. The treaty further extends the 1925 Geneva Protocol by including among its provisions an express prohibition of any use of toxic chemical weapons, including the use in reprisal or in retaliation, that the protocol could not outlaw. Together with the BWC, the CWC is the core of today's CBW governance regime. Initially inspired by the Vietnam War and heavily marked by the Cold War, both treaties are, in terms of membership, nearing universality, but with important holdouts, most conspicuously North Korea, Egypt, Israel, and Syria.[11] Both treaties seek to preclude international transfers of prohibited items, these being defined by their purpose because of the general purpose criteria that the two treaties use to set their scope in order not to interfere with dual-use goods meant for unprohibited purposes. Such an approach to governance of dual-use technology had become more fully developed by the time of the CWC, so much so that the CWC expressly outlaws factories for chemical weapons. The BWC had made no similar provision, its negotiators having been nervous about inhibiting vaccine production and commerce in products of biotechnology. Nor, in contrast to the CWC, does the BWC require disclosure of past biological weapons programs, though one of the confidence-building measures adopted in 1991 provides for it.[12]

Empowerment of the UN Secretary-General to Investigate Use Allegations. In November 1987 the UN General Assembly reaffirmed the powers of the UN secretary-general to investigate allegations of CBW use.[13] Such investigations took place on several occasions in Asia and Africa during 1981–93.[14] Since April 1997, the OPCW has been able, at the request of member states, to investigate allegations of chemical warfare. It has not yet formally done so. What happens if a UN investigation verifies an allegation is left for decision by the processes of international politics. Express provision for sanctions is largely absent from the overall regime.

UNSC Resolution 1540 (2004) and its implementing machinery are elements of the international response to perceptions of impending WMD terrorism. As regards CBW, the resolution seeks to universalize parts of national BWC- and CWC-implementing legislation (including transfer provisions) in regard to non-state entities. Even states not parties to the treaties, being bound as all UN member states are by UNSC resolutions, are now under obligation to enact and enforce such legislation.

Those are the six main components of today's CBW governance regime, all multilateral. Additional components have stemmed from unilateral renunciations outside the treaties and also from three plurilateral initiatives—the Global Partnership against the Spread of Weapons and Materials of Mass Destruction, the Proliferation Security Initiative, and, exclusively concerned with CBW, the Australia Group (AG). The AG began its work in May 1985 at the Australian embassy in Brussels after a year of preparatory activity both there and in other Western capitals. It seeks to harmonize supply-side controls on dual-use technology applicable to CBW by promoting common standards for the formation and implementation of national export-control policies.[15] It was inspired by the discovery that the chemical weapons used by Iraq in its war with Iran were not USSR-supplied but homemade, put together from dual-use commodities and know-how imported from the global marketplace. Its membership and range of activities have expanded over the years, most notably in the early 1990s, when it took on biological as well as chemical export controls and also agreed to controls on specific dual-use equipment applicable to the production and dissemination of CBW agents.[16] As the BWC and the CWC advance closer toward universality of membership, the AG will presumably come to serve mainly as a safety net against noncompliance with the technology-transfer provisions of the two treaties.

The international norm underlying the overall governance regime is CBW nonarmament and, in the case of former CBW possessor states, CBW disarmament. A principle of the regime is that it be nondiscriminatory, making no distinction between the "haves" and "have-nots" among its member states. On the chemical side all of this has been developed into a respected international organization overseeing implementation and compliance procedures, hampered though it is by some remaining gaps in its legal foundation and by the ever-present possibility of governments (or their voters) losing awareness or appreciation of the OPCW's raison d'être.[17] On the biological side, in contrast, there is no such implementing organization to put into effect the terms of the BWC, which on its face is not much more than a statement of the norm plus obligations serving to enhance it that states parties have not always observed. To say this is not at all to disparage the BWC or to suggest that the biological side of the regime is feeble; on the contrary, the norm has clearly drawn much strength from state practice and the support of internationally organized civil society.[18] As Ambassador Donald Mahley, former chief U.S. CBW negotiator, said in Geneva during his valedictory statement on April 28, 2006, civilization, norm, and law are now such that there would be a massive reaction against the use of biological weapons by anyone, whether state or terrorist, in the future.[19] But the BWC regime certainly suffers, as its critics rightly observe, from an "institutional deficit"—the absence of an "OPBW" or anything like it charged with those routine activities of information exchange, assistance networking, and shared international procedure that would embed responsibility for the norm and the obligations within the bureaucracies and legislatures of BWC states parties.

Supranational threats to security, such as these weapons pose, require global solutions involving active international cooperation, as the UK government observed in 2002 in its green paper on strengthening the BWC.[20] Nothing less can suffice. Surprisingly successful though the regime has been, it still needs enlightened policymaking for its further development, not least in view of the newly emergent challenges that are described in the following section.

Challenges to the CBW Governance Regime

A development or change that causes a state to question its continuing allegiance to the CBW governance regime is, by definition, a challenge to that regime. The challenge may be to the regime as a whole or to particular parts of it. If major or many states start such questioning, the challenge is serious, requiring a collective response if the regime is to remain in good order, properly adapted to its ever-changing environment of international relations. For each state party the constant question is whether the benefits flowing from the regime continue to outweigh the attendant costs and also any penalties there may be to the national interest—are we still better off inside the regime than outside it? With that as a framing concept, particular challenges can be identified. Three big ones stand out at present: the emergence of new utilities for CBW, proliferation in a variety of forms, and the creeping legitimation of non-WMD CBW.

New Utilities for CBW

Disarmament, especially WMD disarmament, is an objective widely seen as beneficial, but armament can bring benefit by preserving security. Under some circumstances that could include CBW armament. Military options forgone through renunciation of CBW capabilities might then be significant on the cost side of remaining within the CBW governance regime. The taboo associated with disease weapons means that most states are content with CBW disarmament—except that circumstances now seem to be creating utilities for CBW not previously considered.

At least three types of new utility may now be discerned, and examples of all three seem evident in recent conflicts or in preparedness for war. The first is a consequence of wider changes in the nature of warfare, rather as the shift from "massive retaliation" to "limited war" doctrine in the late 1950s elevated the status of CBW in Western military thinking. A new type of organized violence is taking the place of, for example, those confrontations between highly disciplined and technologically advanced armed forces that characterized the later Cold War. Conflicts these past two decades in the Balkans, the Caucasus, the Horn of Africa, Rwanda, Liberia, Sierra Leone, Angola, Afghanistan, and Iraq have eroded formerly clear distinctions between war, organized crime, and large-scale violation of human rights. These new wars are fought by seeking political control through the displacement or worse of civilian populations and through the sowing of fear and hatred.[21] Because CBW can lend themselves particularly effectively to such objectives, they may have a greater affinity to the new wars than they did to the old, so, notwithstanding the CBW governance regime, they may have an expanding future.[22] This is an additional reason why the latest CBW use allegations, emanating from Sudanese, Israeli, Palestinian, Baluchi, and Lebanese sources, should not remain uninvestigated.

The CWC, though not the BWC, has a compliance-verification system run by the OPCW and its international inspectorate that ought in principle to countervail the new-utility challenge. But the routines of that system were designed against Cold War–period conceptions of utility, meaning that the lists of chemicals and types of industrial facility that the OPCW now has under its immediate surveillance are dictated by the types of chemical weapon that fitted old-war, not new-war, requirements. Basically that meant focusing on toxic chemicals that were so intensely aggressive in their effects that weapons disseminating them would be competitive, in casualty-producing terms, with conventional weapons. Not a great many such toxicants exist, so their coverage in the CWC schedules that govern routine OPCW verification allowed people to suppose that the main threats had thereby been brought under control. In the new wars, however, it is not so much relative aggressivity that determines the utility of CW but rather such other factors as accessibility or availability and terrorizing potential. A whole host of toxic industrial chemicals and other chemicals not hitherto regarded as CW agents might thus find application in new-war contexts. The fact that most of these chemicals are not listed in the CWC control schedules does not mean that their use for CW purposes is not prohibited, nor that the CWC is unavailing against them. It means only that the routine international verification procedures run by the OPCW may not see them. The GPC that the CWC uses to define its scope obliges the national authorities of states parties to ensure that no toxic chemical is abused. The challenge to the regime therefore lies in the degree to which such national controls may fail to exert a constraining effect.

A second major source of novel utility for CBW is the propensity of newly gained knowledge in the life sciences for suggesting novel modes of attack that could be the basis for militarily or politically attractive new forms of weapon. For example, if a hitherto unknown molecular pathway serving a process of life comes to be identified, chemical or biological agents capable of interfering with that pathway might also become identifiable and thus form the basis for a novel weapon. Of course, many considerations other than novelty of effect determine the usefulness of a new weapon, so the new science is not itself the challenge to the regime that is here suggested. But it would be a step toward it, and many such steps can be envisaged.[23] This prospect is not necessarily remote. We should not, for example, disregard the statement reliably attributed to a "former high-level Defense Department official" commenting on the feasibility of U.S. attack on Iranian underground facilities: "We can do things on the ground, too, but it's difficult and very dangerous—put bad stuff in ventilator shafts and put them to sleep."[24] Again, it is the GPC as used in the BWC and in the CWC that is the safeguard provided by the CBW governance regime against such challenges.

A third type of novel utility now becoming manifest is the emerging role of CBW, not so much in the hands of terrorists or other new-war aggressors, but for purposes of counterterrorism. This utility has demonstrably become a stimulus to rich-country questioning of the regime. It is rooted in past counterinsurgency applications of toxic chemicals, which reach back through the Vietnam War to British, French, Italian, and Spanish use of toxic chemicals in colonial situations—a utility that the CWC was intended to suppress. Its reemergence in counterterrorist guise is perhaps to be seen in the proliferation of weapons based

GPC - general purpose criterion

on Agent CR, evident each year in that part of the OPCW Annual Report addressing declarations of "riot control agents," for the potency and other properties of CR have caused it to be widely rejected as suited to civil police use. The utility is also evident in the vigorous advocacy to be heard in some quarters for the arming of counterterrorist forces with more advanced types of "nonlethal" CBW. The readiness with which the U.S. Marine Corps has taken to toxin weapons of this type—devices disseminating Agent OC—is further indication.[25] So is the absence of any serious criticism of the Russian government for having authorized use of toxic chemicals other than riot-control agents by the *spetznaz* forces that, on October 26, 2002, liberated 634 of the theatergoers taken hostage by Chechen separatists in Moscow. The other 129 hostages were killed by the toxicant used, which is said to have been an agent "based on derivatives of fentanyl" that had been developed by USSR special services.[26]

Proliferation of CBW

Nowadays when people speak of CBW proliferation it is not always clear what they are talking about. The concerns expressed most commonly are probably about clandestine acquisition of CBW by nonstate entities, such concerns having supplanted or perhaps augmented earlier concerns about "rogue states." The characteristics that have caused states to be described as rogues include their supposed interest in acquiring CBW, so the concern could have been at root a questioning of the efficacy of the CBW governance regime, in turn becoming stimulus to the various plurilateral initiatives that have since contributed to the regime. Latterly these initiatives have been directed also against nonstate entities. Such entities include business corporations heedlessly serving a lucrative marketplace, criminal organizations feeding a black market, and terrorist groups seeking new weapons.

Proliferation of CBW to terrorists is, for reasons addressed earlier, probably myth. While it is known that certain terrorist groups have indeed looked at CBW options, such intent as they have to acquire CBW has not been translated into capability. Thus far, other means for terrorist violence have proved more attractive or more accessible to them and, since the aberration of Aum Shinrikyo in the 1990s, only the most footling attempts to acquire CBW have been observed.[27] This is not to say that it could not happen: the lesson to draw from the still unresolved "anthrax letters" affair in the United States during late 2001 is that biological weapons can put potential for great harm into the hands of technically competent and skilled individuals.[28] The CWC and BWC in fact place useful tools at the disposal of counterterrorism by obliging states parties to introduce and enforce effective controls on access and use of toxic and infective materials by persons within their jurisdictions. Yet it is at the state level that CBW proliferation is still, on the available evidence, a more serious challenge to the CBW governance regime.

Here it is necessary to differentiate between "vertical" and "horizontal" proliferation. Vertical proliferation describes the process whereby states possessing CBW weapons expand or upgrade existing CBW capabilities. It thus refers solely to states that have opted to remain outside the regime and, for those that have done so in order to preserve CBW capability (as opposed to lack of interest or even awareness), the challenge to the regime is serious on several counts. Above all, it strengthens pro-CBW constituencies in both national and bureaucratic politics, thereby increasing the political costs to the country's leadership if it were to advocate joining the regime. Most probably this process is operating in Egypt, Israel, and Syria, where it has been greatly complicated by nuclear weapons. Syria has been uniquely forthcoming about its avowed CW capability, starting in November 1996 when its ambassador to Egypt told a lecture audience in Alexandria that Syria would retaliate with chemical weapons against Israeli nuclear attack or threat.[29] President Bashar Assad has spoken recently about Syrian rights to possession of CBW as a safeguard against "Israeli aggression."[30] Nor have Israeli officials been reticent about their view of Syrian CW and, by implication, the counter–chemical weapons value of Israeli nuclear weapons.

Horizontal CBW proliferation presents an altogether different kind of challenge to the CBW governance regime, one that is rooted in the otherwise mostly beneficial tendency of industrial and other technologies to diffuse rapidly around the world under the various influences of globalization. The capability of individual states to acquire CBW weapons, if they so choose, is thereby enhanced, and if they still need specialized assistance, clandestine procurement networks have now gained increasingly dense cover within which to operate. That networks of this type can indeed spring up to meet demand was clearly shown by the UNSCOM/UNMOVIC (UN Monitoring, Verification, and Inspection Commission) investigation of Iraqi CBW acquisition and by the Libyan CW program.[31] At the level of know-how and other intangible technology, comparable assistance is increasingly available from another quarter as well. A great proliferation of competence in technological matters relating to CBW is currently underway in the United States as thousands of millions of dollars are dedicated annually to countermeasures against bioterrorism, a competence that may by now surpass whatever is left from the Soviet BW program.[32] Even states that have no immediate wish to acquire CBW may nevertheless move to take advantage of these various possibilities as a hedge against circumstances changing—by, for example, building what could serve as "breakout capacity" into their industrial infrastructure rather as the

USSR created "mobilization capability" for manufacturing BW within its bio-tech industry during 1973–92. Iran, victim on a terrible scale to Iraqi chemical weapons during 1983–88, very probably falls into this category while at the same time being among the most vocal supporters of the CBW governance regime and, especially on the medical side, a proactive participant in its international procedures.[33] Nor is there any clear impropriety in such a position, for all the in-dustrial powers, including ones that menace Iran, have manufacturing industries to which they could turn at short notice for CBW agents (whose full weaponiza-tion would, however, be more demanding). The fact nevertheless remains that horizontal proliferation of this type is a threat to confidence in the regime and therefore a serious challenge to it for as long as the problem of dual use persists.

Creeping Legitimation of Non-WMD CBW

In the ability of CBW agents to target themselves on particular life processes, there is growing scope for users of weapons based on them to "tailor" the nature or severity of their effects to a strategic objective. In that such tailoring could, as has been seen, open the way to weapons suited to hugely malign purpose, CBW present a long-term danger that demands an alert and strong CBW gov-ernance regime. That same tailoring can, however, provide weapons of an al-together more acceptable character, including ones having effects gentler than most other means of violence. Examples include the "tear gas" of police forces; the psychochemical weapons that, according to past U.S. Army teaching, would cause the enemy to "linger in overpowering reverie";[34] and the entirely mythical knockout agents of "war without death" that have figured in science fiction since the nineteenth century. Add to these chemicals the various infective agents that can induce highly debilitating diseases of low mortality, and a category of CBW is created whose features seem far distant from those of WMD, whose possession may appear desirable, and whose constraint by the regime may therefore come to seem a substantial liability, notwithstanding the abyss into which the tailoring could also take us.

A rather wide variety of commercial, political, and military interests stand to benefit from exclusion of some or all of these non-WMD CBW from the gover-nance regime. Sub rosa campaigning to that end has long been under way, most notably during the last months of the CWC negotiation in mid-1992, when the new protagonists of nonlethal warfare (NLW) came up against governmental of-ficials charged with securing consensus on those parts of the CWC text that dealt with "riot control agents" (RCAs). The issue turned then on whether RCA should or should not fall within the definition of "toxic chemicals," subject, thereby, to the GPC that would serve to regulate the duality of their application either in warfare (prohibited) or in law enforcement (permitted). The United States favored exclusion but, finding itself isolated in this position within the Western group, secured a compromise in which the CWC expressly prohibited use of RCA "as a method of warfare" but remained silent on the toxic character of RCAs, thus perpetuating a semblance of ambiguity on whether the toxicity criterion fundamental to the CWC did or did not capture RCAs. The way became open for determined NLW protagonists to argue that, if tear gas was not proscribed by the CWC, then neither should the more modern varieties, for which they coined the category label "advanced RCA technology" (ARCAT). Subsequent ARCAT development projects funded by the U.S. government included work on the fentanyls and other such intensely supertoxic chemicals. The process that can be seen here is a surreptitious equation of toxicity with lethal toxicity, and in this attempt to loosen the CWC constraint on the weaponization of other forms of toxicity we have started to see a creeping legitimation of non-WMD CBW, which is a most serious challenge to the regime. A situation in which some types of toxic weapon are allowed but not others is certain to be unstable.

Strengthening the CBW Governance Regime

Two features stand as bulwarks against the challenges to the CBW governance regime. The first is an OPCW that, despite severe budgetary constraints and opaque operating methods but having constructive U.S. support, is now an effective multilateral institution that is actively suppressing chemical warfare armament in most of the world. Second, in regard to disease warfare more generally, modern customary and conventional international law has transformed an ancient taboo into an enforceable norm of international behavior. Together these are the principal reasons why chemical and biological warfare are rare occurrences even in today's conflict-ridden world. Because of what CBW could become, they are treasure that must not be frittered away.

Loose talk of CBW "nonproliferation" is, as has been seen, a step in that direction, for it carries the implication—no doubt unintended by most of those who use the term—that some states have a right to possess disease weapons; and there are indeed certain states in which some leadership figures actually seem to believe this to be so, at least in the case of disabling chemical weapons having counterterrorist application. Yet as a step in the wrong direction this one is surely far outpaced by that other tendency mentioned earlier, treating CBW as though they can properly be regarded as a subset of WMD. The hazard here is not only the suggestion that non-WMD CBW are acceptable—that as long as CBW do not kill us in large numbers they are legitimate instruments of security. Nor is it only the danger that the fuzzy concept of WMD is now supplanting that long-standing precept of the laws of war whereby weapons employment that does not discriminate between combatant and noncombatant is impermissible, on whatever scale it may occur. No less pernicious is a third implication: that, being in the same category, nuclear weapons are a legitimate, even a necessary, counter to CBW, whether as deterrent instrument of retaliation or as means for destroying CBW capability. We can see this implication displayed in the current pressure in the United States for acquisition of "bunker busting" nuclear weapons and in the entry into the declared national policy of some of the NWS (China is in fact the only clear exception) of stated willingness to use nuclear weapons in response to CBW attack. There is further reason beyond the legitimation it seems to offer for nuclear armament why this last is so dangerous a policy. Any decision on such nuclear release would have to rest on what recent events have shown to be very uncertain ground indeed: intelligence about supposed adversary CBW behavior. Ambiguities, uncertainties, and other peculiarities attach to CBW to such a degree that the methods of intelligence assessment that seem to work adequately outside the CBW field do less well within it. The oddities of CBW, which are rooted mainly in the dual-use nature of much of their contributing technology, are too obtrusive to be swept under a collective WMD carpet. Professional CBW intelligence analysts of course recognize this; it is at the interface between them and their political masters that the attendant misapprehensions are liable to become dangerously misleading or, if not that, the uncertainties then become subordinated to the political imperatives of the moment. The failure to find CBW in Iraq after the last coalition invasion; the cruise-missile bombardment of Al-Shifa Pharmaceutical Industries in the Sudan before that; and, from still earlier times, the Yellow Rain fiasco in which President Reagan's administration mistook bee excrement for BW—all of these and more are cautionary tales.

The sixth BWC review conference (November 20–December 8, 2006) stimulated much work on how best to strengthen the biological side of the present CBW governance regime, and the second CWC review conference (April 7–18, 2008) has begun to do the same for the chemical side. The U.S. government, which has faced criticism for its seemingly hostile attitude toward the BWC since 2001, has put forward suggestions, albeit chiefly of a plurilateral rather than multilateral kind. The often contrasting recommendations of the WMD Commission chaired by Hans Blix of Sweden also merit the most careful attention.[35]

Ordering principles for these and the many other proposed ways forward are needed and, for this, an attractive logic is to prioritize around the two bulwarks of the regime: to put most effort into (a) enhancing the OPCW and (b) strengthening the norm. In comparison, the various other sorts of proposals, such as codes of conduct for scientists, seem mere tinkering at the edges, useful though they are as topics for international discourse at times when real progress is politically difficult.

Enhancing the OPCW means soliciting maximal support for the organization in national politics and as much freedom for it to get on with its CWC-assigned tasks as the international system can countenance. Enhancing the OPCW also means ensuring that, in its necessary pursuit of adaptation to changing international relations, it is protected from having to compromise on principles or procedures that lie at its heart. Undoubtedly the best judge of how to do this is the OPCW technical secretariat. But its institutional memory is now severely challenged by the secretariat having to implement an employment policy that admits only a seven-year job tenure. For this reason, and especially for matters that impinge on political sensitivities and on which the secretariat may therefore be unable to develop its own recommendations, "scapegoat" study by outside specialists may become essential. A clear case in point is the question of how the OPCW should best respond to NLW technology. A second (and not unrelated) example is study of why so many OPCW member states have difficulty implementing the GPC or even recognizing it as the source of the comprehensive nature of the CWC's prohibitions, which is the vital safeguard against adverse technological change and against abuse of dual technology.[36] Both are topics that civil-society friends of the OPCW will expect the second CWC review to examine most carefully. Meanwhile the OPCW's own projects for strengthening the norm should receive the widest possible outside assistance, including that of civil society: the action plans for promoting universality of the CWC and for improving implementation of CWC Article VII on national measures.

Strengthening the norm means, first, not weakening the norm and, second, promoting mechanisms that will ensure the norm is not disregarded at the national level and is more enforceable than it is at present at the international level. How is it possible to weaken a norm that seems to rest on so strong a taboo? Perhaps by fragmentation: by treating BW and CW as though they were entirely different from one another instead of variations on a single theme, that of disease weapons; or by differentiating lethal and "nonlethal" CBW, or WMD and non-WMD. Sometimes, certainly, different types of CBW will require different practical arrangements; but, in the interests of norm integrity, the default position, so to speak, must surely be common treatment wherever possible. Nor is that an unnatural default. As scientific disciplines, chemistry and biology are converging. And the BWC and the CWC anyway overlap strongly in their scope: toxins, for example, are covered by both treaties; and it is not unreasonable to contemplate the routine international procedures of the OPCW being extended into the domain of toxins and other inanimate biological agents.

Beyond that, two different forms of strengthening may now be judged worthwhile. The first is the mechanism noted earlier: machinery for entrenching responsibility for the norm and rules of the BWC into the bureaucracies and legislatures of BWC states parties. For such machinery the CWC has a demonstrably workable model in the obligation it has placed on its states parties to designate or establish national authorities for liaising with other states parties, and with the OPCW, empowered by penal legislation to implement the provisions of the treaty within their jurisdictions. A number of OPCW member states have gone further and created formal lines of communication between their national authorities, their legislatures, their industries, and their civil society, as in the UK's National Authority Advisory Committee. Some of the CWC national authorities already include BWC cells. The necessary precursor of the mechanism being proposed here is an international campaign to ensure that BWC states parties take Article IV more seriously than many seem to do at present. That article contains the obligation upon each state party to "take any necessary measures to prohibit and prevent" all BWC-violative activity within its jurisdiction. The European Union (EU) has already agreed to a joint action to this end and further pressure is emanating from UNSC Resolution 1673 (2006) that has extended 1540 (2004).[37] All that would then be lacking to complete the norm-strengthening mechanism would be some form of standing international secretariat for the BWC. Though there has in the past been resistance to creating any such body, times have now changed, and the BWC institutional deficit has become a disgrace to the states that created it. Their affirmations of support for the BWC are no longer credible.

The second, and complementary, means for strengthening the norm is machinery for better enforcement. Sovereign states do not readily commit themselves in advance to punitive or other reactive sanctions against one another, so a possible way forward is a mechanism for holding *individuals* personally accountable for any such violations. The individual-responsibility approach is already a discernible trend in international affairs. Individuals, or at least substate entities, in their identity as persons involved in WMD proliferation, are the main target of UNSC Resolution 1540 (2004). The former president of Iraq, Saddam Hussein, was found guilty of charges arising out of the CW attacks on Halabja and executed. From among the several categories of stakeholder in the development of biotechnology, individual scientists are being made responsible for impeding access to dual-use materials judged helpful to bioterrorists. All of this is surely good for the norm. Yet the defining feature of a universal norm is not that it should dictate how particular individuals or groups behave but rather how *everyone* should behave, high or low, head of state or simple citizen. All of us are responsible for the continued well-being of the norm against the weaponization of disease, and the onus is therefore on us all, individually, to uphold it. It is all very well saying (as many people continued to do at the time of the 2005 BWC intersessional meetings) that scientists need to think more about conceivable end-applications of their work and be taught about the international treaty that is meant to suppress BW. That treaty, the BWC, codifies the norm, but like the Geneva Protocol and the CWC, it places its primary constraints on the behavior of states, not of individuals. If the norm is to be strengthened, the overall regime must be developed so that its relevance to the individual as well as to the state becomes clear to all. And unless this is done in step with the current moves toward codes of conduct and principles of practice for scientists, those moves will merely become empty acts of discrimination, unpopular and ignored. A more compelling way of inserting the sanction of individual accountability into the regime is needed.

Now that international criminal law is emerging from the constraints of the Cold War, just such a mechanism has become possible. It is a very simple one indeed: a new international convention that would confer on national courts jurisdiction over individuals present in their national territory, regardless of their nationality or official position, who order, direct, or knowingly lend substantial assistance to the acquisition, production, or use of CBW anywhere. Such a convention might take various forms. One possible text, prepared with advice from an international group of eminent jurists, is the Harvard Sussex Draft Convention.[38] This has already attracted favorable notice from a number of governments and now constitutes the basis for a possible further initiative in the WMD area by the EU.

If support could indeed be mustered for the several norm-strengthening and organization-enhancing measures just described, the CBW governance regime would surely be better able to resist the challenges that now face it, even the ultimate challenge of emergent CBW that can change human identity.

Notes

1. The texts of the two treaties are available in many places, including the Web site of the Harvard Sussex Program on CBW, http://www.sussex.ac.uk/Units/spru/hsp, which is cited here because some of the literature referenced later in this chapter, including the *CBW Conventions Bulletin*, is posted on it.

2. United Nations, *Chemical and Bacteriological (Biological) Weapons and the Effects of Their Possible Use*, report of the secretary-general (New York: United Nations, 1969); World Health Organization, *Health Aspects of Chemical and Biological Weapons: Report of a WHO Group of Consultants* (Geneva: World Health Organization, 1970); World Health Organization, *Public Health Response to Biological and Chemical Weapons: WHO Guidance* (Geneva: World Health Organization, 2004).

3. See also Matthew Meselson, "Averting the Hostile Exploitation of Biotechnology," *CBW Conventions Bulletin* 48 (June 2000): 16–19.

4. See "News Chronology: May through August 1997," May 6, 1997, entry, *CBW Conventions Bulletin* 37 (September 1997): 16.

5. Ed Regis, *The Biology of Doom* (New York: Henry Holt, 1999).

6. North Atlantic Treaty Organization, standing group, von Kármán Committee, *Future Developments in Chemical Warfare*, report of Working Group 10 on Chemical, Biological and Radiological Defence, March 1961, as distributed to the UK Ministry of Defence Advisory Council on Scientific Research and Technical Development, paper no. SAC 1928, February 11, 1969, in the National Archive, Kew, file WO195/16864.

7. M. A. Marin, "The Evolution and Present Status of the Laws of War," *Académie de Droit International: Receuil des Cours* 92, no. 2 (1957): 633–749.

8. See World Health Organization, *Public Health Response*, 109–10, 335–40.

9. For the definitive account of the protocol negotiations, see Jez Littlewood, *The Biological Weapons Convention: A Failed Revolution* (Aldershot, UK: Ashgate, 2005).

10. For an unrivaled description of the CWC, see Walter Krutzsch and Ralf Trapp, *A Commentary on the Chemical Weapons Convention* (Dordrecht: Martinus Nijhoff, 1994).

11. North Korea is party to the BWC but not the CWC. Both Egypt and Syria have signed but not yet ratified the BWC; neither has signed or ratified the CWC. Israel has signed but not yet ratified the CWC; it has not signed or ratified the BWC. All four countries are understood to have developed CW and/or BW capability.

12. On which see in particular Nicolas Isla, *Transparency in Past Offensive Biological Weapon Programmes: An Analysis of Confidence Building Measure Form F 1992–2003*, Hamburg Centre for Biological Arms Control Occasional Paper 1, June 2006, http://www.biological-arms-control.org/download/FormF_1992-2003.pdf.

13. UN General Assembly resolution 42/37C.

14. For references see World Health Organization, *Public Health Response to Biological and Chemical Weapons*, 129.

15. Recently the Australia Group (AG), hitherto a secretive organization, has established its own Web site at http://www.australiagroup.net.

16. Robert J. Mathews, "The Development of the Australia Group Export Control Lists of Biological Pathogens, Toxins and Dual-Use Equipment," *CBW Conventions Bulletin* 66 (December 2004): 1–4.

17. For a detailed account of the formation of the OPCW and of how the first eight years of its existence proceeded, see the quarterly reviews published as "Progress in The Hague," *Chemical Weapons Convention Bulletin* 19 (March 1993) through the *CBW Conventions Bulletin* 67 (March 2005): 6–11.

18. See, for example, Julian Perry Robinson, "The Impact of Pugwash on the Debates over Chemical and Biological Weapons," in *Scientific Cooperation, State Conflict: The Roles of Scientists in Mitigating International Discord*, ed. Allison L. C. de Cerreño and Alexander Keynan (New York: New York Academy of Sciences, 1998), 224–52.

19. Graham Pearson, "Report from Geneva: The Preparatory Committee for the Sixth BWC Review Conference," *CBW Conventions Bulletin* 71 (May 2006): 6–15 (14).

20. United Kingdom, Secretary of State for Foreign and Commonwealth Affairs, *Strengthening the Biological and Toxin Weapons Convention: Countering the Threat from Biological Weapons*, Cm 5484, April 29, 2002, http://www.brad.ac.uk/acad/sbtwc/other/fcobw.pdf.

21. Mary Kaldor, *New and Old Wars: Organized Violence in a Global Era* (Cambridge, UK: Polity, 1999).

22. See also Julian Perry Robinson, "The General Purpose Criterion and the New Utility of Toxicants as Weapons," paper presented at the 15th workshop of the Pugwash Study Group on Implementation of the CBW Conventions, Oegstgeest, the Netherlands, June 23–24, 2001.

23. For a particularly rich recent source of information on advances in technology that may be applicable to CBW, see the Institute of Medicine and National Research Council, and the Committee on Advances in Technology and the Prevention of Their Application to Next Generation Biowarfare Threats (Stanley M. Lemon, and David A. Relman, cochairs), *Globalization, Biosecurity, and the Future of the Life Sciences* (Washington, DC: National Academies Press, 2006).

24. Seymour M. Hersh, "The Iran Plans: Would President Bush Go to War to Stop Tehran from Getting the Bomb?" *New Yorker*, April 17, 2006, 30–31, http://www.newyorker.com/archive/2006/04/17/060417fa_fact.

25. See "News Chronology: February–May 1996," March 22, 1996, entry, *CBW Conventions Bulletin* 32 (June 1996): 27.

26. Julian Perry Robinson, "Disabling Chemical Weapons: A Documented Chronology of Events," paper for private distribution, Harvard-Sussex Program, November 1, 2003, 139–42.

27. For an informed review of the evidence of interest in CBW by actual terrorist groups today, see Milton Leitenberg, *Assessing the Biological Weapons and Bioterrorism Threat*, Strategic Studies Institute of the U.S. Army War College, December 2005, 21–42.

28. See, further, Martin Rees, *Our Final Century: Will the Human Race Survive the Twenty-first Century?* (London: Heinemann, 2003); and Milton Leitenberg, *The Problem of Biological Weapons* (Stockholm: Swedish National Defence College, 2004, 137–55.

29. See "News Chronology: November 1996 through February 1997," November 25, 1996, entry, *CBW Conventions Bulletin* 35 (March 1997): 24.

30. See "News Chronology: November 2003 through January 2004," January 6, 2004, entry, *CBW Conventions Bulletin* 63 (2004): 37.

31. On UNSCOM investigations, see especially Tim Trevan, *Saddam's Secrets: The Hunt for Iraq's Hidden Weapons* (London: HarperCollins, 1999); Graham Pearson, *The UNSCOM Saga: Chemical and Biological Weapons Non-Proliferation* (London: Macmillan, 1999); Graham Pearson, *The Search for Iraq's Weapons of Mass Destruction: Inspection, Verification and Non-Proliferation* (Basingstoke, UK: Palgrave Macmillan, 2005); Scott Ritter, *Iraq Confidential* (New York: Nation Books, 2005).

32. Stephanie Chang and Alan Pearson, *Federal Funding for Biological Weapons Prevention and Defense, Fiscal Years 2001 to 2007*, Center for Arms Control and Non-Proliferation, June 21, 2006, http://www.armscontrolcenter.org/assets/pdfs/fy2007_bwbudget.pdf.

33. International Institute for Strategic Studies, *Iran's Strategic Weapons Programmes: A Net Assessment* (London: Routledge, 2005).

34. U.S. Army Chemical Center and School, Fort McClellan, "New Chemical Agents and Incapacitating Agents," lesson plan LP6075, undated (ca. 1965).

35. Weapons of Mass Destruction Commission, *Weapons of Terror: Freeing the World of Nuclear, Biological and Chemical Arms*, final report (Stockholm, Sweden: Weapons of Mass Destruction Commission, June 1, 2006).

36. On these functions of the GPC, see United Kingdom Department of Trade and Industry, *Operation of the Chemical Weapons Act 1996: Annual Report 2004*, 26–28, July 2005, http://www.berr.gov.uk/files/file26554.pdf.

37. Council of the European Union, *Council Joint Action 2006/184/CFSP*, February 27, 2006, http://eur-lex.europa.eu/LexUriServ/ LexUriServ.do?uri=OJ:L:2006:065:0051:0055 :EN:PDF.

38. Matthew Meselson and Julian Robinson, "A Draft Convention to Prohibit Biological and Chemical Weapons under International Law," in *Treaty Enforcement and International Cooperation in Criminal Matters*, ed. Rodrigo Yepes-Enriquez and Lisa Tabassi, 457–69 (The Hague: TMC Asser, 2002).

CHAPTER FIVE

WMD Inspection and Verification Regimes: Political and Technical Challenges

John Hart and Vitaly Fedchenko

Regimes and mechanisms whose purpose is to prevent the spread of nuclear weapons and to prohibit chemical and biological warfare depend on effective implementation. In order for states to satisfy themselves that a given regime is effectively implemented, they must periodically conduct an evaluation, perhaps in cooperation with other states or bodies, of how well the regime is functioning. Verification measures provide the basis for judging compliance, which is generally understood to be the process of successfully implementing an agreement, including the willingness of the parties to actively and in good faith implement agreed-on verification measures. Conducting assessments to resolve uncertainties about possible nuclear, biological, and chemical (NBC) weapon-related activities and the manner in which they are structured presents a variety of political and technical challenges. Any violation should ideally be resolved in an impartial and authoritative manner and be seen as such.

The effectiveness of verification activities and assessments is dependent on the institutional framework in which they are carried out. There are two basic frameworks in which these occur. One is multilateral, while the other is essentially bilateral. The multilateral framework is typically a UN-type organization such as the International Atomic Energy Agency (IAEA) or the Organization for the Prohibition of Chemical Weapons (OPCW), which implement the 1968 Nuclear Nonproliferation Treaty (NPT) and the 1993 Chemical Weapons Convention (CWC), respectively. Such bodies generally make decisions by consensus and consist of three parts: a conference of the states parties, an executive body, and an international inspectorate. Some organizations have standing inspectorates, while others do not. In cases where there is no standing inspectorate, inspection team members are selected from approved national lists shortly before the inspection.

Bilateral and some multilateral arrangements involve direct government-to-government cooperation and coordination and may be of limited duration or ad hoc. These include various "action plans," "joint actions," or the implementation of a UN resolution such as UN Security Council (UNSC) Resolution 1540.[1] In the early 1990s, the United Kingdom and United States engaged in a secret trilateral process with the Soviet Union (then Russia) to ascertain to the status of the former Soviet biological weapons (BW) program with mixed results. In 2003 the United Kingdom and the United States engaged in a similar process with Libya in which the two countries, with the later involvement of the IAEA and OPCW, verified Libya's renunciation of NBC weapons and longer-range missiles. Other arrangements have a more prominent coercive element, including the verification of Iraq's compliance with the terms of UNSC Resolution 687 (1991).

This chapter provides an overview of verification and compliance mechanisms and related factors, including NBC weapon indicators, and of political and technical aspects of inspection and verification regimes in selected multilateral, coercive, and ad hoc arrangements. Related geopolitical factors, current trends, and future challenges are then considered.

Background

The fundamental challenge in carrying out any verification assessment is that, in the absence of an indisputable violation (i.e., a "smoking gun"), uncertainty that the state is adhering to its obligations can exist.[2] A number of measures can be taken to increase confidence that a state is adhering to its obligations, including the provision of information as part of bilateral information exchanges, the regular submission of declarations to an international implementation body, and the subsequent validation of the information through the carrying out of on-site inspections (OSIs) and post-inspection analysis. Nevertheless, analysts and policymakers will, in the absence of positive proof of noncompliance, always be forced to grapple with the question of how much verification is necessary in order to have sufficient confidence the agreement is being observed.

There are two main views regarding the verifiability of an agreement or commitment. One view holds that if a single violation occurs, the usefulness of the agreement or commitment is fundamentally undermined, partly because confidence in its viability is lost. The second view considers verification to be more a process and gives greater consideration to the distinction between a fundamental and a technical violation. In practice, such distinctions can be unclear, and it may be impossible for states to agree when the line has been crossed.

An important issue in verifying agreements is whether and how national technical means (NTM) (i.e., all information available to a state, including that derived from intelligence) can or should be used to support verification activities and compliance assessments. This includes how such information should be used to detect and assess NBC weapon and program indicators. Also, technical analyses (which tend to more narrowly focus on observable facts and capabilities) differ from political analyses (which may provide a net compliance assessment) in that the latter are broader in scope and tend to take into greater consideration the inherently more subjective challenge of assessing intent.

International secretariats that implement treaty regimes are therefore generally precluded from carrying out the type of activities conducted by intelligence services. Otherwise the staff would risk being accused of conducting espionage to support the political agenda of other member states. Uncovering and understanding NBC weapon and program indicators can nevertheless be done to an extent by using open sources or information provided by states participating in the regime through agreed-on procedures such as, in the case of the CWC, a challenge inspection. Any compliance concern that a state may have will, in fact, almost certainly be partly based on information derived from intelligence.

NBC Weapon and Program Indicators

With respect to nuclear weapons, most indicators focus on the nuclear fuel cycle and the stages of manufacturing a deliverable nuclear weapon, namely: obtaining the nuclear explosive material, weaponization, and integration of the explosive device with a delivery system.[3] Above-ground nuclear tests emit a characteristic double flash of visible light which can be detected by means of satellite imagery.[4] Satellites can also detect surface changes associated with such a test. Underground and underwater tests produce seismic signatures, and all nuclear tests produce characteristic nuclear isotopes. Site preparations for any test might also be detected by satellites. Indicators of an enrichment facility would include heat emissions into the air or water and the fact that even the simplest enrichment technologies not only consume a great deal of energy but also require the construction of numerous enrichment stages arranged into "cascades," as well as large buildings, possibly with military or other security-related features, to accommodate them.[5] Although most indicators of weaponization are ambiguous, some equipment or information can be considered to be a "smoking gun."[6] In addition, testing of the nonnuclear elements of an explosive device may, depending on the type of the device, leave distinctive physical traces.[7]

An offensive chemical or biological weapons program may have few or no obvious external indicators.[8] If the program is still at the research and development

(R&D) stage, its elements may be located in a small area such as in part of a building within a larger complex. Agents might also not be produced and filled into munitions until shortly before the munitions are to be used. A traditional, state-run BW program tends to rely on a standby production capacity to a greater extent than do chemical weapons (CW) and nuclear weapons programs where a larger number of operational munitions would be stockpiled. Indicators of possible offensive work include work with primates, work with small particle–size aerosols, and efforts to develop vaccines for rare diseases or those diseases that are not endemic on the territory of the state or in the region.[9] Vaccination capabilities might indicate the agent that a state is prepared to use. Any disease outbreak is routinely analyzed by intelligence communities to determine whether it is naturally occurring or deliberate.[10] With regard to sampling, biological agents may show signs of having been genetically modified by artificial means. It might also be possible to trace a given bacterial or viral strain to a registered pathogen collection held by a facility or researcher. Chemicals can be analyzed against catalogues of possible chemical warfare agents, together with their possible precursors and degradation products, and compared against chemicals that are used for peaceful purposes.[11]

The Dual-Use Dilemma

The principal verification challenge in the NBC field is how to correctly evaluate the purpose for which material, technology, or equipment that can support either a peaceful or prohibited military program is used. For example, nuclear fuel cycle technologies have peaceful applications that might also be used to support a nuclear weapons program. For this reason, there is a view that no state should be allowed to develop a full nuclear fuel cycle and that some key elements of the cycle should be placed under some form of international control.[12]

Much of the dual-purpose problem in evaluating chemical and biological weapons (CBW) programs centers on whether a program is "defensive" or "offensive." The BWC definition has a general purpose criterion (GPC) which bans all microbial or other biological agents or toxins except for nonprohibited purposes. The CWC also has a GPC and defines a CW as consisting of one or more of three elements: (a) toxic chemicals and their precursors except where intended for purposes not prohibited by the treaty (i.e., not as a "method of warfare"), (b) munitions and devices specifically designed to cause death or harm through the use of such toxic chemicals, or (c) any equipment specifically designed to be used directly in connection with such chemicals, munitions, and devices.[13] The GPC is the means by which the two conventions ensure that future technological and scientific developments are covered by the respective regimes. Uncertainties about ambiguous CBW program indicators stem partly from the consideration of how to apply the GPC in practice.

Verification of Arms Control and Disarmament Agreements and Related Arrangements

An important distinction between inspections carried out under multilateral arms control and disarmament agreements and coercive disarmament regimes is that, under the former, inspections are viewed as an opportunity for the parties to demonstrate compliance to each other. Routine inspections under such regimes are therefore generally structured so that inspectors can confirm that declared information is consistent with the findings of the inspection. However, under a CWC challenge inspection or a special IAEA inspection, the inspection mandate will be partly informed by information obtained through NTM provided by one or more member states. With coercive disarmament regimes, such as United Nations Special Commission on Iraq (UNSCOM), the inspection team is authorized to look for evidence of noncompliance, and the inspected party is expected to be fully responsive to information and access requests.

Multilateral Regimes

Major features of traditional multilateral arms control and disarmament regimes include the making of most decisions by consensus and the fact that they are open to universal membership, while ad hoc arrangements, in practice, have more restrictive membership. Also, states generally do not question the legitimacy of traditional multilateral regimes, and great emphasis is placed on the principle of equal treatment of all members. The latter principle may be difficult to reconcile procedurally during the implementation of verification measures. The manner in which states raise compliance concerns can also contribute to a defensive and, therefore, noncooperative reaction by the targeted state.

The Nonproliferation Treaty and the International Atomic Energy Agency. The 1968 Treaty on the Nonproliferation of Nuclear Weapons (Nonproliferation Treaty, or NPT) forms the legal foundation for the global nuclear nonproliferation regime.[14] The NPT obliges the states parties not to "assist, encourage or induce" nonnuclear weapon states from manufacturing or acquiring nuclear weapons, nuclear explosive devices, or acquiring "control over such weapons and explosive devices."[15] The treaty also obliges each nonnuclear weapon state (NNWS) party to place safeguards on "all source or special fissionable material in all peaceful nuclear activities" carried out under its control.

The NPT designates the IAEA as the competent authority for verifying a NNWS party's compliance with its safeguards obligation "with a view to preventing diversion of nuclear energy from peaceful uses to nuclear weapons or other nuclear explosive devices."[16] However, it does not set out detailed provisions as to how this obligation is to be verified. These are contained in a state's bilateral comprehensive safeguards agreement (CSA) with the IAEA, which is modeled on the text of INFCIRC/153.[17] This type of agreement constitutes the legal foundation for the nuclear safeguards system and is based on the concepts of accountancy and control of declared nuclear materials. It gives the IAEA the authority to draft conclusions about both the completeness and correctness of a state's declarations of its nuclear material inventory and fuel cycle facilities. In 1997, in response to the IAEA's failure to detect under traditional INFCIRC/153-type safeguards Iraq's clandestine nuclear weapons program, states began to conclude Additional Protocol (AP) agreements with the IAEA on the basis of INFCIRC/540. This enhanced the organization's ability to detect undeclared nuclear activities as well as to verify the nondiversion of nuclear material.[18]

The IAEA is currently implementing an "integrated safeguards" system that combines traditional safeguards with new safeguards measures allowed under the AP.[19] A number of verification-related implementation issues remain unclear, including whether and under what circumstances the IAEA has the right to investigate R&D of nuclear weapon–relevant activities, especially where no nuclear materials are present. This could include the development of computer codes for simulation and testing of weapons. Although the IAEA updated its approach to verification of the first technological stage of nuclear weapon manufacturing (acquisition of nuclear explosive material), developments in Iran, Iraq, and North Korea prompted the IAEA to proceed to the verification of what some observers have characterized as the second technological stage—weaponization—and to reassess its role in detecting R&D activities related to nuclear weapons. The AP is designed to fill these gaps partly by allowing IAEA inspectors access to undeclared facilities and sites adjacent to declared facilities as well as to conduct environmental sampling.

According to IAEA Director-General Mohamed ElBaradei, "both safeguards agreements and additional protocols are focused on nuclear material—and therefore, the Agency's legal authority to investigate possible parallel weaponization activity is limited, absent some nexus linking the activity to nuclear material."[20] This does not mean that the IAEA would refrain from investigating possible weaponization activities, and the IAEA has, in fact, already been involved in such investigations in Iran, Iraq, Libya, and South Africa. The case of Iran, however, is different because it raises the legal issue of IAEA access rights, which was resolved in the other cases prior to the organization's involvement.

Some states that have concluded a CSA with the IAEA have little or no declared nuclear material or nuclear activities. For such states the IAEA has developed and implemented since 1974 what is known as the Small Quantities Protocol (SQP) to the safeguards agreement. Under this protocol, most of the detailed provisions of the CSA were held in abeyance. This led to concern that the SQP created a loophole in the safeguards system whereby undeclared nuclear activities could be carried out. In 2005 the IAEA Board of Governors therefore concluded that the SQP should be revised. It endorsed some SQP changes that would make an SQP unavailable to a state with an existing or planned nuclear facility, would require states to provide initial reports on nuclear material and notification as soon as a decision has been taken to construct or to authorize construction of a nuclear facility, and would allow for IAEA inspection.[21]

In order to further improve IAEA safeguards, the board of governors established in June 2005 the Advisory Committee on Safeguards and Verification, which was granted a two-year term. In 2006 it considered two documents, both designed to increase the likelihood of discovering undeclared nuclear activities. The first document contained eleven recommendations for improvements to the safeguards system, such as augmenting the capabilities of the IAEA's laboratory network and expanding the list of materials and equipment that NPT member states are required to declare under the AP, while the second document considered ways to increase the IAEA's use of satellite imagery.[22] Significant technical work remains to be done in both cases.

UN Secretary-General's Mandate for Investigating Alleged CBW Use. In 1980 UN General Assembly Resolution 35/144C gave the UN secretary-general the mandate to investigate allegations of use of CW without seeking the prior approval of the UNSC. In 1982 this mandate was expanded to include possible violations of the 1925 Geneva Protocol, thereby including allegations of use of BW. This authority was restricted in 1982 to allow for investigation of allegations raised by UN member states only. It was exercised in the 1980s to early 1990s to investigate allegations of CBW use in Azerbaijan, Iran, Iraq, Mozambique, and Southeast Asia.

It has been suggested that the institutional expertise of the UN Monitoring, Verification, and Inspection Commission (UNMOVIC) be retained to strengthen the UN secretary-general's authority and that UN member states update the list of qualified experts and laboratories that the secretary-general can draw from when exercising this authority.[23] Although UNMOVIC was disbanded in 2007, some of its expertise has been retained partly because some staff now work for the UN Office for Disarmament Affairs (ODA) in New York and other similar organizations. On September 8, 2006, the UN General Assembly adopted the *UN Global Counter-Terrorism Strategy*, which "encourage[s]" the secretary-general to update the roster of experts and laboratories and technical guidelines and procedures in order to help ensure the "timely and efficient" investigation of alleged CBW use.[24] Since 1997, the UN secretary-general's power to investigate alleged CW use has been shared with the OPCW. In 2007 the ODA organized two meetings of technical experts to review the technical guidelines and procedures for carrying out investigations of alleged use of CBW. As of mid-2008 they had not been finalized. In 2007 the ODA also started to develop a Bio-incident database.

Biological and Toxin Weapons Convention. BWC parties do not submit annual, legally binding declarations on activities relevant to demonstrating treaty compliance, and no OSIs are conducted to confirm the veracity of such declarations. There is also no BWC inspectorate to investigate compliance concerns, such as allegations of use. The parties may, however, submit a clarification request to one or more of the treaty's three depositaries.[25] They may also lodge a complaint with the UNSC if they believe that another BWC party has violated the treaty.[26] This mechanism has never been invoked.

On September 8–26, 1986, the Second Conference of the States Parties to the BWC agreed to submit annual, politically binding data exchanges on biologically related information to serve as a confidence-building measure (CBM). The use of the data exchanges as a basis for clarifying concerns and providing increased transparency has provided a mixed benefit because of the uneven submission of data that results from the fact that the submissions are politically binding. The data have, however, been used as a basis for bilateral clarification discussions among the parties.

Some national BWC-implementing legislation and regulations are not sufficiently comprehensive. For example, some states' regulations are rather narrowly focused on public health aspects and do not provide for adequate oversight of pathogen transfers or criminalize all relevant possible activities by nonstate actors under the state's jurisdiction or control.

In 2006 the sixth review conference considered the results of an intersessional process of annual meetings held in 2003–5 on BWC implementation and agreed on a second, similar process for 2007–10.[27] In 2008 these meetings were mandated to "discuss, and promote common understanding and effective action" on (a) national, regional, and international measures to improve biosafety and biosecurity, and (b) oversight, education, awareness raising, and the adoption and/or development of codes of conduct. The sixth review conference also established a temporary three-person Implementation Support Unit (ISU), which has, inter alia, served as a focal point for national implementation assistance and digitized all CBM submissions. The intersessional meetings have mainly consisted of exchanges of information, views, and national offers of assistance. Compliance concerns specific to a given state party are generally not formally considered during such meetings. The negotiations on compliance issues have instead tended to focus on institutional processes in order to better address possible compliance concerns by, for example, taking into better account scientific and technological developments.

Chemical Weapons Convention. The 1993 CWC, which entered into force on April 29, 1997, is implemented by the OPCW, which is based in The Hague, Netherlands. A technical secretariat receives and processes annual declarations from the parties and carries out inspections. The principal CWC verification tasks are (a) ensuring the destruction of all CW, including those that are periodically uncovered on former battlefields, (b) the verifiable destruction of all facilities that produced CW at any time since January 1, 1946, or, in exceptional circumstances, their verifiable conversion for permitted, peaceful purposes, and (c) verification of nonproduction of CW by national defense establishments and in the chemical industry.

Verification issues that have arisen during routine inspections include when and how the "endpoint" of CW destruction is determined, sampling and analysis methodologies, and tagging of munition procedures.[28] Some of the parties believe that additional information ought to be provided by other parties in their declarations, including information on the extent and nature of current defense establishment activities and past offensive CW programs. The United States has expressed concern that Russia has not declared the "full extent" of its CW "agent and weapon inventory."[29] It has also stated that Iran's declaration to the OPCW is incomplete partly because the country did not declare having a CW stockpile (Iran has declared a past CW production capability).[30]

One of the least understood, but important, aspects of the CWC has been the implementation of its provisions on consultations, cooperation, and fact finding (Article IX). Although no challenge inspection has been requested, the other provisions of Article IX, which governs such inspections, have been regularly implemented since the CWC's entry into force.[31] The OPCW continues to periodically conduct practice challenge inspections. A major challenge to the CWC is to ensure that toxic chemicals held by states, such as "non-lethal weapons" and incapacitants, are consistent with law enforcement purposes.[32]

Coercive Regimes: The Case of UNSCOM and UNMOVIC

The UNSCOM and the UNMOVIC verification regimes are unique in terms of their coercive nature in that a failure to provide access or to cooperate could result in further economic sanctions or a military response.[33] The verification regimes under these two bodies also relied much more heavily on NTM.

A fundamental problem faced by UNSCOM in the CBW field was the fact that it could not confirm Iraqi claims that it had unilaterally destroyed weapons and materials. In addition, Iraq pursued a policy of systematic obstructionism and agreed to revise its declarations only when specific information was tabled proving wrong or casting serious doubt on the original information provided. The process by which UNSCOM informed Iraq why it doubted the information also had the effect of revealing some of the NTM capabilities (or lack thereof) of the states that supported the disarmament effort.

The director of the IAEA's Iraq Nuclear Verification Office noted that the inspections took longer than expected (Resolution 687 had foreseen forty-five days for the work on "destruction, removal and rendering harmless" of proscribed materials and equipment). The IAEA also had to learn which verification procedures would be most effective for discovering hidden activities. No-notice intrusive inspections and particle analyses of swipe samples were considered highly effective. Information sharing between the IAEA and its member states also proved important. Thanks to the defection in August 1995 of the former supervisor of all Iraqi WMD programs (General Hussein Kamel) and subsequent events, the IAEA was able to conclude that, by 1998, it had a sufficiently clear understanding of the Iraqi nuclear weapons program.[34]

After the 1998 military operation Desert Fox, the IAEA was no longer able to conduct inspections in Iraq, and only three main verification techniques remained at its disposal: overhead imagery, human intelligence, and the review of import requests. Although overhead imagery had been used by the IAEA since 1991 (when the United States began to share imagery from U-2 overflights), high-resolution commercial satellite imagery was not available to the IAEA until the end of 1999. Although the imagery was useful in preparing for inspections, it was insufficient for determining the presence or absence of nuclear activities. The value of interviewing defectors was uncertain unless the information obtained could be verified through other means, such as an inspection. With the adoption of UNSC Resolution 1409 (2002), the IAEA began to review all contracts for exports to Iraq in order to uncover indications of a possible clandestine nuclear weapons program. This process allowed the IAEA to develop an understanding of Iraqi procurement networks but was insufficient for fully assessing Iraq's nuclear status.

Ad Hoc Arrangements

There is currently a trend toward developing ad hoc arrangements of like-minded states, such as the Proliferation Security Initiative (PSI), to pursue more narrowly focused activities in order to prevent the spread of NBC weapons and to eliminate clandestine NBC weapons programs, if uncovered and where possible.[35]

The Verification of Libya's Renunciation of NBC Weapons. On December 19, 2003, Libya publicly renounced NBC weapons and longer-range missiles and associated programs and agreed to adhere to the NPT, the BWC, the CWC, and the guidelines to the Missile Technology Control Regime (MTCR).[36] As part of a broader commitment to reintegrate itself into the international community, Libya also agreed to allow international inspectors to verify its commitments.[37] In late 2003, Libya hosted at least two visits by British and U.S. teams sent to the country to determine the status of Libya's NBC weapons programs. They found Libya to be cooperative, and the teams were allowed to remove proliferation-sensitive NBC materials and paperwork, including from the A. Q. Khan network. IAEA and OPCW inspectors later visited Libya to confirm the dismantlement of its nuclear weapons program and confirm its CW declaration respectively. The OPCW will continue to monitor the declared CW stockpile and associated facilities until they are destroyed. Libya's nuclear weapons program involved twelve sites, four of which it had not declared to the IAEA. Libya had been unable to manufacture a nuclear weapon partly because of the country's limited technical capability.[38] Libya's CW stockpile was revealed to consist mainly of approximately thirty-five hundred air bombs and just over twenty-three metric tons of sulfur mustard, a blister agent. Libya has consistently maintained that it never had an offensive BW program and, despite doubts by some, perhaps most notably in the United States, this claim has been broadly accepted.[39]

Libya's commitments on nuclear weapons and CW were verified through a system of declarations and OSIs carried out by international bodies. In the case of BW, however, the international community will have to essentially rely on information provided to the member states of the BWC by Libya, the UK, and the United States.

Libya's motivations and the exact sequence of events leading to its 2003 announcement are still not fully understood. Libya is an important case study in terms of how to deal with states that choose to remain outside multilateral arms control and disarmament regimes. It illustrates the impact a mix of long-term economic and political sanctions and consequent isolation coupled with the background threat of military and diplomatic confrontation can have. The future viability of the "Libya model" will partly depend on how well the country appears to do economically and politically in future. The degree to which Libya has been embarrassed politically by acquiescing to international conditions will also probably be a factor in the decision-making process of other states considering a similar decision. Finally, the Libya case demonstrates how verification measures work best in a cooperative environment.

The Soviet Biological Weapons Program and the Trilateral Process. The Soviet Union expanded its offensive BW program on the basis of a secret decision taken in 1973, after it had signed the BWC. A 1979 anthrax outbreak in Sverdlovsk (present-day Ekaterinburg) that resulted in at least sixty-four deaths was shown not to have been caused by the consumption of contaminated meat as maintained by Soviet (and some Russian) officials but rather was the result of the inhalation of *Bacillus anthracis* spores accidentally released from a military facility located in the city. In 1992 Russian president Boris Yeltsin officially confirmed that there had been a delay in his country's implementation of its obligations under the BWC.[40]

As part of a now suspended trilateral process, Russia provided some information and allowed British and U.S. officials to visit some facilities in the early to mid-1990s that had been involved in the Soviet BW program. The UK and U.S. governments decided to pursue the matter in secret because they believed that quiet diplomacy would be more effective partly because of concern that publicly raising this issue could undermine Yeltsin's political control and that other sensitive issues might be adversely affected, such as nuclear disarmament.[41]

The terms of reference of the trilateral process were based on the provisions of the BWC. During the negotiations, none of the states questioned whether the BWC was worthwhile or whether its provisions should be adhered to. In the absence of a BWC, the Soviet Union might have rejected outright any procedure to clarify the status of its military activities in the biological field since there would have been little or no agreed-on basis for such discussions.

Information Baseline and Inspection Experience

Information and experience gained during the implementation of verification measures are desirable partly to overcome logistical and other practical problems and partly to establish a baseline of information and experience that can provide context to the consideration of less frequent serious compliance concerns. A single inspection will probably not provide sufficient assurance that a prohibited activity is not occurring, that previously declared prohibited activities have been ended, or that the declared status and purpose of a facility are correct.

One lesson learned from UNSCOM inspections is the importance of understanding what verification conclusions can be drawn from sampling and analysis results. Such issues include the need to protect against the perception that scientific results have proven or disproven an argument, the need to guard against both false positive and false negative test results, and the need to implement an agreed-on sampling and testing methodology at key points in a facility or location.[42] UNSCOM found that the detection of the conversion of a certain legitimate biological facility for BW purposes was "especially difficult since such activities had taken place only for a short period of time, and the site required only minor adjustments for the production of a biological warfare agent."[43] UNSCOM sometimes assumed that Iraq would or could not carry out certain activities because to do so would risk the health and safety of facility workers.[44] Also, inspectors might not always understand what they were seeing. For example, inspectors missed the modification to some R-400A bombs that enabled them to be used to deliver BW agents. This was partly because Iraq declared the bombs as chemical munitions and partly because Iraq had denied producing BW munitions.[45] The UNSCOM experience also demonstrated the importance of not overly relying on sampling and analysis, building an integrated information baseline, and being able to conduct interviews with Iraqis inside and outside the country.

Implementation of Onsite Inspections

A common theme of inspections and practice exercises is the logistical challenge associated with bringing together an inspection team and its equipment, often on short notice, and transporting the team to the inspection site. Inspection teams must also understand their inspection mandate and clearly communicate its content to the inspected party representatives. If the inspected party wishes to obstruct an inspection, however, it can do so through extended negotiations on issues such as the specific managed access provisions that should be invoked in order to fulfill the inspection mandate, how domestic health and safety regulations should be implemented during the OSI, the modalities for allowing the inspection team to communicate with headquarters, and the role of a third-party observer on the inspection team.

Such challenges can be met partly through the periodic review and updating of standard operating procedures (SOPs) such as the packaging of inspection equipment according to a common configuration.

Technical challenges include the timely approval and acquisition of modern inspection equipment, modifying frequency of inspection procedures, and revising inspection procedures to reflect changes in the chemical, biotechnology, and nuclear industries. Major political challenges to verifying an agreement include understanding how the political process affects technical issues, carrying out the higher-level political assessment of the technical findings of verification measures, and creating follow-up measures to address unresolved compliance issues.

A number of uncertainties remain regarding whether and how the IAEA's wide-area environmental sampling (WAES) procedures will be implemented. There is significant opposition among some states to using WAES partly because of its expense and partly because of its potential to reveal sensitive information unrelated to the IAEA's inspection mandate. Moreover, the United States does not believe that WAES is currently "technically feasible or cost effective as a safeguards measure" and that the situation is unlikely to change unless sampling and analysis technology "improve significantly." The country has also indicated that it would, under present circumstances, invoke a "national security exclusion" to block the use of WAES at military facilities and that it might invoke managed access provisions under the AP to offer alternatives to the use of environmental sampling at locations not subject to the NSE.[46] Such refusals or restrictions on verification measures can be copied by other states. Restrictions can also become codified as a result of implementation practice, including the extent to which an inspection team is allowed to take samples using its own equipment or to remove samples for out-of-country analysis. Two related issues are how states determine what activities and holdings should remain off-limits to outside visitors for national security reasons and the extent to which differences between states on how they define their national security restrictions can be better understood within arms control and disarmament regimes and, therefore, not be misused to conceal prohibited activities.

Organizational Issues

Another trend in international organizations that has implications for the effectiveness of implementing verification regimes is the adoption and implementation of tenure policies for international civil servants. For example, starting in 2003, the OPCW began to implement a seven-year tenure policy for its technical secretariat staff.[47] Such policies, together with uncertainty over the timing of some contract renewals in some organizations, may have the effect of undermining the ability of such organizations to retain individuals who have expertise that is difficult to replace, including inspectors. They can also lead to degradation of institutional memory. A balance needs to be struck between the need to help ensure that staff within the UN system perform and are responsive to the membership as a whole and the need to retain qualified staff with specialized expertise over the longer term, including through select exemptions from or extensions of tenure policies.

Salary levels for some verification-related positions within international organizations are also not compatible with the levels for comparable positions in private industry and some government bodies (e.g., for chemical industry experts working in the OPCW Inspectorate). A related concern is that some scientific or technical people put at risk their future career prospects by taking time out to work in an international organization where they might be unable to keep themselves informed of scientific and technological developments because of their other responsibilities. In order to help attract and retain such staff, study/work furloughs could be arranged and member states could offer to pay the salary of a given position as part of its "national offer" to the international organization. The latter option is a well-established practice that could be further developed. More generally, authority and influence flow from expertise and experience, regardless of the formal relationship among the constituent parts of an organization, such as the interaction between a delegation and a secretariat. Such factors may affect how smoothly compliance assessments are carried out at the operational level.

Current Trends and Future Challenges

In a multilateral framework all states have equal rights and responsibilities, and verification measures can enable the parties to demonstrate their compliance with an agreement. If the inspected party is not cooperative, verification measures can serve to confirm the lack of cooperation and, perhaps, produce useful information regarding noncompliance. The type of verification measures and the cost, level of intrusiveness, and scope required are informed by political decisions. They, in turn, are informed by the perceived importance of the treaty commitment to national interests.

Verification measures should be implemented in a uniform manner. However, at the operational level, there can be differences in how such measures are carried out among different states. Under the CWC, for example, Schedule 2 and Schedule 3 chemicals that appear in mixtures at "low concentration" need not be declared to the OPCW. But states apply different thresholds in their definitions of what constitutes a low concentration. This can affect the number of chemical industry facilities declared and subject to routine inspection and verification. Such variation generally results from the fact that the member states opt to take decisions by consensus, which is not always possible. In cases where a decision is essentially of an administrative or technical nature, international organizations might consider agreeing to use the relevant provisions of a treaty for decisions to be taken by vote. A systematic streamlining of the methodologies for collecting, declaring, and verifying data would also make the verification process more efficient and, in principle, would result in a reduction in the number of man-hours that a secretariat staff would have to devote to disaggregating and reformulating such information into a format more usable for analysis.

Institutional Frameworks

Joint actions, various "action plans" designed to achieve better treaty implementation, and UNSC Resolution 1540 have helped to provide a better understanding of the operational aspects of the verification process.[48] In order to clarify the status of the implementation of national obligations, these mechanisms involve the sending of government and other officials to various states to discuss the status of such implementation. These types of activity offer practical lessons such as identifying the relevant points of contact in various governments responsible for the implementation of treaty obligations and providing insight into aspects of parliamentary and government procedures which may be misunderstood by other states as deliberate obfuscation.

The terms of reference and the framework of these types of activity are structured in a manner that should make it easier for a state or group of states to raise technical noncompliance concerns with other states. A state that is asked to clarify or carry out its commitments should not feel that it is being singled out for political reasons when it is requested to address noncompliance issues that are part of a broader set of agreed-on measures that carry the weight of expectation of all states. Although the dividing line between technical and fundamental noncompliance is not always clear at the operational level, it should be possible to devise joint actions, action plans, and the like which focus on issues that are more closely connected to possible fundamental noncompliance concerns. Attempts could be made to shift the focus of some analyses and related procedures from more or less objective criteria, such as capabilities and holdings, to the more problematic area of assessing intent. In the biological field, for example, this could include requesting that all states implement a system to review the legality of biodefense programs and bioterrorism prevention programs. The existence of such a system would enhance international confidence that the line between defensive and offensive work has not been crossed and that the state is acting in good faith.

Information Issues

The key factors affecting the verification process may be the level and type of information required (or requested) in declarations and information exchanges and the level of responsiveness that can be reasonably expected. This is the case in specific instances, such as whether Iran has complied with its NPT commitments, as well as in the context of general implementation practice. A common phrase that is used in the OPCW Declaration Handbook is that the parties shall provide "all available, relevant information." A party cannot provide information it does not have, and it could decline to provide other information that it believes is irrelevant to fulfilling its declaration obligations. Iran has also justified its removal of topsoil at nuclear facilities before IAEA inspection teams could take environmental samples by referring to environmental regulations. Such issues can be addressed through implementation practice and the establishment and operation of agreed-on SOPs. Every case will possess unique political and technical factors and must be dealt with individually.

How Much Verification?

The issue of how much verification is sufficient to detect possible violations is a basic question that can never be answered with certainty in the absence of a clear violation. How decision makers approach this question reflects a more fundamental disagreement over whether longer-term national security and international stability are better served by having arms control and disarmament agreements, in spite of the risk of secret violations. This risk must be balanced against the cost of foregoing the benefits of having such an agreement. A party contemplating violating an agreement may decide that the risk of detection outweighs the potential security gains of the violation. If the negotiating parties believe that an agreement is worth having as a matter of principle and where there is a suspicion that one or more parties are prone to pursue a clandestine violation, a logical response would be to increase the level of intrusiveness of the verification regime. The financial, political, and other costs that result from more intrusive verification measures must then be weighed against the state's broader security interests.

Such issues can be addressed through quantitative and qualitative cost-benefit analyses. However, a state's decisions on issues such as whether an agreement is worth having and whether verification and compliance mechanisms are sufficient are informed by perceived vulnerabilities and broader political interests. Human psychology, beliefs, philosophical approaches to thinking about international security, and the broader dynamics of political decision making have no "correct" answer. The optimal general strategy for evaluating compliance and verification issues is to systematically and periodically review the technical and political factors of implementing agreements and the relevant broader political processes. These reviews should be reasoned and balanced. If there is disagreement on whether the analyses are "reasoned" or "balanced," one can only attempt to try to elucidate the reasons for this. Open-ended political discussions must, however, be avoided when decisions on possible violations are necessary. The consideration of such issues should therefore not be on process alone.

There is also a need to ensure that common criteria to assess treaty violations are agreed to and implemented. In practice, there is always a risk that the "narrow" versus the "broad" interpretation of treaty text can undermine such attempts. A related risk is that operational procedures are "over-negotiated" to the point where flexibility to exercise common sense is effectively excluded.

Penalties and Restorative Measures

Under the traditional multilateral frameworks, violations or serious unresolved compliance concerns are referred to the UNSC, which, partly because of the veto power wielded by the five permanent members, may be incapable of agreeing on a common position or effective action. The text of any agreed-on statement may be watered down to the "lowest common denominator" of acceptable language and be incapable of providing the basis for effective action. Once a decision is taken, active and sustained political engagement is usually required to achieve success.

Over the long term, the effectiveness of ad hoc arrangements may be undermined by a lack of perceived international legitimacy. This lack of legitimacy may be partly caused by disagreement over the accuracy of a state's status-of-proliferation reports describing other states' activities. Since the underlying data used to support such assessments are generally classified in order to protect intelligence sources and methods, there could be significant scope for those in the international community to question what, if any, violation has occurred. Another issue is how to repair the political damage caused by a violation and how to bring a noncompliant state back "into the fold" of international actors who are in good standing of their international legal obligations. The application of international sanctions or military force may cause such a degree of ill will in the state affected (and, possibly, its political allies) that it may find it difficult to participate in the given regime for many years. Such issues should be periodically considered as they relate to general political processes and individually.

Conclusions

A proper understanding of a disparate amount of information about verification issues is an indispensable prerequisite for informing a decision by states to forego the nuclear weapons option and instead implement effective, long-term strategies to identify and respond to possible NBC threats posed, including by nonstate actors. Threat assessments are the most important factor affecting national policy on NBC weapons. States can be better informed through the establishment of more effective verification measures. The effectiveness of current legal and behavioral norms against NBC weapons is reflected by the fact that no state openly admits to having an offensive CBW program and that, with few exceptions, states decline to acknowledge an interest in obtaining nuclear weapons. Politically acceptable, yet effective, verification regimes are key to closing any gaps between declared and actual defense policies. The political dynamics associated with equal rights and obligations of parties to an agreement and the broader requirements of international diplomacy generally must also be taken into account as verification measures are implemented. This is especially true for cases where there is a high probability of revealing questionable activities or outright violations.

Verification of national obligations will remain an important issue that is distinct from, but nevertheless influenced by, the type of framework in which adherence to the obligations is assessed. There is uncertainty over whether coercive, shorter-term policies that promote verification are more effective than longer-term, more cooperative arrangements in terms of bringing states back into accepted international practice. Doing so can perhaps be more easily achieved without loss of face in the latter case.

Verification mechanisms, including the derivation and use of information that are developed to support them, cannot be a substitute for the settlement of underlying political differences. The verification process should ideally be of a technical nature and be kept separate from political considerations and interpretations. Political considerations and interpretations are nevertheless important and ever present at higher political levels. A distinction should also be made between verification measures that are designed to achieve a given result and the possible other benefits derived from the *process* of implementing such measures (e.g., confidence building).

Even if an agreement is violated, its future viability should not be considered to be lost. The IAEA's integrated safeguards system, for example, is both a response meant to address specific verification weaknesses under traditional safeguards and an example of how a treaty regime can evolve to become more effective. The evolution of treaty regimes can also result from implementation practice (i.e., how treaty provisions are interpreted). To the extent that there is a compliance concern, existing regimes can continue to serve as a basis for engagement that might not otherwise be available.

Notes

1. For information on UNSC 1540, see http://www.un.org/sc/1540.

2. Allan S. Krass, *Verification: How Much Is Enough?* (London: Taylor and Francis, 1985).

3. Nuclear explosive material is almost exclusively highly enriched uranium HEU or plutonium, barring exotic cases of uranium-233 and some actinides. On the integration of the explosive device, see the U.S. Congress, Office of Technology Assessment, *Technologies Underlying Weapons of Mass Destruction*, OTA-BP-ISC-115 (Washington, DC: U.S. Government Printing Office, December 1993), 121–22, 161–71.

4. See Guy E. Barasch, *Light Flash Produced by an Atmospheric Nuclear Explosion*, Los Alamos Scientific Laboratory, November 1979, http://www.gwu.edu/~nsarchiv/NSAEBB/NSAEBB190/02.pdf.

5. Richard Kokoski, *Technology and the Proliferation of Nuclear Weapons* (Oxford: Oxford University Press, 1995), 203–4.

6. E.g., "Data sets for the equation of state of plutonium and uranium at extremely high temperatures and pressures" (James Acton with Carter Newman, *IAEA Verification of Military Research and Development*, Verification Matters, VERTIC Research Report no. 5 [London: VERTIC, July 2006], 27, http://www.vertic.org/publications/VM5%20(2).pdf).

7. E.g., gun-type devices generally include wrapping the HEU into a neutron-reflecting material such as natural uranium, tungsten, or beryllium.

8. In principle, a state could stockpile empty munitions ostensibly for use with conventional explosives.

9. John Hart, "The ALSOS Mission, 1943–1945: A Secret U.S. Scientific Intelligence Unit," *International Journal of Intelligence and CounterIntelligence* 18, no. 3 (Fall 2005): 508–37, and Roger Roffey, "Biological Weapons and Potential Indicators of Offensive Biological Weapon Activities," *SIPRI Yearbook 2004: Armaments, Disarmament and International Security* (Oxford: Oxford University Press, 2004), 557–71.

10. Malcolm Dando, Graham Pearson, and Bohumir Kriz, *Scientific and Technical Means of Distinguishing between Natural and Other Outbreaks of Disease* (Dordrecht: Kluwer, 2001).

11. E.g., a key structural difference between, on the one hand, the organophosphorus nerve agents sarin, soman, V-gas, and VX and, on the other hand, organophosphorus pesticides is that the former have a phosphorus-methyl group ($P-CH_3$) that is absent from the latter. This bond, which is partly responsible for human toxicity effect, is very strong and tends to remain intact in the agents' various degradation products. Thus, the existence of this bond in a known degradation product of the above-mentioned CW agents is a strong indication that the chemical was manufactured for nonpeaceful purposes.

12. Vitaly Fedchenko, "Appendix 13.C: Multilateral Control of the Nuclear Fuel Cycle," *SIPRI Yearbook 2006: Armaments, Disarmament and International Security*, 686–705 (Oxford: Oxford University Press, 2006).

13. Chemical Weapons Convention, Article II, paragraph 1.

14. As defined in Article IX of the NPT, only states that have manufactured and exploded a nuclear device prior to January 1, 1967, are recognized as nuclear weapon states. By this definition, China, France, Russia, the UK, and the United States are the nuclear weapon states parties to the treaty. The text of the NPT is available at http://disarmament.un.org/wmd/npt/npttext.html.

15. NPT, Article I.

16. NPT, Article I, paragraph 1.

17. International Atomic Energy Agency, *The Structure and Content of Agreements between the Agency and States Required in Connection with the Treaty on the Non-Proliferation of Nuclear Weapons*, INFCIRC/153, June 1972, http://www.iaea.org/Publications/Documents/Infcircs/Others/infcirc153.pdf.

18. International Atomic Energy Agency, *Model Protocol Additional to the Agreement(s) between State(s) and the International Atomic Energy Agency for the Application of Safeguards*, INFCIRC/540, September 1997, http://www.iaea.org/Publications/Documents/Infcircs/1997/infcirc540c.pdf.

19. See International Atomic Energy Agency, "Department of Safeguards," n.d., http://www.iaea.org/OurWork/SV/Safeguards/index.html.

20. Mohamed ElBaradei, "Nuclear Non-Proliferation and Arms Control: Are We Making Progress?" statement presented at the 2005 Carnegie International Nonproliferation Conference, November 7, 2005, http://www.carnegieendowment.org/static/npp/2005conference/2005_conference.htm.

21. International Atomic Energy Agency, "Safeguards Statement for 2005, Background to Safeguards Statement and Executive Summary of the Safeguards Implementation Report for 2005," paragraphs 5, 34, http://www.iaea.org/OurWork/SV/Safeguards/es2005.pdf.

22. Paul Kerr, "Efforts to Strengthen IAEA Safeguards Advance," *Arms Control Today* 36, no. 6 (July/August 2006): 46.

23. Trevor Findlay, "A Standing United Nations Verification Body: Necessary and Feasible," Weapons of Mass Destruction Commission (Blix Commission) paper no. 40, December 2005, http://www.wmdcommission.org/sida.asp?id=7.

24. United Nations, "United Nations General Assembly Adopts Global Counter-Terrorism Strategy," Plan of Action, Measures to Prevent and Combat Terrorism, September 8, 2006, paragraph 11, http://www.un.org/terrorism/strategy-counter-terrorism.shtml#plan.

25. This option was exercised once on June 30, 1997. Cuba submitted such a request to Russia, alleging that a U.S. aircraft, which was used for antidrug spraying operations in South America and the Caribbean and which had permission to fly over Cuba, deliberately sprayed *Thrips palmi*, an insect pest that originated from Asia, over Cuban territory. The formal consultative meeting was unable to show that the outbreak was caused by the aircraft overflights. See Raymond Zilinskas, "Cuban Allegations of Biological Warfare by the

United States: Assessing the Evidence," *Critical Reviews in Microbiology* 25, no. 3 (1999): 173–228.

26. Biological and Toxin Weapons Convention, Article VI.

27. The topics were essentially the effective implementation of the treaty, effective oversight and security of biological agents, the detection and investigation of disease outbreaks, and codes of conduct for scientists (Biological and Toxin Weapons Convention, Fifth Review Conference of the States Parties to the Convention on the Prohibition of the Development, Production and Stockpiling of Bacteriological (Biological) Weapons and on Their Destruction, BWC/CONF.V/17, final document, 3–4, Geneva, 2002.

28. Single-stage hydrolysis products are subject to continued OPCW verification measures.

29. U.S. Department of State, *Adherence to and Compliance with Arms Control, Nonproliferation and Disarmament Agreements and Commitments* (U.S. Department of State: Washington, DC, August 2005, 58, http://www.state.gov/t/vci/rls/rpt/51977.htm.

30. Ibid., 55–56.

31. The United States has used the bilateral consultation provisions of this article to "resolve numerous compliance concerns," and recent U.S. bilateral discussions with other parties to the CWC under the article have been "well received" and "useful in laying the groundwork for judging compliance" (U.S. Department of State, *Adherence to and Compliance with Arms Control,* , 5).

32. See Alan M. Pearson, Marie Isabelle Chevrier, and Mark Wheelis, eds., *Incapacitating Biochemical Weapons: Promise or Peril?* (Lanham, MD: Lexington Books, 2007).

33. See UNSCOM Web site, http://www.un.org/Depts/unscom, and UNMOVIC Web site, http://www.unmovic.org.

34. Jacques Baute, "Timeline Iraq: Challenges and Lessons Learned from Nuclear Inspections," *IAEA Bulletin* 46, no. 1 (June 2004): 66, http://www.iaea.org/Publications/Magazines/Bulletin/Bull461/article21.pdf.

35. Christer Ahlström, "The Proliferation Security Initiative: International Law Aspects of the Statement of Interdiction Principles," *SIPRI Yearbook 2005: Armaments, Disarmament and International Security* (Oxford: Oxford University Press, 2005), 741–65.

36. Libya acceded to the CWC on January 6, 2004, and acceded to the BWC on January 19, 1982. On January 14, 2004, Libya deposited its instrument of ratification to the CTBT.

37. Libya also agreed to sever all military ties with Iran, North Korea, and Syria.

38. Many of the components acquired through the A. Q. Khan network had never been unpacked.

39. John Hart and Shannon N. Kile, "Libya's Renunciation of NBC weapons and Longer-Range Missile Programmes," *SIPRI Yearbook 2005: Armaments, Disarmament and International Security* (Oxford: Oxford University Press, 2005), 629–48.

40. Conference on Disarmament, letter dated January 30, 1992, from the representative of the Russian Federation addressed to the president of the Conference on Disarmament, transmitting the text of the statement made on January 29, 1992, by B. N. Yeltsin, the president of the Russian Federation, on Russia's policy in the field of arms limitation and reduction, document CD/1123, January 31, 1992.

41. David Kelly, "The Trilateral Agreement: Lessons for Biological Weapons Verification," in *Verification Yearbook 2002*, ed. Trevor Findlay and Oliver Meier (London: VERTIC, 2002, 93–109.

42. United Nations Security Council, *United Nations Monitoring, Verification and Inspection Commission*, UNSC document S/2006/420, June 21, 2006, 66.

43. Ibid., 67.

44. For example, UNSCOM was initially skeptical that Iraq had progressed beyond the R&D phase of a BW program partly because, in the absence of conclusive evidence to the contrary, inspectors knew that if liquid bacterial agent had been produced at Al Hakam, Iraqi workers would risk airborne contamination. However, it later became clear that Iraq had been prepared to accept such risks. Ibid., 67.

45. Ibid., 67. The R-400 (a more general nomenclature for this type of munition) was designed for chemical fill and later as a binary CW. Most were empty at the time they were destroyed. In the mid-1990s, it was revealed that Iraq had coated the interior of a small number of the munitions with a varnish in order to facilitate taking a BW fill.

46. U.S. Congress, *U.S. Additional Protocol Implementation Act*, Public Law 109-226, April 3, 2006, 15–16.

47. Organization for the Prohibition of Chemical Weapons, *Decision, Tenure Policy of the OPCW*, C-SS-2/Dec. 1, April 30, 2003.

48. The EU Council has carried out joint actions since 2004 that focus on promoting national legislative activities leading to full compliance and enhanced national implementation of the CWC and efforts to bring more states into the regimes. For a review of the OPCW action plans, see Richard Guthrie, John Hart, and Frida Kuhlau, "Chemical and Biological Warfare Developments and Arms Control," *SIPRI Yearbook 2006: Armaments, Disarmament and International Security* (Oxford: Oxford University Press, 2006), 715–16. On the operational aspects of the verification process, see Council of the European Union, *Six-Monthly Progress Report on the Implementation of the EU Strategy against the Proliferation of Weapons of Mass Destruction* (2006/I), EU document 10527/06, June 14, 2006, http://register .consilium.europa.eu/pdf/en/06/st10/st10527.en06.pdf. See also United Nations Security Council, "1540 Committee," http://www.un.org/sc/1540.

CHAPTER SIX

Trade Controls and International Security

Scott A. Jones, Michael D. Beck, and Seema Gahlaut

From the Greek city-states of the classical era to modernity, states and other political entities have used trade restrictions to punish, deter, and weaken adversaries.[1] For example, the United States has a long history of using strategic trade or export controls to achieve economic, political, and security objectives.[2] During the Cold War the United States joined with its allies in the North Atlantic Treaty Organization (NATO) to restrict trade with the Soviet Union and its Warsaw Pact allies, particularly trade in advanced technologies that could strengthen their military capabilities.[3]

The end of the Cold War marked the end of many export restrictions on trade with Russia and former Soviet bloc states. It did not, however, mark the end of export restrictions. The Gulf War startled the United States and other Western states as they came to discover that Iraq had armed itself largely with assistance from Western suppliers.[4] Iraq had launched a major buying spree in Western Europe prior to the Gulf War and found German, Swiss, British, and even American firms willing to provide technological assistance to Iraqi weapons programs. In some cases, Western companies had exported chemicals, goods, and technologies illegally; in other cases, exports were made out of ignorance.

Over the past decade, continuing concerns about Iran and the efforts of other states to arm themselves with weapons of mass destruction (WMD)—nuclear, chemical, and biological (NBC) weapons as well as the missiles used to deliver them—have led the United States and other states to establish and tighten export regulations governing trade in related weapons technologies.[5] Strategic trade controls, as they are most commonly called, are considered critical for U.S. and international efforts to prevent weapons proliferation. The terror attacks of September 2001 and growing concerns about terrorism have also led U.S. and other international policymakers to consider options for strengthening export regulations in order to prevent terrorists from acquiring dangerous weaponry and militarily sensitive technologies.[6]

This chapter is intended as a primer on the what, how, and why of strategic trade controls. The first section provides an introduction, at the national level, to the policies and practices collectively referred to as strategic trade controls. The second section examines the proliferation challenge posed by globalization and the corresponding importance of strategic trade controls. The third section presents a brief introduction to multilateral agreements regarding strategic trade controls. It also briefly assesses the strengths and weaknesses of these multilateral tools for controlling the spread of WMD technologies. The fourth section examines recent United Nations–based efforts to universalize strategic trade controls, in the form of UN Security Council (UNSC) Resolution 1540. The concluding section raises questions about the value of strategic trade controls in a world of globalization and conflict.

What Are Strategic Trade Controls?

Strategic trade controls as a tool for combating weapons proliferation are often overlooked and poorly understood. Many government officials seem to believe that preventing the spread of NBC weapons requires only that these weapons and materials be physically secured. The assumption is that groups or states seeking such weapons will attempt to acquire or steal entire weapons systems. Although this is a real and legitimate concern, it is not typically how most states have acquired WMD. Instead, most states seeking such weapons have purchased the component technologies and materials for such weapons, most of which are "dual use," that is, having both commercial and military applications. For example, Iraq used front companies to purchase commercially the technology needed to build these weapons.[7] Iran has also obtained assistance for developing ballistic missiles from suppliers in Russia. There are now concerns that Russia's decision to build a nuclear reactor in Iran will also aid Iran in acquiring nuclear weapons.[8] Pakistan was able to develop its various ballistics missile programs based upon imported missile components from China and its nuclear weapons with some help from European and U.S. suppliers.[9] In fact, almost all countries possessing and pursuing WMD programs have purchased the necessary components, tools, and technologies from suppliers in other nations. The technologies and components for such weapons include commercially available items—or "dual-use" items—like machine tools and materials like graphite, which can be used for moderating nuclear reactions in a power generation facility or in the enrichment of nuclear fuel for bombs. This suggests that policymakers need to give more attention to strengthening strategic trade controls in order to impede efforts by rogue states or terrorists to acquire the goods and technologies necessary for building weapons of mass destruction. Governments in key supplier states can do a better job of monitoring and tracking exports of sensitive components and technologies.

Strategic trade controls are legal, institutional, technical, and cooperative policies, procedures, and institutions for selectively controlling the import, export, and transit of strategic items. Generally speaking, a country's strategic trade control system is composed of the following functional areas: legal framework, licensing function, enforcement capability, industry-government cooperation, and political commitment and regime adherence. The fifth element, political commitment and regime adherence, explains the government's status vis-à-vis the multilateral strategic trade control regime membership and the various nonproliferation treaties and strives to convey the tenor of the government's attitude toward nonproliferation strategic trade controls. The five elements form an indissoluble interplay of law, policy, and procedures that, ideally, enables licit trade while curtailing the illicit.

What are strategic trade controls capable of doing? First, strategic trade controls can delay a country or group seeking WMD by months, years, and even decades. Although Iraq was able to bypass strategic trade controls in obtaining military-related goods and technology, Saddam Hussein may well have possessed nuclear weapons at the start of the Gulf War had there been no controls in place. Further, strategic trade controls can delay WMD development, which allows for political change or diplomatic pressure to take hold. For example, strategic trade controls appear to have been instrumental in slowing nuclear programs in Argentina and Brazil, allowing for political transitions that led both states to later renounce nuclear arms.[10] Strategic trade controls can also serve as a deterrent by raising the costs of pursuing WMD. States bent on illicitly acquiring weapons must factor in these additional costs and recognize that they could invest billions in covert technology acquisition efforts with no guarantee of a return on investment. Finally, strategic trade controls help to reinforce international nonproliferation norms.[11] States whose WMD programs and ambitions are exposed face limited access to technology and greater international scrutiny. For instance, Iran, which is accused by the United States of pursuing nuclear weapons and supporting terrorism, has suffered both from technology denial and from political isolation resulting from its weapons ambitions.[12]

What can't strategic trade controls do? Strategic trade controls, like all supply-side strategies, are not a solution to the problem of weapons proliferation. Given sufficient time and funding, a country determined to possess nuclear and other mass destruction weapons will eventually be able to acquire the necessary capabilities for such weapons despite the most stringent controls. Strategic trade controls, therefore, need to be complemented by other efforts to reduce or eliminate the threat posed by WMD, including diplomatic and normative measures that reduce the demand for such weapons.

In the next section, we highlight why, particularly in the era of globalization, trade controls are critical nonproliferation tools.

The Nonproliferation Challenge of Globalization

Globalization trends pose several proliferation risks that demand new policy thinking. First, whereas several decades ago, there were only a handful of states selling dual-use technologies, there are now several dozen international suppliers of high-technology items.[13] This means that effective nonproliferation control efforts are only as strong as the weakest link. If a proliferating state cannot purchase from one state the technology and articles needed to build WMD, there is always the opportunity to turn to alternative suppliers in another state that may have more lax strategic trade control systems.

The increasing commercial ties between countries and companies have also altered the economic circumstances surrounding strategic trade control policy. Barriers to the flow of goods, investment, labor, technologies, and services have diminished substantially in Europe, the Americas, and Asia. Volumes of trade and technology transfer have grown dramatically, especially in the 1990s. The total value of advanced technology exports from the United States, for example, grew from slightly more than $69 billion in 1994 to nearly $186 billion in 1998. Moreover, from airlines to software companies, international strategic alliances and acquisitions have reshaped the global economy to make it much more integrated than at any time during the Cold War. The fantastic growth of the Internet and access to the World Wide Web has made possible economic (as well as academic and government) coalitions unimaginable only a decade ago. These new ties have also spawned substantial diffusion of dual-use technologies as companies produce items or support basic and applied research in many countries that were on the margins of the global economy until recently.

Second, there is increased international competition among technology and arms suppliers, which makes it more difficult for countries to reach agreements on regulating their transfer, that is, strategic trade control. Third, the military has also lost its dominance as a source of leading-edge dual-use technologies. Rather than government-funded military research creating "spin-off" high-tech products for the commercial marketplace, the best technologies in most fields now "spin-on" from the private sector to the military. With this shift in the source of technology, government authorities have less control over or knowledge of the pace of technological innovation and application as well, which often creates a lag between the controls and the technological environment. Although the speed and extent of innovation certainly differs from industry to industry and technology to technology, in general effective strategic trade controls now require much more of a partnership between strategic trade control authorities, private and public research institutions, businesses, and others than existed at any time during the Cold War. Some governments, but certainly not all, have responded to these new circumstances by increasing their efforts at transparency and outreach. These efforts have not been uniformly successful across all dual-use industry sectors. Governments must find ways to keep these companies in compliance — or face the risk of these transfers contributing to a WMD program and/or regional conflict.

Finally, the pace of technological change and development has greatly accelerated. This has happened not just for computers and software, but for all forms of high technology products, including communications equipment and weaponry. Programs of contemporary proliferation concern, however, pose a much different target than, for example, the Soviet military. The Soviet Union developed some of the most complex and high-technology weapons systems in the world during the Cold War. Consequently, the United States and its allies concentrated controls on the most advanced dual-use technologies, which they could then apply generally to all communist countries. In contrast, the level of technological development in many projects of proliferation concern today range from the primitive to the sophisticated, sometimes incorporating dual-use technologies long ago decontrolled by the United States and other powers. Not only does this demand innovative new nonproliferation policies, such as those developed under the Chemical Weapons Convention, or "catch-all" strategic trade controls, but identifying what kind of transfers are appropriate to whom has become a much more complex obligation for governments, universities, and companies alike.

Another facet of globalization is the increasing economic unification of states into trading blocs, monetary unions, and free trade areas. The impact of this movement on nonproliferation efforts is little addressed. For example, the European Union (EU), after nearly fifty years in existence, has only recently addressed the need to develop a community-level strategic trade control system as economic borders are collapsed into a single market in which goods, services, technologies, and people will flow freely.[14] Other regions, such as the Southern Cone Common Market (Mercosur) and the Asia-Pacific Economic Conference (APEC) and even the Association of Southeast Asian Nations (ASEAN) and South Asian

Association for Regional Cooperation (SAARC), will face these issues as they continue to merge. Furthermore, how the World Trade Organization (WTO) will address the issue of strategic trade controls remains to be seen.

These global trends will pose new challenges for controlling proliferation-related trade. Consequently, greater policy awareness and international strategies are needed, as currently enshrined in the multilateral strategic trade control regimes.

Multilateral Efforts at Regulating WMD-Relevant Exports

The United States and other supplier states, although united in their resolve to curb WMD proliferation, do not always share the same risk assessments regarding states of proliferation concern or those regarding the proliferation-potential of certain dual-use technologies. To ensure that national economic and diplomatic considerations do not inadvertently help proliferant states to succeed in their goals by playing one supplier against the other, greater cooperation and coordination among supplier states was, and continues to be, necessary. Accordingly, several multilateral agreements came into existence that establish multilateral norms and standards among major suppliers, for transfer of sensitive military and WMD-related items.

Following World War II and the commencement of the Cold War, the United States shared with many of its NATO allies concerns that unrestricted trade with the Soviet Union and its allies could increase the communist threat to the West. As a result in 1949, the United States and a number of its allies formed the Co-ordinating Committee on Multilateral Export Controls (COCOM), with the intention of blocking Soviet access to technology and other sensitive items. These strategic trade controls initially focused not only on items with direct military application but also significantly on commercial items that could be used in developing the industrial base necessary to support a nuclear force. Later the controls were extended to retard the development of missile delivery systems and chemical weapons. Throughout the Cold War, COCOM restricted sales of certain products and was instrumental in maintaining economic pressure—or what some have called economic warfare—on the Warsaw Pact.[15]

The four principal multilateral regimes or arrangements on strategic trade controls include the Australia Group (AG), the Missile Technology Control Regime (MTCR), the Nuclear Suppliers Group, and the Wassenaar Arrangement (WA).[16] The norms and guidelines embodied in these strategic trade control regimes along with the Nuclear Nonproliferation Treaty (NPT), the Biological and

Toxin Weapons Convention (BWC), and the CWC help to de-legitimize and impede efforts to acquire weapons of mass destruction. The following discussion provides a brief introduction to the origins and objectives of these regimes.

The AG was established in 1985 to prevent any contribution to chemical and biological weapons (CBW) programs through the inadvertent supply of chemical precursors, biological agents, and dual-use equipment. The participating governments in this regime agree to common guidelines for chemical and biological export licensing. After the ratification of the CWC in 1995, the Organization for the Prohibition of Chemical Weapons (OPCW) was established. It is charged with the implementation of strategic trade control and verification protocols of the CWC. AG members now view the institution as aiding their efforts to meet obligations under the CWC of 1993 and the BWC of 1972. Although the AG is concerned with regulating trade in CBW articles, it also seeks to ensure that legitimate trade is not inhibited.[17]

The MTCR is an informal and voluntary association of states sharing the goals of nonproliferation of unmanned delivery systems for WMD and seeking to coordinate national export licensing efforts aimed at preventing their proliferation. The group was originally established in 1987, and the number of members has increased steadily to its present total of thirty-four states. It controls exports of missiles (and related technology) whose performance in terms of payload and range exceeds stated parameters. There are two categories of items controlled. Category 1 includes complete systems and subsystems capable of carrying a payload of five hundred kilograms over a range of at least three hundred kilometers and specially designed production facilities for such systems. Category 2 includes missile-related components such as propellants, avionics equipment, and other items used for the production of category 1 systems.[18]

The NSG is an informal institution composed of forty-five states. It establishes common guidelines governing nuclear transfers. The NSG guidelines seek to ensure that nuclear trade is monitored in an effort to prevent the spread of nuclear weapons. The International Atomic Energy Agency (IAEA) first published these guidelines on nuclear strategic trade controls in 1978. In 1991, participating governments were prompted to meet again because of concern about Iraq's attempts to acquire WMD. In 1992, the NSG established additional guidelines for transfers of nuclear-related dual-use equipment, material, and technology. The IAEA (INFCIRC/254) subsequently published these dual-use guidelines as well.[19]

The WA is an informal agreement of forty states established in 1995 to control transfers of conventional weapons and sensitive dual-use goods and technologies. It was designed to promote transparency, an exchange of views and information, and greater responsibility in preventing destabilizing accumulations of advanced conventional weapons and related technologies. Although most adherents agree on restricting transfers to North Korea, Libya, Iraq, and Iran, the institution has no list of target states. There are, however, agreed-on lists of items: tier 1 (basic list) and tier 2 (its very sensitive subset list) that are subject to monitoring. Final interpretation and implementation of these lists is left to the national discretion of participating states. The WA replaced Cold War strategic trade controls (COCOM) that sought to deny the Soviet Union, and its allies, military-related articles.[20]

Despite the commonality of objectives in impeding weapons proliferation, the above multilateral arrangements governing the transfer of strategic dual-use trade continue to give governments "national discretion" in implementing international obligations. In other words, regulation of strategic exports is regarded as a sovereign right. As a result, there are often disputes among member states regarding the advisability of a particular transfer or interpretation of international norms or multilateral strategic trade control agreements. For example, Russian officials do not regard sharing of nuclear technologies with Iran as a breach of international commitments or a significant security risk.[21] U.S. officials, however, view such transfers as highly sensitive because they believe that Iran is covertly pursuing nuclear weapons capability. Thus, although most supplier states agree on the technologies that should be controlled, they have greater difficulty agreeing on particular entities and states of concern and on how to interpret provisions of multilateral strategic trade control agreements.

The end of the Cold War, and a new international environment in which many states are neither "friend" nor "foe," has compounded this problem, resulting in some serious challenges to the operation of these multilateral strategic trade control regimes.[22] First, there are many significant technology suppliers that are not members or do not adhere. As a result, these states are not obligated to observe the same standards of export oversight. Thus, while the United States and its allies may agree not to supply Iran with weapons technology, many states such as China are not bound by either formal or informal agreement to regulating weapons technology trade. Second, as noted above, there is not always agreement on what states are pursuing dangerous weapons. As a result, major suppliers who participate in the strategic trade control regimes do not always agree on what transfers are advisable.

Although there is consensus about the need to deny WMD-related items to Iraq, North Korea, and any country subject to UN sanctions, when it comes to specific issues beyond this overall agreement, the consensus breaks down. For example, Russia and some European states do not view Iran as a "rogue" state that should be the target of comprehensive strategic trade controls while the United States does. Moreover, the United States has been unable to forge consensus on the identity of states seeking WMD or even on state and substate actors supporting terrorism. Even within the United States there are debates as to the extent of technology sharing that should occur with China, given various government reports detailing Chinese efforts to obtain missile and nuclear technologies through civilian channels.[23] Finally, member states of the multilateral strategic trade control regimes also have trouble agreeing on how to respond to India and Pakistan after their public declarations that they intend to develop national nuclear weapons capabilities.[24] States that are not parties to the multilateral regimes also point to the special relationship that the United States has with Israel, which allows technology collaboration on a range of advanced weapon systems, including missiles.

Universalizing Strategic Trade Controls? UNSC Resolution 1540

In 2003, President George W. Bush called on the United Nations to pass a resolution to "criminalize" the proliferation of WMD by and to nonstate actors. The next year, the UNSC obliged, passing Resolution 1540 on the nonproliferation of NBC weapons as well as related delivery systems for WMD. Based on Chapter VII of the UN Charter, the resolution called for states to comply with a battery of legal obligations and report on their progress in implementing the resolution. It also called for the formation of a new UN committee to receive and compile the reports.

Inspired by the terrorist attacks of 9/11 and by revelations surrounding the proliferation network of Pakistani scientist A. Q. Khan, the resolution was explicitly designed to address a gap in current nonproliferation treaties and arrangements, as well as deficiencies in national legislation.[25] The gap concerns "nonstate" actors (today's term of art for terrorist groups or rogue companies or organizations),[26] as the current nonproliferation architecture is predicated upon the nation-state as the primary agent of proliferation. Strictly speaking, these groups are not captured by such treaties as the NPT or the CWC.[27]

Still, the resolution ultimately relies on states to curb such "nonstate" efforts. Resolution 1540 calls on states to put in place "appropriate effective measures to account for and secure" WMD-related items in production, use, storage, or transport and to "maintain appropriate effective physical protection measures" of said items. Most importantly, the resolution seeks to address the absence of universal standards for strategic trade controls, albeit under rather vague provisions, and represents one of the most far-reaching efforts in this regard since the NPT.[28]

The current de facto standards for strategic trade controls are shared among the multilateral strategic trade control arrangements: the AG, the NSG, the MTCR, and the WA. But as their rules are restricted to their limited membership, they also have limited global currency. When strategic technologies were produced by and traded among a smaller number of states, strategic trade controls were effectively applied by and between these supplier states. With an increase in the number of suppliers of and global trade in strategic technologies and dual-use goods, regime nonmember countries with weak strategic trade control can compromise international strategic trade control efforts. Resolution 1540 addresses this need.

Resolution 1540 identifies the key elements of effective strategic trade controls. Specifically, the resolution calls for the creation of "effective" laws to control WMD-related transfers. Leaving aside the ambiguities inherent in the word "effective," the resolution outlines a legal basis that addresses brokering transit, transshipment, and strategic trade controls and sufficient penalties for violations. As the resolution is legally binding, all UN member states must adopt such a legal basis, albeit in a manner according "with their national procedures." Likewise, while outside of the legally compelling paragraphs 1–3, paragraph 6 calls on states to develop "national control lists and calls upon all Member States, when necessary, to pursue at the earliest opportunity the development of such lists."[29]

In addition, states must develop an enforcement capacity to police exports and transfers of sensitive items. States are called on to "develop and maintain appropriate effective border controls and law enforcement efforts to detect, deter, prevent and combat, including through international cooperation when necessary, the illicit trafficking and brokering in such items in accordance with their national legal authorities and legislation and consistent with international law."[30]

To ensure compliance with the "effective" laws the resolution calls on states to "develop appropriate ways to work with and inform industry and the public regarding their obligations under such laws." That's because apart from direct theft of strategic goods and technologies (e.g., fissile material), WMD acquisition efforts are based on otherwise routine commercial transactions; that is, proliferants are purchasing sensitive items from producers.[31] States like Iraq, Iran, Libya, North Korea, and others were able to procure sensitive technology, innocuous-looking dual-use materials, and know-how through direct and semicommercial channels. They did this by using already existing networks of scientists, technologists, and businesspeople who had been cooperating for decades in the WMD procurement efforts of various countries—the Khan network being the most recent example.[32] They operated through real or shell companies, brokerage firms with shady antecedents, and insignificant or overlooked warehousing facilities around the world. Much of the proliferation took place by exploiting loopholes in existing national export control systems of major supplier states whose policies have been shaped by the guidelines of the multilateral regimes.[33]

The resolution acknowledges this reality in its comparative detail of export control standards. Unlike materials accounting, physical protection, and control, export control requirements contain specific references to, for example, brokering and transshipment controls. Both brokering and transshipment controls speak directly to the actual means by which proliferants seek to acquire dual-use items. For instance, the most recent example of dual-use brokering, involving Asher Karni, suggests that proliferation is also being driven by middlemen.[34] Dubai may not be the source of dangerous technologies or materials, but it found itself at the center of the Khan network in a transit and transshipment capacity.[35]

In summary, Resolution 1540 identifies the necessary elements of effective national export controls: legal basis, enforcement capacity, and industry-government relations. Although the resolution's universality is viewed somewhat skeptically by many—since it was approved by the 15 members of the UNSC rather than the 191 members of the UN General Assembly—it was unanimously adopted.[36] Nevertheless, as with similar resolutions, the means and therefore likelihood of implementation are problematic for reasons of scale, resource, and commitment.

Conclusion

Several studies of export controls argue—or simply accept—that increased economic globalization reduces the efficacy of supply-side strategies to control WMD proliferation.[37] Indeed, many developments related to globalization do pose significant challenges for the effective control of trade in militarily relevant goods and technologies—both munitions and dual-use items. Additionally, commercial technologies, vital to many advanced weapons systems and enabling technologies (such as advanced machine tools and high-performance computers), are spreading and developing more rapidly as traditional global barriers to trade (e.g., import duties, discrimination in government procurement, and import substitution measures) are reduced. The pace of innovation in commercial technologies is such that product cycles are measured in months rather than years.[38] This has significant implications for export control.

Implicit in some of these arguments is the assumption that traditional proliferation controls are increasingly futile. A number of factors generate this impression:

- more supplier (and transit) states;
- greater defense industry cooperation and consolidation;
- commercial rather than military-led technology development;

• ease of intangible technology transfers; and
• increasing pace of technological development.

While any one of these factors can diminish the effectiveness of export controls, the cumulative impact of these conditions has convinced some observers that export controls have become, according to one expert, more "speed bumps than real barriers."[39]

Recognition of a long-standing debate over how success should be defined in export controls is relevant here and also informs this conclusion. If one begins with the view that export controls can stop proliferation, then diffusion of WMD technology represents failure. If one starts with the assumption that export controls by themselves can only delay a determined proliferator, then "speed bumps" that buy time for diplomacy or other sanctions are tangible successes. Differing expectations lead to different assessments of effectiveness. Of course, the notion of accurately gauging the impact of export controls on weapons proliferation assumes that we could ascertain the extent to which weapons would spread in a world without export controls. This is clearly not possible. Nevertheless, whether controls are seen as increasingly futile or modestly functional, both sides still agree on their necessity. The real points of contention are what to control, how to control it, and whom to deny.

Observers from many perspectives, however, often ignore the important possibility that governments can adapt export controls to meet these new circumstances. Research in other issue areas suggests that globalization usually produces convergence in national policies that potentially enhance effectiveness as governments are compelled to adapt existing policies and create new forms of coordination to address problems associated with greater connectivity.[40] Diminishing effectiveness of export controls does not necessarily follow from the mere existence of more supplier or transit states. Enhancing effectiveness in a world of growing numbers of dual-use suppliers, however, does demand more dynamic and flexible multilateral policy coordination. Precisely in response to globalization, more states may adopt nonproliferation export controls and reform international export control institutions. Consequently, new nonproliferation export control standards and norms may emerge that make export controls more, not less, effective against existing or emerging patterns of illicit technology transfers. Similarly, while advances in information technology make it easier to transfer technology across borders, such advances may also spur more effective intelligence, licensing, verification, and enforcement activities.

Although these are complicated and constantly changing issues, leaving the future unclear, it is fair to say that export control policies and practices remain vital in restraining the flow of the world's most dangerous technologies. Those concerned with WMD proliferation, including select governments, businesses, think tanks, and individuals, should, and no doubt will, strive to improve export control policy and practice, hoping to meet the challenges. We will learn their successes and failures as we navigate the twenty-first century.

Notes

1. This chapter is based on earlier work by the authors. In particular, it is drawn from Michael D. Beck and Seema Gahlaut, "Introduction to Export Controls," 1–21, and Richard T. Cupitt and Scott A. Jones, "Conclusion," 163–75, in *To Supply or To Deny: Comparing Nonproliferation Export Controls in Five Key Countries*, ed. Michael D. Beck, Richard T. Cupitt, Seema Gahlaut, and Scott A. Jones (The Hague: Kluwer Law International, 2003). It is also derived from various strategic trade control publications at the Center for International Trade and Security at the University of Georgia. See http://www.uga.edu/cits.

2. The current U.S. system of export controls has roots that reach back to the First World War, when the United States cooperated with Great Britain to institute the "navicert" (i.e., naval certification) system for exports and passed the *Trading with the Enemy Act* (TWEA). Following the war and the rearmament of Germany in the 1930s, the United States attempted to avoid foreign entanglements by pursuing a policy of neutrality that restricted the export and re-export of military items. On becoming a combatant in World War II, the United States extended export controls from purely military items to dual-use items, which are goods, services, and technology that while mainly commercial also have defense applications. This policy was primarily intended to ameliorate supply shortages in World War II. See Richard T. Cupitt, *Reluctant Champions: Truman, Eisenhower, Bush, and Clinton: U.S. Presidential Policy and Strategic Export Controls* (New York: Routledge, 2000).

3. Michael Mastanduno, *Economic Containment: CoCom and the Politics of East-West Trade* (Ithaca, NY: Cornell University Press, 1992); Cupitt, *Reluctant Champions*.

4. See Douglas Jehl, "Who Armed Iraq. Answers the West Did Not Want to Hear," *New York Times*, July 18, 1993; Gary Milhollin, *Licensing Mass Destruction: U.S. Exports to Iraq, 1985–1990*, Wisconsin Project on Nuclear Arms Control report, June 1991.

5. Nonproliferation export controls are the laws, regulations, and norms designed to regulate the transfer of weapons of mass destruction components, materials, and technologies. See Jean-François Rioux, ed., *Limiting the Proliferation of Weapons: The Role of Supply-Side Strategies* (Ottawa: Carleton University Press, 1992).

6. Nick Johnson, "War on Terrorism Poses New Challenges for Technology Exports," *Aerospace Daily*, January 2, 2002; Richard T. Cupitt, associate director, Center for International Trade and Security, University of Georgia, testimony before the U.S. Senate Committee on Governmental Affairs, Subcommittee on International Security, Proliferation, and Federal Services, on enhancing export controls to combat terrorism, November 7, 2001; Sharon Weinberger, "Export Control Changes Will Address Old Issues, New Threats, Says

DOD Official," *Aerospace Daily*, March 22, 2002; "House Committee Votes to Toughen Export Controls," *Washington Internet Daily*, March 8, 2002.

7. David Albright, *Preventing Illegal Exports: Learning from Case Studies*, report, Institute for Science and International Security, April 6, 2001.

8. "Concern about Iran-Russia Nuke Cooperation," *RFE/RL Iran Report*, July 1, 2002; "Russia's Risky Iran Connection," *New York Times*, June 10, 2002; Alexander Pikayev, "Strategic Dimensions of the Russo-Iranian Partnership," *Monitor* 7, no. 1 (Winter 2001): 7–10; Stephen Blank, "Russo-Iranian Proliferation: Once More around the Mulberry Bush," *Monitor* 7, no. 1 (Winter 2001): 10–14.

9. U.S., Central Intelligence Agency, *Unclassified Report to Congress on the Acquisition of Technology Related to Weapons of Mass Destruction and Advanced Conventional Munitions, 1 January through 30 June 2001*, January 2002, https://www.cia.gov/library/reports/archived-reports-1/jan_jun2001.htm; Joe Leahy, "U.S. Warns China over Weapons of Mass Destruction," *Financial Times*, January 22, 2002; James Martin Center for Nonproliferation Studies, *China's Missile Export and Assistance to Pakistan*, Monterey Institute of International Studies, July 2000, http://cns.miis.edu/research/india/china/mpakpos.htm#Background; Gordon Oehler, statement at the hearing of the Senate Foreign Relations Committee on Proliferation of Chinese Missiles, June 11, 1998; R. Jeffrey Smith, "China Linked to Pakistani Missile Plant," *Washington Post*, August, 25 1996; Wisconsin Project on Nuclear Arms Control, "Pakistan: Nuclear Helpers," http://www.wisconsinproject.org/countries/pakistan/nukehelpers.htm; Wisconsin Project on Nuclear Arms Control, "Pakistan: U.S. Approves Most Nuclear-Related Exports," *Risk Report* 1, no. 6 (July/August 1995), http://www.wisconsinproject.org/countries/pakistan/usapproves.htm; Gary Milhollin, "Made in America? How U.S. Exports Helped Fuel the South Asian Arms Race," *Washington Post*, June 7, 1998, C1.

10. Tariq Rauf, "Successes of the Nuclear Non-Proliferation Regime: Curbing the Spread of Nuclear Weapons," discussion at Vienna International Centre, October 8, 1999; Wyn Bowen, "Brazil's Accession to the MTCR," *Nonproliferation Review* 3, no. 3 (Spring/Summer 1996): 86–91; Julio Carasales, "The Argentine-Brazilian Nuclear Rapprochement," *Nonproliferation Review* 2, no. 3 (Spring/Summer 1995): 39–48.

11. Kathleen Bailey, "Nonproliferation Export Controls: Problems and Alternatives," in *Proliferation and Export Controls*, ed. Kathleen Bailey and Robert Rudney (Lanham, MD: University Press of America; Fairfax, VA: National Institute for Public Policy, 1993), 49–57; Gary Milhollin, "Can Sanctions Stop The Bomb?" keynote address delivered at the Conference on Economic Sanctions and International Relations, Fourth Freedom Forum and the Joan B. Kroc Institute for International Peace Studies, Notre Dame University, April 3, 1993; Brad Roberts, "Export Controls and Biological Weapons: New Roles, New Challenges," *Critical Review in Microbiology* 24, no. 3 (Fall 1998): 235–54; Janusz Ordover and Linda Goldberg, eds., *Export Controls and Nonproliferation Policy*, Office of Technology Assessment, 1994.

12. Geoffrey Kemp, "Iranian Nuclear Weapons and U.S. Policy," Program Brief 6, no. 2, Nixon Center, January 2000, http://www.nixoncenter.org/publications/Program%20Briefs/

vol6no2iran.htm; "Ever More Perilous Isolation," *Economist*, May 27, 2003; Ali Tajvidi, "'Rogue State' versus 'The Great Arrogance,'" *CSD Bulletin* 5, no. 1 (Autumn 1997): 7, http://www.wmin.ac.uk/sshl/page-114; Geoffrey Kemp, "America and Iran: Road Maps and Realism," monograph, Nixon Center, 1998, http://www.nixoncenter.org/publications/monographs/iran.htm.

13. Dual-use items are those articles or technologies with both peaceful uses and WMD or military applications.

14. Scott Jones, "EU Enlargement: Implications for EU and Multilateral Export Controls," *Nonproliferation Review* 10, no. 2 (Summer 2003): 80–89.

15. COCOM was founded in 1949 by the United States and its allies, mostly NATO members. It arose from a shared concern that uncontrolled trade with the Soviet Union and its allies could increase the communist threat to their own security. See Gary K. Bertsch, *East-West Strategic Trade, COCOM and the Atlantic Alliance*, Atlantic Papers no. 49, Atlantic Institute for International Affairs, 1983.

16. We prefer the term "arrangements" instead of "regimes" because these agreements are informal, and member states are not bound by law to abide by any agreement commonly arrived at by the entire membership. Some experts suggest that the arrangements be called "plurilateral" because unlike the common multilateral agreements, new members cannot be inducted except by consensus among existing members. In this sense, the arrangements are similar to the North Atlantic Treaty Organization, the European Union, the Association of Southeast Asian Nations, the North American Free Trade Agreement, and so forth rather than to the international agreements that are open to all states that want to join.

17. Amy E. Smithson, "Separating Fact from Fiction: The Australia Group and the Chemical Weapons Convention," occasional paper no. 34, Henry L. Stimson Center, March 1997; Jean Pascal Zanders, Melissa Hersh, Jacqueline Simon, and Maria Wahlberg, "Chemical and Biological Weapon Developments and Arms Control," *SIPRI Yearbook 2001: Armaments, Disarmament and International Security* (Oxford: Oxford University Press, 2001); Roberts, "Export Controls and Biological Weapons"; Benoit Morel, "How Effective Is the Australia Group," in Bailey and Rudney, eds., *Proliferation and Export Controls*, 57–68.

18. For background on the MTCR and challenges facing efforts to control missile technology, see Richard Speier, "Can the Missile Technology Control Regime Be Repaired?" in *Repairing the Regime: Preventing the Spread of Weapons of Mass Destruction*, ed. Joseph Cirincione and Kathleen Newland (New York: Routledge and the Carnegie Endowment for International Peace, 2000), 205–16; Richard Speier, *How Effective Is the MTCR?* Proliferation Brief 4, no. 7, Carnegie Endowment for International Peace, April 12, 2001, http://www.carnegieendowment.org/publications/index.cfm?fa=view&id=672&prog=zgp&proj=znpp; Richard Speier, "A Nuclear Nonproliferation Treaty for Missiles?" in *Fighting Proliferation: New Concerns for the Nineties*, ed. Henry Sokolski (Maxwell Air Force Base, AL: Air University Press, 1996); Dinshaw Mistry, "Ballistic Missile Proliferation and the MTCR: A Ten-Year Review," paper presented at the International Studies Association annual meeting, March 19–23, 1998.

19. On the NSG, see Richard Cupitt and Igor Khripunov, "New Strategies for the Nuclear Supplier Group (NSG)," *Comparative Strategy* 16, no. 3 (July/September 1997): 305–15.

20. On the WA, see Christopher Hoelscher and Hans Michael Wolffgang, "The Wassenaar Arrangements between International Trade, Nonproliferation, and Export Controls," *Journal of World Trade* 32 (February 1998): 45–63; Ron Smith and Bernard Udis, "New Challenges to Arms Export Control: Whither Wassenaar?" *Nonproliferation Review* 8, no 2. (Summer 2001): 81–92; Cassady Craft, "New Challenges in Multilateral Efforts to Control the Conventional Weapons Trade," *Monitor* 8, no. 2 (Spring 2002): 15–19; Cassady Craft and Suzette Grillot, "Transparency and the Effectiveness of Multilateral Nonproliferation Export Control Regimes: Can Wassenaar Work?" *Southeastern Political Review* 27, no. 2 (June 1999): 279–302.

21. "Iran-Russia: Russia Is Not Providing WMD Technology, Official Says," *Global Security Newswire*, May 17, 2002; "Russia: Russian President Says Nuclear Cooperation with Iran Poses No Threat," *Global Security Newswire*, May 26, 2002; Yevgeny Zvedre, "The U.S.-Russian Nonproliferation Dialogue: The Iranian Factor and Export Control Cooperation," *Yaderny Kontrol Digest* 5, no. 3 (Summer 2000).

22. Michael D. Beck, "Reforming the Multilateral Export Control Regimes," *Nonproliferation Review* 7, no 2 (Summer 2000): 91–101.

23. For more detail on the problems facing the export control regimes, see Beck, "Reforming the Multilateral Export Control Regimes."

24. Thus, while the United States, United Kingdom, and Canada continue to see civilian nuclear exports to India as a proliferation risk, Russia does not. For a review of Russian perspectives on South Asia, see Seema Gahlaut, "Reducing Nuclear Dangers in South Asia: A Review of Russian Perspectives," *Monitor* (special issue), 7, no. 3 (Fall 2001).

25. The impact of the Khan network was far reaching. As noted by the director-general of the IAEA: "Perhaps the most disturbing lesson to emerge from our work in Iran and Libya is the existence of an extensive illicit market for the supply of nuclear items, which clearly thrived on demand. The relative ease with which A. Q. Khan and associates were able to set up and operate a multinational illicit network demonstrates clearly the inadequacy of the present export control system. Nuclear components designed in one country could be manufactured in another, shipped through a third (which may have appeared to be a legitimate user), assembled in a fourth, and designated for eventual turnkey use in a fifth. The fact that so many companies and individuals could be involved is extremely worrying. And the fact that, in most cases, this could occur apparently without the knowledge of their own governments, clearly points to the inadequacy of national systems of oversight for sensitive equipment and technology. The present system of nuclear export controls is clearly deficient" (speech at the Carnegie Endowment for International Peace Nonproliferation Conference, June 21, 2004).

26. The resolution definition of a nonstate actor is an "individual or entity, not acting under the lawful authority of any State in conducting activities which come within the scope of this resolution."

27. For a recent review of the terrorist WMD threat, see John Eldridge, "Terrorist WMD: Threats and Responses," *Jane's International Defence Review*, September 1, 2005: 83–88.

28. See Wade Boese, "Implications of UN Security Council Resolution 1540," presentation to the Institute of Nuclear Materials Management panel discussion, March 15, 2005, http://www.armscontrol.org/events/20050315_1540.asp.

29. A control list for nonproliferation export controls is the legally established means of verifying the types of goods, services, and technologies that will be controlled and therefore reviewed by the licensing system. Control lists define the products being controlled by describing the technical specifications of items that require a license in order to be exported. A typical nonproliferation export control list contains categories for nuclear, chemical, biological, missile, dual-use, and conventional weapons technologies. Traditionally, national dual-use control lists are derived from the multilateral export control regimes (AG, MTCR, NSG, and the WA) as a minimal basis for control. The EU control list, for example, is becoming the de facto international export control list standard as it is derivative of all of the multilateral export control regimes while allowing for national discretion in adding items. UNSC resolution 1540, however, does not reference the export control regimes in the context of control lists.

30. Resolution 1540 was designed to accommodate the Proliferation Security Initiative. See Jofi Joseph, "The Proliferation Security Initiative: Can Interdiction Stop Proliferation?" *Arms Control Today* 34, no. 5 (June 2004): 6–13.

31. The A. Q. Khan network revealed the extent to which commercial networks were engaged in illicit trade. In addition, studies on terrorist group WMD acquisition efforts indicate they are similarly relying on trade rather than theft. On this last point, see Gavin Cameron, "Multitrack Microproliferation: Lessons from Aum Shinrikyo and Al Qaeda," *Studies in Conflict and Terrorism* 22, no. 4 (October/December 1999): 277–309.

32. Chaim Braun and Christopher F. Chyba, "Proliferation Rings: New Challenges in the Nuclear Nonproliferation Regime," *International Security* 29, no. 2 (Fall 2004): 5–49.

33. Even advanced Western countries were not immune to exploitation by the Khan network, as revealed in a March 2005 article in the trade newsletter *NuclearFuel* discussing an episode in the Netherlands. In 1999, according to the report, the Dutch firm Slebos Research shipped six U.S.-produced absolute capacitance manometers to Pakistan. See "Pakistan's Quest for UF6 Sensors Underlines Limits of NSG Controls," *NuclearFuel*, March 28, 2005.

34. In January 2004, U.S. authorities arrested Asher Karni, an Israeli citizen living in South Africa, for allegedly re-exporting U.S.-made triggered spark gaps from South Africa to Pakistan. Among other things, triggered spark gaps can be used to detonate nuclear weapons. According to a U.S. government affidavit against Karni, Humayun Khan, the CEO of a Pakistani company, Pakland PME, approached Karni around June 2003 in search of triggered spark gaps made by PerkinElmer Optoelectronics of Salem, Massachusetts. The NSG agreed to restrict the export of spark gaps if there is a risk they will be used in nuclear weapons. Based on the NSG guidelines, the United States requires an export license to send them to countries of nuclear proliferation concern, including India, Iran, North Korea, and Pakistan. See Jacob Blackford, "Asher Karni Case Shows Weakness in Nuclear Export Controls," Institute for Science and International Security, September 8, 2004, http://www.isis-online.org/publications/southafrica/asherkarni.html.

35. For example, see Mathew Swibel, "Trading with the Enemy," *Forbes*, April 12, 2004, 86–93, http://www.forbes.com/free_forbes/2004/0412/086.html.

36. Despite its seemingly unobjectionable purpose, however, the U.S.-initiated resolution required several months of debate and revisions before winning approval. See Wade Boese, "Security Council Unanimously Adopts Resolution on Denying Terrorists WMD," *Arms Control Today* 34, no. 4 (May 2004): 34. For more information on the questionable role of the UNSC in legislating international law, see, for example, Stefan Talmon, "The Security Council as World Legislature," *American Journal of International Law* 99, no. 1 (2005): 175, and Eric Rosand, "The Security Council as 'Global Legislator': *Ultra Vires* or Ultra Innovative?" *Fordham International Law Journal* 28, no. 3 (2005): 542.

37. See, for example, Sam Nunn Bank of America Policy Forum, *Executive Summary: Globalization, Technology Trade and American Leadership: A New Strategy for the 21st Century* (Athens: University of Georgia, March 2000; Center for Strategic and International Studies, *Technology and Security in the 21st Century: U.S. Military Export Control Reform* (Washington, DC: CSIS, 2001; Henry L. Stimson Center, *Study Group on Enhancing Multilateral Export Controls For U.S. National Security: Final Report*, April 2001; The Henry L. Stimson Center, and Defense Science Board Task Force on Globalization and Security, Final Report (Washington, DC: Office of the Under Secretary of Defense for Acquisition and Technology, December 1999).

38. According to what is popularly known as Moore's Law, the number of transistors per square inch on integrated circuits has doubled every year since the integrated circuit was invented. Moore predicted that this trend would continue for the foreseeable future, with data density doubling approximately every eighteen months, allowing faster and exponentially more calculations per second.

39. Martin Libicki, "Rethinking War: The Mouse's New Roar," *Foreign Policy*, no. 117 (Winter 1999/2000): 30–43.

40. See, for example, Philip G. Cerny, "Globalization and the Changing Logic of Collective Action," *International Organization* 49, no. 4 (Autumn 1995): 595–625, and Motoshi Suzuki, "Economic Interdependence, Relative Gains, and International Cooperation: The Case of Monetary Policy Coordination," *International Studies Quarterly* 38, no. 3 (September 1994): 475–98. See also Daniel W. Drezner, "Globalization and Policy Convergence" *International Studies Review* 3, no. 1 (Spring 2001): 53–78; and Drezner, "Globalization's Last Hurrah?" (*Foreign Policy*, no. 128 [January/February 2002]: 38–51). Drezner finds little evidence across the literature that policy convergence in response to economic globalization produces a race to the bottom or the lowest common denominator.

PART THREE

Counterproliferation

CHAPTER SEVEN

The Proliferation Security Initiative

James R. Holmes and

Andrew C. Winner

In October 2003, intelligence, law enforcement, diplomatic, and military services from the United States, the United Kingdom, Italy, and Germany collaborated to track and divert the merchant ship *BBC China*, which was carrying a shipment of uranium centrifuge parts to Libya for use in Tripoli's nuclear weapons program.[1] U.S. and British politicians touted the interdiction as a triumph for the newly minted Proliferation Security Initiative (PSI), asserting that it had constituted a critical factor impelling Libya to give up its weapons-of-mass-destruction (WMD) programs. While the operation clearly kept certain uranium centrifuge parts out of Libyan hands, it is less clear, however, whether the interdiction was really the driving force in Libya's overall decision that Western pronouncements claimed. Indeed, considerable debate has ensued over which factors account for the Libyan government's turnaround.[2]

Pointing to the *BBC China* affair, the U.S. government has nonetheless hailed the PSI as an example of "effective multilateralism."[3] This one very public example and the attendant claim that the initiative is "effective" ought to provide some basis for analyzing this new, relatively unique undertaking in multilateral diplomacy dealing with the proliferation of weapons of mass destruction. Drawing on the words of U.S. spokesmen, we propose some indices of effectiveness for the PSI:

- Have participants in the initiative formed solid working partnerships under the rubric of the PSI?
- Have PSI participants integrated diplomacy, intelligence, and military force to good effect?
- Has the initiative shaped the intentions and decision making of proliferators, deterring shipments of weapons-related materiel?
- Has the initiative denied proliferators the weapons capabilities they desire?[4]

Unfortunately, applying these indices is difficult, as the *BBC China* case remains the only one about which details are publicly available for analysts to study. The PSI governments have acknowledged few interdictions publicly, couching their claims for its effectiveness largely in general, negative terms, contending that it lacks certain characteristics that impeded previous multilateral enterprises or that it differs from past enterprises altogether.

The novelty of some of the initiative's operating practices, its relatively quick evolution from idea to ongoing enterprise, and the dearth of empirical data have engendered a number of misconceptions about the PSI, rendering it controversial in some quarters. This chapter seeks to clearly lay out the PSI's origins, characteristics, legal underpinnings, and methods of operation. In addition, the chapter compares its characteristics to those of other multilateral enterprises and assesses what can be gleaned to date about its effectiveness. Finally, the chapter identifies practical and policy issues confronting the initiative, focusing on what these issues imply for its future as a tool to combat proliferation.

What Is the Proliferation Security Initiative?

The PSI is a loose consortium of nation-states, primarily seafaring powers that have a stake in halting shipments of materiel related to nuclear, biological, or chemical (NBC) weaponry or the associated delivery systems, usually ballistic missiles. Unlike other efforts to combat weapons proliferation, the PSI envisions intercepting these items in the transport phase, whether on shore, aloft, or at sea.

The PSI is a counterproliferation initiative, not an international organization.[5] Its spokespeople zealously declare that it is "an activity, not an organization" owing to its lack of a governing treaty, formal structure, and set procedures for applying for membership.[6] Indeed, one refers not to members of the initiative but to "participants." A government becomes a participant in essence by avowing its support—publicly or privately—for the Statement of Interdiction Principles, the initiative's brief founding document, and by backing its declaration of purpose with tangible action. As befits this kind of "coalition of the willing," governments can presumably withdraw their support from the initiative with equal ease or simply abstain from interdiction efforts that imperil their perceived national interests.

According to the U.S. State Department, the PSI now commands the support of well over seventy governments to one degree or another, and in 2005, UN secretary-general Kofi Annan publicly urged all UN member states to throw their support behind its efforts.[7] Some scholars, notably Pace University law professor Mark R. Shulman, have advanced extravagant claims for the PSI, depicting it as a virtual revolution in international affairs. Enthuses Shulman:

The Initiative is both bold and timely. It constitutes one of the most important recent developments in the area of international peace and security and may also add up to the most exciting change in the area of public international law, since it may fundamentally alter the transnational legal framework for the use of force by states.[8]

"By blurring the lines between war and peace," he claims, "the Initiative eventually may permit states to use highly targeted and entirely proportionate force for limited purposes to further security objectives without triggering war and all the horrors that it entails."[9] Perhaps—but for now the reality is something far more modest, as a close reading of the Statement of Interdiction Principles shows.

Unveiled by the PSI governments in September 2003, the Statement of Interdiction Principles declares that participants "are deeply concerned" that the makings of WMD might fall into the hands of terrorist groups, and thus "are committed to working together to stop the flow of these items to and from states and nonstate actors of proliferation concern," namely "countries or entities" intent on developing, acquiring, or transferring WMD or the associated delivery systems.[10] The principles commit PSI participants to the following:

- "Undertake effective measures, either alone or in concert with other states," to interrupt weapons-related cargoes in transit;
- "Adopt streamlined procedures for rapid exchange of relevant information concerning suspected proliferation activity, . . . dedicate appropriate resources and efforts to interdiction operations and capabilities, and maximize coordination" among themselves in these efforts;
- "Review and work to strengthen" national laws and regulations, as well as "relevant international law and frameworks," to support interception operations;
- Refrain from transporting or abetting the transport of weapons-related cargoes to suspect actors, while forbidding their nationals to engage in such activity;
- "[B]oard and search any vessel flying their flag in their internal waters or territorial seas, or areas beyond the territorial seas of any other state," that is reasonably thought to be carrying weapons-related materiel;
- "[S]eriously consider" authorizing other states to board and search their flag vessels when these vessels are reasonably thought to be carrying weapons-related materiel;
- "[S]top and/or search" vessels carrying suspect cargoes in their internal waters, territorial seas, or, when declared, contiguous zones;
- Deny aircraft carrying suspect cargoes permission to transit through their national airspace, or require such aircraft to land for inspection; and
- Inspect and seize weapons-related cargoes at transshipment nodes such as ports, airfields, or railway facilities.

In short, PSI governments promise to work with one another to locate and intercept dangerous shipments where sovereignty is at its apex—on national soil, in internal or territorial waters, in national airspace, or on board ships or aircraft subject to their jurisdiction. While they do not abrogate their right to refuse access to sovereign territory, they pledge to look favorably on requests from fellow participants to board and search their flag vessels and aircraft. To widen the amount of world shipping open to boarding and search under PSI auspices, the United States has negotiated bilateral boarding agreements with major flag states, including Belize, Croatia, Cyprus, Liberia, the Marshall Islands, and Panama. Modeled on similar agreements used for counterdrug operations, these documents expedite U.S. Navy and Coast Guard access to upward of half of world shipping.[11]

How does the PSI perform its mission? As the concept of effective multilateralism suggests, the initiative's strategic objectives include (a) threatening to expose proliferation-related activity, thus deterring rogue regimes, unscrupulous suppliers, or terrorist groups from attempting to transfer weapons-related goods or substances; (b) raising the transaction costs of such transfers to a prohibitive level should deterrence fail; and (c) detecting, thwarting, and publicizing shipments that do proceed. Private actors trafficking in proscribed items face legal action; governments face diplomatic opprobrium, as Libya did in 2003. Thus the PSI sets out to impose a chilling effect on proliferation while reinforcing international accords and regimes.[12]

As noted before, empirical data documenting the PSI's performance are hard to come by, in large measure because of participants' penchant for operational secrecy. "Between April 2005 and April 2006," reported Under Secretary of State Robert G. Joseph in a typical statement, "the United States worked successfully with multiple PSI partners in Europe, Asia and the Middle East on roughly two dozen separate occasions to prevent transfers of equipment and materials to WMD and missile programs in countries of concern," notably Iran.[13]

Monitoring and frustrating proliferation-related transactions anywhere in the world is a task of immense scope. Pooling resources—deploying the full array of resources available to governments, including law enforcement, intelligence apparatuses, customs and border security authorities, coast guards, and military services—is crucial to the success of this venture. Admiral Mike Mullen, the top U.S. naval officer, has spoken of assembling a multinational "1,000-ship navy" for nontraditional operations such as maritime counterproliferation.[14] Even a state with minimal military capabilities can make a valuable contribution to PSI activities by, say, rigorously policing its sovereign territory or by supplying a better-equipped state with actionable intelligence about goings-on in its geographic environs.[15]

What Is the PSI Not?

Despite its seemingly innocuous nature—who could object to states' banding together to enforce proliferation-related laws more efficiently?—the PSI has received substantial criticism since its inception. PSI governments have sought, with mixed success, to dispel misgivings that threaten to inhibit wider participation.

Several factors help account for this ambivalence. First, the precedents leading up to the 2003 founding of the PSI have given many governments and observers pause. Consider the 1993 *Yinhe* incident. In August 1993, U.S. intelligence officials began voicing concerns that the Chinese vessel, detected heading toward Iranian waters, was carrying precursors for use in Tehran's chemical warfare programs. Washington lodged serious, detailed allegations about the vessel. Declared one U.S. intelligence official, "we know these chemicals are bound for Iran's chemical weapons plants and it is a lot of tonnage, tens of tons." An officer from the U.S. Central Command went further, specifying that the merchantman was ferrying thiodiglycol and thionyl chloride to the Islamic Republic.[16]

The Chinese authorities vehemently disputed the U.S. charges. The U.S. case began to unravel when spokesmen for the *Yinhe*'s owner, the Hong Kong–based Guanzhou Ocean Shipping Company, flatly denied that weapons-relevant material was on board the ship. They invited inspectors from a neutral third party to examine the vessel's cargo.[17] Saudi Arabia allowed the ship to enter its port at Dammam, and a Saudi team, including U.S. technical advisers, scrutinized it in concert with Chinese inspectors.

By September, Wu Jianmin, a spokesman for the Chinese Foreign Ministry, was able to report that the joint Sino-Saudi inspections had uncovered no traces of chemical precursors.[18] Insisting that its officials had acted in good faith, Washington refused to apologize for the affair, while Beijing branded the United States a "self-styled world cop"—a charge for which there was no good answer.[19] To this day Chinese officials question how their shippers would be compensated following botched maritime counterproliferation operations.[20] A *Yinhe*-like incident occurring under PSI auspices could taint if not discredit the initiative in the eyes of much of the world.

Less controversial was an incident involving the North Korean freighter *So San*. In December 2002, intelligence tips convinced U.S. analysts the *So San* was hauling ballistic missiles to buyers in the Middle East. As the freighter approached Yemen, the Bush administration requested Spain, which had a warship nearby, to board it. Fortunately for Washington and Madrid, the ship's captain hauled down his flag, turning his ship into a stateless vessel under international law and giving Spain the right to board it.[21] An inspection of the ship's hold turned up Scud missiles buried beneath sacks of cement. Confronted with the evidence, the Yemeni government admitted that it had purchased the North Korean missiles. While Spain could have made a plausible legal case for seizing the cargo or turning it over to the United States, Washington decided to allow the shipment to proceed—reportedly because it valued Yemeni cooperation on counterterrorism more than it feared the minimal threat posed by the Scuds.[22]

Clearly, then, political and economic imperatives impinge on maritime interdiction, promising to complicate future PSI endeavors.[23] Operation Active Endeavor, under which the North Atlantic Treaty Organization (NATO) assets patrol Mediterranean waters and skies, or the multinational flotilla patrolling off the Makran coast, hunting for terrorists fleeing Afghanistan, make better precedents for PSI operations than would the *So San* or especially the *Yinhe* incidents. If the PSI participants played up these precedents, they would stand a better chance of building a reputation as a trustworthy steward of the world's sea-lanes.

Second, many objections to the PSI stem less from what it actually does than from how it might be abused or what it hypothetically might mutate into in the future. As the Statement of Interdiction Principles suggests, most operations will take place not in international waters or airspace—as much of the commentary has it—but within national jurisdictions.[24] The Interdiction Principles do not even contemplate abridging freedom of navigation, which international law generally regards as virtually sacrosanct, without the consent of the flag state. Nor is the PSI a purely military initiative. Indeed, the interception of the *BBC China* was the result of a multinational sting operation. Diplomacy supported by law enforcement and intelligence services made the operation possible; military units simply guided the ship into port for inspection.[25] Explaining that force is only one tool in the PSI's toolkit would do much to quiet worries in world capitals, helping the initiative and the counterproliferation norm it propounds win wider acceptance.

Such misconceptions flourish in part because the PSI participants divulge few details about how they conduct business. The initiative has carried out an ambitious slate of meetings, tabletop exercises, and war games, along with exercises at sea, in the air, and on land in various regions. Most recently, leaders from over sixty participating countries gathered in Warsaw, Poland, to celebrate three years of success while inviting additional countries to take part in the enterprise. Declared President George W. Bush, the PSI has grown

> from a handful of nations to a global partnership. . . . Together, we are working to disrupt the financial activities of networks that support proliferation, as called for in United Nations Security Council Resolutions 1540 and 1673. . . . Together, we are

shutting down front companies and proliferation networks and interdicting cargo carrying these dangerous materials, whether transported by land, air or sea.[26]

Beyond such general statements asserting success, the PSI participants shroud their affairs in strict operational secrecy. As mentioned previously, the few statements wrung out of U.S. officials have amounted to little more than numbers of operations the initiative has executed.[27] While this clandestine mode of operations likely bolsters the efficacy of the PSI's denial function, helping participating agencies detect and interrupt proliferation-related activity without alerting the entities targeted, it is an open question whether deterrence benefits from secrecy. And secrecy certainly raises eyebrows in many capitals and even among analysts favorably disposed toward the initiative in principle. Misconceptions and outsized fears abound in such a climate, especially absent a UN Security Council (UNSC) resolution explicitly authorizing PSI activities.[28]

Third, the venomous tone of international relations in recent years lends itself to suspicions of the PSI. While the initiative is uncontroversial within the United States—indeed, in 2004 the Bush and Kerry campaigns strove to outdo each other on who would prosecute interdiction operations with more vigor—it is reasonable to suppose that some of the bad feelings aroused during the debate over whether to invade Iraq have affixed themselves to the PSI. Indeed, Baghdad fell scant weeks before the Krakow summit at which President Bush announced the new counterproliferation initiative.

And the fact that John Bolton, the firebrand diplomat who inspires disdain in many capitals, was the Bush administration's point man on the PSI may have also created residual animus toward his brainchild, whether or not the initiative's activities are objectionable in legal or operational terms. Bolton's expansive words in the early months of the initiative—on one occasion he proclaimed, "there are essentially an infinite number of potential circumstances and variations and permutations where interdictions could take place"—did little to mollify the PSI's detractors.[29]

Legal Aspects

Indeed, critics and skeptics have questioned the PSI principally on legal grounds. Yet the Statement of Interdiction Principles clearly mandates that actions taken under the initiative shall conform to "national legal authorities and relevant international law and frameworks, including the UN Security Council." The Statement of Interdiction Principles also purports to tie the effort loosely to previous policy documents and statements, such as Group of Eight (G-8) and European Union (EU) statements on proliferation, along with a statement from the UN secretariat.[30]

These past undertakings are thin gruel from a legal standpoint. At most they are politically—as opposed to legally—binding on governments. Since the PSI's inception, however, several international advances have furnished better legal sustenance for interdiction operations. The first of these was UNSC Resolution 1540, enacted unanimously in April 2004. Strikingly, Resolution 1540 was passed under Chapter VII of the UN Charter, binding all UN member states to "refrain from providing any form of support to non-State actors that attempt to develop, acquire, manufacture, possess, transport, transfer or use nuclear, chemical or biological weapons and their means of delivery." It also directs member states to "adopt and enforce appropriate effective laws" forbidding nonstate actors to "manufacture, acquire, possess, develop, transport, transfer or use nuclear, chemical or biological weapons and their means of delivery."[31]

Significantly, Resolution 1540 refrains from codifying PSI operations, despite the efforts of the United States and its partners to insert language to that effect. The elements of Resolution 1540 most pertinent to the PSI relate to transfers and transportation of WMD-related goods and substances and instruct states to impose stringent export control laws on such items. While the resolution covers nonstate actors only, few have objected to a wide interpretation encompassing not only terrorist groups but also proliferation networks like those of Pakistani scientist A. Q. Khan, which clearly operated without official sanction from the Pakistani government.

In addition, Resolution 1540's directive for states to craft laws prohibiting transfers and transportation of WMD-related materials increases the chances that governments will put in place national laws authorizing PSI-related actions within their sovereign jurisdiction. Resolution 1540 instituted a committee (whose mandate was extended in 2006 by UNSC Resolution 1673) to which states report on their progress toward meeting their 1540 requirements. This represents an unusual incentive for positive activity.

A second, potentially more significant legal boost for the PSI came in October 2005, when the 136 parties to the Convention for the Suppression of Unlawful Acts against the Safety of Maritime Navigation (SUA Convention) approved a protocol amending the treaty. Once the protocol elicits the requisite number of ratifications from national legislatures, entering into legal force, it will be unlawful among other things for any person to transport on board a ship the following:

- any biological, chemical, or nuclear (BCN) weapon, knowing it to be a
  BCN [biological, chemical, nuclear] weapon;

- any source material, special fissionable material, or equipment or material especially designed or prepared for the processing, use or production of special fissionable material, knowing that it is intended to be used in a nuclear explosive activity or in any other nuclear activity not under safeguards pursuant to an IAEA [International Atomic Energy Agency] comprehensive safeguards agreement; and
- any equipment, materials, or software or related technology that significantly contributes to the design, manufacture or delivery of a BCN weapon, with the intention that it will be used for such purpose.[32]

In addition, the protocol contains language vis-à-vis flag-state cooperation with at-sea boarding operations that resembles the "reasonable grounds" formulation used in the bilateral U.S. boarding agreements described previously. Once the amendments enter into force, PSI supporters and participants will enjoy a new, treaty-based rationale for their actions.

Despite these legal innovations, countries with considerable proliferation potential and maritime capabilities continue to demur from PSI participation, citing legal impediments. China, to name one, has been troubled by the PSI from the beginning. Beijing accentuates the PSI's flimsy basis in treaty law to justify its refusal to endorse the Statement of Interdiction Principles.[33] Despite its burgeoning strategic partnership with the United States, India discerns legal problems both with the PSI and with the SUA amendments pertaining to proliferation.[34] Having been the objects of nonproliferation and counterproliferation activities over the years, New Delhi and Beijing are wary about seeming to ratify any activity hindering their own nuclear or missile programs.

Other legal analysts see in PSI endeavors an opportunity to midwife a new norm against the transport—particularly at sea—of materials meant to support WMD programs. In particular, Commander Joel A. Doolin, a U.S. Navy lawyer, appraises not just the PSI but also UNSC Resolution 1540 and the amendments to the SUA convention described above, suggesting that these initiatives in aggregate could establish a new international norm allowing ships to be visited and searched for WMD-related materiel on the high seas—perhaps without the consent of the flag state. If states came to perceive such a norm as a duty, it would become embedded in customary international law.[35]

Such a customary law could eventually be codified and added to the short list of exceptions to the right of free navigation—others include piracy, slavery, and illegal broadcasting—permitted under the UN Convention on the Law of the Sea. This will be a long-term project, if it ever comes to pass. Whether the PSI manages to establish a new norm will depend on more than sound legal arguments. It will depend in large measure on the initiative's ability to accomplish its aim of interrupting weapons-related cargoes. States will not back a loser.

Analyzing PSI's Effectiveness

As noted earlier, the PSI is not an international organization in the traditional sense. While policymakers do not speak in such terms, it bears closer resemblance to what international-relations theorists call a "regime," namely a set of implicit or explicit principles, norms, rules, and decision-making procedures around which actors' expectations converge in a given interest area.[36] More specifically, the PSI has the characteristics of a subcategory of regimes known as "global prohibition regimes." Both in domestic and in international law, such regimes forbid state and nonstate actors to take part in particular activities—in the case of the PSI, transportation of items destined for WMD programs.[37] Older, better-known prohibition regimes oppose piracy, slavery, and drug trafficking.

Ethan Nadelmann argues that such regimes only arise when national and bilateral law enforcement measures prove themselves inadequate to defeat criminal activities crossing national borders.[38] The international community's experience with WMD trafficking, exemplified by the evidence uncovered by UN inspectors in Iraq and the cracking of the A. Q. Khan network, seems to have convinced the founders of the PSI that existing nonproliferation and counterproliferation initiatives had failed.

In itself the PSI may not qualify as a global prohibition regime, but it may be part of an emerging one when considered alongside UNSC Resolution 1540, the SUA amendments, and earlier declarations of purpose from groups such as the G-8 and the EU. Nadelmann posits four stages through which prohibition regimes take shape:

- First, the targeted activity is considered legitimate under certain conditions and within circumscribed groups. One could consider the five nuclear weapon states such an exclusive club.
- Second, the activity is redefined as a problem, as in the wake of discoveries about Iraq's WMD programs from 1991 onward.
- Third, regime proponents argue publicly that the activity should be suppressed and criminalized. This has taken over the past several years with regard to proliferation, largely through UN activities but also through the creation of the PSI.
- Finally, the activity becomes the subject of criminal laws and police activity throughout much of the world.

The PSI may supply the vehicle by which a regime opposing shipments of WMD-related materiel reaches the fourth stage. Seventy-plus countries have endorsed the initiative's basic principles, while UNSC Resolution 1540 placed the onus on states to develop robust laws banning WMD trafficking. The PSI represents a mechanism for international police activity regardless of whether military or law enforcement means are used to prosecute an interdiction operation.

Using an approach like Nadelmann's is one way to determine whether the PSI has made progress and whether it qualifies as effective multilateralism. While such an indirect analytical approach is less than satisfactory, certain characteristics of the WMD trade and the PSI render direct measurements of the initiative's efficacy problematic. PSI participants have been reluctant to publicly disclose information about actual interdiction operations, although they have been relatively forthcoming about their military exercises under the initiative. This makes a certain degree of sense given the intelligence and policy sensitivity of these operations, but it complicates independent analysis.

It is worth pointing out that this secretive approach is not confined to the PSI. Nonproliferation supplier regimes like the Australia Group (AG) likewise reveal few details about their efforts. How many export licenses AG members turn down on proliferation grounds each year and how many known proliferators members are able to stop by sharing information about license requests and denials is privileged information.

But even if the precise number of interdictions considered, attempted, and successful within a given time period were publicly known, this would still represent only a crude gauge of merit. Consider the following: The number of interdictions attempted would be a percentage of WMD-related shipments detected (itself a number PSI participants would resist making public). The figure for shipments detected would represent a percentage of all WMD-related shipments that take place—an unknown number owing to proliferators' proficiency at their craft. In this sense, the problem of assessing the effectiveness of the PSI and other counterproliferation and nonproliferation efforts resembles the measurement problem associated with counterterrorist efforts.[39]

Two similarities between counterterrorism and counterproliferation should be borne in mind when evaluating the PSI's effectiveness. First, assessing an effort based on the percentage of acts it successfully stops—even if such a number were knowable—is problematic unless the percentage is one hundred. That is, stopping even one catastrophic terrorist event or deadly weapons-related cargo may be deemed a success if it averts devastating consequences. Warding off the September 11 attacks would have constituted a huge success for the U.S. authorities, even had they missed other, smaller attacks. Some regard preventing centrifuge parts from reaching Libya as an accomplishment of enormous import, since it arguably induced Libya to abandon its WMD ambitions. Governments intent on slowing or halting the proliferation of WMD have shown themselves willing to dedicate significant resources—both political and financial—to such efforts, even if they judge the chances of success low, simply because of the stakes involved.

Second, efforts such as the PSI have a dual purpose. In part they strive to actually deny proliferators certain avenues of transportation, and in part they strive to deter traffickers from ever attempting to ship WMD-related cargoes. While deterrence is not a strategy that gets at the underlying reasons for seeking WMD, it may increase the transaction costs for states and nonstate actors, rendering certain capabilities unaffordable.[40] Or, it may drive up the potential transaction costs for middlemen in proliferation networks to the point where they choose to pursue less risky endeavors or even to go straight.

But this revives the classic problem of deterrence: analysts seldom know whether the target of the strategy was deterred or whether it simply had no interest in the activity one was trying to deter. PSI actions, in other words, could fail in their deterrent mission because covert supply networks do not pass through areas where PSI supporters operate. Buyers of weapons-related technology may have imported enough hardware or know-how that they no longer need to risk taking delivery of international shipments. Or proliferators may simply view the possibility of seeing their cargoes impounded as a routine cost of doing business.

Issues for the Future

That the Proliferation Security Initiative confronts not just questions about its intrinsic efficacy but also a thinking, adaptable foe represents its greatest future challenge. The difficulties the PSI has encountered among potential adherents and the policy analytic community during its first three years of existence stem more from shortcomings in public diplomacy than from any real transgressions against international law. Such shortcomings can be offset through sustained, patient diplomacy. Proliferators, by contrast, will react continuously to PSI strategies and tactics by shifting their operating patterns, diversifying transit networks, and seeking routes that bypass PSI supporters. To keep pace, PSI interdiction efforts will have to become more and more agile and sophisticated, synchronizing effort and resources from participating governments, if they are to realize their goals. And proliferators always have an option of last resort if their shipments are stopped: they can deny responsibility.

In addition, as the number of PSI supporters grows, the likelihood that participants with different interests and perspectives will agree on what constitutes a shipment worthy of interdiction will shrink. Most PSI interdictions will likely involve dual-use items that are—or can be represented as—legitimate items of commerce. Even among the original eleven PSI supporters, which shared similar interests and worldviews, disagreements on whether a shipment was destined for a WMD program were bound to arise. This problem will only grow as PSI ventures become more ambitious and dissimilar governments take part in the initiative.

States are reluctant to share information with foreign states for fear of exposing sources and methods, and they are prone to suspicions about information furnished them by foreign intelligence agencies. Before they will agree to interrupt a shipment, participants must be convinced that it is associated with a WMD program—requiring them to accept the validity of information gathered abroad, predominantly by national intelligence means in partner states. All of the original PSI participants were treaty allies of the United States, accustomed to sharing a variety of intelligence among themselves. As the PSI circle widens to include less trusted countries, U.S. and allied governments will become more reticent about sharing sensitive intelligence. This will reduce the chances of *BBC China*–like operations.

How can the challenges besetting the PSI be met and overcome? Return to the Bush administration's concept of effective multilateralism, which represents a useful set of criteria: have the participating states managed to forge good working relationships among themselves, deploy the requisite implements of national power in a cohesive manner, discourage the transport of WMD-related cargoes, and interrupt shipments that proceed in spite of PSI efforts?

Much of this must remain guesswork for outsiders, so long as the initiative maintains its proclivity for operational secrecy, so the best recommendation for now is for the PSI participants to take a hard, honest look at their efforts, applying these criteria to determine the best way ahead. Should they opt for greater openness in the future, then policy and academic analysts will stand a better chance of generating worthwhile counsel.

To the criteria for effective multilateralism might be added a final benchmark: Are the PSI participants building a new international norm persuasive enough to embed WMD interdiction in customary law? Does the initiative represent the nucleus of a global prohibition regime using Nadelmann's model? Will its activities pave the way for future codification in treaty law, allowing for universal participation?

As they review and improve on their operational practices, PSI supporters would do well to consider whether the costs accruing from their secretive approach, measured in the ambivalence of prospective supporters like China and

India, are worth the benefits in terms of deterring and denying proliferation. A more forthcoming approach might rally wider support, advancing the causes of counterproliferation and international security.

Notes

1. The views expressed in this chapter are those of the authors. They do not reflect the policies or views of the Naval War College, the U.S. Navy, or the U.S. Department of Defense.

2. Bruce W. Jentleson and Christopher A. Whytock, "Who 'Won' Libya? The Force-Diplomacy Debate and Its Implications for Theory and Policy," *International Security* 30, no. 3 (Winter 2005/6): 47–86.

3. Robert G. Joseph, "Combating Weapons of Mass Destruction (WMD): Effective Multilateralism," prepared remarks to the Lawrence Livermore National Laboratory Conference on WMD Latency, Livermore, California, January 20, 2006 (remarks delivered by Ambassador Donald Mahley), http://www.state.gov/t/us/rm/60218.htm.

4. These measures are derived from Robert Joseph's speech coining the phrase "effective multilateralism."

5. On the origins of counterproliferation, see Les Aspin, "Counterproliferation Initiative," PDD/NSC 18, December 1993, http://www.fas.org/irp/offdocs/pdd18.htm; Barry R. Schneider, *Future War and Counterproliferation: U.S. Military Responses to NBC Proliferation Threats* (Westport, CT: Praeger, 1999): 45–62.

6. Robert G. Joseph, "Broadening and Deepening Our Proliferation Security Initiative Cooperation," remarks in Warsaw, Poland, June 23, 2006, http://www.state.gov/t/us/rm/68269.htm.

7. "Recent experience of the activities of the A. Q. Khan network," declared a blue-ribbon panel convened by Annan, "has demonstrated the need for and the value of measures taken to interdict the illicit and clandestine trade in components for nuclear programmes. This problem is currently being addressed on a voluntary basis by the Proliferation Security Initiative. We believe that all States should be encouraged to join this voluntary initiative." Added the secretary-general at the March 2005 Madrid Summit on Democracy, Terrorism, and Security, "I applaud the efforts of the Proliferation Security Initiative to fill a gap in our defenses." Joseph, "Broadening and Deepening Our Proliferation Security Initiative Cooperation"; United Nations, *A More Secure World: Our Shared Responsibility*, Report of the High-Level Panel on Threats, Challenges, and Change (New York: United Nations, 2004), 45; United Nations, "Secretary General Offers Global Strategy for Fighting Terrorism in Address to Madrid Summit," press release SG/SM/9757, March 10, 2005, http://www.un.org/News/Press/docs/2005/sgsm9757.doc.htm.

8. Mark R. Shulman, *The Proliferation Security Initiative as a New Paradigm for Peace and Security* (Carlisle Barracks, PA: Strategic Studies Institute, U.S. Army War College, April 2006, 3.

9. Ibid., viii.

10. U.S., White House, "Fact Sheet: Proliferation Security Initiative: Statement of Interdiction Principles," September 4, 2003, http://www.whitehouse.gov/news/releases/2003/09/20030904-11.html.

11. The figure is 53 percent, counting only the states among the top twenty flag states (measured by gross tonnage of each merchant fleet) that have concluded boarding agreements with Washington or are part of the PSI's Core Group or Operational Experts Group. In all likelihood this understates the actual percentage by a considerable margin, since many PSI participants choose not to disclose their participation in the initiative. International Chamber of Shipping, "Key Facts: Overview of the International Shipping Industry," http://www.marisec.org/shippingfacts/home.

12. The Bush administration's 2002 NSS, which is premised in part on "proactive counterproliferation efforts," declares that Washington will work to "deter and defend" against the threat of catastrophic terrorism "before it is unleashed." U.S., White House, *National Security Strategy of the United States of America* (Washington, DC: Government Printing Office, September 2002) 14, http://www.whitehouse.gov/nsc/nss/2002. The "deny" language appears in the 2006 edition of the NSS. See also White House, *National Strategy to Combat Weapons of Mass Destruction* (Washington: Government Printing Office, December 2002), http://www.whitehouse.gov/news/releases/2002/12/WMDStrategy.pdf; White House, *National Security Strategy of the United States of America* (Washington, DC: Government Printing Office, March 2006, 18–21, 48, http://www.whitehouse.gov/nsc/nss/2006/nss2006.pdf; U.S. Department of Defense, Joint Chiefs of Staff, *National Military Strategy to Combat Weapons of Mass Destruction*, February 13, 2006, esp. 7, 22–25, http://www.defenselink.mil/pdf/NMS-CWMD2006.pdf.

13. Joseph, "Broadening and Deepening Our Proliferation Security Initiative Cooperation." Likewise, Secretary of State Condoleezza Rice has divulged few details about the PSI's activities and successes, noting, for instance, that the initiative acted on eleven occasions between September 2004 and May 2005. Condoleezza Rice, "Remarks on the Second Anniversary of the Proliferation Security Initiative," May 31, 2005, http://www.state.gov/secretary/rm/2005/46951.htm.

14. Mike Mullen, remarks at the U.S. Naval War College, August 31, 2005, http://www.navy.mil/navydata/cno/speeches/mullen050831.txt. In a similar vein, see J. L. Shuford, "President's Forum: Creating a Thousand-Ship Navy," *Naval War College Review* 59, no. 3 (Summer 2006): 17–21.

15. James R. Holmes and Andrew C. Winner, "WMD: Interdicting the Gravest Danger," *U.S. Naval Institute Proceedings* 131, no. 2 (February 2005): 72–75. See also Andrew C. Winner, "The Proliferation Security Initiative: The New Face of Interdiction," *Washington Quarterly* 28, no. 2 (Spring 2005): 129–43.

16. "Chemicals on Chinese Ship Usable for Arms, U.S. Says," *Los Angeles Times*, August 10, 1993, A6.

17. Chris Dobson, "'Blockade' Ship's Cash Call," *South China Morning Post*, August 15, 1993, 5.

18. Lena H. Sun, "China: No Suspect Cargo Found; Official Says Iran-Bound Shipment Carried No Chemicals," *Washington Post*, September 3, 1993, A33; Patrick E. Tyler, "China Says Saudis Found No Arms Cargo on Ship," *New York Times*, September 3, 1993, A3.

19. Patrick E. Tyler, "No Chemicals Aboard China Ship," *New York Times*, September 6, 1993, A4.

20. Author discussions with Chinese officials, Beijing, April 2004, and Washington, DC, July 2006.

21. "Yemen Protests over Scud Seizure," BBC News, December 11, 2002, http://news.bbc.co.uk/2/hi/middle_east/2566207.stm.

22. "U.S. Lets Scud Ship Sail to Yemen," CNN, December 12, 2002, http://www.cnn.com/2002/WORLD/asiapcf/east/12/11/us.missile.ship/.

23. James R. Holmes, Toshi Yoshihara, and Andrew C. Winner, "Maritime Counterproliferation with Chinese Characteristics," *Defense and Security Analysis* 22, no. 1 (March 2006): 5–21.

24. Such impressions have proved difficult to dispel. A prominent Indian commentator, for instance, recently complained that New Delhi was being "pressured to join the Proliferation Security Initiative . . . notwithstanding its apparent contradiction with other international treaties such as the Law of the Sea." R. Ramachandran, "India and the U.S.: Cooperation and Hurdles," *Frontline* 23, no. 15 (July 29–August 11, 2006), http://www.flonnet.com/fl2315/stories/20060811003211200.htm.

25. Michael D. Beck, "The Promise and Limits of the PSI," *Monitor* 10, no. 1 (Spring 2004): 12–16.

26. Jacquelyn S. Porth, "Bush Urges All Nations to Halt Illicit WMD Proliferation Trade," June 23, 2006, http://www.america.gov/st/washfile-english/2006/June/20060623165009sjhtrop0.1716577.html; Jacquelyn S. Porth, "Weapons Proliferation Initiative Seeking More Partners," June 23, 2006, http://www.america.gov/st/washfile-english/2006/June/20060623193821sjhtrop0.3565332.html.

27. See Stephen G. Rademaker, "The Proliferation Security Initiative (PSI): A Record of Success," testimony before the House International Relations Committee, Subcommittee on International Terrorism and Nonproliferation, Washington, DC, June 9, 2005, http://www.state.gov/t/ac/rls/rm/47715.htm.

28. Chinese opposition scuttled a U.S.-sponsored push for UNSC Resolution 1540 to specifically endorse the PSI. China's ambassador to the United Nations, Wang Guangya, boasted that "this interdiction [language] has been kicked out" of the resolution. Colum Lynch, "U.S. Urges Curb on Arms Traffic: UN Is Given Draft Resolution to Ban Transfers to Terrorists," *Washington Post*, March 25, 2004, A20.

29. Wade Boese, "The Proliferation Security Initiative: An Interview with John Bolton," *Arms Control Today* 33, no. 10 (December 2003): 37.

30. U.S., White House, "Fact Sheet: Proliferation Security Initiative: Statement of Interdiction Principles."

31. United Nations Security Council, Resolution 1540, S/RES/1540, April 28, 2004, http://www.un.org/Docs/sc/unsc_resolutions04.html.

32. International Maritime Organization, "Revised Treaties to Address Unlawful Acts at Sea Adopted at International Conference," press release, Diplomatic Conference on the Revision of the SUA Treaties, October 10–14, 2005, http://www.imo.org/About/mainframe .asp?topic_id=1018&doc_id=5334.

33. See Holmes, Yoshihara, and Winner, "Maritime Counter-Proliferation with Chinese Characteristics," 5–21.

34. India, Prime minister's office, *Statement of PM in Rajya Sabha on the India-US Nuclear Agreement*, August 17, 2006, http://pmindia.nic.in/parl/pcontent.asp?id=30.

35. Joel A. Doolin, "The Proliferation Security Initiative Cornerstone of a New International Norm," *Naval War College Review* 59, no. 2 (Spring 2006): 29–57.

36. Stephen D. Krasner, ed., *International Regimes* (Ithaca, NY: Cornell University Press, 1983), 2.

37. Ethan A. Nadelmann, "Global Prohibition Regimes: The Evolution of Norms in International Society," *International Organization* 44, no. 4 (Autumn 1990): 479–526.

38. Ibid., 481.

39. Daniel Byman, "Measuring the War on Terrorism: A First Appraisal," *Current History* 101, no. 659 (December 2003): 411–16.

40. Scott Sagan, "Why Do States Build Nuclear Weapons? Three Models in Search of a Bomb," *International Security* 21, no. 3 (Winter 1996/97): 54–86.

CHAPTER EIGHT

Force, Preemption, and WMD Proliferation

M. Elaine Bunn

North Korea's nuclear weapons test in October 2006 is only the latest illustration of how dramatically the international security environment has changed over the last fifteen years. Given the wider variety of actors that now can inflict mass casualties—not only on the United States but on other states as well—it makes sense to explore the circumstances and situations that may warrant the use—or simply the threat—of force in dealing with the proliferation of weapons of mass destruction (WMD). Such circumstances could arise with regard to either non-proliferation (preventing WMD proliferation from occurring) or counterproliferation (dealing with proliferation once it occurs).[1]

This chapter addresses the threat of force in the context of dissuasion and deterrence and the use of force once a conflict involving WMD has begun, and then it focuses on the preventive or preemptive use of force in the context of forestalling WMD proliferation to regional states of concern or terrorists or dealing with it once it occurs.

The relationships among these pairs of concepts—nonproliferation and counterproliferation, dissuasion and deterrence, prevention and preemption—are complex, sometimes overlapping, and still being debated. But each pair is worth examining in the context of the threat or use of force in dealing with WMD proliferation.

WMD Concerns: Why Consider Use of Force?

The stakes involved in possible WMD proliferation and use mean that those nations seeking to prevent or deal with proliferation will need to consider the role of the threat or use of force. Since the end of the Cold War, analysts in a number of nations, particularly the United States, have focused increasing attention on the dangers of terrorists who seek chemical, biological, nuclear, or radiological weapons, and regional states (sometimes called "rogue states," "problem states," "pariah states," or "states of concern") which have acquired or seek to acquire such weapons. Several new nuclear weapons states have emerged—now including North Korea. Iran appears to be on a quest to acquire the capability to produce nuclear weapons. The uncovering of the extensive network of suppliers led by Pakistani scientist Abdul Qadeer Khan brought home the rise of nuclear know-how, the falling techno-economic hurdles to proliferation in a globalized world, and the increasing ease of acquisition of nuclear and other weapons.

Not surprisingly, U.S. government strategy reflects these concerns. The 2006 *National Security Strategy* (NSS) states that the proliferation of nuclear weapons to rogue states and terrorists poses the greatest threat to our national security.[2] The 2005 *National Defense Strategy* states, "Proliferation of WMD technology and expertise makes contending with *catastrophic* challenges an urgent priority" and calls "particularly troublesome" transnational terrorists and problem states that possess or seek WMD.[3] The 2006 *Quadrennial Defense Review* states that the "principal objective of the United States is to prevent hostile states and nonstate actors from acquiring WMD."[4] In a May 2006 speech at West Point, President George W. Bush reiterated: "The greatest threat we face is the danger of terrorists armed with weapons of mass destruction."

Given these concerns about WMD in the hands of rogue states and terrorists, what should be the policy to deal with them?

Nonproliferation, Counterproliferation, Consequence Management

If there is substantial agreement about the gravity of WMD proliferation, there is substantial disagreement about how to deal with it. Some emphasize nonproliferation and the need to focus on keeping nuclear and other WMD materials out of the hands of potentially hostile regional states and nonstate entities in the first place, including thorough export controls and the safety and security of these materials at the source. Others believe that somehow, some way, someone will attain WMD materials or weapons, so the focus must be on counterproliferation—with many views about the best methods and most pertinent capabilities as well about when the use of force is warranted. Others emphasize that since neither of those approaches is foolproof, the focus should be on consequence management, attribution, and response. Of course, these three areas—preventing capabilities from getting into the wrong hands; detection, deterrence, and defense if they do; and consequence management in the case of an event—are not mutually exclusive. Efforts are needed in all three areas to deal with the possibility of terrorists and rogue states with WMD capabilities. The 2006 NSS, like the 2002 version, calls for a "comprehensive strategy involving strengthened *nonproliferation efforts* to deny these weapons of terror and related expertise to those seeking them; *proactive counterproliferation efforts* to defend against and defeat WMD and missile threats before they are unleashed; and *improved protection* to mitigate the consequences of WMD use."[5]

The options available for dealing with potential or actual proliferation will vary, depending on how far along a country or nonstate actor is in seeking or acquiring WMD. On a hypothetical acquisition-to-use timeline, there are opportunities all along the spectrum. Some involve the use of force, and some do not. In addition to military options, there are diplomatic, informational, and economic options—including sanctions, or cutting off bank accounts for rogue states or supporters of terrorism—and law enforcement to arrest suspected terrorists or those involved in proliferation networks. Preferably, these types of actions can preempt the need for preemptive use of force. But in some cases, consideration of the threat or use of force may be warranted.

The *use* of force, however, does not necessarily mean actual *employment* of force; a broader connotation would include the threat of use of force—including everything we do for dissuasion and deterrence. Even *having* military capabilities which cast a shadow could be thought of as "preventive use of force."

Dissuasion and Deterrence

With regard to preventing WMD acquisition and use, dissuasion and deterrence are separate concepts, both of which can include the *threat* of the use of force. Both deterrence and dissuasion seek to influence the decisions of an adversary or competitor. The goal of deterrence is to prevent aggressive action or WMD use by ensuring that, in the mind of a potential adversary, the risks of the action outweigh the benefits, while taking into account the consequences of inaction. While deterrence is focused on convincing an adversary not to undertake acts of aggression, dissuasion is aimed at convincing a potential adversary not to compete with the United States or go down an undesirable path, such as acquiring, enhancing, or increasing threatening capabilities.[6] One *deters* aggression but *dissuades* acquisition (or improvement) of the means of aggression. More specifically, one deters WMD use but dissuades acquisition of WMD. In general, dissuasion is before acquisition, and deterrence is after acquisition but before use.

Capabilities for deterrence are not limited to military capabilities; diplomatic, economic, informational, and law enforcement capabilities can also influence an adversary's decision about whether to take the action we wish to prevent. For example, U.S. nonmilitary homeland security efforts, such as the ability to sustain economic activity, may reinforce deterrence by denying adversary objectives in attacks on the American economy or infrastructure. U.S. diplomatic or economic sanctions can impose costs, while economic aid in the context of an adversary *not* taking an action can reinforce the benefits of restraint. Legal capabilities, such as threats of war crimes prosecution for any commander involved in the use of WMD, may affect the decision-making calculus of lower-level adversary leaders. U.S. diplomatic commitments to allies, embodied in treaties and agreements and reinforced by a web of economic and industrial relationships, can reinforce deterrence of aggression against allies by convincing adversaries that U.S. stakes are high.

Nonetheless, military capabilities—with the inherent implication of the possibility of the use of force—certainly play a key role in deterrence. Military capabilities for deterrence, furthermore, are not limited to nuclear weapons, as many thought was the case during the Cold War; there is a broad set of military capabilities needed for, and applicable to, deterrence.

One view, expressed in the 2006 *Quadrennial Defense Review*, is that the New Triad capabilities are the primary ones for deterrence. The 2001 Nuclear Posture Review (NPR) described the New Triad as composed of (a) offensive strike systems—nuclear and nonnuclear, kinetic and nonkinetic, such as cyber attack; (b) defenses of all types, both active (including missile defense) and passive (such as protective gear for troops and vaccines); and (c) a revitalized and responsive defense infrastructure.[7] This New Triad is bound together by enhanced command and control, intelligence, and planning. The concept of the New Triad was developed during the 2001 NPR to expand "strategic" capabilities beyond just nuclear weapons.[8]

From the deterrence standpoint, the capabilities of the New Triad can be seen as affecting different sides of an adversary's calculus. Offensive forces, broadly defined, increase potential risks to aggressors; defensive forces decrease potential gains by denying the aggressor the political or military objectives they hoped to achieve.

Credibility has long been viewed as a key aspect of deterrence: to deter, the adversary must perceive the ally as having both the capability and the will to carry out threatened actions, whether to impose costs or deny benefits. To strengthen the credibility of its threats to act against an adversary, the United States needs to develop capabilities across the spectrum and develop a range of deterrence options. The NPR recognized that large-scale nuclear attacks in response to some actions taken by some adversaries are simply not credible. The 2001 NPR was, in essence, an early attempt to tailor capabilities for the multiple deterrees and situations of the twenty-first century.

Other analysts understandably take a much broader view of military capabilities needed for tailored deterrence beyond the New Triad, such as forward presence (U.S. forces—people and hardware—stationed abroad), force projection (the ability to send forces where needed), and cooperation with a range of allies and partners. This approach to deterrence is explicit in the 2006 *Deterrence Operations Joint Operating Concept* developed by U.S. Strategic Command.[9] It breaks down the capabilities needed for deterrence into two categories: those that directly and decisively influence an adversary's decision calculus, and those that enable such decisive influence. *Direct means* include force projection; active and passive defenses; global strike (nuclear, conventional, and nonkinetic); and strategic communication. *Enablers* include global situational awareness; command and control; forward presence; security cooperation and military integration and interoperability; and deterrence assessment, metrics, and experimentation. Thus, the *Deterrence Operations Joint Operating Concept* goes beyond the capabilities explicitly, or even implicitly, included in the New Triad, particularly by including overseas presence and allied/coalition military cooperation and integration.

The deterrence capabilities to be emphasized and their specific mix will vary by the adversary and situation; that is, how much one relies on defenses versus offenses (probably more reliance on defenses, broadly defined, in the case of rogue states and terrorists than in the case of major powers), and how much one emphasizes nuclear versus nonnuclear or kinetic versus nonkinetic. Likewise, the roles of forward-deployed forces and allies in deterrence will vary.

Deterrence—by threat of force, denial, or other (nonmilitary) means—may not always work. U.S. policymakers should not have as much confidence in their ability to deter rogue sates such as Iran and North Korea as their counterparts did in deterring the Soviet Union during the Cold War. The United States should have even less confidence in its ability to deter terrorists armed with WMD. But that does not mean that efforts aimed at deterrence are fruitless. If nonproliferation efforts fall short of their goals, and the United States and others are confronted with WMD-armed rogue states or terrorists, it will be essential to do everything possible to reinforce deterrence.

Both dissuasion and deterrence focus on influencing the decisions of others, and both require "getting into their heads." Dissuasion and deterrence succeed when an opponent decides not to do something, not when he or she is physically prevented from doing it. Without influencing an opponent's decision, states could still try to block or disrupt an opponent's acquisition of threatening capabilities or develop measures to defeat or defend against their use. In that case, however, those would not constitute dissuasion or deterrence because they do not rely on altering adversary decisions and mental calculus. That is not to say that the United States should stint on its efforts to prevent, deny, disrupt, or defeat; those remain valuable capabilities. Indeed, U.S. ability to prevent, deny, defeat, and disrupt may well influence the calculations of the adversary and contribute to dissuasion and deterrence.

It could be argued that "deterring terrorists" is an oxymoron, given the apparent appeal of suicide or "martyrdom" operations for some groups. As recently as May 2006, President Bush asserted, "The terrorists have no borders to protect, or capital to defend. They cannot be deterred—but they will be defeated."[10] This hypothesis requires scrutiny and reconsideration. At its essence, terrorism seeks political goals. Even terrorists with suicidal inclinations want to die to accomplish something. Consequently, defensive deterrence—denying them the fruits or "benefits" of their actions—rather than threatening punishment may, over time, be the more effective way to deter terrorists.[11] Indeed, in the case of some terrorists, an overwhelming response may be precisely what they are trying to goad the United States into, if they believe it would advance their objectives, such as increasing animosity toward the United States to enhance recruitment and drive wedges between the United States and its partners.

While deterring terrorists will require new thinking, deterring and dissuading rogue states also presents challenges. Arguably, the threat of force—particularly, the threat of regime change—may be counterproductive and can spur or reinforce the determination of a rogue state to acquire WMD. On the other hand, it is not clear that taking the threat of force off the table will have a beneficial effect in convincing a party not to pursue WMD capability or to give up a program already under way. In the case of North Korea and other rogue states, removing the threat of force may well be insufficient to compel a regime to give up WMD, or dissuade it from acquiring WMD. The threat of force in some form remains a staple of deterrence—at least among states.

Before we turn to an examination of preventive/preemptive force, two other potential "uses of force" deserve mention: extended deterrence and reactive use of force. Extended deterrence also involves the threat—or perhaps it is better to say the promise—of use of force in allies' defense. The assurance of allies has proven to be one of the most effective nonproliferation tools in history—for instance, convincing Japan, South Korea, Germany, and Turkey to forego acquiring their own nuclear weapons, under the belief that U.S. conventional and nuclear weapons were available to deter and respond to aggression against them.

Force also may be used reactively, after conflict with a WMD-armed adversary has erupted or even after WMD are used. Objectives of such a use of force include preventing first or follow-on WMD use in order to limit damage or disrupting or defeating aggression. This well-accepted and well-documented category of the use of force requires no further elaboration in the context of this chapter.

Preventive/Preemptive Force

While deterrence and dissuasion involve only the threat of force, and responsive use of force once a conflict has begun is widely accepted, it is the preventive or preemptive use of force that generates the greatest controversy. Since the concept of preemption was publicly introduced by the Bush administration—first in the president's June 2002 West Point speech, and then elaborated in the NSS in September 2002—it has been a lightning rod for controversy. While some commentators hailed preemption as a valuable concept whose time had come, others condemned it as a dangerous precedent that could damage U.S. interests, strain relations overseas, and make the United States a feared unilateralist in the international system. All the hue and cry has done little to clarify the issues and choices that policymakers face in weighing the utility and limits of the concept of preemption. Many critics have conflated preemptive/preventive force exclusively with the Iraq war. Nonetheless, in the context of concerns about the proliferation of WMD to North Korea, Iran, and terrorist organizations, policy analysts should move the discussion beyond the complete "Iraqification" of the issue, while understanding that the war in Iraq will necessarily have an effect on how preemption and prevention are viewed, both domestically and internationally. The question remains, what should be the role of preventive or preemptive military force in both nonproliferation (preventing WMD proliferation from occurring) and counterproliferation (dealing with proliferation once it occurs)?

In popular usage, preemption is often thought to be synonymous with the use of force, particularly with military strikes. But "preempt" is defined in *Merriam-Webster's Collegiate Dictionary* as "to prevent from happening or taking place: forestall; preclude." Indeed, the concept as used by the Bush administration has a broader meaning and application, as implied by the administration's careful emphasis on preemptive action. Both President Bush and his spokesmen have emphasized the inclusion of, and preference for, nonmilitary types of preventive/preemptive action. President Bush said in April 2006, "The doctrine of prevention is to work together to prevent the Iranians from having a nuclear weapon. I know—I know here in Washington prevention means force. It doesn't mean force, necessarily. In this case, it means diplomacy." White House spokesman Tony Snow averred in a press briefing in July 2006 that "there's a misconception that preemption means war. It doesn't. Preemption means stopping somebody before they can do you harm. There are diplomatic ways to do that, and that is always preferable to using major force."[12] In fact, many of the preemptive actions that the United States is likely to undertake will be nonmilitary, such as financial, diplomatic, or law enforcement measures: for example, going after terrorist bank accounts or arresting the terrorist Khalid Sheik Mohammed. However, the nonmilitary methods of action are likely to be less controversial than military prevention/preemption—that is, the use of force.

It is useful to examine what recent U.S. strategy documents have to say about preemptive and preventive force. The 2002 NSS, widely considered to be the foundation document for U.S. policy on preemption, states that "the United States will, if necessary, act preemptively" to prevent rogue states or terrorists from threatening or using WMD against the United States or friends and allies; "[t]he greater the threat, the greater is the risk of inaction—and the more compelling the case for taking anticipatory action to defend ourselves, even if uncertainty remains as to the time and place of the enemy's attack." The NSS acknowledges the change in U.S. security posture that this emphasis on preemption represents (noting that "[t]he United States can no longer solely rely on a reactive posture as we have in the past"). At the same time, the NSS argues that preemption has long been a tool of U.S. policy. Importantly, it adds, "The United States will not use force in all cases to preempt emerging threats."

The 2006 NSS reiterates the policy on preemption; most of the key points, as well as the concluding sentences, are taken verbatim from the 2002 version. On closer inspection, however, some differences emerge. Possibly to ameliorate the reaction to the 2002 NSS, the 2006 NSS stresses the earlier point that military action is not the sole strategy to combat WMD—even adding to the summary of the 2002 NSS, "Our preference is that nonmilitary actions succeed." The 2006 version also highlights this point in its concluding paragraph: "Taking action need not involve military force. Our strong preference and common practice is to address proliferation concerns through international diplomacy, in concert with key allies and regional partners."

Another difference between the 2002 and 2006 versions of the NSS is the acknowledged relationship between strategies to combat proliferation and deterrence posture. The 2006 version includes references to the New Triad forces as one of the key "new approaches to deterrence and defense." The document then, in turn, ties extended deterrence back into strategies to prevent proliferation and observes that "security commitments have played a crucial role in convincing some countries to forgo their own nuclear weapons programs, thereby aiding our nonproliferation objectives." The 2006 NSS also places greater emphasis on the denial of acquisition of WMD by denying terrorists and rogues states "access to the essential ingredient of fissile material."

It is worth noting that most Bush administration documents use the term "preemptive" to apply both to actions classically defined as preventive (that is, before the threat is imminent) and actions classically defined as preemptive (when the threat is imminent). There are two possible reasons for the Bush administration labeling both preemptive.

The first is to gain greater legitimacy and acceptance for actions taken before WMD aggression is imminent. Preemption, as classically defined, has long been seen as both legal and legitimate in terms of international law and public opinion. Indeed, according to a 2005 UN report, "[i]mminent threats are fully covered under Article 51, which safeguards the inherent right of sovereign States to defend themselves against armed attack," but "[w]here threats are not imminent but latent, the Charter gives full authority to the Security Council [not the State] to use military force, including preventively, to preserve international peace and security."[13] It may be that the Bush administration, by using the term "preemption" to cover both classic preemptive force as well as preventive force, is seeking to blur the distinction and expand the range of situations perceived to be legitimate for a state to use force before an enemy attack has occurred.

A second reason could be to focus attention on the need for a redefinition of what is considered imminent. Preemption is a term usually used when an attack is imminent, not when acquisition of a capability is imminent. There are a number of reasons a redefinition may be warranted: when it is difficult to know how close an adversary is to either acquisition or use; when it may not take years to develop WMD, but may be acquired from another party, either in whole or in part, reducing significantly the amount of time it takes to acquire WMD. But how far back on the timeline from imminent threat must the action occur in order to be in the *prevention* category rather than *preemption*? The distinction between prevention and preemption is not always clear-cut; some have suggested (somewhat tongue in cheek) that a term such as "prevemption" may better describe the gray area between the two. It really boils down to an interpretation of what constitutes an imminent threat. Indeed, the NSS argues the need to "adapt the concept of imminent threat to the capabilities and objectives of today's adversaries" including rogue states and terrorists with weapons of mass destruction—"weapons that can be easily concealed, delivered covertly, and used without warning."[14]

Some consider the Bush administration statements to constitute a doctrine of preemption rather than just an option. The question of "option or doctrine" is not purely a semantic distinction. To call preemption a doctrine implies that it is a central organizing principle for marshaling the instruments of national power in support of national objectives and that in relevant cases action will be taken in accordance with established governing principles of the doctrine. Seen in this light, the recent use of force against Iraq may be the first application of a new doctrine of preemptive action.

On the other hand, preemption may have been an option employed in that specific situation, without its rising to the level of doctrine. With respect to North Korea, the Bush administration has downplayed the idea that Pyongyang's nuclear program constitutes a crisis or that military force might be required, and it has insisted that a diplomatic solution is possible. The same is true for Iran; President Bush dismissed press reports that his administration was studying options for military strikes against Iran and its nuclear program as "wild speculation" and emphasized that the administration preferred diplomacy in that case as well. This could lead to the conclusion that since preemptive/preventive force has not been chosen in all cases where it conceivably applies, it must not be a doctrine. But the administration also reportedly moved B-52s and B-1s to Guam so that they would be available for military options in North Korea—one of which might be preemptive action, and reports and rumors of military plans for Iran also resurface periodically, particularly recently as U.S. claims of Iranian support for insurgents in Iraq have increased. That said, the difficulty—both politically and militarily—of another war while the conflict in Iraq is ongoing should not be underestimated. Probably only in hindsight, with historical perspective, will we be able to judge the administration's application of preemptive/preventive force, and whether it constituted a doctrine.

Preemption sometimes is taken to mean preemption with nuclear weapons. However, it is an understatement to say that the threshold of any U.S. presidential decision for nuclear preemption would be higher than for conventional strike. It is difficult to imagine that a president would preempt with nuclear weapons in other than the most dire circumstances, with no other option to prevent massive American or allied casualties. The use of nuclear weapons would be among the most difficult decisions a president could make, given their destructiveness, the breaking of the fifty-plus-year barrier to nuclear use, and the international opprobrium likely to follow. It would be hard enough for any president to make the decision to use nuclear weapons in response to the use of WMD; deciding to preempt with nuclear weapons would be far more difficult. U.S. officials argue that the purpose of nuclear weapons is (still) largely for deterrence—so that in the mind of a rogue state leader, it is credible that the United States might use nuclear weapons and thus conclude that the risks are not worth the gains.

Although the resort to preemptive/preventive force is not aimed at influencing the decisions of the immediate adversary, it may have a dissuasive or deterring effect on the next would-be WMD proliferant or aggressor downstream. On the other hand, it may spur them to acquire WMD to deter U.S. preemptive or preventive use of force or to use it sooner in order to forestall U.S. preemption. Preventive or preemptive use of force is certainly no substitute for deterrence, and it is difficult to compare the two. And as one analyst observed, "One of the great difficulties of evaluating the comparative advantages of and disadvantages of deterrence versus preemption is that once we have taken preemptive action, it is almost never possible to know whether deterrence would have worked as well or better."[15]

History

The preventive or preemptive use of military force is not new as an option for dealing with WMD. There are a number of historical examples of the United States contemplating preventive or preemptive military actions including against WMD-armed adversaries (at least partially motivated by preemption or prevention, sometimes in addition to other motives), but only a small number of examples in which preemptive military action was actually taken.

U.S. government deliberations in the late 1940s and early 1950s considered attacking Soviet nuclear capabilities while they were a fledgling force, and discussions in the early 1960s debated whether to take out Chinese nuclear capabilities.[16] In neither case did the United States go forward with preemptive strikes.

During the Cuban Missile Crisis of October 1962, the quarantine or blockade of Cuba was intended to prevent any further buildup of offensive arms (medium-range ballistic missiles and nuclear warheads were already on the island, although the presence of nuclear warheads was not clear at the time).[17] The Cuban Missile Crisis has been cited repeatedly by Bush administration officials as an example of preemptive action (as opposed to a preemptive strike).

In 1989–90, America threatened to take military action to shut down a Libyan chemical facility at Rabta, which the United States suspected was intended to produce mustard or nerve gas.[18] Qadhafi subsequently shut down the Rabta facility, claiming that a fire had destroyed it. U.S. officials in 1996 also threatened military strikes against a suspected chemical weapons plant that Qadhafi was building under a mountain near Tarhunah.[19]

In 1994, when North Korea threatened to remove fuel rods from the Yongbyon nuclear reactor, U.S. officials considered a preemptive strike on the reactor with conventional precision weapons. Former officials have recently testified that they were confident that such a strike would have eliminated the facilities at Yongbyon without causing any radioactive plume to be emitted downwind, but they also recognized that the result might well have been a very destructive North Korean conventional attack on South Korea.[20] (Such a war was averted by the negotiation of the 1994 Agreed Framework.)

The United States is not the only country that has considered or carried out preemptive actions. The classic case involving WMD is the 1981 Israeli attack on Iraq's Osirak nuclear facility because of concern that Iraq would use the reactor to produce highly enriched uranium for a weapons program. (Iran had previously bombed Osirak in the opening days of the Iran-Iraq war in 1980, lightly damaging the facility.)[21] After its 1981 attack, Israel claimed it was exercising its inherent right of self-defense, consistent with Article 51 of the UN Charter. Despite Israeli claims, the UN did not concur; the UNSC censured Israel, and the U.S. ambassador to the UN spoke against Israel for its action.[22]

Types of Preventive/Preemptive Force

Because there is a tendency to equate preemption and Iraq, it is important to lay out the range of scenarios that could include the preventive/preemptive use of military force.

Even when focusing more specifically on the use of force, the term delineates this from use of diplomatic, economic, or political tools, but it still leaves much room for interpretation. Does it mean *force* or *forces*—that is, is any use of military forces, including anyone in uniform, in activities prior to conflict considered preemptive or preventive use of force? This broader usage would imply that military forces involved in interdiction activities (exclusive of combat) would be included in the definition of preventive/preemptive use of force. A narrower definition would imply combat environment, or at least a nonpermissive environment, and include primarily military strikes or war. The discussion below considers both the broader and narrower categories—use of military *forces* as well as *force*—in the range of preventive/preemptive force.

On one end of the spectrum is preventive war—the Iraq-type situation—often with the objective of regime change and with all the follow-on action required in that type of scenario.

On the other end of the spectrum is the use of military forces to interdict WMD before a state or nonstate actor can acquire all the materials and parts needed for WMD capability. This category could include the PSI, aimed at interdicting proliferation-related shipments that export controls fail to stop. In cases where PSI involves the use of military force, it could be considered a type of either preventive or preemptive (depending on how imminent the threat is deemed to be) use of force—albeit at the low end of the spectrum of force.

Somewhere in the middle of the spectrum is the one-time, in-and-out military strike or raid. That usually means bombs on target, though other means such as special operations forces or computer attack could be used. An example would be the Israeli strike on the Osirak reactor in 1981 or the 1998 U.S. strike on the suspected chemical facility in Sudan. Of course, one of the problems is uncertainty about when the one-time strike may escalate to an all-out war, which would move it to the far end of the spectrum.

Each of these three illustrative types of military preemption—preventive war, interdiction, and the one-time strike—has different objectives, requires different capabilities, and has different planning implications. Interlocutors in the debates on preventive/preemptive force often talk past each other, because they are implicitly speaking of different types of force to achieve fundamentally different goals—some use the term synonymously with the regime change/preventive war end of the spectrum, while others are talking about the one-time strike but don't make that clear.

A thought-provoking example of a proposed one-time, in-and-out strike was offered in an editorial by William Perry and Ashton Carter prior to North Korea's July 4, 2006, missile tests. Perry, who was secretary of defense during the Clinton administration, and Carter, who was an assistant secretary of defense at the time, suggested that if North Korea persisted in its launch preparations, "the United States should immediately make clear its intention to strike and destroy the North Korean Taepodong missile before it could be launched." They asserted that a conventionally armed cruise missile strike would puncture the thin-skinned, fueled missile and probably cause it to explode; the test bed for North Korea's nascent nuclear missile force would be destroyed; and there would be no damage to North Korea outside the immediate vicinity of the missile gantry. They argued that the Bush administration had applied the doctrine of preemption to Iraq, "where the intelligence pointed to a threat from weapons of mass destruction that was much smaller than the risk North Korea poses. (The actual threat from Saddam Hussein was, we now know, even smaller than believed at the time of the invasion.) But intervening before mortal threats to U.S. security can develop is surely a prudent policy." Perry and Carter further argued that it is unlikely in such a scenario that North Korea would escalate to an all-out attack on South Korea, since South Korea has been working to improve North-South relations (sometimes at odds with the United States), and so it would likely oppose the U.S. attack, and since "an invasion of South Korea would bring about the certain end of Kim Jong Il's regime within a few bloody weeks of war, as surely he knows." Still they argued that "it would be prudent for the United States to enhance deterrence by introducing U.S. air and naval forces into the region at the same time it made its threat to strike the Taepodong." While they acknowledged that their proposal undoubtedly carried risk, Perry and Carter determined that the risk of continuing inaction in the face of North Korea's race to threaten the United States would be greater. They concluded that "diplomacy has failed, and we cannot sit by and let this deadly threat mature. A successful Taepodong launch, unopposed by the United States, its intended victim, would only embolden North Korea even further. The result would be more nuclear warheads atop more and more missiles."[23]

The Bush administration elected not to carry out such an attack on North Korea. Several weeks after the Perry/Carter proposal, the North Koreans conducted flight tests of seven missiles, including one longer-range Taepodong missile which failed early in its flight; several months later, North Korea conducted a nuclear test. It is unclear what the effect of the strike proposed by Perry and Carter would have been—an end to the North Korea missile program, a long or short delay in it, or a longer war on the Korean peninsula. Still, it provides an example of a contemporary situation in which former senior Defense Department officials, from a different administration, believed that the risks of inaction outweighed the risks of "intervening before mortal threats to U.S. security can develop."[24]

On the issue of timing, there are several ways to think about a *preemption timeline*. One is the traditional peacetime-to-crisis-to-conflict-to-postconflict timeline, in which preemptive action is taken in peacetime or during a building crisis. Another, in the case of WMD, is where on the timeline an adversary is in the process of acquiring or actually using WMD. There are some cases on the WMD acquisition-to-use timeline that most agree satisfy the "imminence test"; for instance, intelligence that North Korea was fueling missiles in preparation for launch. Even the director of the Japanese Defense Agency has said that a strike against North Korea in that scenario would not be preemption—the war would already have begun. Agreement on the imminence of the threat becomes more difficult as one backs up the timeline from there to where an adversary has a useable WMD capability but is not on the verge of using it, to a point where the adversary has scientists and is gathering WMD knowledge, components, and material, all the way back to the initial decision to acquire WMD or pursue research and development. All along that spectrum, there are preemptive or preventive actions one can take—not all of them are military—but even with use of force, there are a variety of options.

It is ironic that the closer to the "imminent use" end of the spectrum a situation falls, the easier a preventive/preemptive use of force is to justify politically, but the harder it may be to be operationally decisive (because the adversary will likely have protected the intended targets of preemption through deception, hardening, burial, dispersal, or predelegation of release). Conversely, the farther from (ahead of) the imminent use end of the continuum a situation lies, the less acceptable it is likely to be to world opinion, though preventive/preemptive use of force at that stage is more likely to be effective in eliminating or postponing the WMD threat.

Another consideration for decision makers contemplating preventive/preemptive use of force is the need to think through their objectives, and the effectiveness of any operation in achieving those objectives, as well as how to measure that. If the overriding objective of preventive/preemptive force is *regime change*, the measure of effectiveness is fairly straightforward—although not necessarily easy to achieve, as the situation in Iraq demonstrates.

On the other hand, if the objective is limited, say, to disarm or eliminate a specific offensive capability or category of weapons, rather than to remove the leadership of the adversary, the measure of effectiveness may be more temporal, delaying rather than eliminating the latent threat. For example, the Israeli attack against the Osirak reactor may have set the Iraqi nuclear program back—it is unclear whether by several months or several years—but as the inspections after Operation Desert Storm in 1991 found, the attack did not end the Iraqi program.

It is useful to consider what degree of confidence would be required, in both the intelligence information and the U.S. ability to effectively carry out the mission, in order to support any future decision to use preventive/preemptive force. If, for example, the objective were to destroy WMD, there should be a determination of how much of it must be destroyed for the preventive/preemptive use of force to be considered effective. Furthermore, because there is unlikely to be absolute confidence in the intelligence capability to locate all of an adversary's WMD or in the military capability to destroy it, consideration must be given to preemption prompting the adversary to use the remainder or resort to counterattacks, such as terrorist attacks. If so, assessments must balance whether the United States would be better or worse off after executing such a preemptive option.

The final assessment depends fundamentally on the assumptions made about the likelihood of use. For instance, would a threatened leader use WMD in any event, either early as a last gamble to save the regime or later as the regime falls, in an effort to inflict as much pain as possible? If such a leader were going to use WMD anyway, and the United States destroys even some of them, preemption makes sense. On the other hand, if U.S. action prompts adversary use of WMD capability that otherwise would not have been employed, preemption could turn out to be a poor option. The difficulty is in knowing the answer in advance. Decision makers also must ask whether terrorists present a different case from rogue states. If the assumption that "possession equals use" applies to terrorist groups, as some maintain, then the "better-or-worse-off" presumption in terrorist cases would be in favor of preemption.

In the one-time strike scenario, since preemptive action is unlikely to be 100 percent effective, the role defenses play in preemption must also be considered. Defenses of all types—ballistic missile defense, cruise missile and other air defense, defenses of borders and ports—should probably be put on a higher state of alert or readiness prior to preemptive strikes. But raising the alert level of defenses may have an adverse effect on tactical surprise. We can also ask: is the U.S. government more likely to consider preemption if it believes its defenses can be effective against any WMD capabilities that it fails to destroy? Or conversely, do effective defenses allow the United States to hold off on preemption because we can defend against the initial bad things that are thrown our way? Defenses may decrease the pressure on the decision maker to strike first in a threatening situation.

The decision maker also must ask: militarily, can we do it? The long pole in the tent is likely to be the adequacy of intelligence. In addition, a state has to be sure it has the appropriate military forces to carry out the desired preventive/preemptive action.

Effect of Iraq

Certainly, the war in Iraq will have an effect on the preventive/preemptive use of military force in the future. Depending on the context, it has both raised and lowered the bar.

Again, a more nuanced look at the *spectrum* of types of preventive/preemptive use of force is necessary, because the type will affect future decisions about preventive/preemptive military action and will require fundamentally different kinds and amounts of capabilities.

For war in pursuit of regime change—which could involve hundreds of thousands of ground troops, significant casualties and costs, and long-term reconstruction responsibilities—the bar is significantly higher now. In the aftermath of Iraq, the credibility of intelligence will likely be questioned and scrutinized more carefully at home and abroad. Concerning preventive war involving regime change, future U.S. leaders are likely to be very cautious and more conservative in their assessments of intelligence and U.S. capabilities.

On the other end of the spectrum, preventive/preemptive force for interdicting WMD or components at sea or elsewhere requires very different capabilities, such as ships at sea and intelligence to monitor the flow of components. These activities are consistent with PSI and other international efforts to thwart proliferation. The United States may be willing to act on less certain intelligence, since the implications of being wrong are not as severe as in the other types of preventive/preemptive action. Indeed, the bar to this kind of military preemption may be lower post-Iraq—partly because much of the world does not want to see the United States going to the other end of the preventive/preemptive spectrum.

In the middle of the spectrum is the one-time, in-and-out strike. This type of preemption could employ conventional strategic strike capabilities or perhaps special operations forces or cyber attacks against adversary command and control capabilities. It would also require a different type of intelligence, such as detailed location and characterization of the target to be struck. The bar for one-time strikes would probably be lower than for regime change, but higher than for

PSI-like interdiction, with special consideration needed as to whether it would lead to all-out war.

In addition to the type of preventive/preemptive military action, another key variable in the degree of controversy is the nature of the target; that is, a terrorist target or a regional state. For most domestic and foreign audiences, it seems that in the case of terrorist groups or facilities, prevention or preemption—even use of military force—is relatively noncontroversial (although extremely difficult to do). It is the use of preemptive military force against nation-states, even those labeled rogue states, that raises the greatest controversy.

The preventive or preemptive use of military force remains an *option* any administration is likely to want to have available to address future contingencies. Depending on the administration, preemption will be emphasized more or less and talked about to a greater or lesser extent. Nevertheless, it is difficult to imagine a U.S. president who would give up the option completely; there may be situations where it represents the best in a set of bad options. Therefore, instead of equating all preemption with the regime change in Iraq, it is worth carefully assessing the military and operational implications of possible future scenarios for preemption, the factors to be weighed in considering it, and the capabilities required to carry it out.

Conclusion

Given the dangers of WMD proliferation, many tools are needed in the effort to prevent it from occurring and to deal with it when it does occur: diplomatic, economic, informational, law enforcement, and military. Military options may involve either the threat—implicit or explicit—or the actual use of force.

Dissuasion and deterrence have not, as some argue, been replaced by the concept of preemption. Dissuasion and deterrence both involve the threat of the use of force (among other tools) in trying to change the mind of a potential adversary: for dissuasion, about acquiring or improving WMD capabilities, and for deterrence, about using WMD. Dissuasion and deterrence will continue to be the preference over other options, but the possibility of their failure will mean that other options may be needed.

Preventive/preemptive action is more than just military use of force, since it too can include law enforcement, diplomacy, and financial measures. Even when the military tool is used, preventive/preemptive use of force is more than just regime change, or precision strike and raids; for example, it could include interdiction or boarding ships at sea. Even preventive/preemptive strike is more than just kinetic strike; it could include the use of special operations forces or information operations. Any of these types of preventive/preemptive action could take place anywhere along the WMD acquisition-to-use timeline; useful capabilities will vary with the particular actor and situation.

Preventive and preemptive use of force should be seen as a subset of all of the potential threats or uses of force options to dissuade, prevent, deny, or disrupt WMD proliferation and deter or defeat its use. There are unlikely to be many cases where the preventive/preemptive use of *military strikes* or preventive war will be chosen as the best option.

Notes

1. The glossary of the 2006 *National Military Strategy to Combat Weapons of Mass Destruction* defines "nonproliferation" as "[a]ctions to prevent the proliferation of weapons of mass destruction by dissuading or impeding access to, or distribution of, sensitive technologies, material, and expertise," and "counterproliferation" as "[a]ctions to defeat the threat or use of weapons of mass destruction against the United States, U.S. Armed Forces, its allies, and partners." U.S., Department of Defense, Joint Chiefs of Staff, *National Military Strategy to Combat Weapons of Mass Destruction*, February 13, 2006, http://www.defenselink.mil/pdf/NMS-CWMD2006.pdf.

2. U.S., White House, *National Security Strategy of the United States of America* (Washington, DC: Government Printing Office, March 2006), 19, http://www.whitehouse.gov/nsc/nss/2006/nss2006.pdf.

3. U.S., Department of Defense, *National Defense Strategy of the United States of America*, March 2005, 3, http://www.defenselink.mil/news/Mar2005/d20050318nds1.pdf.

4. U.S., Department of Defense, *Quadrennial Defense Review Report*, February 6, 2006, 33, http://www.defenselink.mil/pubs/pdfs/QDR20060203.pdf.

5. U.S., White House. *National Security Strategy of the United States of America*, March 2006, 18.

6. This definition is influenced by the discussion of dissuasion in the 2001 and 2006 *Quadrennial Defense Reviews*, as well as Andrew Krepenevich's work on dissuasion at the Center for Security and Budgetary Affairs.

7. See the secretary of defense's foreword to the NPR, www.defenselink.mil/news/Jan2002/d20020109npr.pdf. The report itself remains classified (despite the fact that excerpts were leaked and posted on the Internet).

8. In fact, the 2001 NPR was misnamed; it should have been called the *Strategic* Posture Review, since it addressed more than just nuclear capabilities.

9. U.S., Department of Defense, U.S. Strategic Command, "Deterrence Operations Joint Operating Concept," final draft, version 2.0, August 2006, http://www.dtic.mil/futurejointwarfare/concepts/do_joc_v20.doc.

10. George W. Bush, "President Delivers Commencement Address at the United States Military Academy at West Point," May 27, 2006, http://www.whitehouse.gov/news/releases/2006/05/20060527-1.html.

11. See, for example, Paul K. Davis and Brian Michael Jenkins, *Deterrence and Influence in Counterterrorism: A Component in the War on Al Qaeda*, MR-1619 (Santa Monica, CA: RAND, National Defense Research Institute, 2002). See also Center for Global Security Research (CGSR), Lawrence Livermore Laboratory, "'Whither Deterrence?' Final Report of the 2001 Futures Project," May 2002.

12. Press briefing by White House spokesman Tony Snow, James S. Brady Briefing Room, July 10, 2006.

13. United Nations, *In Larger Freedom: Towards Development, Security and Human Rights for All*, report of the secretary-general, March 21, 2005, section 3.

14. U.S., White House, "Prevent Our Enemies from Threatening Us, Our Allies, and Our Friends with Weapons of Mass Destruction," ch. 5 in *National Security Strategy of the United States*, September 2002, http://www.whitehouse.gov/nsc/nss/2002/nss5.html.

15. Alan M. Dershowitz, *Preemption: A Knife That Cuts Both Ways* (New York: W. W. Norton, 2006), 10.

16. William Burr and Jeffrey T. Richelson, "Whether to 'Strangle the Baby in the Cradle': The United States and the Chinese Nuclear Program, 1960–64," *International Security* 25, no. 3 (Winter 2000/2001): 54–99.

17. Anatoli I. Gribkov and William Y. Smith, *Operation ANADYR: U.S. and Soviet Generals Recount the Cuban Missile Crisis* (Chicago: Edition Q, 1994).

18. This was against the backdrop of earlier tensions with Libyan leader Muammar Qadhafi and the 1986 U.S. bombing of Libyan leadership sites (Operation El Dorado Canyon) following the bombing of a Berlin nightclub that killed two Americans.

19. Richard J. Newman, "The Qadhafi Question," *U.S. News and World Report*, April 15, 1996, 15.

20. Ashton B. Carter, "Three Crises with North Korea," prepared testimony before the Senate Foreign Relations Committee, February 4, 2003.

21. Rebecca Grant, "Osirak and Beyond," *Air Force Magazine* 85, no. 8 (August 2002): 74. Grant cites a statement issued by the official Iraqi news agency following the 1980 Iranian bombing of Osirak: "The Iranian people should not fear the Iraqi nuclear reactor, which is not intended to be used against Iran, but against the Zionist entity."

22. Anthony Clark Arend, "International Law and the Preemptive Use of Military Force," *Washington Quarterly* 26, no. 2 (Spring 2003): 89.

23. Ashton B. Carter and William J. Perry, "If Necessary, Strike and Destroy; North Korea Cannot Be Allowed to Test This Missile," *Washington Post*, June 22, 2006, A29.

24. Ibid.

CHAPTER NINE

International Legal Responses to WMD Proliferation

Daniel H. Joyner

This chapter contributes to the theme of this volume by discussing how the processes of globalization have affected trends in proliferation of the means of violence, i.e., weapons, particularly of the nonconventional variety (i.e., weapons of mass destruction [WMD]) and related items and technologies, and by reviewing the international legal efforts which have been adopted by the international community in response to this threat to international peace and security.[1]

The chapter begins by reviewing the efforts which have been undertaken in the contexts of multilateral treaties, safeguards arrangements, and informal export control arrangements at the international level to try to control the proliferation of WMD, with a particular discussion of the recently passed United Nations Security Council (UNSC) Resolution 1540. It concludes with a discussion of international legal issues relevant to the trend in some states' policies away from the nonproliferation treaties and regimes system and toward more forceful and proactive counterproliferation strategies.

Nonproliferation Efforts

The following sections consider the legal and diplomatic efforts which have been undertaken, and which are currently being undertaken internationally, to deal with the problem of the proliferation of WMD. The treatment begins with a review of the relatively long history of multilateral treaties regulating possession and proliferation of WMD by states. It then considers supplementary regimes to these treaty systems, such as the safeguards regime of the International Atomic Energy Agency (IAEA), as well as multilateral nonproliferation export control regimes.

A. Treaties

During the period of East-West superpower rivalry that has come to be known as the Cold War, while on one level there was almost unbridled development of WMD programs and production and operational fielding of the most lethal WMD systems ever seen by the superpowers, there were concurrently at another level significant efforts involving those actors as well as other members of the international community to limit the proliferation of WMD outside of a very select group.[2] The clearest example of this effort is found in the nuclear weapons area, particularly in the establishment of the Treaty on the Nonproliferation of Nuclear Weapons, also referred to as the Nuclear Nonproliferation Treaty (NPT), in 1968, which forms the cornerstone of the modern multilateral nuclear non-proliferation regime.[3]

The NPT was signed after twenty-five years of Cold War nuclear tension, for the purposes of providing a normative basis for coordination of peaceful uses of nuclear technology and for encouragement of international efforts of disarmament and decommissioning of existing nuclear stockpiles, and of prevention of further proliferation of nuclear weapons. The NPT's provisions established two classes of state parties. In Article I it obligated five acknowledged nuclear weapon states (NWS)—the United States, Russian Federation, United Kingdom, France, and China—not to transfer nuclear weapons, other nuclear explosive devices, or their technology to any recipient state not of their number and prohibited them "in any way to assist, encourage, or induce any non-nuclear-weapon State to manufacture or otherwise acquire nuclear weapons or other nuclear explosive devices, or control over such weapons or explosive devices." Nonnuclear weapon state (NNWS) parties to the NPT obligate themselves under Article II not to acquire from any other states, or produce on their own, nuclear weapons or nuclear explosive devices and not to receive foreign assistance in weapons development programs. As of this writing, there are 189 parties to the NPT.

In the context of chemical and biological weapons (CBW) as well there emerged during this era and afterward binding multilateral legal instruments addressing both the proliferation and, in more absolute terms, the development and possession of related materials and technologies.[4] Building from the 1925 Geneva Protocol, which addressed the use of chemical and biological agents in war, the 1972 Convention on the Prohibition of the Development, Production and Stockpiling of Bacteriological (Biological) and Toxin Weapons and on Their Destruction (Biological and Toxin Weapons Convention [BWC]) banned the development, production, stockpiling, or acquisition by other means, or retention of microbial or other biological agents or toxins, as well as of weapons, equipment, or means of delivery designed to use such agents or toxins for hostile purposes in armed conflict.[5] It further prohibited the transfer of such agents, toxins, weapons, equipment, or means of delivery to "any recipient whatsoever." Unlike the NPT, however, the BWC does not separate states parties into categories with some having privileges for retention differing from those of others.

Like the NPT, the BWC is a multilateral disarmament and nonproliferation treaty which addresses both vertical (intrastate) and horizontal (interstate) proliferation. While it does include a commitment to engage in the "fullest possible" exchange among parties of biological agents, toxins, and equipment for the processing, use, or production of such agents, its prohibition on transfers is controlling. In terms of disarmament the BWC's central and most remarkable feature is the blanket requirement for all parties to destroy or divert to peaceful purposes (such as nonmilitary scientific research) all biological agents, toxins, weapons, equipment, and means of delivery no later than nine months after entry into force of the convention or later accession.

Similarly, following the 1990 U.S.-Soviet Chemical Weapons Agreement—which bilaterally provided for a halt to the production of chemical weapons, a reduction of chemical weapon stockpiles to equal, low levels, and a mechanism to verify compliance—and building on a number of other regional initiatives, in January 1993 the multilateral Chemical Weapons Convention (CWC) was opened for signature.[6] The CWC prohibits to all parties the development, production, other acquisition, stockpiling, retention, or transfer to anyone of weaponizeable toxic chemicals and their precursors, except where intended (as shown through consistent types and quantities) for nonprohibited peaceful purposes such as industry, agriculture, medicine, and related research. To implement the provisions of the CWC, toxic chemicals and their precursors are listed in three attached schedules, corresponding to the level of concern applicable to them and detailing their respective destruction and transfer requirements. States parties are further obligated under the CWC to implement the provisions of the CWC through national laws prohibiting natural or legal persons anywhere in their territory or elsewhere under their jurisdiction or of their nationality from undertaking any activity prohibited to a state party.[7]

B. Safeguards and Export Controls

However, recognizing the characteristic, and politically necessary, vagueness and nonspecificity of these binding multilateral legal instruments, further related efforts of nonproliferation have included supplementary mechanisms for verifying compliance with treaty obligations and for coordinating and harmonizing national export control laws and policies. In the NPT context, for example, these additional mechanisms are explicitly provided for in Article III of the treaty. Under Article III.1, NNWS are required to accept the imposition of safeguards administered by the IAEA to verify compliance with the provisions of the NPT and specifically to detect diversions of nuclear materials from peaceful uses, such as civilian power generation, to the production of nuclear weapons or other nuclear explosive devices.[8] Each NNWS agrees under Article III.1 to conclude an independent bilateral safeguards agreement with the IAEA. Under the terms of these safeguards agreements, all nuclear materials in peaceful uses at civilian facilities within the jurisdiction of the NNWS must be declared to the IAEA, whose inspectors are to be given regular access to the facilities for purposes of monitoring and inspection. Because of its comprehensive character, this NPT safeguards system is referred to as the "full-scope safeguards system" (FSS).[9] Compliance with IAEA safeguards agreements is verified under this inspection scheme and reports are submitted to the IAEA Board of Governors. If that body determines that there has been a breach either of a safeguards agreement or of the provisions of the NPT itself, it can in accordance with its statutory procedures refer the matter to the UNSC for that body's deliberation and action, and for its potential authorization of measures to remedy the breach. These measures may include at the extreme the use of the UNSC's powers under Chapter VII of the UN Charter.

Article III.2 provides the international legal basis for all nuclear export controls.[10] It specifies that all parties to the treaty will not transfer nuclear (fissionable) materials, as well as "any equipment or material especially designed or prepared for the processing, use or production of special fissionable material" to NNWS for peaceful purposes unless such material is subject to the safeguards specified in Article III.1. Although not formally part of the NPT treaty regime, shortly after the NPT's entry into force, a group of NPT-member supplier states and potential supplier states of nuclear materials gathered for the purpose of clarifying the technical implications of NPT export controls as well as to establish a continuing forum for interpretation of Article III.2's broad export control provisions.[11] This meeting was the nucleus of a group which came to be known as the Zangger Committee, after its first chairman, Professor Claude Zangger. The Zangger Committee continued to meet periodically and eventually established both a set of Understandings adopted by all committee members and a Trigger List composed of items the export of which should "trigger" the requirement of safeguards.

The explosion of a nuclear device by India in May 1974, in addition to increased activity among other NNWS to create a full nuclear fuel cycle, led to heightened concern among supplier states regarding nuclear proliferation.[12] In 1975 a new group of supplier states met in London with the purpose of supplementing the Zangger Committee's work in the field of nuclear export controls. Over successive meetings, this group became known unofficially as the London Club and officially as the Nuclear Suppliers Group (NSG).

In 1976 NSG member states produced a document entitled "Guidelines on Nuclear Transfers," which was accepted by all fifteen members in 1977 and published in February 1978 as IAEA document INFCIRC/254. The NSG guidelines incorporated the Zangger Committee Trigger List and largely mirrored the Zangger Committee's Understandings, with the notable addition of going beyond the context of the NPT to cover nuclear transfers to any nonnuclear weapon state. The NSG guidelines further tightened export control standards in a number of areas including the transfer of nuclear facilities and technology supporting them.[13]

In 1992 the NSG produced a supplementary regime for the coordination and harmonization of national export controls on dual-use items (i.e., those materials and technologies with both legitimate commercial as well as potential WMD-related use). The chief catalyst for the addition of this supplementary regime was the revelation that one of the greatest facilitators of the formidable yet clandestine Iraqi nuclear weapons program was the importation, through various methods ranging from open purchase to covert indirect acquisition, of dual-use items from Western companies. The NSG arrangement for dual-use nuclear export controls, now referred to as NSG Part 2, consists of a set of guidelines for transfers of nuclear dual-use items and a list of approximately sixty-five items including equipment and technology. The basic principle of the guidelines states that suppliers should not authorize transfers of equipment, materials, software, or related technology identified on the list if (a) they are to be used by a nonnuclear weapon state in a nuclear explosive activity or an unsafeguarded nuclear fuel cycle; (b) there is in general an unacceptable risk of diversion to such an activity; or (c) when the transfers are contrary to the objective of averting the proliferation of nuclear weapons.[14] Other important provisions in the guidelines specify criteria for assessing the risk level specified in the basic principle and conditions for transfers and retransfers (i.e., end-use statements or assurances of nonuse for explosive or unsafeguarded nuclear fuel cycle activity). This arrangement was formally adopted by the twenty-seven NSG members at the 1992 plenary meeting in Warsaw, and both the resulting guidelines and trigger list were published by the IAEA in July 2002 as INFCIRC/254/REV 1.Part 2.[15]

A comparable system of safeguards and multilateral export control regimes exists in the chemical weapons area, coordinated through and monitored by the Organization for the Prohibition of Chemical Weapons (OPCW) and the Australia Group (AG). The latter covers, under its mandate, the coordination and harmonization of national export controls in the areas of both chemical and biological weapons–related materials.

Challenges to the Nonproliferation System

The "treaties and regimes" approach to nonproliferation described above, however, has some very real and important limitations with regard to its comprehensive character and ability to effectively combat WMD proliferation.[16] The first limitation is the fact that all of these instruments and organizations are entirely dependent on the voluntary participation of states. One of the foremost problems challenging the effectiveness of such treaties and regimes, linked particularly to the emergence of new supplier states after the Cold War as described above, is that many of these states remain outside of the nonproliferation treaties and regimes frameworks. This is what is known in proliferation studies circles as the "secondary proliferation" problem.[17]

Secondary proliferation has occurred for a variety of reasons. For some states, resistance to international nonproliferation regime membership has been a decision based upon political or philosophical dissent from the perceived aims of such regimes. Trade in nuclear dual-use items, for example, is of particular interest to developing states at the early stages of energy production capacities. Many such states have voiced concern that the NSG's regulation in this area is overly restrictive and, on a more fundamental level, that the NSG itself is outside of the legal regime for multilateral regulation of nuclear materials, with the NPT as its cornerstone. They have protested the characterization of NSG standards and policies as being authoritatively or normatively incumbent on non-NSG members, whether NPT parties or not.[18] They have argued that the NSG is essentially a supplier-state cartel whose policies unduly target states legitimately attempting to develop civilian power generation facilities, and whose primary objective is to keep nuclear technologies within the fairly tight-knit community of existing nuclear states. This is only one example of the debates, often split along developed/developing and North/South lines, of the character and overall aims of the nonproliferation regime system. In large measure due to these disagreements, a number of states (importantly, including India and Pakistan) have remained outside of the nuclear nonproliferation regime system.

For some other states, resistance to inclusion in nonproliferation regimes has been grounded rather on economic interest and the opportunity to remain free to trade in weapons-related goods without restriction and to profit through the ability to undercut nonproliferation regime member states by trading with states and nonstate entities, and also in items and technologies, that are proscribed by the various regime instruments. One perennial state of concern in this vein is North Korea.

Many states, however, have not joined the regime system because they are not supplier states of sensitive items and technologies themselves, have either insufficient resources or simply no intentions to acquire or produce WMD, and therefore have a fairly low foreign policy priority in joining multilateral nonproliferation regimes. This position, however, overlooks the dangerous reality that such states—and particularly those with insufficient resources to effectively police their territory and borders against illicit traffic in WMD-related technologies—are often prime trans-shipment targets for smuggling rings of varying levels of sophistication. This is particularly the case in troubled regions of the world such as Eastern Europe, the Middle East, and Central and South Asia.

A second major challenge to the nonproliferation treaties and regimes system is the fact that all existing restrictions within the regimes on manufacture, possession, and trafficking in weapons-related technologies are addressed to states. Thus at the international level there is no substantive restriction on private parties, including business entities as well as other nonstate actors, engaging in any of these activities. Of course, states that are members of the various regimes undertake to remedy this problem through national-level legislation and regulation. However, even for regime members these undertakings have traditionally only been enshrined in "soft law" or nonbinding declarations and agreements. National export control systems for WMD-related goods and technologies are underdeveloped and underresourced in many regime member states and are virtually nonexistent in some others. Again, for many states, creating and maintaining effective export control and border protection systems within their territories is not high on their resource-allocation priority list for a variety of reasons, outlined above. Thus, the ability of nonstate actors in many countries of the world to engage in WMD development programs and activities—essentially legally—can be seen as a major shortcoming of the classical nonproliferation regime system.

UN Security Council Resolution 1540

On April 28, 2004—not coincidentally, shortly after the details of the A. Q. Khan network came to light in February—the UNSC passed Resolution 1540, in which it undertook to address these challenges. Before getting to the specifics of the resolution itself, it is significant first to note that this resolution represents a significant milestone in the history of nonproliferation regulation in international law.[19] Until its passing, all such regulation had been adopted on the basis of the voluntary consent of states to be bound to their commitments in this area legally, in the case of treaties, or politically, in the case of informal export control regimes. In passing Resolution 1540, however, the UNSC in effect imposed additional nonproliferation-related obligations on states nonconsensually, i.e., according to states' existing obligations to uphold UNSC mandates under Article 25 of the UN Charter, and ordered even the reticent to undertake specified nonproliferation efforts, including the adoption of national legislation.

From an institutional perspective, this represents a significant departure from the traditional practice of the UNSC and the established jurisprudence of UNSC resolutions. The scope of this treatment will not allow a thorough review of Resolution 1540 from the perspective of the limitations on the power of the UNSC imposed by the UN Charter. However, the author has covered this subject extensively elsewhere.[20] It must suffice herein to say that the legal foundations of Resolution 1540 as a statement of binding international law are dubious at best.

Although its legal status remains in some doubt, Resolution 1540 at least ostensibly, and at least in part, filled some of the major gaps identified above in the nonproliferation treaties and regimes system. Its first substantive target is the problem of nonstate actors and their ability to traffic in WMD-related goods legally in states that do not choose, or who feel unable to choose, to construct and maintain national legal and enforcement structures to stop them. In operative paragraph (OP) 1 the UNSC decides that "all States shall refrain from providing any form of support to nonstate actors that attempt to develop, acquire, manufacture, possess, transport, transfer or use nuclear, chemical or biological weapons and their means of delivery." In OP 2 it decides further that "all States, in accordance with their national procedures, shall adopt and enforce appropriate effective laws which prohibit any non-State actor to manufacture, acquire, possess, develop, transport, transfer or use nuclear, chemical or biological weapons and their means of delivery, in particular for terrorist purposes, as well as attempts to engage in any of the foregoing activities, participate in them as an accomplice, assist or finance them." OP 3 then turns to the dual problems of insufficient sensitive materials protection, control, and accounting (MPC&A) programs and the lack of effective export and transshipment controls in the legal systems of many UN member states. The Council

[d]ecides also that all States shall take and enforce effective measures to establish domestic controls to prevent the proliferation of nuclear, chemical, or biological weapons and their means of delivery, including by establishing appropriate controls over related materials and to this end shall:

  a) Develop and maintain appropriate effective measures to account for and secure items in production, use, storage or transport;

b) Develop and maintain appropriate effective physical protection measures;
c) Develop and maintain appropriate effective border controls and law enforcement efforts to detect, deter, prevent and combat . . . the illicit trafficking and brokering in such items in accordance with their national legal authorities and legislation and consistent with international law;
d) Establish . . . and maintain effective national export and trans-shipment controls over such items, including appropriate laws and regulations to control export, transit, trans-shipment and re-export and controls on providing funds and services related to such export and trans-shipment such as financing as well as establishing end-user controls; and establishing and enforcing appropriate criminal or civil penalties for violations of such export control laws and regulations.

As in Resolution 1373, the UNSC in OP 4 decides to establish a standing committee to be made up of representatives of all council members and advised by chosen experts. This committee is to "report to the Security Council for its examination, on the implementation of this resolution." In order to facilitate the committee's report, furthermore, the UNSC in the same article "calls upon States to present a first report no later than six months from the adoption of this resolution . . . on steps they have taken or intend to take to implement this resolution."

Counterproliferation

Even with this latest attempt by the UNSC to fill in some gaps in the nonproliferation system, there are clearly still loopholes left in the system that can be exploited by states and nonstate actors intent thereon. For example, Resolution 1540 still only binds UN member states to establish laws in their domestic jurisdictions regulating sensitive exports and nonstate actor behavior with regard to sensitive items and technologies and to deny them state support. This does, again at least ostensibly, establish international legal obligations for states, but it is not clear exactly what those obligations are with regard to direct and official state transfers of WMD-related items and technologies. These may in fact not be covered by domestic export controls, which are as a rule focused on regulating exports by private parties and can generally be overridden by state policy imperative. Even more poignantly, nonstate actor behavior is still not made the subject of international legal coverage under Resolution 1540 so as to give rise directly to breaches of international law by private parties engaging in WMD-related materials transfer.

And then, of course, there is the separate and perennially difficult issue of imperfect implementation of all of these legal frameworks in both states' foreign policies and national legal structures, whether the result of intentional abrogation, negligence, or simple incapacity. On this last point, and highlighting the "un-funded mandate" nature of Resolution 1540, Cassady Craft has recently written:

> Export controls and materials safeguards are best conceptualized and built as a system, as opposed to individual components that work in isolation from one another. Neither can one consider the establishment of a viable legal basis for export controls or mate-rials safeguards in isolation from the institutions to staff, manage, and implement the laws. Likewise, highly task-specific equipment is needed in many areas of nuclear, chemical, and biological control, not to mention extensive operational training so that officials are not exposed to life-threatening substances while performing their duties. Developing such a system requires resources in addition to time and expertise. Although UNSCR 1540 directs UN member states to develop such systems, it does not provide the requisite resources.[21]

In light of these imperfections in both coverage and implementation of non-proliferation norms contained in international treaties and regimes, particularly in the policy positions of the United States and a small number of other powerful states, the momentum of policy has begun to swing toward an increased empha-sis on proactive, forceful, and often unilateral or small coalition–based counter-proliferation activities and away from more multilateral and diplomacy/interna-tional law–based efforts of nonproliferation.

A. The Proliferation Security Initiative

The PSI is one important example of this phenomenon. As explained in chapter 7 of this volume, through the PSI a group of states (including the most powerful European states, Japan, Australia, Russia, and the United States) seeks to coordi-nate efforts in intelligence gathering and in land, sea, and air force capabilities to interdict shipments of WMD-related goods and technologies being transported either from or to states or nonstate actors of proliferation concern. Of course the political parameters of this exercise are highly contentious, and so too are the legal parameters regarding threatened uses of force against shipments of goods from and to third states, particularly if those interdictions are made in areas not under the full sovereign control of PSI member states.[22]

The PSI is part of this resetting of emphasis in the United States and in a lim-ited number of other countries to favor counterproliferation efforts. It is closely akin to what has become known as preemption policy, as iterated inter alia in recent U.S. policy documents.[23] Both ideas share the classic, general nonprolif-eration aim of preventing the development and use of WMD and yet differ from traditional nonproliferation approaches in that they prescribe action in situations in which that use is not an imminent reality but rather is perceived to be a serious developing threat.[24]

B. Self-Defense

It is this distinction and emphasis on anticipatory activity instead of preventive normativity—the very aspects of appeal to counterproliferation proponents—that makes preemption as a more general policy, as well as the particular strategies embodied in the PSI, a focus of concern for international lawyers.[25] Since the right of self-defense in international law has been offered as one justificatory rubric not only for preemptive action in the broader sense but also specifically for the PSI, this chapter proceeds now to briefly consider the contours of the modern right of self-defense particularly as it bears on the idea of a state using force against another state before an attack by that target state has been commenced.[26]

A review of principles of law currently governing international uses of force reveals a significant legal distinction between two categories of actions and related justificatory rubrics often lumped together in recent debate and discussed under the heading of "preemption." Properly distinguished, however, these are anticipatory self-defense and preventive self-defense.[27]

Anticipatory self-defense may be defined as an attack on another state which actively threatens violence and has the capacity to carry out that threat, but which has not yet materialized or actualized that threat through force. Anticipatory self-defense does have a solid historical foundation in international law as a principle developed in state practice throughout the classical period and was originally an extension of states' understanding of their right to self-preservation.[28] However, by the mid-nineteenth century the right of anticipatory self-defense as a matter of customary international law was circumscribed by the important limiting principles of imminence, necessity, and proportionality.[29]

The correspondence between U.S. Secretary of State Daniel Webster and British officials during the famous *Caroline* incident is widely understood as offering a correct iteration of customary international law pertaining at the time:

> Mr. Webster to Mr. Fox (April 24, 1841)
> It will be for . . . [Her Majesty's] Government to show a necessity of self-defense, instant, overwhelming, leaving no choice of means, and no moment for deliberation. It will be for it to show, also, that the local authorities of Canada, even supposing the necessity of the moment authorized them to enter the territories of the United States at all, did nothing unreasonable or excessive; since the act, justified by the necessity of self-defense, must be limited by that necessity, and kept clearly within it.[30]

Ian Brownlie has suggested that state practice between 1841 and 1945 served to even further limit the flexibility of the principle of anticipatory self-defense, leaving it in a tenuous state of existence at the time of drafting of the UN Charter.[31] This position would seem to be supported through even more recent events, such as the 1981 preemptive attack by Israel against a suspected Iraqi nuclear weapons site at Osirak. Resolution 487 of the UNSC, which was adopted unanimously, denounced the Israeli attack as a "clear violation of the Charter of the United Nations" notwithstanding Israel's believable (and later validated) claim regarding Iraq's clandestine WMD program and its connection to the site.[32]

For parties of the UN Charter, resort to a right of anticipatory self-defense must be seen to be highly questionable in light of the plain meaning of the text of Article 51 of that document.[33] Nevertheless some have contended that the "inherent right" language in Article 51 has worked a retention of the rights of self-defense operable under pre-Charter customary law for UN Charter parties.[34] This is a plausible position but in the final analysis does little to help those wishing to justify a broad preemptive right. For even if this contention is granted, the right of anticipatory self-defense must still be held to be limited at least by the *Caroline* factors of imminence, necessity, and proportionality, if not in an even more restrained fashion as Brownlie urges.[35]

Under these limiting factors particularly, anticipatory self-defense would seem an inapposite and unworkable principle in the context of the PSI, as in most incarnations of counterproliferation policy. The entire thrust of the principles underlying the PSI, as well as preemption policies more broadly, is a preventive one, i.e., to prevent the acquisition of potentially dangerous technologies by states and nonstate actors of concern. Proponents of the PSI have never expressed an understanding of an imminence of threat from particular foreign target vessels, which under the *Caroline* formula would trigger even the customary right of anticipatory self-defense on the part of interdicting states.

The idea of preventive self-defense, which may be described as an attack against another state (or in the PSI context a vessel under the jurisdiction and flag of another state) farther back down the *ex ante* chronological line when a threat is feared or suspected but there is no evidence that materialization or actualization of the threat is imminent, was never a part of scholastic international legal rights argumentation in the classical period. It finds no foundation as a principle of customary international law in modern times, and any attempt to justify this extreme interpretation of a right includable in the legal concept of the right of self-defense by reference to the UN Charter is a clear exercise in futility.

The material point of the current discussion is that the right of states to self-defense, under either of the possible subcategories thereof comprising the concept of preemption, currently is not sufficient to act as a broad justifying principle for the PSI.

Considerations of Nonproliferation and Counterproliferation

Returning to the shift in some influential states' policies toward counterproliferation programs and strategies and a lessening emphasis on traditional nonproliferation efforts, the observation is made that the PSI can be taken at least to some extent as a representative case study which, while not of course comprehensively exemplary, is useful in its illustration of a number of poignant distinctions between the methodologies imperfectly differentiated as falling into these two categories. It further raises significant questions, sure to be recurring, of the harmony of such policies, both in their specific application through discrete methodologies and programs and also in their theoretical foundations, with international law.

Squaring nonproliferation efforts with international law has not classically been problematic, due largely to the consensual nature of international legal instruments and other normative regimes which form their foundation and reference. And even nonproliferation-related sanctions programs, while not usually consensual on the part of target states, have as a general rule been conducted under the auspices of international legal regimes, most notably the UNSC, and have not been found to be in breach of states' obligations under Article 2(4) of the UN Charter to refrain from acts violating the "territorial integrity or political independence" of other states.

Counterproliferation strategies, because of fundamental aspects of their character, design, and purpose, are often much harder to square with international law. This observation includes not only the PSI but also the larger issues of preemption discussed above. Counterproliferation tactics tend generally to be more forceful, interventionist, and nonconsensual. They also tend to be carried out either unilaterally or by small coalitions, due in no small part to the difficulties of intelligence sharing among large numbers of diverse partner states at the grade of sensitivity necessarily involved in the detection of WMD-related materials possession or transfer. The question becomes how to square this fact of disharmony with established international law and the rules of international legal regimes, with the fairly well supported imperative expressed by many both within national governments and without that, despite its virtues and successes, the current nonproliferation regime system is ineffective at curbing WMD proliferation to a troubling degree. And even the promised effectiveness of the less invasive strategy of economic sanctions—which it should be noted has received a positive shot in

the arm through recent revelations of the crippled state of Iraqi WMD development programs—must be understood to be limited in its attractiveness as a policy
option due to its lengthy timetable and collateral damage to civilian economies
and infrastructure.[36]

As much as one—particularly if that one is an international lawyer—attempts
to avoid it, the observer is led down a path of analysis that almost inescapably
leads to the conundrum that, at least in reference to some of the more modest and
persuasively supported applications of counterproliferation principles, a calculus
must be employed by which the value of maintaining compliance with international law must be set against the value of increasing the effectiveness of efforts to
stop WMD proliferation where those are mutually exclusive desired outcomes.

In some cases, as in the case of the PSI, the question seems to become one of
a fairly limited marginal contribution to antiproliferation efforts on one hand as
compared to the cost in terms of the strategy's rather considerable potential violence to the substance of international law in an important area of legal regulation
and the consequences—likely more long term than immediate—flowing there-
from. As with the PSI, where there cannot be shown to be a significant marginal
contribution to the international community's efforts to stem the proliferation of
WMD, yet the danger of either per se or potential abuse of settled and important provisions of international law is great, this balance would seem to tilt away
from the supportability of the maintenance of such counterproliferation policies.

In other cases, such as in some of the better-argued cases for propriety of application of preemptive strike principles, there is a much stronger argument to
be made that an international legal right to act against WMD possession and
proliferation could be of significant strategic usefulness and national security prudence for states who genuinely feel they are intended targets of such weapons in
the not-distant future.[37] This is a harder case as it is difficult to argue against the
legitimate interest of states to defend themselves under circumstances of threat
wildly altered from those obtaining in 1945 when Article 51 of the UN Charter
was written and accepted as a norm sufficient to protect state interests and allowing of adequate measures of defense against conventional attack by means in
customary usage at the time. The WMD age, however, particularly in its current
advanced moment, has forced a very different set of security realities on states,
and it is not unreasonable for governments both to expect and demand that international law recognize this fact and give legitimacy to reasonable state actions
done in consideration of it.

This conclusion obviously leads directly to considerations of changing current
international law to reflect modern proliferation realities. And such efforts may
be both prudentially sound and even practically feasible in some such persuasive cases and worth the potentially immense political capital the expenditure of

which will be necessary to bring such changes about. However, particularly poignant in this regard is the fact that it is very unclear whether a system of international use of force law could possibly be developed which would allow the kind of flexibility (including on issues of intelligence sharing mentioned above) that an effective preemption doctrine would require, while keeping any semblance of an objectively verifiable rule of law in the regulation of international uses of force.

Although the confines of the present examination do not permit a thorough discussion of these important larger issues, in the present author's opinion it is unclear whether we can much longer spare ourselves the rather imposing question of whether it is possible to have in the modern "postproliferated" age a real and viable international use of force law system, based on rule of law principles, that yet legitimizes the kinds of actions states would reasonably need to be allowed in order to significantly increase the effectiveness of international antiproliferation efforts.[38] The author thus agrees with former UN Secretary-General Kofi Annan in his judgment when speaking of the proposed logic of preemption as a counterproliferation strategy and the argued legitimacy of its prosecution by states acting unilaterally or through ad hoc coalitions (i.e., outside of the framework of the United Nations). In considering these proposals the secretary-general has insightfully stated:

> This logic represents a fundamental challenge to the principles on which, however imperfectly, world peace and stability have rested for the last 58 years. . . . If it were to be adopted, it could set precedents that resulted in a proliferation of the unilateral and lawless use of force, with or without justification. . . . But it is not enough to denounce unilateralism, unless we also face up squarely to the concerns that make some states feel uniquely vulnerable. . . . We must show that those concerns can, and will, be addressed effectively through collective action. We have come to a fork in the road. This may be a moment no less decisive that 1945 itself, when the United Nations was founded.[39]

Conclusion

This chapter has reviewed and analyzed issues of international law pertaining to the efforts of states to combat the spread of WMD technologies, both through the traditional treaties and regimes system and through the more recent shift in some countries' policies toward counterproliferation strategies.

As in other areas of high politics and national security sensitivity, the role that international law can play in both coordinating and regulating state behavior in this area is constrained by the fundamental limitations of international law as a legal system. Thus, it is unclear, for example, what role international use of force law will be able to play in regulating state uses of preemptive force against perceived WMD proliferation threats.

However, the institutions of international law can, at least to a degree, continue to aid in coordination and harmonization of the nonproliferation efforts of states and give iteration to the developing values of the international community with regard to WMD possession and proliferation. With regard to counterproliferation strategies as well, as the ongoing counterproliferation-based war in Iraq has amply shown, even with its imperfections there is wisdom to be found in the reserve imposed on states' actions through the norms and institutions of international law, which states ignore at their peril.

Notes

1. This chapter is a substantial reproduction of a paper previously published by the author in *Globalization of Political Violence*, ed. Christopher W. Hughes and Richard Devetak (London: Routledge, 2007), and is reprinted by permission of Taylor and Francis.

2. On WMD proliferation and related international legal instruments generally see Jozef Goldblat, *Arms Control: The New Guide to Negotiations and Agreements*, 2nd ed. (London: Sage, 2002); Julie Dahlitz, *Nuclear Arms Control with Effective International Agreements* (London: Allen and Unwin, 1983); Jayantha Dhanapala, ed., *Regional Approaches to Disarmament: Security and Stability* (Aldershot, UK: Dartmouth, 1993); Richard Kokoski, *Technology and the Proliferation of Nuclear Weapons* (Oxford: Oxford University Press, 1995); Julian Perry Robinson, *CB Weapons Today* (Stockholm, SIPRI, 1973).

3. Treaty on the Nonproliferation of Nuclear Weapons, opened for signature July 1, 1968, 21 U.S.T. 483, T.I.A.S. no. 6839, 729 UNT.S. 161. On the NPT see Goldblat, *Arms Control*, chs. 4–6; Jozef Goldblat, *The Nuclear Non-Proliferation Regime: Assessment and Prospects* (The Hague: Martinus Nijhoff, 1997); John Simpson and Darryl Howlett, eds., *The Future of the Non-Proliferation Treaty* (New York: St Martin's Press, 1995).

4. For CBW proliferation generally see Erhard Geissler, ed., *Biological and Toxin Weapons Today* (Oxford: Oxford University Press, 1986); Robinson, *CB Weapons Today*; Nicholas Sims, *The Diplomacy of Biological Disarmament: Vicissitudes of a Treaty in Force, 1975–1985* (Basingstoke, UK: Macmillan, 1988).

5. Protocol for the Prohibition of the Use in War of Asphyxiating, Poisonous or Other gases, and of Bacteriological Methods of Warfare; Convention on the Prohibition of the Development, Production and Stockpiling of Bacteriological (Biological) and Toxin Weapons and on Their Destruction, opened for signature April 10, 1972, 26 U.S.T. 583, T.I.A.S. no. 8062, 1015 UNT.S. 163.

6. See Convention on the Prohibition of the Development, Production and Stockpiling and Use of Chemical Weapons and on Their Destruction, opened for signature, Paris,

January 13, 1993, entered into force April 29, 1997, 32 I.L.M. 800. See generally Thomas Bernauer, *The Projected Chemical Weapons Convention: A Guide to the Negotiations in the Conference on Disarmament* (New York: United Nations, 1990).

7. In addition to these instruments, during this era and up to the present there have been concluded as well a complex web of treaties and agreements addressing in more targeted fashion vertical proliferation through measures of strategic arms control and limitation. Notable examples of such agreements in the nuclear context include the SALT 1, SALT 2, START 1, START 2, and SORT treaty regimes.

8. On nuclear weapons proliferation generally see David Fischer and Peter Szasz, eds., *Safeguarding the Atom: A Critical Appraisal* (London: Taylor and Francis, 1985); David Fischer, *History of the International Atomic Energy Agency: The First Forty Years* (Vienna: IAEA, 1997); Goldblat, *Nuclear Non-Proliferation Regime.*

9. Fritz Schmidt, "NPT Export Controls and the Zangger Committee," *Nonproliferation Review* 7, no. 3 (Fall/Winter 2000): 136–45.

10. On the role that export controls can play in nonproliferation efforts as well as the limitations of export controls see Kathleen Bailey, "Nonproliferation Export Controls: Problems and Alternatives," in *Proliferation and Export Controls*, ed. Kathleen Bailey and Robert Rudney (Lanham, MD: University Press of America, 1993), 49–57; U.S., Congress, Office of Technology Assessment, *Export Controls and Nonproliferation Policy* (Washington, DC: Government Printing Office, 1994), OTA-ISS-596, May 1994; Gary K. Bertsch and Suzette Grillot, eds., *Arms on the Market: Reducing the Risk of Proliferation in the Former Soviet Union* (New York: Routledge, 1998); Richard Cupitt and Suzette Grillot, "COCOM Is Dead, Long Live COCOM: Persistence and Change in Multilateral Security Institutions," *British Journal of Political Science* 27, no. 3 (July 1997): 361.

11. On the Zangger Committee and the NSG see generally Richard Cupitt and I. Khripunov, "New Strategies for the Nuclear Supplier Group (NSG)," *Comparative Strategy* 16, no. 3 (1997): 305–15; Fritz Schmidt, "The Zangger Committee: Its History and Future Role," *Nonproliferation Review* 2, no. 3 (Fall 1994): 38–44; Daniel H. Joyner, "The Proliferation Security Initiative: Nonproliferation, Counterproliferation and International Law," *Yale Journal of International Law* 30, no. 2 (2005): 507–48.

12. Tadeusz Strulak, "The Nuclear Suppliers Group," *Nonproliferation Review* 1, no. 1 (Fall 1993): 2–10.

13. Ibid.

14. Ibid.

15. Daniel H. Joyner, "The Nuclear Suppliers Group: History and Functioning," *International Trade Law and Regulation* 10, no. 2 (2005): 33–42.

16. On patterns of technology dissemination and the challenges presented thereby, see William W. Keller and Janne E. Nolan, "The Silent Arms Race: The Arms Trade: Business as Usual?" *Foreign Policy*, no. 109 (Winter 1997/98): 113–25; Michael Hirsch, "The Great Technology Giveaway," *Foreign Affairs* 77, no. 5 (September/October 1998): 2–9.

17. See a full discussion of the current weaknesses of the multilateral export control regimes and proposals for restructuring in Center for International Trade and Security, *Strengthening Multilateral Export Controls: A Nonproliferation Priority*, CITS report, September 2002.

18. One basis for such characterizations is provided in the NSG part 2 guidelines, paragraph 9, which states, "In the interest of international peace and security, the adherence of all states to the Guidelines would be welcome."

19. On Resolution 1540 generally see Gabriel Oostuizen and Elizabeth Wilmshurst, *Terrorism and Weapons of Mass Destruction: United Nations Security Council Resolution 1540*, Chatham House Briefing Paper 04/01, September 2004.

20. Daniel H. Joyner, *International Law and the Proliferation of Weapons of Mass Destruction* (Oxford: Oxford University Press, 2008).

21. Cassady Craft, *Challenges of UNSCR 1540: Questions about International Export Controls*, Center for International Trade and Security Issue Brief, October 20, 2004.

22. For more on the PSI and counterproliferation in general, see Joyner, "Proliferation Security Initiative," 507–48.

23. See U.S., White House, *National Security Strategy of the United States of America* (Washington, DC: Government Printing Office, September 2002), http://www.whitehouse.gov/nsc/nss/2002, and U.S., White House, *National Security Strategy of the United States of America* (Washington, DC: Government Printing Office, March 2006), http://www.whitehouse.gov/nsc/nss/2006/nss2006.pdf. See also Robert S. Litwak, "The New Calculus of Pre-emption," *Survival* 44, no. 4 (Winter 2002): 53–79.

24. The U.S. 2002 NSS document argues for a changed conception of the principle of imminence in light of the "capabilities and objectives of today's adversaries," 15.

25. See Ian Brownlie, *Principles of Public International Law*, 6th ed. (Oxford: Oxford University Press, 2003), 702; Michael Byers, "Preemptive Self-Defense: Hegemony, Equality and Strategies of Legal Change," *Journal of Political Philosophy* 11, no. 2 (June 2003): 171–90; Richard A. Falk, "What Future for the UN Charter System of War Prevention?" *American Journal of International Law* 97, no. 3 (July 2003): 590–98.

26. Greg Sheridan, "U.S. 'Free' to Tackle N. Korea," *Australian*, July 9, 2003.

27. See Anthony Arend and Robert J. Beck, *International Law and the Use of Force: Beyond the UN Charter Paradigm* (London: Routledge, 1993); Ian Brownlie, *International Law and the Use of Force by States* (Oxford, UK: Clarendon Press, 1963); Christine Gray, *International Law and the Use of Force* (Oxford, UK: Oxford University Press, 2000).

28. Brownlie, *Principles of Public International Law*.

29. George A. Lopez and David Cortright, "Containing Iraq: Sanctions Worked," *Foreign Affairs* 83, no. 4 (July/August 2004): 90–103.

30. See Daniel Webster, *The Papers of Daniel Webster: Diplomatic Papers, 1841–1843*, ed. Kenneth E. Shewmaker, vol. 1 (Hanover, NH: University Press of New England, 1983), 43. The *Caroline* was a U.S. registered steamer hired to ferry provisions across the Niagara river to supply Canadian rebels taking part in the insurrection against British colonial rule of Canada in 1837. On December 29, several boatloads of British soldiers came across the river onto the U.S. side and set fire to the *Caroline*, dragged it into the river current, and sent it blazing over Niagara Falls, killing one man in the process. The ensuing diplomatic correspondence between U.S. and UK officials has come to be regarded as a reliable statement of contemporary customary international law on self-defense.

31. Brownlie, *Principles of Public International Law*.

32. See Louis Rene Beres and Yoash Tsiddon-Chatto, "'Sorry' Seems to Be the Hardest Word," *Jerusalem Post*, June 9, 2003.

33. See Bruno Simma, ed., *The Charter of the United Nations*, 2nd ed. (Oxford: Oxford University Press, 2002); Ahmed Rifaat, *International Aggression: A Study of the Legal Concept* (Stockholm: Almquist and Wiksell, 1979); Brownlie, *International Law and the Use of Force by States*.

34. See Myres S. McDougal and Florentino P. Feliciano, *Law and Minimum World Public Order: The Legal Regulation and International Coercion* (New Haven, CT: Yale University Press, 1961); Derek Bowett, *Self-Defence in International Law* (Manchester, UK: Manchester University Press, 1958).

35. On the principles of necessity and proportionality in customary international law, see Brownlie, *International Law and the Use of Force by States*, 257–64.

36. See Lopez and Cortright, "Containing Iraq," 90–103.

37. Israel's destruction of the Iraqi nuclear reactor at Osirak in 1981 presents a more compelling case. See Beres and Tsiddon-Chatto, "'Sorry.'"

38. See Daniel H. Joyner, *Jus ad Bellum in the Age of WMD Proliferation*, forthcoming.

39. Address of the secretary-general to the UN General Assembly, September 23, 2003, http://www.un.org/webcast/ga/58/statements/sg2eng030923.htm.

PART FOUR

Regional and Country Issues

CHAPTER TEN

The Role of the European Union in WMD Nonproliferation

Ian Anthony

Decisions taken at the highest political level of the European Union (EU) have established that the fight against proliferation of weapons of mass destruction (WMD) is one of its highest foreign and security policy objectives. In statements and documents produced in the space of eight months during 2003 the European Council established an ambitious program to combat the proliferation of WMD. Through subsequent decisions and actions a considerable momentum was generated at the European level for a program of practical action that was intended to contribute to the wider, global nonproliferation effort.

The EU gave a much higher political profile to the issue of nonproliferation of weapons of mass destruction after the then Swedish minister for foreign affairs, Anna Lindh, called for a new strategy to combat WMD in April 2003, a suggestion that was quickly picked up and actively promoted by the Greek EU presidency and endorsed by the EU. At the time Lindh formulated her proposal, Europeans were acutely aware of the negative impact of internal divisions over how best to resolve the issue of noncompliance by Iraq with disarmament-related UN Security Council (UNSC) resolutions. Not only did these divisions prevent a collective response during the Iraq crisis (in spite of full agreement over EU objectives in Iraq), but they also handicapped individual efforts by European countries to develop national initiatives. At a particularly difficult time for trans-Atlantic relations, nonproliferation also offered a framework for cooperation with the United States on an issue of mutual concern.

The proposition advanced by Lindh was that the EU must go beyond declaratory policy and aim to become a leading player in the global effort to reduce the threat of WMD by working with like-minded countries in other parts of the world to implement a practical agenda. The April 14–15 General Affairs and External Relations Council (GAERC) accepted this idea and tasked the council secretariat to produce a draft document outlining the EU's strategic aims in the field of nonproliferation of WMD.

In a separate but interconnected development in June 2003, the EU High Representative for the Common Foreign and Security Policy, Javier Solana, presented the elements of a European Security Strategy (ESS) in his document *A Secure Europe in a Better World*. In a final and revised version of that document, adopted in December 2003, the proliferation of WMD is described as "potentially the greatest threat to our society."[1]

The view that proliferation is a very grave threat was still strongly held by senior decision makers in 2006. At their summit meeting in St. Petersburg in July 2006 the leaders of the G-8 group of industrialized states confirmed their collective view that the proliferation of WMD and their means of delivery, together with international terrorism, remained the preeminent threat to international peace and security. The leaders reaffirmed their "determination and commitment to work together and with other states and institutions in the fight against the proliferation of WMD, including by preventing them from falling into hands of terrorists."[2]

This chapter is an evaluation of the efforts by the EU since 2003 to combat proliferation.

Background

In June 2003 the European Council secretariat presented the Political and Security Committee (PSC) with two documents. The first was *The Basic Principles for an EU Strategy against Proliferation of Weapons of Mass Destruction*.[3] The principles restated the commitment of the EU to strengthen existing multilateral arms control, nonproliferation, and disarmament processes. In adopting the principles the PSC underlined that policies should be based on a common assessment on the EU level of global proliferation threats, and the EU Situation Centre was duly tasked to prepare a threat assessment "using all available sources" that was to be maintained and continuously updated. Moreover, the intelligence services of the member states were to be instructed to engage in this process.

The second document adopted in June was an *Action Plan for the Implementation of the Basic Principles for an EU Strategy against Proliferation of Weapons of Mass Destruction*.[4] The Action Plan describes measures to be undertaken by the EU, grouped into two categories: measures for immediate action and measures to be implemented over a longer time frame.

At the Thessaloniki European Council on June 19–20, 2003, a Declaration on Nonproliferation of Weapons of Mass Destruction was adopted. The council declared that the EU members "are committed to further elaborate before the end of the year a coherent EU strategy to address the threat of proliferation, and to continue to develop and implement the EU Action Plan as a matter of priority."

The *EU Strategy against the Proliferation of Weapons of Mass Destruction* (the WMD Strategy) was duly adopted at the European Council meeting in Brussels on December 9, 2003.[5] It addressed the root causes of proliferation, emphasizing both state and nonstate dimensions of the contemporary proliferation challenge. The WMD Strategy is not confined by geography but is global in application.

In the past, the term "proliferation" has been taken to mean the process by which the armed forces of states come into possession of or gain the ability to use chemical, biological, radiological, or nuclear (CBRN) weapons. This understanding reflected concern about the use of such weapons in conflicts between states or between alliances of states. However, threat assessments have changed significantly in recent years, and in its documents the EU has taken a more modern and nuanced view of what proliferation is and how it needs to be fought. The EU certainly takes into account the threat from weapons in the hands of the armed forces of states but also underlines the risk associated with the acquisition of CBRN goods and materials by nonstate actors intending to use them in acts of mass-impact terrorism. Moreover, the WMD Strategy is a recognition that this modern definition is not rhetorical but should be reflected in the activities carried out by the EU to achieve its nonproliferation objectives.

It has been pointed out that the practical impact the WMD Strategy will have is to be closely tied to the effectiveness of its implementation.[6] The need for efficient implementation of measures to achieve the goals laid out in the WMD Strategy has been recognized by the EU. A review mechanism was established linking the implementation of the strategy to the discussions among high-level decision makers—something that was intended to maintain a certain momentum behind the WMD Strategy for as long as nonproliferation is close to the center of public concern.

In October 2003, the EU High Representative appointed his personal representative on nonproliferation of WMD to coordinate, help implement, and further develop the WMD Strategy and to give sharper focus to these issues in dialogue with third countries. The personal representative and her office have provided a focal point within the EU and provided momentum to the implementation of the WMD Strategy. One innovation in this regard has been the preparation of a six-month progress report on the implementation of the WMD Strategy, which is periodically accompanied by a list of priorities for its implementation. The report and the priorities are discussed by senior officials from EU member states in the PSC and subsequently endorsed by EU foreign ministers in the General Affairs and External Relations Council (GAERC).

The WMD Strategy is guided by the collective EU belief that a multilateralist approach to security, including disarmament and nonproliferation, provides the best way to maintain international order. In the past EU member states have tended to emphasize national compliance with the relevant treaties and conventions as the central element of their approach to arms control. However, the EU can never achieve the more ambitious goals of the WMD Strategy by complying with formal international instruments. The armed forces of EU member states hold no biological weapons, no radiological weapons, and no chemical weapons. The number of nuclear weapons within the possession of EU member states represents a small share of the total global nuclear weapons inventory, and this share is progressively diminishing over time.

The contemporary nonproliferation agenda now encompasses actions targeted on different types of CBRN weapon–related materials, equipment, and expertise. These actions are not planned and implemented under the umbrella of a single international organization or body or exclusively within the frameworks established by the main treaties and conventions.

The treaties and conventions remain one vital part of the contemporary framework for nonproliferation. However, in the recent past a significant number of other instruments have been created, or in some cases existing instruments have been reformed and revitalized. These include not only legal instruments but also political understandings that have come to play an increasingly important role in shaping "soft law" in the area of arms control and nonproliferation.

The WMD Strategy makes clear that the effective multilateralism that is the cornerstone of the WMD Strategy not only requires full implementation of treaties and conventions but also demands a strengthening and the further development of other legal and political instruments that together create the international nonproliferation regime. By making effective multilateralism the main pillar in its nonproliferation strategy, the EU has pointed to the need for a complex response to a complex problem.

Many of these programs developed to tackle particular CBRN-related problems under the umbrella of this wide nonproliferation regime are, by nature, of a technical character, and their scale and complexity mean that implementation cannot be accomplished in a short period. A number of such programs have been developed under the initiative and leadership of the United States or, when pursued in cooperation, in the framework of the G-8 group of industrialized states. The WMD Strategy makes clear that close cooperation with key partners is crucial for the success of the global fight against proliferation.

The WMD Strategy points to a range of instruments that the EU has at its disposal to combat proliferation, including strengthening the system of multilateral treaties and verification mechanisms, applying national and internationally coordinated export controls, carrying out cooperative threat reduction programs, using political and economic levers (including trade and development policies), interdicting illegal procurement activities, and, as a last resort, applying coercive measures in accordance with the UN Charter.

In order to combat the contemporary proliferation challenge, the EU needs to work as part of a complex and fast-moving nonproliferation effort worldwide. To summarize, implementing the WMD Strategy therefore requires that the EU be able to shape the policies and behavior of states that are not EU members by applying the full range of instruments at its disposal to create a mix of incentives and pressure. Doing this requires cooperation not just with states but also with international organizations and nonstate actors. This is not an activity that is either limited in time or confined to particular locations. Rather, nonproliferation is expected to become a permanent element of the external policy of the EU.

Mainstreaming Nonproliferation into EU External Policy

Sustained EU engagement required that the issue of nonproliferation should be raised in all of the various elements of external policy and actions undertaken across the EU and at all levels. A consistent and coherent message should be delivered by the representatives of the European Council, the European Commission, and the member states both through activities organized under the Common Foreign and Security Policy (CFSP) and in actions managed by the commission.

Achieving this level of coherence across all aspects of external policy and in the interactions with a wide range of countries is undoubtedly a major challenge for the EU. After 2001 the EU drew up a Constitutional Treaty to contain the fundamental rules related to the working of EU institutions, the division of powers between them, and the rules that would be used to implement agreed-on policies. The text of the Constitutional Treaty, which was signed in October 2004, provided for a number of institutional changes including the appointment of a foreign affairs minister who would also be a vice president of the commission. The treaty also foresaw the appointment by the European Council of a president of the EU with a term of two and a half years and responsible for representing the EU on issues concerning CFSP, replacing the current arrangement of member states holding the office of president on a rotating six-month basis. The creation of a European External Action Service would have made a direct connection between these central authorities and the European Commission staff on the ground around the world.

Once in force these provisions of the Constitutional Treaty would have significantly increased the likelihood of coherent implementation of all EU external policies but would perhaps have been particularly important in an area like nonproliferation where the EU has little past experience on which to draw. However, in May and June 2005 the Constitutional Treaty was rejected by voters in France and the Netherlands, respectively, making it very uncertain whether the treaty will ever enter into force.

There has been an early and difficult test of the extent to which the EU can achieve coherence in responding to doubts about the future trajectory of the Iranian nuclear program. There is also some experience of how the EU approaches the issue of mainstreaming nonproliferation in its relations with some other countries, including several that are important from a nonproliferation perspective.

The Case of Iran

During the years 2002–3, evidence emerged that Iran had secretly pursued a range of nuclear fuel-cycle technologies, including those that are the most sensitive from a nuclear weapons–proliferation perspective—uranium enrichment and reprocessing of spent nuclear fuel—without declaring these activities to the International Atomic Energy Agency (IAEA) (as required under the terms of its 1974 Safeguards Agreement with the agency).[7] The lack of transparency contributed to concerns that Iran might be putting into place, under the cover of a civil nuclear energy program, the facilities needed to produce fissile material for a nuclear weapon.

In September 2003 the IAEA adopted a resolution that urged Iran to provide full transparency with respect to developments related to its nuclear program by October 31.[8] In mid-October, amid public statements that Iran's nuclear program might become an issue for the UNSC if the IAEA resolution was not complied with, Iran began negotiations with the director-general of the IAEA about the signing of an additional protocol to Iran's existing safeguards agreement with the agency. Under such a protocol Iran would allow inspectors open access to all of its suspected nuclear facilities. As the October 31 deadline approached without agreement on the additional protocol, Iran invited the foreign ministers of three EU countries (France, Germany, and the United Kingdom) to visit Tehran for discussions on resolving the nuclear issue.

The result of these discussions between Iran and the EU3 was positive and led to Iran signing an additional protocol with the IAEA and agreeing to suspend its uranium enrichment–related activities for the duration of negotiations over a permanent resolution of outstanding questions about the Iranian nuclear program.

The EU3 established a steering committee with working groups on political and security issues to develop negotiating positions and to carry out negotiations with Iran. Subsequently, the European Council secretariat was represented in these bodies through participation by the office of the personal representative on nonproliferation of WMD of the EU High Representative. Although negotiating positions were developed by three countries, rather than by all twenty-five EU member states, the full membership was kept informed of developments through various EU mechanisms—notably the Political and Security Committee—that also allow for comments and suggestions on the approach chosen by the EU3.

In contrast to the IAEA, which seeks clarification and transparency related to Iran's nuclear program, the EU3 set for themselves the very ambitious objective of modifying the Iranian program to exclude the most proliferation-sensitive elements permanently. It must be admitted that the initial success achieved by the EU3 did not immediately lead to a resolution of the problems associated with Iran's nuclear program in line with this EU objective. According to the Paris Agreement reached with the EU3 in November 2004, Iran suspended all of its uranium enrichment and nuclear fuel–reprocessing activities during negotiations to secure a long-term arrangement that provided "objective guarantees that Iran's nuclear program is exclusively for peaceful purposes."[9] Philippe Errera, the director of the policy planning staff at the French Ministry for Foreign Affairs, subsequently made clear that for the EU3 an objective guarantee required the permanent cessation by Iran of all activities leading to the production of nuclear materials.[10] This would exclude keeping uranium enrichment, plutonium reprocessing, and heavy water facilities on Iranian territory.

To this effect, the EU3 developed a *Framework for a Long-Term Agreement* that was put to Iran as the basis for a package deal by which Iran would be offered technical and financial assistance for its civilian nuclear program in exchange for a permanent renunciation of proliferation-sensitive activities and a commitment by Iran never to withdraw from the Nuclear Nonproliferation Treaty under any circumstances. The EU3 also offered to try to facilitate progress in the discussions concerning the application to accede to the World Trade Organization (WTO) lodged by Iran in September 1996, after which there has been no agreement within the WTO to start the accession negotiation process.

For the EU3, there was no urgent need to reach a final agreement as long as Iran continued to suspend sensitive activities under international monitoring arrangements. However, Iran made clear to the EU3 that it could not under any conditions accept the approach proposed as the basis for an agreement and instead pointed to a form of reverse conditionality—that the suspension of sensitive activities would only last for as long as Iran believed that talks continued to show progress. In the autumn of 2005 Iran informed the IAEA of its decision to resume uranium conversion activities, and at the beginning of 2006 Iran resumed all of the nuclear activities that had been suspended since 2003 on a voluntary basis while discussions with the EU3 took place.[11]

In the latter part of 2005 the EU3 also began to work for a referral of the Iranian nuclear problem to the UNSC—something that the United States had argued in favor of for several years. The EU3 drafted a proposal to this effect for presentation to the IAEA Board of Governors, a proposal that formed the basis for a resolution adopted by the IAEA at the end of September 2005. Subsequent to that resolution the IAEA referred the case of Iran to the UNSC in February 2006. The discussion in the UNSC has been supported by a series of discussions between six countries—the P5+1, namely the five permanent members of the UNSC and Germany—who have worked to ensure that they present, to the degree possible, a unified and coherent position on the Iranian nuclear program.

The process of widening the discussion has led to a modification in the position of the EU3 in that the text of the nuclear package of incentives offered to Iran by the P5+1 (or, put another way, the EU3 plus China, Russia, and the United States) suggested that Iran would restore its suspension of uranium enrichment immediately but did not exclude eventual enrichment on Iranian soil, subject to certain conditions.[12] For the United States to accept the possibility that Iran could engage in uranium enrichment, albeit far in the future and under different conditions from those prevailing, can be presented as a significant change in U.S. policy brought about by the EU3. However, the revised package presented in 2006 is still not acceptable to Iran, which objects to the conditions laid down in the offer for resuming enrichment.

While there is currently an impasse in negotiations between the EU3 and Iran, there is also an impasse in the negotiation of an EU-Iran agreement on trade and economic cooperation. The EU and Iran do not currently have a framework agreement—in effect, a contract—as the basis for their bilateral relationship. The lack of such an agreement has limited the development of specific cooperative projects and programs in most areas. However, the Council of the European Union agreed in June 2002 to open negotiations with Iran on a so-called mixed agreement—that is, an agreement covering political aspects as well as trade and cooperation. The negotiations were launched in Brussels in December 2002 but were later suspended as the atmosphere in bilateral talks between the EU3 and Iran on the nuclear issue deteriorated.

Taken as a whole, the interactions between the EU and Iran over the nuclear issue have not produced a very satisfactory outcome from a European perspective at the time of this writing. Iran continues to develop the more sensitive parts of its nuclear program with no sign that the package of incentives and disincentives in large part crafted by European negotiators could influence this state of affairs. However, in terms of the management of the process a number of significant successes can be pointed to. The EU3 have managed to maintain solidarity among themselves, which was never achieved during the crisis over Iraq.

Moreover, they have consistently been supported in their efforts by the wider EU membership in spite of some misgivings about the fact that actions taken by the three states would inevitably be perceived internationally as EU actions although they were decided without advance consultations with all twenty-five member states. This achievement is notable given that the EU3 have set ambitious objectives for themselves in regard to the Iranian nuclear program and have taken a rather hard line in pushing for those objectives to be accepted. The EU3 have persuaded the United States to modify its national position on the Iranian nuclear program in two respects.[13] Finally, the EU3 persuaded two permanent members of the UNSC—China and Russia—that were seen as implacable opponents of any coercive element in a package of measures to address the Iranian nuclear program to vote in favor of UNSC Resolution 1696 (2006), which envisions "appropriate measures under Article 41 of Chapter VII of the Charter of the United Nations" (i.e., economic sanctions) to persuade Iran to suspend its sensitive nuclear activities.[14]

The Use of the Nonproliferation Clause in EU Agreements

More broadly than the particular and very difficult case of Iran, in November 2003 the EU decided that because nonproliferation of WMD was a major concern for the EU it should from that point onward constitute a "fundamental element" of the decision to enter into negotiations with a third country or the decision to establish a contractual relationship. The European Council decided that as a general rule future agreements between the EU and third countries should include a "nonproliferation clause" as an essential element.[15] This would mean that subsequent violation of the clause could be a basis for termination of the contract, with the loss of associated benefits (such as trade preferences and project financing). At the same time the European Council asked the European Commission to examine a wider conditionality linked to EU assistance programs by considering linking noncompliance by a given country with its nonproliferation commitments and suspension of assistance.

The general message that the nonproliferation clause is intended to convey is that the failure to strengthen export controls and work actively for nonproliferation will be seen as a serious matter by the EU and that while the EU will consider helping states to meet the highest standards in these areas, it will also consider punishing those who refuse such an undertaking or who agree to it but do not comply with it in good faith. The potential preventive value of such an approach has been noted by analysts, but so has the inherent difficulty in implementing, monitoring, and controlling the mainstreaming effort. Roberto Aliboni has noted that "while its preventative policies predicated on economic instruments and geared to enhance development and increase economic growth or welfare in the middle-long term look generally acceptable to its partners, policies involving political and security questions may be less so. The attempt of the EU is, however, legitimate and positive."[16]

The nonproliferation clause formed part of the Association Agreement initialed by Syria and the EU on October 19, 2004, and in other early cases was also part of agreements concluded with Tajikistan and Albania. The EU negotiators also included the text in interregional agreements with Mercosur, the Gulf Cooperation Council, and as part of the Cotonou agreement between the EU and African, Caribbean, and Pacific states. In one or other form the language of the nonproliferation clause also found its way into the various Action Plans being negotiated as part of the European Neighbourhood Policy with Israel, Ukraine, Moldova, Jordan, Morocco, and Tunisia.

The model language put forward for the nonproliferation clause states that "full compliance with and national implementation of their existing obligations under international disarmament and nonproliferation treaties and agreements and other relevant international obligations" is an essential element of the bilateral agreement. The EU and the other party concerned agree to cooperate with two ends in mind: to take steps "to sign, ratify, or accede to, as appropriate, and fully implement all other relevant international instruments"; and to establish "an effective system of national export controls, controlling the export as well as transit of WMD related goods, including a WMD end-use control on dual use technologies and containing effective sanctions for breaches of export controls."

The desirability of cooperation with the EU and the possible risk that cooperation would be lost represent strong incentives that would make countries think carefully about the balance of advantages and disadvantages associated with proliferation. The way in which the issue of mainstreaming nonproliferation into external action has been framed also holds out the possibility of EU support for measures to enhance the effectiveness of national measures taken to prevent proliferation. However, a number of difficulties have been pointed to in implementing the approach that has been decided upon.

The question of how to judge compliance with nonproliferation commitments has been underlined in the recent past by EU differences over the extent of Iraqi violations of UNSC resolutions on WMD disarmament. Clear legal criteria have proved elusive, and it may be challenging for the EU to assemble, distribute, and analyze the information needed as the basis for a decision to cancel a bilateral agreement on the basis of noncompliance.

In negotiations the EU would need to decide whether to insist on uniformity in the language and content of a nonproliferation clause or whether to modify the language on a case-by-case basis. According to Roberto Aliboni, Syria at first requested modifications to the language of the model clause but finally accepted the proposed text of the nonproliferation clause in its Association Agreement with the EU. Given Syria's nonparticipation in the Chemical Weapons Convention (CWC), this was a potentially difficult case for the EU, but it should be noted that the Association Agreement does not make Syrian accession to the CWC a condition of economic and technical cooperation.

Article 5.1 of the Association Agreement with Syria commits both parties "to contribute to countering the proliferation of weapons of mass-destruction, nuclear, biological and chemical and their means of delivery through full compliance with their *existing* obligations under international disarmament and nonproliferation treaties and agreements and their other existing relevant international obligations, as well as United Nations Security Council resolutions and ensuring their effective implementation" (emphasis added). The parties agreed that *this* provision constitutes an essential element of this agreement. In article 5.2 the parties agreed to take action "towards the signature, ratification or accession, as appropriate, and full implementation of all other relevant international instruments" and to set up "effective national systems of export, transit and end-use controls of WMD-related goods and technologies, including dual use, and containing enforcement procedures with appropriate penalties."[17] However, this obligation (which does not have a specific set of procedures or timetable attached) does not represent an essential element of the agreement. Its realization depends on the willingness of the EU and Syria to cooperate in this field as well as on the resources the EU would be willing to devote to capacity building and technical assistance to Syria rather than on conditionality.

In April 2004 the European Commission concluded a new cooperation agreement with another difficult case, Pakistan. As a European Community (EC)–only agreement (i.e., an agreement dealing with issues that fall under the commercial policy of the EU) it did not mention nonproliferation for reasons linked to the EC's legal competences. The European Council decided in 2003 that in these circumstances the principle of introducing an essential nonproliferation element in the EU–third country relationship would still apply but would be approached through the conclusion of a parallel instrument establishing a link with the EC agreement. The EC-only agreement provides the framework for commercial, economic, and development cooperation—and therefore contains the elements needed for the conditionality proposed by the EU as its main approach—and has been concluded. However, the EU has made a declaration of intent to propose to Pakistan a cooperation mechanism of an undefined kind to deal with issues related to WMD and counterterrorism.[18] With the Cooperation Agreement already in place, it is not clear what incentive Pakistan would have to join such an arrangement or what the implications of failing to reach an agreement would be for economic and technical cooperation.

The EU has taken a somewhat different approach in regard to Pakistan's neighbor, India. The EU has a contractual relationship with India based on a partnership and cooperation agreement signed in 1993. This was also an EC-only agreement and would not therefore include a nonproliferation clause even if renegotiated. Unlike the Pakistan case, the EU has reached an important bilateral agreement with India after the WMD Strategy was adopted and after the decision was taken to mainstream nonproliferation into bilateral agreements with partners. However, the EU did not insist on the insertion of the nonproliferation clause in this agreement.

The EU has held a regular political dialogue with India since 1993, and since 2000 annual bilateral high-level summit meetings have been held. At their summit meeting in 2004 the EU and India decided to upgrade their bilateral relationship by relabeling it a "strategic partnership." The EU and India decided to jointly elaborate a comprehensive EU-India Action Plan for a strategic partnership and a new joint political declaration.

This work was duly carried out, and the resulting *India-EU Strategic Partnership Joint Action Plan* was adopted in September 2005. One element of the partnership is the arrangement of a bilateral India-EU security dialogue at senior official level to include "regular consultations on global and regional security issues, disarmament and nonproliferation."

According to the November 2003 decision, a new "parallel instrument" with a partner was intended to contain a provision according to which the parties would commit themselves to full compliance with and national implementation of their existing obligations under international disarmament and nonproliferation treaties and agreements and other relevant international obligations (this commitment forming an essential element of the agreement). The EU and its partner would also agree "to cooperate and to contribute to countering the proliferation of weapons of mass destruction and their means of delivery by: taking steps to sign, ratify, or accede to, as appropriate, and fully implement all other relevant international instruments; the establishment of an effective system of national export controls, controlling the export as well as transit of WMD related goods, including a WMD end-use control on dual use technologies and containing effective sanctions for breaches of export controls."

These elements are not contained in the India-EU Strategic Partnership Joint Action Plan, where the text is limited to a general agreement that "effective export control measures for dual use goods can play an important role in preventing proliferation, and at the same time, such measures should not hamper international cooperation in materials, equipment and technology for peaceful purposes."[19]

The Strategic Partnership Joint Action Plan also falls some way short of the language in the statement that accompanied the 2003 mainstreaming decision in that no link with the EC agreement has been established in this parallel instrument. The element of conditionality is therefore missing in the nonproliferation element of the EU-India relationship, and actions India takes (or doesn't take) in this field would not offer a legal basis for canceling the partnership and cooperation agreement.

The EU has clearly made efforts to "mainstream" nonproliferation into external agreements with some success. Although the overall impact of the effort cannot yet be evaluated, the manner of implementation so far suggests a direct link between the way in which the EU will determine noncompliance with obligations contained in contracts with partners and the determination of compliance with existing multilateral arms control and disarmament treaties and conventions. A finding of noncompliance with existing commitments would probably trigger the denial of opportunities for trade and technical cooperation with the EU. The EU must hope that the perceived risk of denial will provide an additional incentive for partner countries to comply with the treaties to which they are committed. From this point of view mainstreaming could be seen as one way in which the EU is helping to strengthen the enforcement of treaties.

At the same time, there is a degree of differentiation in the way that the EU has carried out mainstreaming in that the element of conditionality is sometimes strong, sometimes weak, and sometimes absent in the documents that provide the framework for bilateral relations with partners.

European Union Nonproliferation Instruments

One part of the logic of mainstreaming is to create leverage for the EU in addressing particular cases of proliferation concern. However, there is a significant range of other instruments that the EU has at its disposal in implementing the WMD Strategy.

Negotiating and Strengthening Multilateral Treaties

As noted above, the EU WMD Strategy emphasizes the point of view that "a multilateralist approach to security, including disarmament and nonproliferation, provides the best way to maintain international order" and the "commitment to uphold, implement and strengthen the multilateral disarmament and nonproliferation treaties and agreements." In this context the WMD Strategy underlines a "determination to support the multilateral institutions charged respectively with verification and upholding of compliance with these treaties." Another prominent element in the WMD Strategy is a commitment "to strong national and internationally-coordinated export controls."

All EU member states have signed and ratified all of the most important multilateral arms control and disarmament treaties. In the framework of treaty regimes states parties meet periodically to review their status and examine the need for modifications to the treaties. The EU has, for some years, been trying to coordinate the positions adopted by member states at such review meetings and then to work for the adoption of agreed-on EU positions.

The European Council working groups that deal with WMD nonproliferation (first and foremost the EU Working Group on Nonproliferation [CONOP]) meet roughly once a month, bringing together officials from EU member states to discuss issues of mutual concern and interest. The agenda of CONOP has predominantly been taken up with preparing the positions that the EU will take in multilateral events or conferences. The outcome of these working group activities may be reflected in EU legislative acts (for example, in recent years it has become normal practice for the EU to formulate a common position prior to important meetings regarding the framework of the major nonproliferation and disarmament treaties). They might also lead to drafts of joint statements to be issued on behalf of the EU.

The EU appears to have developed an effective method for managing its collective contributions to multilateral treaty processes. These treaty processes have not borne fruit in recent years, and in a number of cases have failed completely, sometimes in spectacular fashion. However, these failures cannot reasonably be laid at the door of the EU, which has been among the most energetic supporters of and creative contributors to review meetings.

The EU will face a significant test of its ability to take a coordinated approach when the long-anticipated treaty to ban the production of fissile material for use in nuclear weapons (fissile material cut-off treaty or FMCT) reaches the point of negotiation. The EU position will need to reconcile the perspectives of two nuclear weapon states (France and the United Kingdom) that will be important targets for the FMCT with those of other EU member states on issues such as the scope of any ban and the specific verification provisions attached to the treaty.

Preventive Measures Taken by the European Union: Export and Customs Controls

Two instruments that contribute in an important way to the overall EU nonproliferation effort are grounded in EU law. The first is the legal framework controlling exports of dual-use items out of the EU, which was established in a European Council regulation.[20] The second is the EU Community Customs Code, which establishes a uniform set of procedures to be used by national customs authorities across the EU and has recently been modified to incorporate a security dimension.[21]

The dual-use export regulation and the Customs Code both form a part of the primary legislation under the first pillar of the EU. Each of these instruments is based on an agreed set of standards that should be implemented in the same way across the EU, and that can therefore also be the basis for collective external actions.

The EU has recently worked to enhance the effectiveness of its export controls. A "peer review" of the export control systems of member states and accession countries as regards dual-use items was conducted in 2004. The review was intended to strengthen the coordination of the dual-use export control activities of member states and to provide opportunities for mutual learning in order to enhance the effectiveness of implementation of European Council Regulation 1334/2000 in an enlarged EU.

A peer review task force included representatives of the European Council secretariat, the European Commission (the directorates-general for trade and for external relations), and one member state (Finland). The review process was organized around clusters of countries, comprising two member states and one acceding country. Experts from member states visited the acceding country, which in turn made return visits. The review covered around twenty fundamental issues relevant to export licensing, enforcement, industry awareness programs, and control of technical assistance.

The peer review revealed discrepancies regarding implementing legislation, industrial awareness programs, the technical capacities available to national authorities to evaluate license applications and classify items, and the intelligence infrastructure. The review also found that the application of the dual-use regulation differed in important respects across countries.

The peer review task force produced a report and recommendations for future action and the General Affairs Council subsequently decided that these recommendations should be "acted upon without delay." As a result, in order to improve EU export controls a number of concrete actions should be taken by EU member states. The peer review is therefore likely to lead to substantive changes in the dual-use export control systems of countries and to a revision of the European Council regulation on which the system rests. In combination, this should strengthen controls and increase the consistency of practice throughout the EU.

After 2003 the European Commission has brought together the elements of a new security-management model for the external borders of the enlarged EU based on two pillars: a set of common control standards to be used as the basis for customs procedures throughout the EU and a set of trade facilitation measures that will be available to exporters that can demonstrate a responsible approach to exporting. The elements of the model were the basis for security amendments to the Community Customs Code.

With these amendments the EU introduced three important changes to the customs code. First, the new regulation requires traders to provide customs authorities with prearrival and predeparture declarations containing information on goods prior to import to or export from the EU. Second, the new regulation introduces the status of authorized economic operators (AEO) that, once conferred, will provide reliable traders with the right to receive certain trade facilitation measures. Third, the new regulation introduces a mechanism for setting uniform community risk-selection criteria for controls, supported by computerized systems.

Subsequently, the European Commission has been drafting implementing provisions (published in July 2005) and managing an open consultation in order to prepare a final draft provision for discussion by EU member states in the EU Customs Code Committee. It was hoped that revised implementing regulations for the Community Customs Code could enter into force in 2006 and go into full effect in 2009. However, this timetable may not be achieved as European industry associations have made a joint request for a delay in implementation.

The new system is intended to help protect the internal market of the EU as well as helping to secure international supply chains. However, the new mechanisms being developed as part of this process can also strengthen the implementation of dual-use export controls by helping customs authorities to recognize sensitive shipments, stop them at the border, and inspect them more closely. The pre-arrival and pre-departure declarations required under the new system could also provide the information needed to control the transit and transshipment of dual-use goods across the EU.

The EU has worked to enhance the effectiveness of export controls and customs procedures, which could be important preventive nonproliferation instruments. However, implementing the revised controls is a formidable undertaking.

The peer review identified a need to improve EU performance in some of the most challenging aspects of export control implementation, such as the recognition of dual-use items subject to control at the border, the implementation of controls on nonlisted items (the so-called catch-all), and controlling intangible transfers of technology.

The revisions to the customs code will require national customs authorities and industry to develop automated systems to meet data reporting requirements. The industry response to the revised customs code has been to argue that this will be much easier said than done. These systems must be compatible both between national customs authorities and between customs authorities and exporters. Moreover, advance shipment data will probably have to be provided by the carriers of goods (who are experienced in filing customs documents but have little prior experience working with security-related controls) rather than the exporters. Therefore the automated system will probably have to link together information collected from a number of different industry actors in order to generate complete reports.

Nonproliferation and Disarmament Assistance

After the end of the Cold War a number of programs have developed to provide financial, economic, and technical assistance to states (in the first instance the Russian Federation) that lack the means to implement shared disarmament, nonproliferation, and counterterrorism objectives. International nonproliferation and disarmament assistance (INDA) differs from the traditional approach to arms control, which depends on each state that is party to a treaty or an agreement to implement in good faith and at its own initiative and expense obligations codified in that particular document. Practical assistance measures have been jointly implemented on the territory of one state by a coalition of parties that may include states, international organizations, local and regional government, nongovernmental organizations, and the private sector.

The EU is not new to the delivery of assistance in this area. Through its regular budget the EC has financed projects in the following functional areas of direct relevance to nonproliferation and disarmament:

- programs to redirect scientists formerly employed by the Soviet Union in programs to develop and produce WMD;
- projects to support the conversion or destruction of former Soviet chemical weapons production facilities to civilian use;
- projects to help create modern and effective regulations to govern nuclear material control and accountancy;
- projects to improve the quality of methodologies and techniques used to account for and control the fissile materials that are the essential element of nuclear weapons or of a nuclear explosive device;
- projects under the Northern Dimension of EU external actions to secure and store radiological waste and spent nuclear fuel that contain such fissile materials and that are located in northwestern Russia; and
- projects to strengthen the national dual-use export control systems of countries whose exports could contribute to nuclear, biological, and chemical (NBC) weapons programs of concern.

The EC has also financed an extensive border management assistance program in countries around the periphery of the EU.

The European Council has used joint actions to define and finance a number of INDA activities and programs. In particular, attention can be drawn to a number of joint actions that have financed the following:

- a European Cooperation Programme for Nonproliferation and Disarmament in the Russian Federation;
- the strengthening of the physical protection of a nuclear site in the Russian Federation;
- the Organisation for the Prohibition of Chemical Weapons (OPCW) to help implement and strengthen the CWC;
- the IAEA Nuclear Security Program; and
- IAEA activities in the areas of nuclear security and verification.

In an evaluation of the effectiveness of past and current EU activities in this area the Stockholm International Peace Research Institute (SIPRI) concluded that the EU has the financial resources, project management skills, and technical expertise to make a very significant contribution to international nonproliferation and disarmament assistance (INDA) efforts should it choose to do so. The EU has used INDA as one element of its fight against proliferation in the past but has not by any means fully exploited the possible applications of this approach in light of its capacity to act. When it comes to addressing WMD issues the EU includes this approach as one element in its overall response and should do so by developing a well-conceived, well-coordinated set of projects that command adequate resources.

There is some evidence that the EU will follow this path, but it is far from certain. Since there are significant financial costs associated with INDA the discussion has been closely linked to the process of agreeing on the next general budget of the EU, which is based on a medium-term financial framework that is agreed on between the European Parliament, the Council of the EU, and the European Commission. The annual budget sets the amount of expenditure to be allocated to each policy area in which the EU is involved, including external action, based on that agreed-on framework.

In 2005–06 the overall framework of the budget in the period 2007–13 was established and new financial instruments to implement external action using that budget were fixed after the Commission argued that changes that have taken place since the public finances of the EU were reformed in 1988 justify a new start and fresh thinking not only about policy but also about the nature and number of instruments at its disposal to implement that policy.

In 2003 the commission prepared a broad communication called *Building Our Common Future: Policy Challenges and Budgetary Means of the Enlarged Union 2007–2013* addressing the need for budget reform. The Commission argued that over time the size and complexity of the budget for financing external actions has outstripped the administrative capacity available to implement it. Three problems can be pointed to in particular: (a) unclear and divided responsibilities for relevant issue areas; (b) a chronic staff shortage in certain functional areas; and (c) excessively complex administrative procedures in conditions where there are at least thirty different geographical budget lines and around fifty different thematic budget lines.

On September 29, 2004, there followed legislative proposals to establish a new catalogue of financial instruments better adapted to the current and future needs of the EU. The Commission proposed replacing all the geographical and thematic budget instruments that had grown up over the previous sixteen years with six instruments. Of these six, two were existing instruments that would be retained without modification and four were entirely new.

The European Council undertakes initiatives within the CFSP framework in the form of joint actions to address specific issues. A joint action may prescribe the resources to be made available for its implementation as well as define objectives, procedures, and conditions for its implementation. One part of the title for external action within the general budget is reserved to finance joint actions in the field of CFSP. The CFSP budget will continue to exist alongside new instruments.

One of the new instruments proposed by the European Commission was a stability instrument, and one suggested purpose of it was to deliver financial, economic, and technical assistance in ways that help the EU combat the proliferation of WMD. The general budget has been financing projects whose sole rationale is nonproliferation—such as the redirection of scientists formerly employed in WMD research and development—for more than a decade. Nevertheless, in April 2005 the European Council Legal Service provided a written opinion on the proposal to create a stability instrument. While recognizing that the objective of combating proliferation is an important part of the CFSP, the opinion found that general support for this EU goal is insufficient to justify the initiation of specific actions by the European Commission. Any such actions would need a clearer legal basis. Moreover, the legal opinion stated that the specific legal basis suggested in the European Commission proposal as the basis for actions to fight the proliferation of WMD was not adequate because the treaties in which they are contained do not give the EC general competence to act in that field.

Against that background the stability instrument was revised. The version of the stability instrument that was agreed to by the Committee of Permanent Representatives in May 2006 included a provision for technical and financial assistance to address specific global and transregional threats that have a destabilizing effect. One part of this assistance was set aside for risk mitigation and preparedness relating to chemical, nuclear, and biological materials or agents.[22] Furthermore, the use of the resources was not linked to any named location, but instead it was stated that particular emphasis should be put on assistance projects in "those regions or countries where stockpiles of such materials still exist and where there is a risk of proliferation of such material." The financial reference amount established for the stability instrument for the period 2007–13 was €2.254 billion, and as a guideline it was stated that no more than 15 percent of that amount (approximately €340 million) should be used for these kinds of assistance projects.

As part of the agreement on the overall budget a minimum of €1.74 billion has been set aside to finance measures related to the CFSP. The CFSP budget (which is intended to be flexible and to respond to need) is not earmarked in advance. However, a proportion of this money is very likely to be used for nonproliferation-related activities, and the increase in the CFSP budget from an annual amount of roughly €60 million to an annual average of €250 million could give scope for increased financing from this source.

The lack of a clear budget line within the EC budget makes it difficult to calculate past and current expenditure on nonproliferation- and disarmament-related projects. To find this information it is necessary to look at each of the specific projects in the different parts of the external action program and make a judgment about their nonproliferation relevance. Within the external action part of the EC budget the average annual commitment of funds to finance future projects that can be considered to be relevant to nonproliferation and disarmament is estimated to be €31 million over the period 1994–2006. The data in the general budget for the CFSP budget for 2006 indicate that €14.845 million was allocated to support nonproliferation and disarmament in 2004 and €7.2 million was allocated for the same purpose in 2005. However, this money was intended to finance measures that contribute to the reduction of WMD as well as financing operations to combat the distribution of light arms and illicit arms trafficking.

In the next financial perspective, 2007–13, the EU will have both significant resources to devote to international nonproliferation and disarmament assistance and the financial instruments that would allow those resources to be applied. This does not mean that such a program will be developed, however. That depends primarily on the willingness of the European Council and the European Commission to prioritize the INDA effort and cooperate to develop a program that can be implemented systematically over the medium term.

Assessment: Problems and Prospects

After the leaders of the EU made nonproliferation an important element in their collective foreign and security policy, the EU has progressively tried to assemble the various instruments at its disposal in order to implement a complex and fast-moving nonproliferation effort worldwide. Nonproliferation has now become embedded into the budget and into the bureaucratic structures of the EU. Therefore, nonproliferation will be part of the everyday activities of the EU indefinitely. Given that the proliferation problems that need to be addressed are persistent and do not lend themselves either to short-term measures or to purely technical solutions, the EU is now in a position to emerge as a constructive part of the wider attempt to resolve a difficult problem that can undermine international security. At this early stage it is not possible to draw firm conclusions about the impact of EU actions on global proliferation trends. If successful, the nonproliferation effort could also be a building block in the effort to make the EU a more coherent and influential international actor.

The effort to mainstream nonproliferation has helped to bring coherence to the EU in process terms but has also underlined the scale of the proliferation challenge in some locations. The EU3 have been the motor for policy development in regard to Iran, while the United Kingdom pursued a bilateral dialogue with Libya that focused directly on the elimination of Libyan WMD capacities. However, EU colleagues were informed of these initiatives, and the states concerned ensured that their activities were within the agreed-to framework established at the European level.

In cases where there have not been innovations of this kind, it has been more difficult for the EU to prepare and carry out coherent nonproliferation initiatives. In particular, it can be noted that the relevant European Council working groups have not been able to act as a forum for preparing country- or region-specific approaches for presentation to senior decision makers. Neither is it clear whether the working groups would be able to implement any country- or region-specific approaches that were developed. The CONOP has not examined specific country or regional proliferation threats and problems in any systematic manner, assessed the range of potential EU responses to identified threats, or prepared proposals for an EU approach to the given problem.

As a result, no such discussion has taken place in the PSC or at the ministerial level. The EU still lacks leadership in its effort to engage with important countries from a nonproliferation perspective, such as India, Iraq, Israel, North Korea, Pakistan, and Syria.

The working groups have developed an effective approach to setting common objectives within multilateral treaty processes. In recent years these processes have not been the main forum for the most interesting efforts to combat proliferation. However, this may change if negotiations begin on a FMCT. Developing a common approach to the FMCT will be an important but challenging task for the EU.

The EU has taken important steps to strengthen its export controls and border security but faces formidable implementation challenges. Nevertheless, the EU is in the process of establishing a body of legislation that is coming to be seen and accepted as setting an international standard in the area of dual-use export controls. The recent changes to the European law establishing rules of procedure for customs authorities could, once implemented, have the same impact in the field of border control.

The EU has equipped itself with the legal basis and budget to apply technical and financial assistance to help other countries combat proliferation. This capacity has not yet been translated into a coherent program of action, but the next budget contains the possibility that the EU will expand the geographical scope and the scale of its nonproliferation actions.

The next steps in developing effective tools to combat proliferation will depend on the level of cooperation that can be achieved between the various parts of the EU. There is a general difficulty in securing coherent and regular inputs from member states on the implementation and further development of the WMD Strategy as a whole. This is partly a reflection of the different levels of capacity and interest in regard to the issue of WMD proliferation among the twenty-five member states. However, it also reflects the particular mechanisms used by the EU when dealing with the multifaceted and complex nonproliferation issue.

European Council working groups largely consist of officials who travel from national capitals for periodic meetings, meaning that the composition of personnel at the meetings changes. The timetable of meetings is challenging for officials who have national responsibilities to attend to, yet too infrequent for sustained attention to complex problems or oversight of large projects. If input to the development and implementation of the WMD Strategy drew more systematically on representatives of member states based in Brussels, then a stable group of individuals could work on a more regular basis with counterparts in the European Council secretariat and the European Commission. However, there has not been a tradition of staffing missions with specialists on WMD-related issues and a number of member states would have concerns that this Brussels-based group might lose contact with important national priorities, in effect "going native." In practical terms, smaller EU countries in particular would find it difficult to staff their delegations with permanent representatives who were specialists on particular issues while also maintaining expertise in the capitals.

A more regular series of consultations with a smaller group of states that have larger human resources and a strong interest in the issue of nonproliferation would have practical advantages but might be difficult to establish in relation to the elaboration and implementation of the WMD Strategy—a process that is necessarily EU-wide.

The six-month review of the implementation of the WMD Strategy presented to the PSC has the potential to become a focal point for the work of a group of officials from the capitals that meet more regularly than the current working groups. In that way the six-month reporting document could become an important working instrument drawing in information and insights from member states. A broad parallel might be the important role that preparing the annual report on the implementation of the EU code of conduct on conventional arms exports now plays in stimulating cooperation and information exchange among officials from member states.

Within the European Commission, the opportunity offered by the new financial instruments and the new budget guidelines will not be capitalized on effectively unless the problem of unclear and divided responsibilities for relevant issue areas is addressed. Expertise on nuclear and biological issues as well as export controls and border security are distributed across different parts of the European Commission directorates–general, and it is not clear that an efficient system exists for developing cooperation even within different parts of the same directorate-general. The programming and delivery of technical and financial assistance will not be possible without a team that is specifically tasked with the job, sufficient in size, and technically competent. Therefore there is a need for senior European Commission officials to bring the administrative aspects of managing nonproliferation assistance in line with the political priority assigned to the issue by the most senior European decision makers.

Notes

1. Javier Solana, *A Secure Europe in a Better World: European Security Strategy*, December 12, 2003, 3, http://ue.eu.int/uedocs/cmsUpload/78367.pdf.

2. G-8 Summit 2006, "Statement on Non-Proliferation," St. Petersburg, July 16, 2006, http://en.g8russia.ru/docs/20.html.

3. Council of the European Union, "The Basic Principles for an EU Strategy against Proliferation of Weapons of Mass Destruction," 10352/03, June 10, 2003, http://www.sipri.org/contents/expcon/eu_wmd.html.

4. Council of the European Union, "Action Plan for the Implementation of the Basic Principles," 10354/03, June 13, 2003, http://www.sipri.org/contents/expcon/eu_wmd.html.

5. Council of the European Union, "EU Strategy against the Proliferation of Weapons of Mass Destruction," 15708/03, December 12, 2003, http://www.consilium.europa.eu/cms3_fo/showPage.asp?id=392&lang=EN&mode=g.

6. Joanna Spear, "The Emergence of a European 'Strategic Personality,'" *Arms Control Today* 33, no. 9 (November 2003): 13–18.

7. Described in International Atomic Energy Agency, Implementation of the NPT Safeguards Agreement in the Islamic Republic of Iran: Report by the Director General, GOV/2003/40, June 6, 2003.

8. International Atomic Energy Agency, Implementation of the NPT Safeguards Agreement in the Islamic Republic of Iran, GOV/2003/69, September 12, 2003.

9. EU-3, Paris Agreement, November 15, 2004, has been reproduced as an IAEA document, INFCIRC/637, November 26, 2004.

10. Philippe Errera, "The E3/EU-Iran Negotiations and Prospects for Resolving the Iranian Nuclear Issue: A European Perspective," Tehran, March 5–6, 2006, http://www.globalsecurity.org/wmd/library/report/2005/errera.htm. It should be noted, however, that Iran has never accepted this EU position and that no such language is found in the Paris Agreement.

11. On January 3, 2006, Iran informed the IAEA that it would resume research and development associated with the enrichment of uranium as of January 10, 2006 (A. A. Soltanieh, "Statement by the Resident Representative of the Islamic Republic of Iran to the IAEA," Vienna, Austria, February 2, 2006, http://www.iaea.org/NewsCenter/Focus/IaeaIran/index.shtml).

12. "Text of P5+1 Nuclear Package of Incentives Offered to Iran," *Iran Focus*, July 18, 2006, http://www.iranfocus.com/modules/news/article.php?storyid=7946.

13. In 2006 Secretary of State Condoleezza Rice stated that the United States would be prepared to join talks on nuclear issues with Iran and the EU3, reversing a previous refusal to engage in direct talks with Iranian government officials. In subscribing to the P5+1 offer to Iran the United States accepted that Iran should suspend proliferation-sensitive activities and that this moratorium would be subject to future review. Unlike previous U.S. statements, the P5+1 offer does not exclude that the future review would permit sensitive activities to resume.

14. United Nations Security Council, Resolution 1696, S/RES/1696/2006, July 31, 2006, paragraph 8, http://www.un.org/Docs/sc/unsc_resolutions06.htm.

15. Council of the European Union, *Fight against the Proliferation of Weapons of Mass Destruction: Mainstreaming Non-Proliferation Policies into the EU's Wider Relations with Third Countries*, 14997/03, November 19, 2003, http://trade.ec.europa.eu/doclib/html/118532.htm.

16. Roberto Aliboni, "The Non-Proliferation Clause in a Preventive Perspective," *Conflict in Focus* 1, no. 4 (December 2004): 3.

17. European Commission, "Proposal for a Council Decision on the Conclusion of a Euro-Mediterranean Association Agreement between the European Community and Its Member States of the One Part, and the Syrian Arab Republic, of the Other Part," COM

808/2004 final, December 17, 2004. The agreement was initiated by the parties on October 19, 2004, but has not been approved by the EU Council.

18. European Commission, "Cooperation Agreement between the European Community and the Islamic Republic of Pakistan on Partnership and Development," April 22, 2004.

19. European Commission, "India-EU Strategic Partnership Joint Action Plan," New Delhi, September 7, 2005.

20. European Commission, "Council Regulation (EC) No. 1334/2000 of 22 June, 2000," setting up a European Community regime for the control of exports of dual-use items and technology.

21. European Commission, "Council Regulation (EC) No. 648/2005 of 13 April, 2005."

22. European Parliament, "Draft Regulation of the European Parliament and the Council Establishing an Instrument for Stability," A6-0157/2006, May 24, 2006.

CHAPTER ELEVEN

South Asia and the Nonproliferation Regime

Seema Gahlaut

South Asia—namely India and Pakistan—is often considered the greatest challenge to the nonproliferation regime. Despite sanctions, diplomatic pressure, and international opprobrium for several decades, neither country agreed to join the Nuclear Nonproliferation Treaty (NPT) or the Comprehensive Test-Ban Treaty (CTBT). Then in 1998, both conducted a series of nuclear tests and asserted their arrival into the international community as nuclear weapons states (NWS)—regardless of the NPT-defined criteria for such a status. Apart from the challenge to the normative authority of the international nonproliferation regime, these two states are considered the most likely to break the post–WWII taboo on the use of nuclear weapons and thereby cause a human and environmental catastrophe several times more serious than that caused by U.S. bombing of Hiroshima and Nagasaki. In this decade, another concern has been added to the ones described above: proliferation of WMDs or WMD technologies from South Asia to states of international concern or to terrorist groups. The revelation of the A. Q. Khan network transformed these concerns into an undeniable reality for the nonproliferation regime. Finally, how the major powers deal with these two countries— despite their refusal to accept the NPT norms—might also have consequences for the future of the nonproliferation regime. India's and Pakistan's actions, therefore, are likely to have a lasting impact on the normative and institutional efficacy of the nonproliferation regime.

This chapter examines in detail three aspects of the proliferation/nonproliferation challenge emanating from India and Pakistan. Section 1 examines the issue of vertical proliferation. What is the current status of the India-Pakistan rivalry? Why is this rivalry uniquely dangerous? How likely is the predicted nuclear use in a war between them? What are the prospects for peace between them? The second section examines the issue of horizontal proliferation. What were the causes

and consequences of the Pakistan-based A. Q. Khan network for the nonproliferation regime? Is a similar proliferation network likely to arise in India? What have
the two countries learned from the revelations about this network? The third section examines the changing relationship between the United States and India.
What is involved in the U.S.-India nuclear deal? How are other major stakeholders in the international system reacting to it? What consequences will such a
deal have for the legitimacy and effectiveness of the nonproliferation regime?
The concluding section sets forth a few predictions on the future of proliferation
in South Asia, explores what changes we can expect in the policies of India and
Pakistan regarding the issue of nuclear nonproliferation, and offers some recommendations to induce them to cooperate with the nonproliferation regime.

I. Vertical Proliferation: The Danger of Nuclear War

Until the 1990s, the focus of the nonproliferation regime was on vertical proliferation by India and Pakistan. There was, and continues to be, the concern that
as India and Pakistan engage in a conventional arms race, it will lead to a nuclear
arms race, which, in turn, would increase the probability of a conventional war
escalating into a war with missiles and nuclear weapons. According to experts,
the region continues to be a major risk for nuclear weapons use because of two
reasons: (a) their growing arsenal, which includes nuclear weapons and various
delivery systems for them (submarines, fighter aircraft, ships, and missiles); and
(b) their long-standing and intense rivalry. The size and composition of their respective arsenals is monitored by several research groups, and the data are largely
undisputed.[1] It is the so-called unique characteristics of the India-Pakistan dyad
that are worthy of closer scrutiny. Nonproliferation experts believe that nuclear
weapons in the hands of these two states are particularly dangerous because (a)
these are contiguous states with aspirations for regional leadership; (b) both have
a long-standing dispute over territory; (c) they have fought several wars and continue to maintain large armies; and, finally, (d) neither is a member of the NPT
and, thus, neither accepts the moral taboo against the development and use of
nuclear weapons. These factors, accordingly, make them more likely to start
armed conflict and use nuclear weapons against each other.

However, a quick look at a parallel dyad within the extended region—China-
India—would show that neither of these characteristics is unique to the India-
Pakistan dyad. Through the Cold War, India and China too competed within
South and Southeast Asia for regional leadership, share a large border, and have a
much larger area under dispute. They fought a war in 1962 and maintained large
armies deployed in contiguous areas. Finally, China did not accept the NPT until

1992.[2] Yet rarely do experts see the likelihood of a nuclear war between India and China as anything but a remote possibility. The only unique factor in the India-Pakistan dyad might be the so-called religious divide: an Islamic Pakistan versus a Hindu India.[3] However, the same religious divide that would hypothetically cause a Hindu India to attack Pakistan might also work against an atheist China—which has not happened yet, and the possibility appears to be growing more remote in the coming decade.

An alternate way to assess the likelihood of war might be to look at the characteristics and behavior of the two countries in each dyad. In the case of India-Pakistan, each of the conventional wars until 1998 started with the attempt by the weaker party—Pakistan—to gain preemptive advantage by first using low-intensity conflict to secure disputed territory and, later, escalating it into a conventional conflict. By most accounts, after the 1980s, Pakistan used an implicit nuclear threat to warn India of major consequences if it attempted to use its conventional forces to deal with the subversive groups located on Pakistani territory. In contrast, the India-China border has rarely been considered "active" except for minor skirmishes over border posts. Although Chinese nuclear weapons have long been deployed in Tibet, and India has enjoyed a 2:1 conventional superiority on its border with China, nuclear weapons have never come into play in any such skirmishes. In other words, it is not the "objective" factors but the nature of the regimes composing the dyad that makes analysts more or less inclined to see the use of nuclear weapons as an active option. Pakistan's military and its civilian leaderships have always been more risk acceptant and willing to engage in nuclear brinkmanship than India's. This has been shown through the 1980s and the 1990s in Pakistan's policy of supporting insurgency and terrorism in India with the confidence that Pakistan would not have to face major consequences because India will refrain from starting a conventional war that has a high probability of escalating into nuclear war.[4]

After the 1998 tests, first by India and then by Pakistan, the bombs literally came out of the basement and entered the domestic public discourse on national security. Experts from both countries began discussions on how to secure them and how to manage their deployment through the establishment of a clear chain of command. Doctrines, deployment postures, and confidence-building measures (CBMs) to reduce the dangers of nuclear war began to be discussed as bilateral priorities. In February 1999, Indian prime minister Atal Bihari Vajpayee traveled to Lahore by bus, signaling a new beginning to the bilateral peace process. However, within a few weeks of this "historic" trip came reports of Pakistani infiltration across the Line of Control (LOC). The subsequent war between the two countries in and around the area called Kargil is now logged as the first conventional war between two nuclear-armed states since the advent of the NPT.

The Kargil war shattered the argument of nuclear optimists that possession of nuclear weapons makes states more cautious about starting conventional wars.[5]

The Indian and Pakistani armies had maintained their tradition of withdrawing from their most advanced positions in the mountains (along the LOC) during winters and returning to them in the spring. The two armies respected each other's deployment pattern and did not try to take advantage of this seasonal change.

> In the winter of 1999, however, Pakistani backed Kashmir militants and regular army units moved early into evacuated positions of the Indians, cheating on the tradition. The Pakistani backed forces thus gained a significant tactical advantage over the only ground supply route Indian forces can use to bring in supplies to the most remote eastern third of Kashmir. By advancing onto these mountaintops overlooking the Kargil highway, Pakistan was threatening to weaken Indian control over a significant (yet barren) part of the contested province.[6]

By June 1999, U.S. leadership was worried by the intelligence reports pointing toward the danger of full-scale war becoming a real possibility:

> The danger was that the Indians would grow weary of attacking uphill (actually up-mountain) into well dug in Pakistani positions. The casualties the Indian forces were taking were mounting. New Delhi could easily decide to open another front elsewhere along the LOC to ease its burden and force the Pakistanis to fight on territory favorable to India. . . . [By July 4th] there was more disturbing information about Pakistan preparing its nuclear arsenal for possible use.[7]

This forced the United States to demand that Pakistan withdraw to its original position at the LOC and agree to follow the Lahore peace process.[8]

Clearly, Pakistan's leadership—civilian and military—saw the utility of their new nuclear status as a shield for their subconventional forces engaged in "solving" the territorial dispute with India. Kargil also brought forth the disturbing knowledge that Pakistan actively considered use of nuclear weapons in support of its conventional forces. It also set forth a series of red lines—possible nonnuclear actions by India in response to actions by Pakistan and by Pakistan-supported substate groups—that would justify Pakistan's first use of nuclear weapons. This Pakistani doctrine of first use still exists despite a No-First-Use policy being adopted by India in 2000.

The Kargil war, which was stopped with the help of forceful diplomacy by the Clinton administration, led to a number of domestic changes within both India and Pakistan. General Musharraf came to power in October 1999 through a military coup that removed the democratically elected leader—Prime Minister Nawaz Sharif. There is widespread agreement in Pakistan that the coup that deposed Nawaz Sharif and brought General Musharraf to power was in a large degree the result of the prime minister's handling of the Kargil conflict.[9] According to the reviews of General Musharraf's 368-page autobiography, contrary to Pakistan's public declarations to the contrary, Pakistani soldiers, and not mujahideen or freedom fighters, were involved in the military operations during Kargil, and the Pakistan Army "established outposts to act as eyes and ears, and made raids and ambushes."[10] General Musharraf's own perception about this war is that the "bravery, steadfastness, and ultimate sacrifice of our men in that inhospitable, high altitude battlefield, against massive Indian forces will be written in golden letters," which led him to award soldiers of the Northern Light Infantry by converting them into a regular group of the Pakistani military: "They now exist as a proud segment of the army's 'queen of battle': the infantry."

In India, the coalition led by the right-wing nationalist Bharatiya Janata Party won a second term but also faced the reemergence of the rival Congress Party and its leader, Mrs. Sonia Gandhi.[11] "Indians perceived Kargil, which was planned even as the Lahore peace process was underway, as a betrayal by Pakistan; and ever since then they have hardened their posture over dialogue with Pakistan."[12] At the same time, "India has instituted various changes in its higher defense management, operational deployments in Kashmir, and nuclear command and control structure. The concept of limited war has become a buzzword of Indian strategic thinking, which also is the outcome of the Kargil conflict."[13] Public discourse and media coverage in the two countries during and immediately after the war shows the differences in the lessons each side learned from this experience.[14]

To this day, there are conflicting reports from Pakistani elite as to what really transpired during and after the Kargil war. According to Shireen M. Mazari, Prime Minister Nawaz Sharif was very much "in the loop" on Kargil. He had been thoroughly briefed by the chief of the army staff, General Pervez Musharraf. Moreover, the Kargil operation was necessary and legitimate from Pakistan's viewpoint, and it was not a military failure—it was botched up by Sharif's panicky visit with President Bill Clinton on July 4, 1999.[15] General Musharraf's autobiography confirms this account.

However, in his own memoirs, ousted prime minister Sharif asserts that he got to know about the "Kargil misadventure" from then Indian prime minister Atal Bihari Vajpayee when the latter telephoned him.[16] Sharif is quoted as saying in this book that Musharraf "literally begged" him to involve America (Bill Clinton) after twenty-seven hundred soldiers of the Pakistani Northern Light Infantry were killed during the Kargil operation. Accordingly, Sharif contacted then U.S. president Bill Clinton to seek his help to save the Pakistan army. Sharif contends that Musharraf moved nuclear warheads for use against India without his approval, and that he, despite being the prime minister of Pakistan, came to know about this only from Clinton.[17]

Whatever the truth behind the calculations and processes of the Pakistan army in planning and executing this war, it has since been followed by a series of good and bad events in the mercurial relationship between India and Pakistan. The lowest period followed a terrorist attack on the Indian Parliament in December 2001 and led to a serious breakup of diplomatic relations, the mobilization of Indian forces in Kashmir, and the end of any bilateral dialogue. Since May 2003, however, the peace dialogue has begun again and continues despite occasional setbacks.[18] The process has even been able to ignore the terrorist attacks in India and the changing domestic scenarios in Pakistan.[19]

Several reasons have prompted each side to keep the bilateral dialogue inured from the exigencies of changing events. In Pakistan, General Musharraf is facing growing opposition from political parties regarding his plan to manipulate the legislature into anointing him president for yet another term. The civil society networks and the political parties have mobilized to denounce his removal of the chief justice of Pakistan's Supreme Court. In the province of Baluchistan, the assassination of a Baloch leader in 2006 has intensified an insurgency aimed at garnering more political and economic resources for Balochis from the regional industrial projects supported and financed by China. The pro-Taliban tribal leaders in the North West Frontier Province oppose any operations by the Pakistan army to capture terrorists who have been inflicting casualties on the European forces operating across the border in Afghanistan. International pressure on the General and his regime has increased with demands that Pakistan take active and visible steps to fight Islamic terrorists and their supporters within Pakistan. The U.S. Congress has now made further economic and military aid to Pakistan conditional on positive and periodic reports on Pakistan's contributions to fight terrorism in the region.

In India, Prime Minister Singh's administration is facing domestic opposition to the U.S.-India nuclear deal, and the international community, led by the United States, is pressing India to sustain the bilateral peace process in visible and concrete ways. Moreover, the pro-economic reform lobby in the ruling coalition favors a mutually acceptable resolution to the Kashmir dispute in the long term and a deflection of national and international attention away from the bilateral dispute in the short term. Indian focus currently is on opening up more people-to-people links and an increase in bilateral trade—although a final resolution of Kashmir is seen as being a few years away. Meanwhile, the continuous Indian dialogue with Pakistan also seeks to diminish the confidence of the pro-independence groups in Kashmir: these groups are now divided between those who seek a separate place at the bilateral table, those who want Pakistan not to compromise the struggle of Kashmiris by responding to Indian overtures, and those who are disillusioned with both countries and denounce the peace process as a sham. The current violence is most likely a product of the militant supporters of the latter two groups: they seek to scare the pro-dialogue constituencies or to disrupt the process entirely by inciting adverse nationalist public opinion. They have not succeeded thus far.

II. Horizontal Proliferation: The A. Q. Khan Network

International concern about horizontal proliferation from India and Pakistan is of relatively recent origin. As discussed earlier, the traditional focus was on stopping technologies and materials from going to these countries. Few experts considered the possibility that these countries might have something (other than complete nuclear weapons themselves) that might be of interest to proliferators.[20] The episodic outreach of the Nuclear Suppliers Group (NSG) and the Missile Technology Control Regime (MTCR) to South Asia throughout the 1990s attempted to convince the two countries to abide by their guidelines regarding nonexports of nuclear and missile technology as a way to induce them to undertake non-NPT obligations. These efforts became more pronounced after the 1998 nuclear tests, when these export control obligations were enshrined into the "benchmarks" that India and Pakistan had to accept in order to show their good faith regarding their pronouncements on nonproliferation.[21] While the other benchmarks lay forgotten or mired in domestic controversy, both countries asserted their intention to abide by the export control benchmarks and, indeed, engaged in sustained bilateral dialogue with the United States on these issues.

However, the discovery of the proliferation network being masterminded from Pakistan by Dr. A. Q. Khan shook the foundations of the common international assumptions about what might or might not be considered tradable by Pakistan. Dr. Khan had long been on the radar of the international nonproliferation community as the architect of Pakistan's enrichment program. He was implicated in the first publicized case of intangible technology transfer—from Dutch consortium Urenco in the 1980s—when he fled to Pakistan with blueprints, designs, and other technical information regarding this centrifuge facility.[22] Despite this case, Dr. Khan traveled freely through Europe and maintained contacts with technical experts spread across several countries such as Germany, Switzerland, and the Netherlands.[23] Reportedly, even after his flight to Pakistan, he continued to use the same network of subcomponent and materials suppliers that had been supplying to Urenco. In 2002, the *Wall Street Journal* quoted unnamed "senior Pakistani government officials" as conceding that Dr. A. Q. Khan's dismissal from Khan Research Lab had been prompted by the U.S. government's suspicions of his involvement in nuclear weapons technology transfers with North Korea. But this removal was followed by his appointment as the special science and technology adviser to the president of Pakistan with a ministerial rank—a position he held until he was implicated in proliferation activities along with his fellow scientists. He offered a televised public confession to President Musharraf and was granted a pardon by the national legislature the next day.[24] He has since been put under house arrest in Islamabad and only the Pakistan government (GoPak) has access to him.[25] Questions raised by the International Atomic Energy Agency (IAEA) and U.S. investigations into the network's activities are now relayed to him through GoPak, and his answers are conveyed to the outsiders after expunging information that might compromise Pakistan's defense and security. Concerns, however, remain about many of his unexplained activities:

> A. Q. KHAN, the Pakistani metallurgist, is known to have peddled nuclear secrets to Iran, North Korea, and Libya. What is not known—at least by U.S. intelligence—is what he did on visits to Afghanistan, Egypt, Ivory Coast, Kazakhstan, Kenya, Mali, Mauritania, Morocco, Niger, Nigeria, Saudi Arabia, Senegal, Sudan, Syria, Tunisia, and the United Arab Emirates.[26]

Although the European members of the multilateral export control regimes continued to monitor Dr. Khan's travels and activities in Europe throughout the 1990s, none acted to stop these until after his public confession. Several explanations have been proffered in the European press for this lapse.[27] First, under European law, exports are considered a right of the citizens and not a privilege. Governments cannot curtail export-related activities of its citizens without a rationale that can hold up in the courts. The evidentiary bar for proving wrongdoing by a citizen is therefore much higher than in the United States, where courts tend to rule in favor of the government.[28] Since the European governments could not find "enough" evidence to prosecute Khan or their own citizens who worked with him, they did not try. Another explanation is that most of these governments assumed that Dr. Khan was procuring items and expertise for Pakistan's national program—which was a known danger—and unless it was something really serious, they might have decided that such activities might allow them to gather intelligence about the state of the Pakistani program. Another explanation is that Pakistan was seen as an ally during the Cold War and continued to be useful for U.S. interests; therefore, ignoring these "Pakistani" activities was not a big deal and, in some cases, may have been a favor to the United States. They did not know when Khan morphed from being a procurer for Pakistan into a seller to, and broker between, third countries.

Whatever the major explanations for inaction, the revelation of the Khan network has renewed concerns throughout Europe and the United States that secondary proliferation—sales and transfers of controlled technologies by new suppliers that are not members of the multilateral regimes—will be a major challenge to the efficacy of the regimes. Indeed, as a 2007 report produced by the International Institute for Strategic Studies concludes, the Khan network itself has continued to operate in a morphed form even after the neutralization of Dr. Khan himself.[29]

The Pakistan government denied any involvement in authorizing Khan's activities and has since projected him as a "lone ranger" and a money-hungry megalomaniac who exploited his privileged position in the Pakistani establishment for his narrow and misguided personal aims. As there is no way to cross-question Dr. Khan to affirm or deny this GoPak claim, several explanations and speculations have been offered to explain how he could operate this independent network while evading Pakistani security and military establishment. The primary scenario being offered is that Dr. Khan had a unique position within the Pakistani establishment—nuclear and defense. For over two decades he had been given complete discretion over vast amounts of funds and the institutional autonomy to do *whatever it took* to give Pakistan its nuclear deterrent against India. His success in establishing and running the centrifuge program and in developing the missile capability of Pakistan had earned him highest national accolades and the public status as the Father of the Pakistani nuclear and missile program. As such, few could question or curtail his activities.[30] Moreover, until September 2004, GoPak departments and agencies of the armed forces were exempt from the requirements of the Pakistani export control law.[31] Thus, when Dr. Khan transferred the Chinese-origin nuclear weapons design to Libya, or the P-1 and P-2 centrifuges and centrifuge designs to Iran, or possibly enrichment technology to North Korea, he did not violate Pakistan's export controls per se—although he probably did violate the Official Secrets Act and the material protection, control, and accounting system of Pakistan.[32]

Those who are skeptical about the total ignorance of GoPak regarding Khan's activities point toward the contradictory evidence. First, the nuclear weapons program and related assets have been under the complete control of the Pakistan military almost since inception. As befits a professional national security organization, one would expect that the military had established multiple layers of security around these national assets. Moreover, Dr. Khan had been under the security cordon of GoPak intelligence services for decades—because of his own status as a national asset and the threats to his well-being from Pakistan's enemies. As such it would have been extremely difficult for him to keep his unauthorized activities—such as trips to Europe, Asia, and Africa, and contacts with foreign nationals—secret from the military and the intelligence services.

Another disputed aspect of this episode relates to the motivations of Khan, his associates, and his "bosses" in Pakistan. For several months before his arrest,

Dr. Khan had been giving public statements about his service to the nation as a patriot, noting that he had never done anything without permission of the national leadership.[33] He had even named a few ex-generals—including General Musharraf—as having authorized activities that they and he believed would promote Pakistan's national interest.[34] He was also quite vocal about his ideological commitment to strengthening fellow Islamic states by sharing defense technologies. He was one of the earliest public proponents of the idea that the Pakistani bomb was an Islamic bomb—meant to counter what he saw as the Christian, Jewish, and Hindu bombs.[35] This ideology was shared by many military generals and nuclear scientists who envisioned Pakistan as a modern, technologically advanced leader of the Islamic world.[36] Few people within Pakistan—outside of GoPak—believe either that Khan worked alone or did it all solely for money. The United States and other countries have given the Pakistan government the benefit of the doubt partly because it would encourage positive changes in the relevant Pakistani laws and institutions governing transfers of WMD technologies. The other reasons are strategic: Pakistan is an ally in the war on terror, rounding up al Qaeda and Taliban members in Pakistan and Afghanistan, and it has total control over access to Dr. Khan. Without GoPak support, U.S. and International Security Assistance Force (ISAF) efforts would not succeed in countering Islamic terrorists, nor would the international community have any means of getting even limited answers from Dr. Khan to help its ongoing investigations into his network's past activities.

After the international furor over the revelations of Khan's alleged activities, Pakistan established a new export control law, which closes the loopholes of the earlier law—no exemptions and clearly defined, strict penalties for violations.[37] The system of control over nuclear assets has also been strengthened—to ensure clarity in the chain of command and more focus on export control issues by the armed forces who control all the facilities engaged in research and development (R&D) and production of WMD-relevant technology in Pakistan. The GoPak has also become more responsive to U.S. and international overtures regarding dialogue and engagement on export control issues.[38] However, as of 2007, there was little to no information available on the implementing regulations for the 2004 law. Nor was there information on the division of responsibilities to clarify the process and procedures for issues such as licensing, outreach to government-owned or private entities with dual-use capabilities, and corresponding changes to the powers of enforcement agencies such as customs, border guards, armed forces, and so forth.

In India, the Khan case did not come as a surprise. Indian experts had long suspected the transfer of technology between Pakistan and some of the Islamic states (primarily Libya, Iraq, and Saudi Arabia) that had provided financial support to Pakistan's nuclear and missile programs in the 1970s and 1980s.[39] India it-self had been contacted by some of the same states during the Cold War—with offers of financial support in return for access to India's nuclear weapons ca-pabilities. The Indian government felt vindicated and hoped that this episode would—once and for all—sever the India-Pakistan linkage in the traditional in-ternational view: the Indian record of not proliferating to other states would dif-ferentiate it clearly from Pakistan—the irresponsible and risk-acceptant constitu-ent of the generic "South Asia" or India-Pakistan dyad. However, armed with the notional certainty that "what happens in Pakistan must happen in India," the international nonproliferation community increased its pressure on India to do more on export controls.[40] Some Indian experts responded by highlighting the differences in the institutional context within which Indian and Pakistani WMD programs operate.[41] Unlike Pakistan, Indian programs have always been under the control of the civilian leadership. Moreover, because they are slow and bureaucratic, the Indian programs did not concentrate power within one per-son or one agency. They worked on the basis of standard operating procedures, which required multiple clearances and checks before any activities could be authorized. However, these experts recommended that India not become com-placent but instead upgrade some of its procedures to ensure that it closed any loopholes that the Khan episode uncovered. Other Indian experts took an oppos-ing path and warned the government against trying to please the international community, which they saw as irrevocably biased against India. They noted the unseemly haste with which GoPak's version of the Khan network was accepted by the leaders of the nonproliferation community and the deafening silence that greeted Libya's revelation that it had acquired a tested *Chinese* weapons design from Khan. For the past few years, the Indian government has been trying to follow a middle path between these two positions when responding to interna-tional calls for upgrading its export control system. India, however, passed a com-prehensive export control law in 2005, established implementing regulations in 2006, and harmonized its control list with those of the NSG and the MTCR by July 2006.[42] It has also maintained a sustained dialogue and exchange with the United States on export controls and has been sharing information on its processes and procedures with government and nongovernment entities around the world.

The Khan case strengthened the international demand that states criminal-ize all unauthorized WMD-relevant activities of their citizens. The UN Security Council (UNSC) Resolution 1540 (2004) was a direct product of this demand.[43] Both India and Pakistan took advantage of this resolution and justified their ex-port control initiatives at home as fulfilling its universal mandate rather than as a response to pressure by particular countries. Both have shared compliance information with the 1540 committee, which has provided a useful transparency measure vis-à-vis each other as well as third parties.[44]

III. A Case of Exceptionalism: The U.S.-India Nuclear Deal

The United States and India have had a strange relationship, especially since the 1970s. Leaders from both sides have sought to portray their own countries as an example to the rest of the world and as exceptions to the rule. Both take pride in being democracies and multiethnic, multilingual, secular states. Just as the United States saw pre–WWII European wars as unrelated and detrimental to U.S. economic interests, India saw the Cold War as a preoccupation of the advanced industrialized countries of the East and the West. For developing countries like India, there was no reason to pick sides—they needed help in economic development and wanted it from all states. Although this perception was similar to the early twentieth-century U.S. view of remaining disengaged from other countries' wars, the resulting Indian commitment to the Nonaligned Movement became a bone of contention between the two countries. This problem was further exacerbated after India's refusal to sign the NPT as a nonnuclear weapon state and because of its repeated calls for universal nuclear disarmament.

The mainstream view of U.S.-India relations from the 1970s is focused around a simple narrative. India refused to sign the NPT, signed a treaty of Peace and Friendship with the USSR in 1970, detonated a device in 1974, and continued to keep its indigenously produced nuclear facilities out of the IAEA safeguards. The United States was forced to be suspicious of India's nuclear intentions. It had to devise institutions like the NSG to ensure that India and other developing states refrained from proliferation. At the same time, the United States had to support the weaker but avowedly anticommunist Pakistan—which was also a valuable conduit for establishing relations with China.[45] The supply of U.S. advanced conventional weapons and other military aid to Pakistan was intended to assuage its insecurity against a bigger and more aggressive India, to ensure its support against the forces of communism in the region, and to provide it a disincentive for developing its own nuclear deterrent. The actual record is a bit more complicated.

The United States and India maintained a steady stream of cooperation in the field of civilian science and technology throughout this period, although there were no conventional arms transfers. India's 1974 test did not come as an earth-shattering surprise—most U.S. intelligence reports had suggested that with a little help or determination, India could have exploded a weapon in the 1960s—immediately before or after the Chinese tests of 1964. The Tarapur nuclear power plant, the focus of much controversy in the 1980s, did get its fuel from alternate suppliers (France, USSR, and China) with the active consent of the United States. The spent fuel at Tarapur was supposed to be shipped back to the United States—but U.S. environmental concerns have precluded it to this day. The fuel now remains under IAEA safeguards, although the bilateral U.S.-India agreement, the original reason for the safeguards, expired in 1993. In 1974, Henry Kissinger developed the idea of a multilateral regime of nuclear suppliers to ensure that unilateral U.S. denials of technology were not undercut by others and to bring in France—a non-NPT supplier—within the ambit of such multi-lateral obligations. Kissinger believed that India was already past the threshold of controls and would inevitably follow the path of other NWS. Thus, it needed to be co-opted rather than sanctioned. Accordingly, India was offered the chance to become part of the NSG—and it declined. Interestingly, the U.S.-India Business Council was set up the same year to establish a business-to-business channel of communication with a country that was not amenable to U.S. propositions in bilateral political communications.

India, for its part, saw its own nuclear behavior as above reproach in that it was keeping its nuclear weapons option open and building its nuclear R&D capacity while waiting for the Article VI promises of the NPT to be honored by the sig-natories.[46] It remained unmoved by the U.S. proposition that it should prove its nonproliferation credentials by unilaterally adhering to NSG and MTCR guide-lines as a nonmember. Indian negotiators asserted that their record and policy on horizontal nonproliferation was better than many members of these regimes, and that they saw no reason to pledge allegiance to the regimes that continued to target India for technology denials. This "uncooperative" stance undoubtedly caused a severe hardening of U.S. nonproliferation policy vis-à-vis India. Indeed, looking at most of the unilateral U.S. technology denials to India during the Bush (senior) and Clinton administrations, it seems clear that catch-all controls were being used for punitive rather than technical/nonproliferation reasons.

There were periodic affirmations of U.S. nonproliferation objectives in South Asia, including the goal of making India and Pakistan sign the NPT. But by the early 1990s, this goal was seen as unrealistic. Indeed, the CTBT was promoted as an alternate means of affecting disarmament in the region. The Chemical Weapons Convention (CWC) was readily accepted by the two South Asian countries—giving further confidence to the U.S. nonproliferation community. However, by the time it became a treaty and was taken out of the CD and into the UN General Assembly—over India's objections—there was little hope that India would sign it. The Clinton administration, however, introduced the Entry into Force clause—confident that it would be successful in bending India to the international will. Some Indian experts have argued that the Indian decision to conduct nuclear tests was a direct result of these pressure tactics.

The initial U.S. reaction to the 1998 Indian tests was strongly negative. Over two hundred Indian entities were targeted for technology denials and sanctions. All ongoing science and technology cooperation projects were put on hold. India did not seem to be as affected by the sanctions as the nonproliferation community had hoped. However, when the same sanctions were applied against Pakistan, within a few months it was clear that significant U.S. constituencies would be adversely affected by these sanctions, and that Pakistan appeared to be on the brink of becoming a failed state. Accordingly, the Clinton administration and the Congress began the process of waiving sanctions against both countries. The dialogue with India resumed in earnest as U.S. policymakers attempted to understand the extent of India's determination to develop a "credible minimum deterrent" and to assess where external pressure would be effective in limiting this determination. The Talbott-Singh talks achieved the first U.S. objective but—according to Talbott—failed in the second.[47]

The Kargil war of 1999 became one of the first turning points in U.S.-India strategic relations. Indian officials were pleasantly surprised when the Clinton administration criticized Pakistan for provoking this crisis and demanded unconditional withdrawal of Pakistani forces to their original positions across the LOC. It gave confidence to many pro-U.S. constituencies in India that the United States had indeed shed its Cold War baggage and was willing to engage each country (India and Pakistan) on its merits. This was further bolstered by Clinton's visit to India—the first by a U.S. president since Jimmy Carter in the 1970s.

Nonproliferation, however, continued to be a major point of contention between the two countries until the end of the Clinton administration.[48] By this time, business-to-business links had grown much stronger, and U.S. industry, beyond the information technology (IT) sector, was looking at India as both a market and as a venue for technology-embedded manufacturing for the global market. Comparisons with China on fundamental and long-term economic strengths began to show India in equally favorable if not more favorable light. Influential Republicans began to perceive India as a useful counterweight to China in Asia—in both the economic and security spheres. Accordingly, when George W. Bush became the president, his administration turned the nonproliferation debate regarding India on its head. It saw India as being a part of the solution rather than a problem. The Bush administration argued for a strategic partnership with India based on some clear markers of the inevitable future: India's determination to develop its civilian nuclear sector for its growing energy needs, its growing defense procurement budget, and its burgeoning capacity to become an alternate supplier of WMD-relevant technologies. With or without U.S. intervention, India was set to move on these tracks, and it would be in U.S. interest to co-opt rather than sanction India. What helped to popularize this new formulation in the United States was India's excellent record at preventing horizontal proliferation, its democratic government, the national consensus to continue economic liberalization and pursue poverty reduction, and its desire to diversify its foreign partnerships beyond Russia.[49] The lobbying by U.S. businesses and Indian Americans helped in convincing the strategic community that thirty years of sanctions had not worked, that India's nuclear and missile programs were now more insulated from international sanctions, and that it really did not make good strategic sense to trade in dual-use items with a communist China but ignore an equally large and democratic India.

The results of these efforts bore fruit in the shape of a series of bilateral agreements and dialogue processes such as the High-Technology Cooperation Group, the Next Steps in Strategic Partnership, and the Framework Agreement for Defense Cooperation. The July 2005 U.S.-India agreement between President Bush and Prime Minister Singh was a culmination of the limited agreements that preceded it. In essence, this revolutionary agreement expanded and formalized an Indian offer to "island" its weapons facilities and open some of its civilian nuclear facilities to international safeguards, in return for access to foreign nuclear fuel and reactor-related technologies for generating energy.[50]

Critics of the agreement point to a few major flaws in the U.S. reasoning that undergirded this "deal." First, it overturns decades of U.S. and international policy of denying civilian nuclear cooperation to countries that seek to develop nuclear weapons and do not abide by the NPT. It sets a precedent for other NPT and non-NPT states to demand similar treatment from the supplier states. Second, it delegitimizes and undercuts international efforts to stop nuclear weapons development by countries such as North Korea and Iran. Moreover, it would encourage these and other countries to develop nuclear weapons to overcome their security concerns and decide to weather any international sanctions as temporary inconveniences. Third, the deal assumes that India will now change its foreign policy priorities: it will eschew its relations with Iran, support international nonproliferation sanctions against that country, and enter into a strategic alliance with the United States against China. Fourth, the deal will not bring any significant nonproliferation benefits to the international community. India will keep its weapons program intact, and its Fast Breeder Reactor will remain outside the IAEA safeguards. Since India has already been restrained about horizontal proliferation, there is no reason to offer it any incentives for continuing its policy of restraint. Moreover, the access to foreign nuclear fuel will help India divert its own limited uranium resources to build an even larger arsenal. Fifth, if the United States will treat India as an exception, other countries, notably China, might ask for a similar exception for their own friends, for example, Pakistan. Finally, the appearance of a strategic alliance between India and the United States would make both China and Pakistan insecure and force them to cooperate closely on nuclear issues. In short, the nuclear deal will severely weaken the nonproliferation regime because it allows India to be treated as an exception.

However, most of these criticisms can be easily countered.[51] First, the NPT is a weak treaty for today's world. Its weaknesses have been exacerbated over the years as much by technological developments as by its signatories. Almost all of its "rules" have been broken under one exception or another.[52] The most serious problem for the NPT is the fact that none of the eight NWS today pay anything more than lip service to it: there are no plans in place to fulfill disarmament commitments (Article VI) and although the purists feel morally satisfied in distinguishing between the "legitimate" and "nonlegitimate" NWS based on fixed NPT criterion, in operational terms it makes little difference to the insecurity of their neighboring states. Worse, this distinction ensures that after failing at controls on vertical proliferation, the NPT has no way to curb any horizontal proliferation by these outsiders. Second, states do not develop nuclear weapons by contagion from far-away developments. The list of states seeking nuclear capabilities has not varied very much since the 1960s. And those that had given up their quest did so under the force of external incentives (the U.S. nuclear umbrella) or domestic changes (regimes with vastly different perspectives on national security). I would argue that hitherto quiescent states will begin to seek nuclear capability because of changes in the above two factors and not because of what India might or might not be doing.[53]

Third, a complete break in India's relations with Iran is indeed unlikely: India would not turn away from one of its energy suppliers and a long-term supporter in the Islamic world—especially when the U.S.-Pakistan relationship continues to provide succor and cover to the military junta in Pakistan—to downplay its support to anti-India terror groups and its proven proliferation record. India has already recalibrated its position regarding the Iranian nuclear program and voted with the United States twice in the IAEA. But it is more likely to respond to growing Israeli security concerns rather than punitive U.S. policies when it further delimits its links with Iran. Fourth, Indian restraint regarding proliferation has been a result of political decisions across the policy strata. But these strata are now populated by a more pragmatic and assertive generation of politicians and bureaucrats who routinely compare international treatment of known proliferators in the Indian neighborhood (China and Pakistan) and question the need for Indian restraint. Taking this restraint as a given for the foreseeable future would not be prudent. Besides, India already has enough uranium reserves to build an arsenal several times larger than what it currently has—without significant downgrading of its energy ambitions in the next two decades.[54] Its slow-paced buildup has not been because of a lack of domestic resources, but rather a political decision to have a "credible minimum deterrent"—not unlike the Chinese decision for a limited but adequate nuclear arsenal that allows assured second strike. Finally, what most critics seem to forget is that the U.S.-India deal came about almost one year after the China-Pakistan nuclear agreement—which was signed just a few weeks before China joined the NSG. Under this agreement, China will build several nuclear power plants in Pakistan—under IAEA safeguards—but without any of the other requirements and commitments that the United States has placed on India. In any case, the China-Pakistan nuclear and missile link is far older as well as far more opaque and questionable in terms of contributing to proliferation. One could argue that the Bush administration saw the China-Pakistan deal as unstoppable and responded by forging its own linkage with a more transparent and responsible partner.

The India deal, therefore, brought the United States up to speed on vying for new markets and new partners in Asia—and sought to even out the growing asymmetry with its strategic competitor, China.[55] India had already become an exception in the nonproliferation regime: it was treated as a pariah despite having a democratic political system, a good record on horizontal proliferation, the largest civilian nuclear sector outside the NPT, and the fifth largest economy. The U.S.-India deal provides a way for the international nonproliferation community to tap into its institutional, diplomatic, and technological strengths; to shore up its procedural weaknesses that might lead to proliferation; and to cool the domestic ardor for vertical proliferation.

Conclusion

South Asia will continue to present normative and structural challenges to the nonproliferation regime in the coming years. The major challenges that the nonproliferation regime will face include challenges to its legitimacy and to its efficacy. The legitimacy issues derive from Article VI issues of the NPT and the fact that the NSG and MTCR remain self-selected groups of nuclear and missile suppliers. Now, the existence of four non-NPT states—all of them with nuclear weapons capability—presents a problem for the regime to explain the practical difference between NPT-sanctioned NWS and these other NWS. The prospect of nuclear proliferation networks operating with the help of a mix of state and nonstate entities also challenges the state-focused approach of the NPT. On the efficacy side, the IAEA Additional Protocol (AP), the NSG, and UNSC Resolution 1540 have attempted to close some of the major gaps in the NPT-centric regime and those stemming from the lack of a treaty to control missile proliferation. Yet technological developments and spread of weapons know-how continues unabated, with no international consensus on whether the existing mechanisms will stem the proliferation of tomorrow.

The black-and-white criterion of good guys and bad guys is no longer tenable when identifying proliferation activities and potential. Nowhere is this starker than in South Asia. If the nonproliferation regime seeks to deny technology to al Qaeda and the Taliban operating in Pakistan and Afghanistan, it has to perforce rely on the government of Pakistan to ensure success. The Pakistan government has to develop the commitment and ability to (a) secure its arsenal and facilities from sabotage and insider threats; (b) induce its scientists and military to put nonproliferation as a higher priority than support to fellow Islamists; and (c) increase its vigilance and action against groups that might seek to deal a mortal blow to India by attacking its nuclear facilities. All of this commitment would require that the nonproliferation regime be willing to offer something to the Pakistan government in return. It has traditionally fallen on the United States to craft a side payment to support such endeavors—and it has had to overlook some Pakistani transgressions as a result—which, in turn, sets another bad precedent in terms of nonproliferation purity.

Similarly, if we want India to strengthen the nonproliferation regime, it will have to commit resources to (a) regulate and monitor its fast-growing dual-use industry; (b) enforce regulations that limit its exports and diplomatic relations with some countries on whom it depends; and (c) continue to weather domestic criticisms for ceding control over a large part of its nuclear establishment to the international community. The price for this vigilance on India's part would be greater technology-embedded partnerships with supplier states, which, in turn, would enhance its technical capacity as an alternate supplier of dual-use technologies around the world.

Beyond this, there is little to no likelihood that either India or Pakistan will join the NPT in the near future. And any amendment to the NPT structure that would allow the formation of a third category of states—nuclear capable states rather than NWS—is equally unlikely. Any cooperation with India and Pakistan, in the meantime, would inevitably have the effect of "legitimizing" their nuclear pursuits—again affecting the purity of the nonproliferation principles. The one possible alternative of partially justifying cooperation but allowing India and Pakistan to remain outside the NPT would be to induce them to adopt multilaterally developed guidelines (AP, NSG) and voluntary compliance with international industrial best practices regarding the management of strategic trade. India has already adopted many of these guidelines as part of its agreement with the United States.

Pakistan has so far linked all its potential decisions on joining old and new nonproliferation initiatives to the decisions made by India. Therefore, we can begin by examining the possibility of Indian participation in the CTBT and the proposed fissile material cut-off treaty (FMCT). However, given the growing power disparity between Pakistan and India, it would be interesting to see if Pakistan will actually follow suit if India agrees to some nonproliferation measure.

One of the major issues in the U.S.-India deal is India's insistence that it too—like the United States—will remain outside the CTBT but continue to abide by the voluntary moratorium on testing. It is also hinting that it will reserve the right to test if other countries break their own moratoria. On the FMCT, the Indian position has been closer to that of the United States in the CD: both see the treaty as primarily an agreement to cut-off further increments to the fissile stockpile and production rather than to destroy existing stockpiles. As the domestic politics in the United States undergoes "regime change" there may be greater support for negotiating a verifiable ban on fissile materials production, and it would certainly put greater pressure on India and Pakistan to fashion defensible responses to such internationally popular proposals.

In sum, the state of proliferation today highlights trends not foreseen by the nonproliferation regime. The normative and practical challenges represented by nuclear and missile proliferation in South Asia necessitates innovative approaches aimed at eliciting cooperation from *all* countries—sometimes including the problem countries themselves. While statesmen debate how to overhaul the regime, government officials around the world are attempting to forge limited consensus on implementation and enforcement practices. Such attempts, although piecemeal and confined to "coalitions of the willing," nevertheless suggest the way the regime will have to be maintained and sustained in the near future.

Notes

1. See, for instance, the nuclear notebooks published by the *Bulletin of the Atomic Scientists* and compilations by SIPRI (Stockholm). For 2007 data on Pakistan, see http://thebulletin .metapress.com/content/k4q43h2104032426/fulltext.pdf, and for India, see http://www.sipri .org/contents/expcon/India.pdf.

2. China's entry into the NPT in 1992 has not significantly changed the parameters of its declared no-first-use (NFU) policy. China reserves the right to use (introduce) nuclear weapons to defend its territorial integrity. In essence, the NFU would not stop China from using nuclear weapons against India to defend the (disputed) territory that both countries claim.

3. Technically though, Pakistan has a Muslim majority and is an avowedly Islamic state, whereas India has a Hindu majority but the state is secular.

4. This is usually explained in terms of Glenn Snyder's stability-instability paradox that has characterized South Asia from the mid-1980s until now. See Glenn H. Snyder, "The

Balance of Power and the Balance of Terror," in *The Balance of Power*, ed. Paul Seabury (San Francisco: Chandler, 1965), 198–99. For a discussion on how this has operated in South Asia, see S. Paul Kapur, "India and Pakistan's Unstable Peace: Why Nuclear South Asia Is Not Like Cold War Europe," *International Security* 30, no. 2 (Fall 2005): 127–52.

5. Although one can argue that the two countries have possessed nuclear weapons since before the 1998 tests. These tests were merely a means to formally announce their intent and status to the world.

6. Bruce Riedel, *American Diplomacy and the 1999 Kargil Summit at Blair House*, Center for the Advanced Study of India Policy Paper, 2002, http://www.ccc.nps.navy.mil/research/kargil/reidel.pdf.

7. Ibid.

8. For a timeline of events in this conflict, see the Center for Contemporary Conflict, Naval Postgraduate School, Department of National Security Affairs, http://www.ccc.nps.navy.mil/research/kargil/important_events.pdf.

9. Sharif himself feared such a fate even before his July 4, 1999, meeting with Clinton and later after the cessation of hostilities. See Riedel, *American Diplomacy*.

10. "Musharraf vs. Sharif: Who's Lying?" *Weekly Voice*, October 2, 2006, http://www.weeklyvoice.com/site/index.php?option=com_content&task=view&id=1443&Itemid=66; Pervez Musharraf, *In the Line of Fire: A Memoir* (New York: Simon and Schuster, 2006).

11. The Bharatiya Janata Party's A. B. Vajpayee was the first Indian prime minister since 1971 to win a second consecutive term in office. In 1999, Mrs. Sonia Gandhi—Italian-born widow of assassinated prime minister Rajiv Gandhi—emerged as a major force in Indian politics. She won her first race for a parliament seat in that year.

12. Rajesh Basrur, quoted in Center for Contemporary Conflict, "Asymmetric Conflict in South Asia: The Cause and Consequences of the 1999 Limited War in Kargil," conference report, Monterey, CA, May 29–June 1, 2002, http://www.ccc.nps.navy.mil/events/recent/may02Kargil_rpt.asp.

13. Ibid.

14. See Ashley J. Tellis, C. Christine Fair, and Jamison Jo Medby, *Limited Conflicts under the Nuclear Umbrella: Indian and Pakistani Lessons from the Kargil Crisis* (Santa Monica, CA: RAND, 2001).

15. Shireen M. Mazari, *The Kargil Conflict 1999: Separating Fact from Fiction* (Islamabad, Pakistan: Institute of Strategic Studies, 2003).

16. The memoirs (*Ghadaar Kaun? Nawaz Sharif Ki Kahani, Unki Zubani* [*The Traitor Within: Nawaz Sharif's Story in His Own Words*]) were originally written in Urdu by senior Pakistani journalist Suhail Warraich and published in the summer of 2006.

17. "Musharraf vs. Sharif: Who's Lying?"

18. For an excellent recap of this process since 1988, see the South Asia Confidence Building Measures (CBM) Timeline at http://www.stimson.org/southasia/?SN=SA20060207948.

19. Samrat Sinha, *Major Terrorist Attacks in India 2000–2006*, IPCS special report 27, July 2006, http://www.ipcs.org/IPCS-Special-Report-27.pdf; Paula Newberg, "Pakistan: The Eye of a Coming Storm?" *YaleGlobal*, February 28, 2007, http://yaleglobal.yale.edu/display.article?id=8838.

20. Experts believed that these countries developed nuclear weapons because of their quest for prestige, national security and nationalist ideology—these logics would not allow them to share/transfer/export these weapons to third countries. Moreover, the common assumption was that these countries would not like to prop up competitors and/or would not dare to incur the wrath of the international community by doing so.

21. Strobe Talbott, *Engaging India: Diplomacy, Democracy, and the Bomb* (Washington, DC: Brookings Institution Press, 2004), 268.

22. David Albright and Corey Hinderstein, "Unraveling the A. Q. Khan and Future Proliferation Networks," *Washington Quarterly* 28, no. 2 (Spring 2005): 111–28; David Albright and Corey Hinderstein, *Documents Indicate A. Q. Khan Offered Nuclear Weapon Designs to Iraq in 1990: Did He Approach Other Countries?* Institute for Science and International Security, February 4, 2004, http://www.isis-online.org/publications/southasia/khan_memo.html.

23. For the Dutch connection, see Aaron Gray-Block, "The Dutch Role in Shady Nuclear Deals," Expatica, February 20, 2004, http://www.expatica.com/actual/article.asp?subchannel_id=1&story_id=4878

24. Seymour Hersh, "The Deal," *New Yorker*, March 8, 2004, 32–37, http://www.newyorker.com/archive/2004/03/08/040308fa_fact.

25. Declan Walsh, "'Dr Khan Isn't Taking Calls Today': Disgraced Father of Pakistan's Nuclear Arsenal Is Kept under Guard after Selling Secrets Abroad," *Guardian* (London), November 20, 2004.

26. "Pakistan's Secrets," editorial, *Boston Globe*, December 30, 2004, http://www.boston.com/news/globe/editorial_opinion/editorials/articles/2004/12/30/pakistans_secrets?mode=PF.

27. Craig S. Smith, "Roots of Pakistan Atomic Scandal Traced to Europe", *New York Times*, February 19, 2004, A3. See also ANP (Netherlands National News Agency), "CIA Asked Us to Let Nuclear Spy Go, Ruud Lubbers Claims," August 9, 2005, http://www.expatica.com/actual/article.asp?subchannel_id=1&story_id=22629. For a more systematic examination of the results of European investigations after Khan's confession, see Kenley Butler, Sammy Salama, and Leonard S. Spector, "Where's the Justice?" *Bulletin of Atomic Scientists* 62, no. 6 (November/December 2006): 25–34, 62–63, and Mark Hibbs, "The Unmaking of a Nuclear Smuggler," *Bulletin of the Atomic Scientists* 62, no. 6 (November/December 2006): 35–41, 63.

28. In the U.S. system, the underlying assumption is that exports are a privilege granted to citizens by the state and can be curtailed based on national security concerns.

29. Mark Fitzpatrick, ed., *Nuclear Black Markets: Pakistan, A. Q. Khan and the Rise of Proliferation Networks* (London: International Institute for Strategic Studies, 2007), 103–5, 117, 167.

30. See, for instance, Chris Clary, "Dr. Khan's Nuclear Walmart," *Disarmament Diplomacy* 8, no. 76 (March/April 2004), http://www.acronym.org.uk/dd/dd76/76cc.htm. See also F. Hassan Khan, "Nuclear Proliferation Motivations: Lessons from Pakistan," *Nonproliferation Review* 13, no. 3 (November 2006): 501–17.

31. Anupam Srivastava and Seema Gahlaut, "Curbing Proliferation from Emerging Suppliers: Export Controls in India and Pakistan," *Arms Control Today* 33, no. 7 (September 2003): 12–16.

32. Seema Gahlaut, "Plugging the Proliferation Loopholes in Pakistan and Beyond," *Defense News*, March 22, 2004, 53.

33. B. Raman, *Madrid Impressions I: Pakistan, the Nuclear Walmart*, South Asia Analysis Group Paper no. 1303, March 25, 2005,http://www.saag.org/%5Cpapers17%5Cpaper1638. html http://www.southasiaanalysis.org/%5Cpapers14%5Cpaper1303.html; Benazir Bhutto, "Musharraf Knew about A. Q. Khan's 'Private' Proliferation," *New Perspectives Quarterly* 21, no. 2 (2004): 39–43.

34. Massoud Ansari, "Daddy's Girl," *New Republic*, March 27, 2004, 12–13.

35. Bill Powell and Tim McGirk, "The Man Who Sold the Bomb," *Time*, February 14, 2005, 22–30, http://www.time.com/time/magazine/article/0,9171,1025082-2,00.html.

36. Some of Pakistan's nuclear scientists believe that the bomb should be shared with all of the Muslim community, even — or especially — with al Qaeda. See David Albright and Holly Higgins, "A Bomb for the Ummah," *Bulletin of the Atomic Scientists* 59, no. 2 (March/April 2003): 49–55.

37. For the complete text of the export control law, see http://www.iaea.org/Publications/ Documents/Infcircs/2004/infcirc636.pdf.

38. Command and control changes have been explained to foreign audiences in workshops, conferences, and bilateral exchanges.

39. On Pakistan's links with Saudi Arabia, see "Saudi Arabia Special Weapons," http://www .globalsecurity.org/wmd/world/saudi/index.html. See also Albright and Hinderstein, *Documents Indicate A. Q. Khan Offered Nuclear Weapon Designs*. For Khan's contributions to the Libyan program, see Wyn Q. Bowen, "The United Kingdom and Nuclear Deterrence," *Adelphi Papers* http://www.informaworld.com/smpp/title~content=t713662270~db=all~tab =issueslist~branches=46 - v4646, no. 380 (May 2006): 7–10. On his contributions to the Iranian program, see Douglas Jehl, "CIA Says Pakistanis Gave Iran Nuclear Aid," *New York Times*, November 24, 2004.

40. See, for instance, Seema Sirohi, "Hyphen Begone!" *Outlook*, March 2, 2004, http://www.hvk.org/articles/0304/48.html, and Kaushik Kapisthalam, "Sleeping with the Nuclear Snake," *Kashmir Telegraph* 3, no. 10 (March 2004), http://www.kashmirtelegraph .com/0304/one.htm.

41. Manoj Joshi, "Why Indian N-tech Won't Leak ," *Times of India*, February 2, 2004, http://timesofindia.indiatimes.com/articleshow/msid-469288,curpg-1.cms.

42. Seema Gahlaut and Anupam Srivastava, *Export Control Developments in India: Update 2005*, CITS report for Carnegie Corporation of New York, July 2005, http://www.uga .edu/cits/documents/pdf/EXEC%20SUMMARY%2020050616.pdf.

43. For a debate on the legitimacy and future of this "international law" see Daniel Joyner, *UNSC Resolution 1540: A Legal Travesty?* CITS Issue Brief, August 2006, and Seema Gahlaut, *UNSC Resolution 1540: A Principled Necessity*, CITS Issue Brief, August 2006, both at http://www.uga.edu/CITS.

44. Pakistan's and India's reports are available at http://disarmament.un.org/Committee1540/ report.html.

45. Presumably, the communistic repression of freedoms was deemed less evil in the case of China as it was internally directed, unlike that of the Soviet Union.

46. For a detailed look at the Indian position, see Seema Gahlaut, "India and the Non-proliferation Regime," in *India's New Dynamics in Foreign Policy*, ed. Subrata K. Mitra and Bernd Rill, 93–106, Studies and Comments 4, (Germany: Hanns Siedel Foundation, 2006).

47. See "Jaswant Achieved More of His Objectives Than I," Rediff interview with Strobe Talbott, September 21, 2004; http://www.rediff.com/news/2004/sep/21inter.htm.

48. See Gary K. Bertsch, Seema Gahlaut, and Anupam Srivastava, "U.S.-India Relations in the Coming Decades," in Mitra and Bertsch, *India's New Dynamics in Foreign Policy*, 107–27.

49. Seema Gahlaut, *Indian Export Control Policy: Political Commitment, Institutional Capacity, and Nonproliferation Record*, CITS Issue Brief, May 2006, http://www.uga.edu/cits/documents/pdf/Briefs/Indian%20XC%20Brief%20Final.pdf.

50. For a detailed list of obligations assumed by India and the United States under this agreement, see Anupam Srivastava and Seema Gahlaut, "The New Energy in the U.S.-India Relationship," *Defense and Security Analyses* 22 http://www.informaworld.com/smpp/462288586-72732537/title~content=t713412200~db=all~tab=issueslist~branches=22 - v22, no. 4 (December 2006): 353–72.

51. For some major flaws in the NPT-related arguments of the critics, see Seema Gahlaut, "Mis-firing at the India Nuclear Deal," *ForeignPolicy.com*, March 2006.

52. Seema Gahlaut, "A Critical Look at the Opposition to the U.S.-India Agreement," in *Nuclear Cooperation with India: New Challenges, New Opportunities*, ed. Wade L. Huntley and Karthika Sasikumar, Simons Centre for Disarmament and Non-Proliferation Research, Vancouver, BC, Canada, March 2006, 18–22.

53. The lessening credibility of U.S. extended deterrence, for instance, is far more likely to affect the calculations of Taiwan and Japan. Libya made a decision to give up its pursuit during the time when a nuclear India was being "rewarded" with U.S. attention. Iran, Libya, Iraq, and North Korea did not learn the right lessons from the period when India was being sanctioned by the international community. Finally, the extent of adherence Saudi Arabia, Syria, and Egypt have maintained to their NPT commitments remains to be seen—as we dig deeper into the Khan network.

54. On this, see the detailed and systematic examination by Ashley Tellis, *Atoms for War? U.S.-Indian Civilian Nuclear Cooperation and India's Nuclear Arsenal*, Carnegie Endowment Report, June 2006.

55. Almost all of the U.S. allies in Asia now depend on China for trade. China has replaced the United States as the largest trading partner for Japan, South Korea, Australia, and Taiwan. In India today, China is a close second to the United States in terms of two-way trade.

CHAPTER TWELVE

China's Changing Approach to Nonproliferation

Bates Gill

China's approach to nonproliferation has been a much-watched and often contentious aspect of international security affairs at least since China detonated its first nuclear weapon more than forty years ago.[1] In recent years, as China has become an increasingly important geopolitical actor and as international proliferation concerns have increased, especially involving possible terrorist access to weapons of mass destruction (WMD), Beijing's approach to these questions becomes all the more critical to understand, engage, and strengthen in positive ways. Today, given China's steadily advancing military-technical capabilities, particularly in its strategic forces, and given China's relations with key proliferating states—such as India, Iran, North Korea, and Pakistan—it is all the more vital to understand the motivations and likely outcomes of the country's approach to nonproliferation. For better or for worse, China will have an increasingly significant influence on the future of nonproliferation in Asia and in the rest of the world.

This chapter examines these issues more deeply by first reviewing China's past approach to nonproliferation. Second, the chapter details and analyzes China's evolving and increasingly constructive policies and practices on nonproliferation. In a concluding section, the chapter highlights issues of continuing concern with China's nonproliferation record and assesses Beijing's likely future approach to the horizontal and vertical spread of sensitive weapons and technologies.[2]

China's Past Approach to Nonproliferation

For its first four decades, the People's Republic of China vigorously opposed international nonproliferation and arms control efforts and was an active proliferator in its own right. This skepticism and opposition toward international nonproliferation efforts was guided in part by important historical and ideological viewpoints rooted in China's self-perception as weak and as a "victim" in the international system, a victim duty-bound to leverage what influence it had to advocate for the interests of the developing world. Chinese proliferation activities also derived from more straightforward strategic, political, and economic interests.

For example, as the target of nuclear threats first from the United States in the 1950s and later from the Soviet Union, China saw little other choice but to pursue nuclear weapons as a means to deter what they expected to be inevitable aggression by those powers. In some cases, China's exports of sensitive weapons and technologies were—as was the case for other major powers—part of a broader national security effort to maintain active and beneficial strategic ties with certain states.

At the conceptual level, the People's Republic of China emerged on the international scene in the 1950s and 1960s as a relative "newcomer" to the arms control and nonproliferation framework that was established over the course of the Cold War without Chinese participation. Even as Chinese policy in the late Cold War and early post–Cold War period came to favor certain arms control and nonproliferation efforts, Beijing often argued that the global framework on these questions was largely established without China's involvement, either as part of negotiations between the United States and the Soviet Union or as part of larger multilateral efforts to which China was not invited, or in which China chose not to participate.

In addition, Beijing in the past found fault with what it viewed as a wrong-headed and even cynical international nonproliferation approach that gave dominant emphasis to "supply side" denial rather than more nuanced and balanced mechanisms that sought to address the "demand side" of proliferation by dealing with the security threats driving states and substate actors to pursue WMD in the first place. Moreover, Beijing expressed the view that a supply-side approach unfairly denied developing world states access to legitimate technologies, while allowing the "haves" in the developed world to continue their pursuit of ever more advanced weaponry, including WMD, with little concern for commensurate security assurances for weaker states. This view focused particularly on what China termed supply-side "cartels"—such as the Nuclear Suppliers Group, the Zangger Committee, the Missile Technology Control Regime (MTCR), the Australia Group (AG), and the Wassenaar Arrangement (WA)—which were primarily made up of like-minded, Western-oriented, and developed states.

Beijing saw an even more sinister rationale for the global nonproliferation framework of the time: to keep weak states weak so they could not challenge the military, technical, and economic dominance of the major powers, especially the United States. Beijing was particularly affronted by the fact that other major countries—such as the Soviet Union and particularly the United States—dominated the international arms export market in supplying their client states (such as Taiwan by the United States, a place of enormous strategic importance to Beijing) with a range of sophisticated weapons, and even tolerated the development of nuclear weapons in states such as India and Israel, while demanding China take a more responsible approach to weapons exports.

China's past approach to nonproliferation can be more sharply detailed by examining Chinese policies related to three key cases of concern: Pakistan, Iran, and North Korea.

The Case of Pakistan

China's most sensitive and long-standing proliferation relationship is with Pakistan and dates back to the mid-1960s. No other Chinese client has received more weapons from Beijing than Pakistan. Even during past years when Pakistan maintained friendly and strategic relations with the West, China remained its most dominant weapons supplier.

The greatest nonproliferation concerns about this relationship focus on China's active support for Pakistan's nuclear weapon and ballistic missile programs.[3] Such assistance may have included acquisition of highly enriched uranium (HEU), assistance in HEU production, and confirmation of Pakistani nuclear weapons designs. Nuclear weapon design blueprints and other documents that Libya handed over to the United States in 2003 "yielded dramatic evidence of China's long-suspected role in transferring nuclear know-how to Pakistan in the early 1980s."[4]

Beginning in the mid- to late-1980s, significant Sino-Pakistan ballistic missile-related cooperation was another area of proliferation concern. At the time, China held discussions with a number of countries, including Pakistan, to sell its newly developed, made-for-export, M-series ballistic missiles. Moreover, from the mid-1990s onward, China also provided significant support in helping Pakistan establish its domestic missile development and production programs such as the Shaheen-I and -II and the Haider-I.

The Case of Iran

The military-technical relationship between China and Iran is over a quarter century old. But the most provocative proliferation activities between China and Iran involve Chinese transfers of nuclear weapon–, missile-, and chemical weapon–related technologies. From the late 1980s to the late 1990s, China reportedly provided Iran with a range of nuclear-related exports and other assistance, such as cooperation in uranium mining, uranium enrichment and conversion technologies, research reactors, production facility blueprints, and technical training and assistance.

Leaked CIA analyses in the mid-1990s reported that China transferred possibly hundreds of missile guidance systems and computerized machine tools, as well as gyroscopes, accelerometers, and test equipment, all bound for Iran's indigenous missile development programs.[5] Chinese companies and individuals have also been suspected of transferring sensitive chemical weapons-related materials to Iran since the mid- to late 1990s.

The Case of North Korea

China's extensive military-technical assistance to North Korea, particularly between the 1950s and mid-1980s, was dominated by large supplies of conventional weapons, but also various forms of assistance to Pyongyang's nuclear and missile programs. In addition, based on the uranium enrichment technology which China provided, Pakistan in turn assisted North Korea's nuclear weapons in return for North Korea's help with Pakistan's missile program, probably beginning around 1997.[6]

China also actively assisted the North Korean missile development program at least through the late 1970s. Some of the most important Chinese transfers were HY-1 antiship missiles and HQ-2 missiles (Soviet-designed surface-to-air missiles of 1950s vintage) in the early 1970s that North Korea was able to utilize in the development of its ballistic missile programs. According to a number of reports, Chinese missile-related assistance continued to North Korea through the 1980s and into the 1990s, including the provision of design and metallurgical assistance, propulsion and guidance technologies, specialty steels, and scientific training and exchanges.[7] In addition, it is possible that Chinese missile specialists assisting indigenous missile development in Pakistan and Iran have had some professional interactions with North Korean specialists also working in those countries, know-how that could be applied to North Korean missile development. According to its most recent report on global proliferation concerns, the Office of the Director of National Intelligence reported that in 2004 "firms in China provided dual-use missile-related items, raw materials, or assistance to Libya and North Korea."[8]

China's Evolving, More Constructive Approach

Since the mid- to late 1990s China's policies and practice on nonproliferation have changed in substantial ways. Beijing has dramatically reduced its exports of weapons and sensitive technologies, taken a more active international role on certain high-profile nonproliferation challenges such as Iran and North Korea, and gradually implemented a number of new international, bilateral, and domestic nonproliferation commitments. Despite these positive developments, China's nonproliferation record still raises concerns, and in many quarters it is hoped Beijing will do more to help rein in the proliferation ambitions of countries such as Iran, North Korea, and Pakistan. But China's overall approach to nonproliferation has shown significant change in a direction more consistent with international norms.[9]

This evolving, more constructive approach to nonproliferation is best seen in China's policies toward Pakistan, Iran, and North Korea, and in Beijing's acceptance and implementation of important international and domestic nonproliferation measures.

The Case of Pakistan

Since the mid- to late 1990s, China has reduced its weapons and sensitive technology exports to Pakistan, though a number of concerns persist. For example, regarding nuclear-related exports, following revelations in early 1996 that Chinese exporters had supplied Pakistan's Kahuta nuclear research laboratory with some five thousand ring magnets and subsequent intense negotiations with Washington, Beijing publicly pledged in May 1996 it would no longer provide nuclear assistance to unsafeguarded nuclear facilities, such as the Kahuta facility. In another positive step, China and the United States issued a joint statement in June 1998, following the nuclear tests of India and Pakistan a month earlier, pledging that the two sides would "prevent the export of equipment, materials or technology that could in any way assist programs in India and Pakistan for nuclear weapons."[10]

Beijing has made a number of pledges to the United States since the early 1990s that it would take steps to stem the flow of missiles and missile-related technology to Pakistan. After it was discovered that China had shipped some thirty-four M-11 missiles to Pakistan, in spite of its previous pledges, Beijing agreed in October 1994 not only to abide by the basic guidelines of the MTCR but also to apply the concept of "inherent capability" that would apparently obligate Beijing to halt further M-11–related exports.[11] In June 1998, during the U.S.-China summit, and shortly after Pakistan detonated several nuclear devices to become a de facto nuclear weapons state, China joined the United States to reaffirm its October 1994 pledge, stating its policy is to "prevent the export of equipment, materials or technology that could in any way assist programs" in Pakistan working on ballistic missiles capable of carrying nuclear weapons, and that the two sides would "strengthen our national export control systems."[12]

China made a number of additional commitments in the early 2000s. In November 2000, China agreed not to "assist, in any way, any country in the development of ballistic missiles that can be used to deliver nuclear weapons (i.e., capable of delivering a payload of at least 500 kilograms to a distance of at least 300 kilometers)" and to "further improve its export control system."[13] China issued long-awaited missile export control regulations and an associated control list in 2002.[14] However, it is important to note that in spite of these constructive steps, serious concerns persist that Chinese companies continue to assist Pakistan's missile development programs, probably with the tacit acknowledgment of Chinese government authorities.

The Case of Iran

Similar to the case of Pakistan, Beijing began in the early- to mid-1990s to cut back on its proliferation activities with Iran, often under pressure from the United States. Washington's efforts led to the cancellation by China of two ostensibly civilian nuclear deals in the mid-1990s, and in 1997 China made a number of additional and important commitments regarding its nuclear cooperation with Iran.

As part of a U.S.-China presidential summit that year, Beijing provided a written pledge to the White House that it would not provide any new nuclear assistance to Iran, following the completion of two projects—a zero-power research reactor that uses natural uranium and heavy water and a zirconium cladding production factory, which were not of proliferation concern to the United States. China also agreed not to provide the nuclear power reactors and the UF6 conversion facilities that China and Iran were negotiating at the time.[15] Beijing also agreed to join the Zangger Committee. Furthermore, Beijing pledged to stop the future export of antiship cruise missiles to Iran.[16] It is widely believed that China has adhered to these agreements, especially with regard to exports of nuclear technologies and antiship cruise missiles to Iran. However, as discussed below, a number of concerns continue about Chinese exports of missile- and chemical-related materials to Iran.

More recently, China has also taken a more active and high-profile stance along with other members of the international community to address the Iranian nuclear issue. As concerns about Iranian nuclear ambitions mounted in 2004–5, Beijing at first preferred to maintain a low profile, keep the issue out of the United Nations Security Council (UNSC) and quietly support a negotiated solution between Tehran and the European troika of France, Germany, and the United Kingdom. However, in the early months of 2006, as these talks proved fruitless and International Atomic Energy Agency (IAEA) concerns about Iran's lack of cooperativeness increased, international pressure grew to take up the question within the United Nations Security Council (UNSC). Again, Beijing preferred negotiations outside of the Security Council: in June 2006, Beijing joined the other permanent members of the UNSC and Germany to present Iran with a political and economic incentive package in the hopes of gaining Tehran's agreement to suspend its enrichment activities.

But as Iran continued to defy international appeals, Beijing joined with all the permanent members as well as nine additional UNSC members to support the relatively tough-worded Resolution 1696. That resolution called on Iran to suspend "all [nuclear] enrichment-related activities and reprocessing activities, including research and development . . . or face the possibility of economic and diplomatic sanctions." The resolution also "expresses the intention" of the UNSC "to adopt appropriate measures under Article 41 of Chapter VII" of the UN Charter—which opens the possibility that force could be used to back up the will of the UNSC—should Iran not comply with the resolution.[17] At the time, this was the most forceful language China had yet supported regarding the Iranian nuclear issue and was indicative of a greater willingness to get behind more stringent international nonproliferation efforts.

The Case of North Korea

There remain some lingering concerns that Chinese entities continue to assist North Korean missile-related programs. But at the same time Beijing has become far more proactive in addressing the concerns related to North Korea's nuclear weapons and missile testing programs.

China's more active involvement is a decided shift from previous policy. With the onset of the first North Korean nuclear crisis in 1993–94, Beijing chose against participating in the Korean Peninsula Energy Development Organization (KEDO). Beijing did take part in the short-lived four-party talks between December 1997 and August 1999, another attempt to negotiate a diplomatic solution to roll back Pyongyang's nuclear ambitions.

However, as those ambitions became clearer and closer to reality in 2002—with North Korea acknowledging a clandestine uranium enrichment program in

October 2002, ousting IAEA inspectors in December 2002, and announcing its withdrawal from the Treaty on the Nonproliferation of Nuclear Weapons (NPT) in January 2003—China took more focused action. China initially encouraged bilateral discussions between Pyongyang and Washington and was willing to serve as a host, but not an active participant, in talks in Beijing. However, with Washington's insistence, and as China grew increasingly frustrated with its North Korean neighbor, Beijing came to support a multilateral approach. By 2006, Beijing had hosted several sets of multilateral talks aimed at resolving the North Korea nuclear standoff. The first, involving China, North Korea, and the United States, was held in April 2003. The second set of talks was held in August 2003 and was expanded by an additional three parties: Japan, Russia, and South Korea. A second, third, and fourth round of six-party talks were convened in Beijing in February 2004, June 2004, and July 2005. In September 2005, China was praised for its role in facilitating a breakthrough during resumption of the fourth-round of talks, in particular the drafting of a joint statement in which North Korea agreed to halt its nuclear weapons programs and allow international inspections in exchange for economic cooperation, aid, and security assurances from the United States. Following a short and fruitless fifth round of six-party talks in November 2005, this process stalled over the course of 2006, in spite of Chinese efforts to keep the parties together.

Outside of the six-party talks, Beijing apparently took other, more aggressive steps to stem North Korea's nuclear ambitions. According to U.S. Assistant Secretary of State for Arms Control Stephen Rademaker, Chinese authorities worked with the United States in the fall of 2003 to interdict a chemical shipment destined for North Korea's nuclear weapons program.[18] Since North Korea's revelations of a nuclear weapons program in October 2002 and its claims to possess nuclear weapons in May 2003, Chinese leaders have issued highly public statements insisting that the Korean Peninsula should be free of nuclear weapons.[19]

Beijing has also taken some positive steps to dampen North Korea's enthusiasm for pursuing ballistic missiles. In July 2006, China joined all members of the UNSC in unanimously supporting Resolution 1695 in response to North Korea's missile tests. The resolution expresses "grave concern" and "condemns" the launch of the North Korean missiles, and demands that Pyongyang "suspend all activities related to its ballistic missile program" and reestablish a moratorium on missile launches. The resolution also requires all United Nations member states to "exercise vigilance" and prevent the transfer of missile-related parts and technology to or from North Korea's missile or nuclear weapons development programs.[20] However, China had earlier opposed a draft resolution proposed by Japan that would have levied more serious economic sanctions against North Korea and opened the possibility for the use of force to enforce the demands of the resolution.

Beijing faces a complex set of political, economic, and security interests in dealing with North Korea — trying to balance its interest in maintaining good relations with the United States, realizing a nonnuclear peninsula where Chinese interests hold sway, and avoiding chaos, collapse, or conflict on the Korean Peninsula — all of which constrains a tougher approach from Beijing.[21] Nevertheless, China has taken progressively more positive steps to rein in Pyongyang nuclear and ballistic missile proliferation in recent years and will likely continue to do so, even though these steps may not fully satisfy expectations in other capitals such as Washington and Tokyo.

International and Domestic Measures

Beginning in the mid-1990s, China became especially active in joining and adhering to a range of global and regional nonproliferation and arms control mechanisms.[22]

In addition, China joined other major powers to oppose the nuclear tests by India and Pakistan in 1998 and was a principal drafter of UNSC Resolution 1172 (1998) setting out a framework for the denuclearization of Indo-Pakistani rivalry. In recognizing the link between terrorism and the spread and potential use of WMD, China joined the U.S.-sponsored Container Security Initiative (CSI) in July 2003 and has called for multilateral arms control discussions to address the threat of terrorism and WMD.[23]

Since 2004, China has also taken more active part in support of other multilateral nonproliferation initiatives. Beijing voiced support for efforts by the Association of Southeast Asian Nations (ASEAN) Regional Forum to combat proliferation and supports steps to bring nonproliferation and other security issues onto the agenda of the Asia-Pacific Economic Cooperation (APEC) group. China has also been favorably cited by American officials for its work to achieve a strengthened Convention on the Physical Protection of Nuclear Material.[24] Beijing has also signed on to support nuclear weapon–free zone agreements, most recently those in Central Asia and in Southeast Asia.

As noted above, over the course of the 1990s and into the early 2000s, Beijing took on a number of bilateral commitments with the United States that pledged to limit China's proliferation-related activities with certain countries of concern, such as Iran, Pakistan, and others.

Consistent with these steps on the international scene, beginning in the mid- to late 1990s, China promulgated a host of domestic export control regulations and control lists in order to better govern and limit the transfer of sensitive exports.[25] This process began in December 1995, when China issued a control list based on the control list used by the Chemical Weapons Convention (CWC). Subsequent regulatory guidelines issued by the Chinese government in March 1997, August 1997, June 1998, and October 2002 further strengthened China's chemical export controls.

In September 1997, China publicly released regulations to govern nuclear material and technology exports. These regulations incorporate a control list identical to the one used by the Nuclear Suppliers Group (NSG); China later formally joined the group in 2004.

In the area of conventional weapons exports, China issued its "Regulations on Export Control of Military Items" in October 1997; they became effective in January 1998 and were further revised in October 2002. They listed a detailed set of procedures by which conventional weapons could be exported, the government agencies responsible for overseeing these procedures, and the penalties for violating them. They also stated that only certain companies would be approved to engage in conventional weapons transfers. China does not belong to the Wassenaar Arrangement. However, in November 1998, China expanded its export controls for conventional weapons by issuing a list of 183 dual-use technologies that would be subject to tighter controls, many of which are also covered in the WA's "core list" of dual-use technologies.[26]

The Chinese government published a twenty-four-article set of missile export control regulations and a related control list in August 2002.[27] With some exceptions, the regulations and technologies described in these documents hew closely to procedures and items found within the approach of the MTCR, both in terms of the Chinese "presumption of denial" approach and in terms of the specific items and technologies to be controlled.[28] The regulations outline the proper procedures to register as an exporter of missile-related technologies and to obtain export licenses for controlled items and technologies, require end-user certificates for recipients of controlled items, and set out penalties for violations. A close analysis of the regulations reveals that while they cover nearly all the systems and technology exports that led to U.S. sanctions in the past, the regulations leave open the possibility of some exports of concern that could create disputes in the future.[29] In May 2004, Beijing announced that it had fined two unnamed companies for violating the country's missile export control laws.[30]

In October 2002, Beijing issued regulations and a control list to cover exports of "dual use biological agents and related equipment and technologies." The twenty-five-article set of regulations stipulate a licensing procedure for exporters of dual-use biological agents, requirements for end-user certificates and declarations, the bureaucratic process by which export licenses for such items would be granted, and the fines and penalties for violators of the regulations. The accompanying control list is understood to parallel similar control lists within the international community, such as that employed by the AG.

Encouraging Progress, Continuing Concerns

Explaining Beijing's More Constructive Approach

China's more constructive policies on nonproliferation derive from what might be called its "new security diplomacy." This more constructive approach to international affairs in recent years seeks to maintain a stable regional security environment to facilitate China's domestic social and economic development, reassure China's neighbors and key international partners that its rise as a more powerful global player will be peaceful and constructive, and avoid a confrontational relationship with the United States.[31]

In seeking a more stable regional environment, Beijing increasingly came to see that this interest was directly affected by proliferation developments, especially those close to the Chinese periphery or in areas of strategic concern to Beijing. This is most true regarding North Korea. Even though it is unlikely that Pyongyang actively contemplates the use of WMD or ballistic missiles against China, nevertheless their possession by North Korea greatly complicates Beijing's security calculus. At a minimum, China wishes to avoid military action by the United States and its allies against North Korea, a situation that could possibly destabilize China's northeast border region, lead to refugee flows into China, and result in a significantly increased American and allied military presence on China's doorstep. In addition, as the United States and Japan increase their missile defense capability in response to North Korea's missile programs, this can weaken China's relative military position in the region as well.

Similarly, Beijing's interests would be threatened by potential instabilities and conflict that might result from nuclear-related tensions in South Asia between Pakistan and India, or in the Persian Gulf over Iran's nuclear ambitions, between Iran and the United States. China clearly favors a stable status quo in South Asia, although it appears resigned to the open nuclearization of the region. China's interests would not be served should Iran's actions result in conflict and war in the Persian Gulf, events that would disrupt the flow of energy resources from the region, spike energy prices, and probably result in an extensive and extended American military presence in this strategically critical part of the world. Beijing will try to manage proliferation problems on its periphery in a way that avoids external distractions and resource commitments that conflicts might bring, in order to focus instead on more pressing problems of economic, social, and political development at home.

China's more constructive approach to nonproliferation also flows from Beijing's strategic aim of reassuring regional neighbors and other international players about the peaceful and constructive nature of China's emergence on the global scene. By accepting, promoting, and adhering to nonproliferation commitments,

Beijing can burnish its image as a "responsible great power" and as a more constructive and less menacing international citizen.

For example, such expectations help explain China's willingness to abandon past opposition to "supply-side cartels" and become an active member of such nonuniversal nonproliferation regimes as the Zangger Committee and the NSG and to establish domestic export control regulations consistent with other such mechanisms such as the MTCR, the WA, and the AG. In supporting the establishment of nuclear weapon–free zones in Central and Southeast Asia, China again burnishes its image, especially in the developing world, as a responsible great power.

Beijing's more positive approach to nonproliferation in recent years can also be attributed to its long-term strategic interest in avoiding an openly confrontational relationship with the United States. The best examples of this approach are found in the many occasions Beijing took on additional nonproliferation commitments in order to avoid an open and damaging confrontation with Washington and instead develop a more beneficial and stable bilateral relationship. Time and time again throughout the 1990s and into the 2000s, Beijing steadily conceded ground to the United States on a range of nonproliferation questions, principally having to do with Pakistan and Iran. But in so doing, Beijing also signed up to more far-reaching nonproliferation and arms control commitments with global applications.[32]

But these steps were not for Washington's benefit alone, or simply meant to avoid a clash with the United States. Beijing too steadily came to recognize the interests it has in stemming the proliferation of weapons and technology, especially to areas of potential instability around its periphery. Moreover, in finding common ground on nonproliferation with the United States, Beijing has expectations of possibly limiting the power of other states and promoting Chinese interests as well. Even in cases when China accepts verifiable limits on its own military capabilities—such as Beijing's agreement to sign on to the CWC and the Comprehensive Test Ban Treaty—it does so having reached the self-interested expectation that such restraints would apply to other powers as well.

Continuing Future Concerns

However, in spite of China's increasingly positive and genuine interest in nonproliferation, many concerns persist. These concerns include the level of Chinese commitment to nonproliferation, continued worries over China's military-technical relations with particular countries, the problem of "third party" proliferation, and the possible proliferation effect of China's ongoing missile buildup and strategic modernization program.

For example, while Beijing has increasingly taken more and more nonproliferation commitments on board, concerns remain that in some cases it has done
so on a cautious and contingent basis. In the past, Beijing appeared to distinguish
its commitments between those reached on an international, multilateral level,
those reached at a bilateral level with the United States, and those steps that
China undertook at home. China's strongest commitments—in principle and
in practice—were to international, multilateral agreements. More questionable
were China's commitments—for reasons of principle, politics, and practice—to
agreements made on a bilateral basis such as to the United States or commitments made in the form of Chinese domestic laws and regulations, such as export controls. It is apparent that Beijing will need to do more to fully implement
and enforce its own export control laws, including more effective dissemination
of nonproliferation information among its domestic producers and building a
greater nonproliferation "norm" or "culture." Greater financial resources for personnel, training, monitoring, and interdiction are also needed. Overall, China's
"contingent" approach to nonproliferation commitments can still be seen today,
though not as obviously as in the past.

A more pressing and immediate concern relates to China's continuing military-
technical relations with particular countries, especially Pakistan and Iran. For example, U.S. intelligence sources report that Pakistan will continue to require China's assistance to Pakistan's solid-propellant ballistic missile and that one "cannot
rule out" continued contacts between Chinese entities and elements of Pakistan's
nuclear weapons program.[33] As noted above, the United States continues to sanction Chinese individuals and companies for their trade in missile and chemical
weapons-related exports with Iran. As the CIA found, "Although Beijing has taken
steps to improve ballistic missile related export controls, Chinese firms continue
to be a leading source of relevant technology and continue to work with other
countries on ballistic missile-related projects."[34]

A related and continuing concern involves the problem of third-party proliferation, situations in which sensitive Chinese exports are passed on from the original
recipient to a third party. For example, North Korea has become a far greater
proliferation concern in recent years, including as a conduit for technologies and
systems apparently originating in China. North Korean cooperation with Pakistan
on nuclear weapons and on missile development is particularly disturbing: in return for North Korea's help with ballistic missiles, Pakistan assisted Pyongyang's
clandestine bomb program utilizing uranium enrichment technology, the same
method Islamabad used, with Chinese assistance, for its bomb program. In another case, which was noted above, Pakistan provided Libya with nuclear weapons
designs and other documents that, once they were turned over to the United States
in November 2003, revealed that significant nuclear know-how had originated
from China. Pakistani scientist A. Q. Khan later resold these designs to Libya.[35]

North Korea is also known to have cooperated with Iran in the development of Iran's missile programs, some technology of which may have originated in China.

In another example of the third-party phenomenon, in July 2006 Hezbollah fighters in Beirut fired an Iranian-made C-802 antiship cruise missile, which struck an Israeli naval corvette; the C-802 missile was shipped in large quantities to Iran by China in the early to mid-1990s, and Iran subsequently developed its own version designated the *Noor*, possibly with Chinese assistance.[36] A future scenario of this kind might come to pass should Pakistan—armed with nuclear weapons in part through Chinese assistance—fall under the authority of a more radicalized leadership willing to export nuclear materials and know-how to other state and substate actors.

Finally, China's continued *vertical* weapons proliferation—especially its ongoing conventional and strategic missile buildup—is a source of global alarm. This buildup has sparked Taiwan to recontemplate its ballistic missile programs, devote more resources to its cruise missile development programs, and consider other potential offensive, preemptive strike capabilities. Looking ahead, other governments in the region—such as the United States, Japan, South Korea, and others—will also feel compelled to respond to China's steady military modernization process, particularly regarding its missile buildup, with both offensive and defensive (such as missile defense) countermeasures.

Future Prospects

Looking ahead, it appears likely that China's record of nonproliferation will be a mix of both steady progress and continuing concerns. Beijing will probably continue to strengthen its overall proliferation efforts as it improves its domestic capacity to enforce its export control regulations. At the same time, Beijing is likely to steadily increase its cooperation in conjunction with other major powers in response to clear threats to the international nonproliferation regime and especially in cases where Chinese national security interests are closely affected, such as with regard to North Korea and to a lesser extent Iran. However, on the other hand, for the near to medium term, Chinese entities will continue to be important suppliers of sensitive nuclear-, chemical-, and ballistic missile–related technologies and components to Iran and nuclear- and ballistic missile–related technologies and assistance to Pakistan. Other low-level proliferation may also occur between China and North Korea, and the third-party phenomenon will no doubt continue to cloud China's proliferation record for the foreseeable future.

The international community can take steps to curb the downside of China's proliferation record while bolstering more encouraging steps. First and foremost, concerned parties in the international community should intensify their focus on persistent Chinese violations of nonproliferation norms and China's own export control laws. Beijing should be reminded that enforcing its nonproliferation commitments is not a matter of doing a "favor" for the international community but is in fact consistent with its own laws, not to mention its interests in seeking a secure and stable regional and global environment.

It appears China's full participation in most of the major international nonproliferation treaties and supply-side control regimes has helped Beijing develop a more sophisticated and like-minded appreciation for the importance of stemming the flow of sensitive and destabilizing weapons and technologies. China should be encouraged to deepen its commitment to these regimes, and its willingness to join others should be seriously considered. Countries with well-developed domestic export control systems should increase their level of interaction with Chinese customs and law enforcement officials with the aim of learning more about China's export control system and should assist in improving it.

China's approach to proliferation has come a long way in a more positive direction over the past two decades. As its record of proliferation steadily improves, the international community will place more and more scrutiny on how China responds to emergent cases of proliferation concern in the years ahead, as in the cases of Iran and North Korea. In this sense, China's approach to new proliferators in the future will be of far greater strategic importance than its approach to proliferation in the past.

Notes

1. This chapter draws in part from Bates Gill, *Rising Star: China's New Security Diplomacy and Its Implications for the United States* (Washington, DC: Brookings Institution Press, 2007), especially ch. 3, and Bates Gill, "The Growing Challenge of Proliferation in Asia," in *Strategic Asia 2003–04: Fragility and Crisis*, ed. Richard Ellings et al. (Seattle: National Bureau of Asian Research, 2003), 365–97.

2. Past studies on the motivations, evolution, and implications of China's arms transfer policies include Evan S. Medeiros, *Reluctant Restraint: The Evolution of China's Nonproliferation Policies and Practices, 1980–2004* (Stanford, CA: Stanford University Press, 2007); Wendy Frieman, *China, Arms Control, and Nonproliferation* (London: RoutledgeCurzon, 2004); Bates Gill, "Two Steps Forward, One Step Back: The Dynamics of Chinese Nonproliferation and Arms Control Policy-Making in an Era of Reform," in *The Making of Chinese Foreign and Security Policy in an Era of Reform*, ed. David M. Lampton (Stanford, CA: Stanford University Press, 2001), 257–88; Evan S. Medeiros and Bates Gill, *Chinese Arms Exports: Policy, Players and Process* (Carlisle Barracks, PA: Strategic Studies Institute, U.S. Army War College, August 2000; Zhu Mingquan, "The Evolution of China's Nuclear

Nonproliferation Policy," *Nonproliferation Review* 4, no. 2 (Winter 1997): 40–48; Bates Gill, *Chinese Arms Transfers: Purposes, Patterns, and Prospects in the New World Order* (Westport, CT: Praeger, 1992).

3. Central Intelligence Agency, *Unclassified Report to Congress on the Acquisition of Technology Relating to Weapons of Mass Destruction and Advanced Conventional Munitions, 1 January through 30 June 2000*, February 2000, http://www.cia.gov/cia/publications/bian/bian_feb_2001.htm.

4. Joby Warrick and Peter Slevin, "Libyan Arms Designs Traced Back to China," *Washington Post*, February 15, 2004, A1. The Pakistan nuclear weapons program also received critical assistance from other sources as well. For example, centrifuge designs stolen from the Netherlands were essential to the development of the Pakistan bomb.

5. See, for example, Elaine Sciolino, "CIA Report Says Chinese Sent Iran Arms Components," *New York Times*, June 22, 1995; Jeffrey Smith and David Ottaway, "Spy Photos Suggest China Missile Trade," *Washington Post*, July 3, 1995; Bill Gertz, "China Sold Iran Missile Technology," *Washington Times*, November 21, 1996.

6. On Pakistan's aid to the North Korean nuclear program, see Seymour M. Hersh, "The Cold Test," *New Yorker*, January 27, 2003, 42; "North Korea I: Pakistan Probably Gave Nuclear Aid Recently, Officials Say," *Global Security Newswire*, November 13, 2002, http://www.nti.org/d_newswire/issues/newswires/2002_11_13.html; David E. Sanger, "In North Korea and Pakistan, Deep Roots of Nuclear Barter," *New York Times*, November 24, 2002.

7. See, for example, Bill Gertz, "China Assists North Korea in Space Launches," *Washington Times*, February 23, 1999; Bill Gertz, "China Breaks Vow, Sends N. Korea Missile Materials," *Washington Times*, January 6, 2000; Bill Gertz and Rowan Scarborough, "China Connection," *Washington Times*, November 19, 1999.

8. See Central Intelligence Agency, *Unclassified Report to Congress on the Acquisition of Technology Relating to Weapons of Mass Destruction and Advanced Conventional Munitions, 1 January through 31 December 2004*, November 2004, http://www.dni.gov/reports/2004_unclass_report_to_NIC_DO_16Nov04.pdf.

9. A number of studies have examined China's changing approach to nonproliferation. See, for example, Medeiros, *Reluctant Restraint*; Frieman, *China, Arms Control, and Nonproliferation*; Gill, "Two Steps Forward."

10. United States, Department of State, *Text: U.S.-China Joint Statement on South Asia*, June 27, 1998, http://www.fas.org/news/china/1998/sasia.htm.

11. Even though China argued the M-11's advertised range, at about 280 kilometers, fell below the basic MTCR threshold, Beijing acknowledged the missile was still "inherently capable" of longer ranges if its payload was reduced slightly.

12. People's Republic of China, Embassy, *Sino-U.S. Joint Statement on South Asia*, June 27, 1998, http://www.china-embassy.org/eng/zmgx/zysj/kldfh/t36228.htm.

13. "PRC FM Spokesman On Non-Proliferation Issue," *Xinhua*, November 21, 2000, translated in Foreign Broadcast Information Service, CPP20001121000110.

14. People's Republic of China, Ministry of Foreign Affairs, *Regulations of the People's Republic of China on Export Control of Missiles and Missile-Related Items and Technologies*, August 22, 2002, http://tr.china-embassy.org/eng/xwdt/t161702.htm; "Regulations of the People's

Republic of China on Export Control of Missiles and Missile-Related Items and Technologies," August 22, 2002, http://www.gov.cn/english/laws/2005-07/25/content_16957.htm.

15. "China Agrees to End Nuclear Trade with Iran When Two Projects Completed," *NuclearFuel*, November 3, 1997, 3–4.

16. United States, White House, "Fact Sheet: Accomplishments of the U.S.-China Summit," October 30, 1997; see also Steve Erlanger, "U.S. Says Chinese Will Stop Sending Missiles to Iran," *New York Times*, October 18, 1997.

17. S/RES/1696, July 31, 2006.

18. U.S.-China Economic and Security Review Commission, testimony of Stephen G. Rademaker, assistant secretary of state for arms control, U.S. Department of State, March 10, 2005, http://www.uscc.gov/hearings/2005hearings/written_testimonies/05_03_10wrtr/rademaker_stephen_wrts.htm.

19. See, for example, Jeremy Page, "Putin and Hu Find Common Ground on Korea and Iraq," Reuters, May 27, 2003; "China, Russia Issue Joint Statement," *People's Daily*, December 4, 2002, http://english.peopledaily.com.cn/200212/03/eng20021203_107822.shtml; "Chinese, U.S. Presidents Talk over Phone," *People's Daily*, March 19, 2003, http://english.peopledaily.com.cn/200303/19/eng20030319_113538.shtml.

20. S/RES/1696, July 31, 2006, http://www.un.org/Docs/sc/unsc_resolutions06.htm.

21. These complexities are discussed in more detail in Bates Gill and Andrew Thompson, "A Test for Beijing: China and the North Korean Nuclear Quandary," *Arms Control Today* 33, no. 4 (May 2003): 12–14.

22. See the favorable comments from a senior U.S. official in U.S.-China Economic and Security Review Commission, testimony of Stephen G. Rademaker.

23. See, for example, Information Office of the State Council, *China's National Defense in 2004* (Beijing: Information Office of the State Council, December 2004), ch. 10.

24. U.S.-China Economic and Security Review Commission, testimony of Stephen G. Rademaker.

25. This discussion of Chinese export controls draws in part from the Web site of the East Asia Nonproliferation Project, James Martin Center for Nonproliferation Studies, Monterey Institute of International Studies, http://cns.miis.edu; Jing-dong Yuan, Phillip C. Saunders, and Stephanie Lieggi, "Recent Developments in China's Export Controls: New Regulations and New Challenges," *Nonproliferation Review* 9, no. 3 (Fall/Winter 2002): 153–67.

26. See a translation of these regulations in Foreign Broadcast Information Service, Daily Report: China, January 17, 1999; see also, "China Approves New Export Controls on Sensitive Technology," Reuters, December 2, 1998.

27. People's Republic of China, Ministry of Foreign Affairs, *Regulations of the People's Republic of China*; People's Republic of China Ministry of Foreign Affairs, *Missiles and Missile-Related Items and Technologies Export Control List*, August 22, 2002, http://www.fmprc.gov.cn/eng/33981.html.

28. For two analyses of the Chinese missile export control regulations, one by a Chinese and one by an American, see Phillip C. Saunders, *Preliminary Analysis of Chinese Missile Technology Export Control List*, James Martin Center for Nonproliferation Studies, Monterey Institute of International Studies, September 6, 2002, http://cns.miis.edu/cns/

projects/eanp/pubs/prc_msl.pdf; and Li Bin, "Comments on the Chinese Regulation on Missile Technology Export Control," August 26, 2002, http://learn.tsinghua.edu.cn/homepage/S00313/eexctl.htm.

29. Yuan, Saunders, and Lieggi, "Recent Developments in China's Export Controls," 160–62.

30. See Central Intelligence Agency, *Unclassified Report to Congress on the Acquisition of Technology Relating to Weapons of Mass Destruction and Advanced Conventional Munitions, 1 January Through 31 December 2004*, http://www.dni.gov/reports/2004_unclass _report_to_NIC_DO_16Nov04.pdf.

31. China's new security diplomacy and its motivations are examined in depth in Gill, *Rising Star.* See also Avery Goldstein, *Rising to the Challenge: China's Grand Strategy and International Security* (Stanford, CA: Stanford University Press, 2005).

32. Evan Medeiros demonstrates the critical influence of the United States in shaping China's approach to nonproliferation in *Reluctant Restraint.*

33. Central Intelligence Agency, *Unclassified Report to Congress on the Acquisition of Technology Relating to Weapons of Mass Destruction and Advanced Conventional Munitions, 1 January through 30 June 2001*, January 2002, https://www.cia.gov/library/reports/ archived-reports-1/jan_jun2001.htm; Central Intelligence Agency, *Unclassified Report to Congress on the Acquisition of Technology Relating to Weapons of Mass Destruction and Advanced Conventional Munitions, 1 January through 30 June 2002*, April 2003, https://www .cia.gov/library/reports/archived-reports-1/jan_jun2002.html.

34. George J. Tenet, "The Worldwide Threat 2004: Challenges in a Changing Global Context," testimony of director of Central Intelligence George J. Tenet before the Senate Select Committee on Intelligence, February 24, 2004, https://www.cia.gov/news-information/ speeches-testimony/2004/dci_speech_02142004.html.

35. Warrick and Slevin, "Libyan Arms Designs Traced Back to China."

36. Alon Ben-David, "Hizbullah Hits Israel's INS Hanit with Anti-Ship Missile," *Jane's Defence Weekly*, July 18, 2006.

CHAPTER THIRTEEN

North Korea's Nuclear Weapons Program to 2015: Three Scenarios

Jonathan D. Pollack

Executive Summary

This essay evaluates three alternative scenarios for North Korea's nuclear weapons development over the coming decade: (1) pursuit of a symbolic nuclear capability, (2) pursuit of an operational nuclear deterrent, and (3) a deficient or failed effort to achieve an operational capability.[1]

Main Argument

North Korea's weapons are now a fact, not a bargaining chip. Absent fundamental internal change in North Korea or extraordinary changes in the negotiating strategies of the United States and other powers, there is virtually no possibility that North Korea will irrevocably yield the totality of these capabilities.

Given that Pyongyang still confronts major technical hurdles if it expects to proceed to an operational deterrent force, however, the most likely outcome would be a symbolic nuclear capability. North Korea may be prepared to restrict some nuclear activities in return for guarantees and commitments from the United States and other powers. This possibility warrants careful consideration by the United States and others seeking a negotiated end to Pyongyang's nuclear program, even if it would not entail a definitive end to the program. It would not be prudent, however, to anticipate an early end to Pyongyang's program or to the dangers it poses for security in East Asia and for the future viability of the nonproliferation regime.

Policy Implications

There are four immediate policy considerations that the international community would benefit from exploring:

- determining additional measures to discourage or impede North Korea's future weapons development, which in the near term should focus on convincing North Korea to forego additional nuclear tests or further tests of ballistic missiles
- reiterating to Pyongyang that any transfer of nuclear materials, technologies, or completed weapons outside its borders would constitute a grave danger to the international community as a whole
- imposing additional costs on North Korea for any further nuclear tests
- fully weighing the trade-offs in pursuing partial steps to restrict nuclear weapons development versus pursuit of maximal policy goals

On October 9, 2006, the Democratic People's Republic of Korea (DPRK or North Korea) undertook its first ever test of a nuclear device in open defiance of repeated warnings from the United States, China, and other states. This essay examines possible scenarios for North Korea's future nuclear development in light of this initial test, focusing on three research issues: (a) the North Korean leadership's assessment of the purposes of nuclear weapons development; (b) the feasibility of the DPRK, in light of its current and projected technical capabilities, achieving various posited goals; and (c) the potential policy options for constraining North Korea's future nuclear development.

The policy consequences of a sustained North Korean nuclear weapons program are hugely worrisome both for the future of the nonproliferation regime and for regional security. The DPRK is the first state ever to withdraw from the Nuclear Nonproliferation Treaty (NPT), a move that has created a very troubling precedent for other states that might contemplate such actions. Should North Korea opt to transfer abroad any of its nuclear technologies, materials, and weapons, the dangers to international peace and security would be exceedingly grave. Additionally, the regional consequences are also highly worrisome. Without nuclear weapons, the latent possibilities of a highly destructive military conflict on the Korean Peninsula remain very high; with nuclear weapons, the potential consequences of renewed conflict for the Republic of Korea (ROK), Japan, and for U.S. forces are incalculably greater. Quite apart from the potential for armed conflict, North Korea's possession of nuclear weapons seems very likely to prompt major security reassessments on the part of all the states of Northeast Asia.

The prospective directions in North Korea's nuclear development over the next decade nonetheless remain uncertain. For one, international observers are uncertain of what value the DPRK leadership attaches to the possession of such capabilities; an additional factor is the possibility that the international community might be able to induce North Korea to limit its programs without definitively foregoing its capabilities. At the same time, however, Pyongyang also faces major technical and other hurdles in proceeding to a credible nuclear force. This essay thus posits three alternative outcomes: (1) a largely symbolic or political deterrent, (2) a more operational capability, and (3) a failure to fully realize a credible deterrent.

Of the three scenarios, the first outcome seems the most likely, and would be the least disruptive to regional and global security. Though Pyongyang may prefer a genuine operational force, achieving this goal may simply be a bridge too far, though North Korea has no incentive to disclose a failure to reach its goals. Pyongyang's test of a nuclear device was inherently destabilizing, but pursuit of a deployed nuclear capability (whether it succeeds or fails) would be far worse. The United States and other powers must therefore undertake all feasible steps to reduce the possibilities of either of the latter outcomes.

This essay is organized in four sections. The first describes the near-term implications of the nuclear test and then proposes assumptions for the remainder of the analysis. The second section assesses the DPRK's presumed objectives in undertaking the test. The third section analyzes the technical and resource questions that are likely to govern North Korea's nuclear and missile development. The fourth section provides overall conclusions and offers policy implications.

North Korea's Nuclear Breakout

North Korea's October 9, 2006, test of a nuclear device marks a fundamental divide in the nearly two-decade effort to prevent the emergence of the DPRK as a nuclear-armed state. The ability of a small, isolated, economically vulnerable, and acutely self-referential regime to sustain a nuclear weapons program and to conduct a nuclear test—drawing primarily on indigenous materials, technology, and scientific and engineering skills—validates at least three conclusions. First, as Richard Betts has observed, no state develops nuclear weapons by accident or inadvertence. It reflects purposive, long-term commitment and the dedication of substantial resources toward such a goal.[2] Second, building and testing a nuclear device and moving toward an operational delivery system are very difficult and time-consuming tasks, all the more so for a state as economically challenged as the DPRK. Third, under prevailing circumstances there is no meaningful possibility that Pyongyang will either yield the totality of its capabilities or forego what the leadership deems as North Korea's entitlement as a nuclear-armed state.

The DPRK's nuclear weapons are a fact, not a bargaining chip, even if the quantitative and qualitative characteristics of North Korea's capabilities remain to be determined. The leadership believes that nuclear weapons will enable North Korea to punch above its weight. In addition, the possession of such capabilities solidifies Kim Jung Il's symbiotic relationship with the North Korean military. A coalition of outside powers is intent on denying the DPRK any opportunity to convert its test into tangible political-strategic gains. External actors are seeking to exact added costs on North Korea for Pyongyang's nuclear test, inhibiting its limited dealings with the outside world, and moving quickly to impose additional restrictions on technology transactions that could enhance North Korea's capabilities for weapons development or export. Though likely to continue, these efforts (all mandated under UN Security Council [UNSC] Resolution 1718) are very unlikely to compel Pyongyang to alter North Korea's basic commitment to nuclear weapons development. Absent a fundamental leadership transformation in the DPRK or extraordinary changes in the negotiating strategies of the United States and others, it is virtually inconceivable that North Korea will dismantle the entirety of its nuclear inventory and weapons potential. There may have been a time when this goal was feasible, but the opportunity has passed.

Pyongyang may still be prepared to "trade," "rent," or otherwise limit some of its nuclear activities in return for guarantees and commitments from external powers. One such possibility, for example, was broached in meetings in Berlin in mid-January 2007 between North Korea's lead nuclear negotiator, Vice Minister of Foreign Affairs Kim Kye-gwan, and his U.S. counterpart, Assistant Secretary of State for East Asian and Pacific Affairs Christopher Hill. Kim purportedly informed Hill that in exchange for a U.S. commitment to resume economic and energy assistance to the DPRK and a parallel commitment to unfreeze $24 million held in North Korean accounts at the Banco Delta Asia in Macao, Pyongyang would agree to suspend various nuclear activities, including operations at its 5-megawatt electric reactor at Yongbyon. Kim also reportedly indicated that North Korea would be prepared to permit resumed monitoring at Yongbyon by the International Atomic Energy Agency (IAEA).[3] These would be at best preliminary (and reversible) measures to end North Korea's nuclear weapons development and in no way would constitute the definitive end of the program. Policymakers therefore need to weigh carefully the options, trade-offs, and potential liabilities both in reducing the scope, scale, and pace of Pyongyang's nuclear development and in mitigating the more worrisome possibilities associated with North Korea's possession of nuclear weapons.

A single nuclear test establishes a baseline but does not confirm a particular trajectory. In light of the longer-term pattern of North Korean nuclear and missile development, what kinds of capabilities are imaginable? Does Kim Jung Il or anyone else in North Korea have a specific goal in mind for the nuclear program? Is such a goal realistic or achievable in light of the DPRK's economic, scientific, and technical circumstances?

To assess these issues, this essay examines alternative scenarios for North Korean nuclear weapons development to 2015. This requires examination at three levels: (a) policy calculations within the DPRK leadership, (b) the technical and financial resources available to the program, and (c) the policy options of external powers to inhibit the DPRK's future nuclear and missile development. Notwithstanding the leadership's insistence that it will protect the North Korean system at all costs, Pyongyang might be compelled to limit its future nuclear options. For example, although North Korea might have specific nuclear objectives in mind, other countries may be able to deny Pyongyang the means to realize these goals, or North Korea may simply lack the resources to achieve them. Yet projecting the DPRK's future forces in the absence of fuller insight into its nuclear intentions remains daunting. There is also a tendency in the aftermath of the first tests of new nuclear entrants to overstate a country's prospective capabilities. One need only recall the hugely inflated U.S. estimates of the Chinese nuclear force dating from the mid- and late 1960s, following Beijing's initial test, though many of these estimates were generated with justifications for a "thin" ABM system in mind. This essay cautions against linear projections based on a single presumed nuclear trajectory.

It is necessary to make two additional assumptions. The first is to assume the basic stability of the North Korean system over the next ten years. Since many analysts (and more than a few officials outside the DPRK) deem this outcome almost unimaginable, this essay does not discount the possibility of significant shifts in leadership and policy. For example, very little is known about potential succession arrangements following the death or physical incapacitation of Kim Jung Il. Kim will be sixty-seven years old in February 2009. Is it reasonable to assume that a decade hence the DPRK will still be in the era of General Kim? Thus, change within the regime or true regime change might well occur, but for purposes of analysis this essay posits neither.

The second assumption this essay makes is to preclude a highly optimistic scenario (i.e., a North Korean "zero option"). This scenario assumes that the DPRK would be prepared to forego the totality of its nuclear programs in exchange for three basic goals long sought by the leadership: validation, compensation, and assurance, in particular from the United States. A grand bargain posits both that there is a price that external powers are prepared to pay for denuclearization of the peninsula and that Pyongyang will deem this payment sufficient to ensure the survival and legitimation of the regime. This argument, however, minimizes or neglects the internal considerations that have shaped and sustained North Korea's nuclear program. For North Korea, the Cold War has never ended; in the aftermath of North Korea's nuclear test, it is not even clear that the leadership *wants* the Cold War to end. Thus, a future where the DPRK would no longer be able to characterize itself as under acute threat might undermine the system more than its current siege mentality, since prevailing circumstances justify highly centralized control and major limits on the foreign presence inside North Korea.

The remainder of this essay addresses three questions pertaining to the North's potential nuclear capabilities in 2015:

- What are the leadership's presumed objectives in developing a nuclear weapons capability?
- What resources would be required to fulfill these goals?
- How are the policies of outside powers likely to affect North Korea's ability to achieve its objectives?

Assessing the DPRK's Nuclear Goals

Very little is known about how North Korea assesses its nuclear requirements, other than the obvious conclusion that the leadership believes it is now more secure with a demonstrated nuclear weapons capability than without one. The DPRK first claimed status as a nuclear-armed state on February 10, 2005, when it announced that it had manufactured an unspecified number of nuclear weapons. Though it is possible that Pyongyang believed this declaration would elicit initiatives from the United States and others to forestall an actual test, no such initiatives were forthcoming. Thus, the October 2006 test was designed in part to demonstrate definitively North Korea's ability to build and test a nuclear device. The test was also an act of assertion directed against prevailing international arrangements that Kim Jung Il opposes, including U.S. alliance commitments to the Republic of Korea (ROK). It also revealed Kim's conviction that the DPRK is not accorded appropriate political weight by outside powers, especially by the United States.[4]

Yet what kind of nuclear capability does North Korea seek? Leaders in Pyongyang have revealed little about their thinking; it is entirely possible that they have yet to give serious consideration to this issue. Moreover, as Peter Hayes has argued, "There are no grounds to believe that the DPRK will employ a U.S. or Western conceptual framework of nuclear deterrence and crisis management in developing its own nuclear doctrine and use options."[5] This does not mean, however, that leadership calculations are unfathomable.

The fullest evidence of the DPRK's declared nuclear goals is contained in a Foreign Ministry statement of October 3 (six days prior to the nuclear test) and in another on October 17, immediately following passage of UNSC Resolution 1718.[6] The October 3 statement justified the impending test on the basis of "the United States' extreme war threats and sanction and pressure maneuvers." A "nuclear deterrent" was therefore deemed necessary as "a corresponding defensive countermeasure." There was also a pledge that the DPRK would "never use nuclear weapons first" and would "thoroughly prohibit threats through nuclear weapons and nuclear transfer." In addition, the statement argued:

> Our nuclear weapons will serve, to all intents and purposes, as a reliable war deterrent for protecting the supreme interests of our state and the security of our nation from the United States' threat of aggression and preventing a new war . . . on the Korean peninsula. We will always sincerely implement our international commitment in the field of nuclear nonproliferation as a responsible nuclear [weapons] state. . . . Our ultimate goal [in advocating the denuclearization of the Korean Peninsula] is not a denuclearization to be followed by our unilateral disarmament . . . but the denuclearization aimed at settling the hostile relations between the DPRK and the United States and removing the very source of all nuclear threats from the Korean peninsula and its vicinity.

Pyongyang's statement bears immediate comparison with those of other new nuclear entrants, all of whom have contended that they were compelled to test under acute threats to national security, with parallel assurances that they would exercise utmost prudence as a nuclear-weapons state. The North Korean statement is especially reminiscent of China's postdetonation announcement of October 16, 1964. In late October 2006 a senior Chinese Foreign Ministry official stated that North Korean diplomats (in an effort to justify their program) reminded Chinese interlocutors that "we are only doing what you did four decades ago." Chinese officials supposedly retorted that the circumstances prevailing in the 1960s were very different from those of the early twenty-first century.[7]

Such a judgment, however, is very much in the eye of the beholder. North Korea's essential circumstances are eerily similar to those confronting China in the early to mid-1960s. China then and North Korea now constitute embattled, isolated states experiencing extreme economic deprivation (including parallel experiences with famine), with the supreme leader in both systems prepared to devote extraordinary efforts to build nuclear weapons and thereby achieve notional equivalence to their major adversaries. In addition, it is unsurprising that North Korea did not explicitly threaten to export nuclear technology, fissile material, or finished weapons. Any such threat would wholly negate Pyongyang's repeated claim that its weapons are intended only for deterrence, without specifying what it deems necessary for deterrence. The DPRK may also have concluded that any such threat would have been too overt a challenge to the United States. Thus, North Korea has not made explicit or detailed reference to the scenario that the United States in particular finds most worrisome—namely, that Pyongyang might choose to transfer nuclear material, technology, or even a fabricated weapon to another state or to a nonstate actor.

What would the DPRK's basic logic, if accepted by the outside world, indicate about how much capability would be required to achieve the goal of deterrence? Three alternative nuclear futures for 2015 emerge:

- a largely political nuclear capability
- an operational deterrent capability
- a deficient or failed effort to achieve an operational capability

These respective outcomes seem relatively straightforward, though it would be the height of conceit to specify how each "translates" in quantitative terms. The remainder of this essay identifies some relevant signposts and possibilities that might indicate movement along one of these three paths.

Technical and Resource Requirements

Most of what the outside world knows about North Korea's nuclear weapons potential concerns the DPRK's inventory of fissile material.[8] The ancillary technology, materials, equipment, and know-how needed to build an operational nuclear force (i.e., miniaturizing warheads, mating a warhead to a missile, and readying an alternative means of delivery, such as aircraft) represent equally or even more daunting technical and engineering challenges.[9] The ability to build nuclear warheads and integrate such capabilities with a delivery system, however, would indicate whether the DPRK either is advancing toward specific goals or will remain highly constrained in what it can achieve. In the event of scenario one, in which the DPRK's nuclear achievement is by and large symbolic, the characteristics of a North Korean nuclear weapon would matter far less. Development of a credible warhead, however, would be decisive in determining whether North Korea is on the path to scenario two. Failed efforts to achieve such a goal would indicate scenario three.

The DPRK's production of fissile material for weapons development appears entirely homegrown and self-sustaining. The prospects for denying North Korea technology relevant to such production therefore seem dubious. It is reasonable to assume that North Korea long ago stockpiled or developed the necessary technologies and materials for fissile material production, utilizing the spent fuel from its graphite-moderated reactor. Some analysts and U.S. government officials believe that the DPRK might ultimately possess a uranium enrichment capability as an alternative source of fissile material. Such a prospect remains highly questionable, however. Pyongyang pursued this option in transactions with A. Q. Khan (including acquisition of centrifuges with which North Korea may have undertaken experimentation or exploratory work); it also sought to procure substantial quantities of industrial materials needed for an enrichment program through black markets in Europe. Yet there is still no definitive evidence of a proven production capability, and it is possible that North Korea long ago shelved major efforts to develop one.[10] Enhanced international monitoring of North Korea's foreign technology acquisition further complicates any possibilities of an enrichment capability, whereas the DPRK claims to "have mastered the entire plutonium production cycle."[11] It therefore seems highly likely that the DPRK will continue to rely on its plutonium option, since it possesses the requisite experience and know-how, a functioning technological and industrial infrastructure, and a proven weapons design. This bears in particular on warhead miniaturization, in view of the smaller size of plutonium-based weapons.

In comments to a visiting U.S. delegation three weeks after the nuclear test, North Korean officials stated that the DPRK planned to accumulate additional fissile material by reloading its 5-megawatt electric reactor at Yongbyon with fresh fuel rods in 2007 and by reprocessing the spent fuel at appropriate intervals. This would be the third major reloading of the reactor since North Korea's pullout from the NPT in early 2003. According to Siegfried Hecker, a prominent nuclear scientist on the U.S. delegation, complications at the fuel fabrication facility seem likely to slow the production rate of new fuel rods. Ri Hong Sop, director of the Yongbyon Nuclear Complex, also informed Hecker that possible changes in the "political situation" could dictate a less than optimal schedule for the unloading of spent fuel.[12] He acknowledged that North Korean engineers still hope to resume work on the 50-megawatt electric reactor that was under construction at the time of the establishment of the Agreed Framework. Technical progress has been slowed, however, by the physical deterioration of equipment placed in storage more than a decade ago as well as by difficulties in assembling all the materials for the 50-megawatt electric reactor. To date, there has been no meaningful resumption of work at the site. (According to Hecker, plans in the early 1990s for a 200-megawatt electric reactor are fully in abeyance at this time.) If construction did resume on the 50-megawatt electric reactor, and it became operational, however, the reactor could enable a tenfold increase in the annual production of plutonium.[13] An enhanced production capability would enable much more ambitious goals for the nuclear program. Reliance on the single operational reactor will therefore impose inherent limitations on the scope of the program, though the consequences of a slow but steady production rate should not be minimized.

Yet North Korea has not reinvented the laws of physics. Its extant reactor can produce approximately 5–7 kilograms of plutonium annually, or enough for approximately one additional weapon per year, assuming no major problems either in the operation of the reactor or in the reprocessing of spent fuel. Estimates for North Korea's plutonium inventory vary. A higher-end estimate (prepared by the Institute for Science and International Security) credits North Korea with a total amount of separated plutonium in mid-2006 of 20–53 kilograms, or enough to fabricate between 4 and 13 nuclear weapons. (This estimate posits that 4–5 kilograms of plutonium would be required to build a weapon; other assumptions about the required amounts of plutonium for a weapon are somewhat higher.) By mid-2008 (i.e., when the spent fuel currently in the reactor has been unloaded, cooled, and fully reprocessed), the Institute for Science and International Security (ISIS) estimate increases to 40–68 kilograms, or enough for 8–17 weapons.[14] The October 2006 test reduced both estimates by one. Assuming no additional plutonium production capability between now and 2015 and steady-state production at the Yongbyon facility, a "guesstimate" would be a maximal inventory of 14–23 weapons. A more conservative estimate, prepared by Siegfried Hecker, posits a total inventory in November 2006 of 40–50 kilograms, which he judges sufficient for 6–8 weapons. According to Hecker's assumptions, this would enable a total weapons inventory by 2015 of perhaps 14–16 weapons, assuming that all the separated plutonium was converted into finished weapons.[15]

Two additional considerations directly affect judgments about the sufficiency of the plutonium supply: how Pyongyang evaluated the results of the first test and whether North Korea deems a political deterrent sufficient for its strategic purposes. External analysts have offered a range of views on the technical results of the October 2006 test. There are no indications that North Korean officials judge the test either a political or a technical disappointment, but we should hardly expect otherwise. The predominant view outside of North Korea, however, is that the test (though not an outright failure) was far from a full success.[16] If the DPRK wanted principally to demonstrate the ability to conduct a nuclear detonation, then even a problematic test result would have been sufficient. If North Korean expectations were greater, however, then Pyongyang has incurred "the onus without the bonus."

Separate assessments of the test results, one undertaken by Richard Garwin and Frank von Hippel and another by Siegfried Hecker, suggest two possibilities: the test either involved a low yield based on a larger, simple device or was a far more sophisticated design geared to configuring the weapon for use on a Nodong medium-range missile. Though acknowledging that any judgment is speculative, Hecker considers the first hypothesis far more plausible.[17] He believes that there is only one proven means to ensure a practicable, reliable design for a warhead: North Korea would need to test and more than likely test on multiple occasions. This creates added political and resource dilemmas for the DPRK. If North Korea's goals are more ambitious (i.e., scenario two, not scenario one), Pyongyang would have little alternative but to test again, which could readily entail heightened penalties against North Korea, including those China might impose. The resource issue concerns what might be termed the nuclear credibility paradox. Further tests might move North Korea closer to the goal of an operational capability, but each additional test would also reduce the size of the DPRK's potential nuclear weapons inventory. In addition, it is always possible that a future test or tests would fail to achieve satisfactory results. As noted in another post-test assessment, "amidst Pyongyang's post-test bravado, the options to enhance its incomplete deterrent remain inauspicious."[18]

North Korean technical personnel and military planners presumably perceive the need for additional tests, but this will very likely be a political rather than a technical decision. Despite some early reports that North Korea was preparing for another test, none has occurred. Pyongyang may be holding the tacit threat of an additional test (or tests) in reserve, depending on how leaders in North Korea assess the diplomatic and political responses of outside powers to their nuclear weapons development and on whether the DPRK believes its expressed concerns are being satisfactorily addressed. According to South Korean press reports, when Chinese state councilor Tang Jiaxuan met with Kim Jung Il on October 19, 2006, Kim reportedly informed Tang that the DPRK had "no plans" for a second test.[19] Kim also reportedly told Tang, however, that future North Korean actions would be contingent on the policies of other powers, in particular the United States. The Stanford University group visiting the DPRK observed: "None of the officials we met gave us the impression that they are planning a second nuclear test."[20] Though these are only impressions, and remarks from North Korean officials should be scrutinized with ample care, the observations of the group seem credible at this time.

A decision to proceed with additional testing would constitute compelling evidence both that the DPRK deemed the first test results unsatisfactory and that Pyongyang's goals for its nuclear program are more ambitious than a one-time demonstration of strategic autonomy. To be sure, there is every reason to believe that North Korea will proceed with the refinement of its nuclear capabilities, even without further tests. Pyongyang's situation would then be somewhat akin to what India in the more than two decades between its "peaceful nuclear explosion" of 1974 and nuclear weapons tests of 1998 characterized as a "recessed deterrent." Though still not having consented either to full disclosure of its weapons program or to binding limitations on its nuclear activities, North Korea would not, however, trigger the major international responses that would undoubtedly result from additional tests. Deterrence through uncertainty and ambiguity, though entailing major risks, would be a far less consequential outcome in strategic terms than vigorously pursuing a deployed nuclear force. In a technical and operational sense, however, development without additional testing can proceed only so far. Will Pyongyang ultimately be prepared to incur additional risks by further tests, or will it remain content with a more ambiguous nuclear status? As Jungmin Kim and Peter Hayes argue,

> Having tested and failed, the DPRK can no longer rely on opacity as the basis for . . . a credible nuclear force. . . . The DPRK might believe that a half kilotonne "mininuk" still provides it with a measure of nuclear deterrence and compellence; but . . . other nuclear weapons states . . . [will not] perceive it . . . [as] anything more than an unstable, unreliable and relatively small nuclear explosive device.[21]

This suggests an uncertain and potentially unstable nuclear environment.

North Korea's ability to deliver a nuclear weapon also assumes intrinsic importance in any assessment of its nuclear weapons potential. This is not an issue with respect to targeting the ROK since—with or without nuclear weapons—North Korea already holds South Korea hostage. (Targeting of U.S. bases in the ROK with nuclear weapons, however, would constitute a much more worrisome possibility.) Even in the event of a recessed deterrent, the DPRK wants to demonstrate a capability for strategic reach, in particular the ability to target Japan and U.S. military facilities in Japan and beyond, beginning with Guam. These missiles are reportedly armed with conventional warheads at present, though there are scattered indications that some might be armed with chemical weapons. In addition, some analysts also speculate about the possibility of a missile armed with a biological warhead, but the available data does not enable an informed judgment on the credibility or feasibility of this claim.

The pivotal issue is whether North Korea is undertaking major efforts to pair a nuclear warhead with extant or future ballistic missiles. There is the additional question of whether the DPRK deems the ability to reach the continental United States, Alaska, or Hawaii with a ballistic missile either feasible or necessary. Repeatedly over the past decade, the DPRK has threatened to retaliate for any U.S. strike on North Korea by launching strikes against U.S. assets anywhere in the world or even against U.S. territory. For example, a December 1998 statement proffered the following warning:

> We have our own operation plan. "Surgical operation" style attack and "preventive strike" [by the United States] are by no means an exclusive option of the United

States. The mode of strike is not a monopoly of the U.S., either. It must be clearly known that there is no limit to the strike of our People's Army and that on this planet there is no room for escaping the strike.[22]

Though the DPRK has yet to demonstrate the capability for building and testing such a missile, such threats not only cannot be discounted but also must necessarily be a factor in long-term U.S. planning. A successful launch of a multistage missile would also help validate Pyongyang's self-perception of its presumed equivalence with U.S. strategic power.

Pyongyang's more immediate requirement is to put its neighbors and U.S. regionally deployed forces at risk. North Korea already possesses a daunting array of conventionally armed short- and medium-range missiles and other weapons systems such as long-range artillery that can be directed against targets in South Korea. These capabilities are based on indigenous production capabilities as well as the continued development of new or improved capabilities.[23] According to General B. B. Bell, commander of U.S. Forces Korea (USFK), North Korea currently deploys over 800 missiles, comprising "over 600 Scud missiles of various types and as many as 200 Nodong missiles."[24]

Siegfried Hecker's observation about the need for nuclear testing applies with equal relevance to ballistic missiles. Pyongyang cannot expect to achieve a credible longer-range missile capability simply by having tested a prototype first in 1998 and a more advanced version eight years later, with no testing in between. (This long interregnum, however, reflected North Korea's pledges of a moratorium on the testing of longer-range missiles, with advancement of multistage missile capabilities during this period limited principally to engine testing at static test beds.) The contrast between the clear success of three Nodong missiles and three Scud variants—all proven, reliable systems—in North Korea's July 2006 tests as well as the conspicuous failure of the Taepodong 2 highlights an inescapable conclusion: additional testing of missiles, especially multiple stage missiles, is essential to any North Korean plans to more fully operationalize its delivery capabilities, whether or not the missiles are armed with nuclear warheads.[25] Though it is possible that after October 9 North Korea will feel less constrained in pursuing a longer-range missile option, resource constraints and technology and engineering requirements may impose serious constraints on any such plans relative either to the continued investment in more "tried and true" missile systems or to the pursuit of less ambitious nuclear goals.

The DPRK might, however, have an alternative and less obtrusive path to missile enhancement through its long-standing relationship with Iran. Tehran has been among North Korea's closest and longest-term customers and collaborators. Iran has purchased and tested versions of the Nodong, designated the Shahab-3, with a range of approximately 1,500 kilometers.[26] Tehran is engaged in a vigorous testing program, purportedly based on an indigenous manufacturing capability.[27] Iran claims to have developed a new model of the missile, with an estimated range of 2,000 kilometers; other reports suggest an additional missile variant with a range of 1,300–1,400 kilometers. Recent innovations have also encompassed new configurations in warhead design. The accuracy of the missile has also reportedly been enhanced and the estimated weight of the warhead reduced to seven hundred kilograms. In view of the lengthy, close collaboration between the DPRK and Iran, there is a real possibility that design innovations and test data are being shared between them. If so, North Korea may be an indirect but substantial beneficiary of this collaboration. Such cooperation might enable Pyongyang to accelerate progress toward ultimately "mating" a Nodong missile with a nuclear warhead.

These judgments presuppose that the DPRK will be able to develop a workable miniaturized warhead that could be placed atop such a missile, thereby putting Japan and U.S. forces at increased risk, and even potentially extending beyond Japan. For these reasons alone, therefore, we should anticipate heightened missile defense efforts by Japan as well as the United States. Yet the outside world knows very little about the status of North Korea's research and development (R&D) efforts. Based on the problematic results of the first nuclear test, this is a stage in nuclear weapons development that North Korea has yet to approach and (as Hecker also notes) would almost certainly require additional nuclear weapon tests: but this highlights yet again the potential implications of North Korea having definitively crossed the nuclear divide without a clear sense of how the country proceeds from here. It is likely that the DPRK has only begun to ponder fully what an operational nuclear capability might entail. This is not intended to suggest that there is a single path to nuclear and missile advancement. Entirely possible, however, is that Pyongyang's weapons scientists and missile builders are only now beginning to come to grips both with the new realities that they face and with a still problematic path to becoming a more credible nuclear weapons state.

Some Policy Implications

North Korea's test of a nuclear device attests to its ability to undertake a technically demanding long-term program and see it to fruition but reveals very little else about where or how Pyongyang proceeds from here. Not at all clear is whether anyone in North Korea could answer this latter question. Even if someone could, equally uncertain is whether the DPRK has the wherewithal to get there from here on a practicable timetable. Added to this is the question of whether the actions of the outside world will matter very much in North Korea's future decisions. As a seasoned and appropriately cynical former U.S. official has observed, if for sake of argument the United States directly approached Kim Jung Il to achieve a political breakthrough, would the North Korean leader be able to say what he wants and needs from the United States? The answer is not at all certain.

North Korea has tested a nuclear device, even if the results may not have been what Pyongyang expected. This act cannot be "undone." The DPRK is, however, one of the world's most impenetrable states. The immediate policy questions relate to what outside powers can do both to minimize the risks posed by North Korean actions and to make it as difficult as possible for North Korea to achieve significant headway in its nuclear goals without triggering responses from Pyongyang that make the existing situation even more dangerous. In this context, it is imperative that communication channels remain open to North Korea and that new ones be considered. Though the persistent efforts by China to induce Pyongyang's return to the six-party talks are welcome, this is an episodic diplomatic venue, rather than an ongoing process. There is the obvious risk that the DPRK will endeavor to "pocket" the political gains that would derive from more sustained efforts to open doors to North Korea's leaders, but this should be the least of the outside world's concerns. The U.S. willingness to meet bilaterally with North Korea in Berlin in mid-January 2007 constitutes evidence of flexibility that may yield meaningful results; even if failing to produce a significant or sustained breakthrough, it is heartening that the effort has been undertaken.[28]

Notwithstanding its isolation, open defiance of nonproliferation norms, and acute internal vulnerabilities, North Korea has grimly persisted in its nuclear weapons efforts. Its indigenous technological and industrial base will likely enable it to make continued progress toward longer-term goals in weapons development, though this progress will remain halting and incomplete. The question is whether external powers can meaningfully inhibit or slow the DPRK's further nuclear development. North Korean trading companies and military-scientific personnel will maintain and even enhance their efforts to acquire a wide array of dual-use equipment and industrial items to advance the DPRK's weapons testing and development programs; limiting its access to these technologies must therefore be a high-priority, coordinated policy endeavor. This task is now made easier both by the international community's obligations under UNSC Resolution 1718 and by the heightened efforts among the five other members of the six-party process to communicate and coordinate their respective actions. Yet what if (as seems much more likely than not) North Korea is able to continue its programs, all the while reminding the outside world of its ability to inflict harm on its neighbors, even as its neighbors remain equally concerned by the risks to regional stability posed by an internal meltdown in North Korea? The DPRK is a hugely repressive state and very possibly an endangered species, but what are the policy alternatives if North Korea either refuses to fold its tent or undertakes additional, even riskier steps to counter perceived threats to its survival? What if the regime is able to revive its economy through a process of incremental reform without foregoing its nuclear capabilities and longer-term nuclear potential? These questions remain deeply sobering and require full and frank discussion among all affected states, unburdened by unrealistic preconceptions about North Korea and without remaining tethered to past policy decisions and their consequences.

Notes

1. This chapter previously appeared in *Asia Policy* 2, no. 3 (January 2007): 105–23, and is reprinted with permission from the National Bureau of Asian Research. The views in this paper are those of the author and should not be attributed to the U.S. government, the Department of Defense, or the Naval War College.

2. Richard K. Betts, "Universal Deterrence or Conceptual Collapse? Liberal Pessimism and Utopian Realism," in *The Coming Crisis: Nuclear Proliferation, U.S. Interests, and World Order*, ed. Victor A. Utgoff (Cambridge, MA: MIT Press, 2000), 57.

3. "N. Korea 'Ready to Suspend Nuclear Activities,'" *Chosun Ilbo*, January 22, 2007, http://english.chosun.com/w21data/html/news/200701/200701220011.html.

4. On the latter issue, see Peter Hayes, *The Stalker State: North Korean Proliferation and the End of American Nuclear Hegemony*, Nautilus Institute Policy Forum Online 06-82A, October 4, 2006, www.nautilus.org/fora/security/0682Hayes.html.

5. Ibid.

6. Statement of the DPRK Foreign Ministry, Korean Central Broadcasting Station and Korea Central News Agency (KCNA), October 3, 2006; and statement by DPRK Foreign Ministry spokesman, Korean Central Broadcasting System, October 17, 2006. Though a Foreign Ministry statement might sound like a routine pronouncement, analysts of the North Korean media indicate that such statements are very rare, highly authoritative, and only released following approval at the highest levels of the leadership.

7. Author's interview with senior Chinese Foreign Ministry official, Beijing, October 30, 2006.

8. See, for example, David Albright and Paul Brannan, *The North Korean Plutonium Stock Mid-2006*, Institute for Science and International Security, June 26, 2006, http://www.isis-online.org/publications/dprk/dprkplutonium.pdf.

9. For a comprehensive overview, see *North Korea's Weapons Programmes: A Net Assessment*, International Institute for Strategic Studies, January 21, 2004, http://www.iiss.org/publications/strategic-dossiers/north-korean-dossier.

10. For a very useful compilation of available information, see Sharon Squassoni, *Weapons of Mass Destruction: Trade between North Korea and Pakistan*, Congressional Research

Service Report for Congress, March 11, 2004, 4–9, 11–15, http://fpc.state.gov/documents/organization/30781.pdf.

11. Siegfried S. Hecker, *Report on North Korean Nuclear Program*, Center for International Security and Cooperation, Stanford University, Stanford, CA, November 15, 2006, 6. This trip report is based on the results of a late October to early November visit of Hecker and three other colleagues to the DPRK. Hecker, former director of the Los Alamos National Laboratory and a plutonium specialist, is the only foreign scientist known to have examined plutonium metal produced at the DPRK nuclear complex. Siegfried Hecker, "Visit to the Yongbyon Scientific Research Center in North Korea," testimony before the Senate Foreign Relations Committee, Washington, DC, January 21, 2004, http://www.fas.org/irp/congress/2004_hr/012104hecker.pdf.

12. Hecker, *Report on North Korean Nuclear Program*, 5.

13. Ibid., 6.

14. Albright and Brannan, *North Korean Plutonium Stock Mid-2006*, tables 1–2.

15. Hecker, *Report on North Korean Nuclear Program*, 8.

16. Space constraints preclude more detailed discussion here. See Jungmin Kang and Peter Hayes, *Technical Analysis of the DPRK Nuclear Test*, Nautilus Institute Policy Forum Online 06-89A, October 20, 2006, http://www.nautilus.org/fora/security/0689HayesKang .html; Richard Garwin and Frank N. von Hippel, "A Technical Analysis: Deconstructing North Korea's October 9 Nuclear Test," *Arms Control Today* 36, no. 9 (November 2006): 14–16; and Hecker, *Report on North Korean Nuclear Program*, 2–4.

17. Hecker, *Report on North Korean Nuclear Program*, 3–4.

18. International Institute for Strategic Studies, "North Korea's Nuclear Test: Continuing Reverberations," *IISS Strategic Comments* 12, no. 8 (October 2006), http://www.iiss.org/publications/strategic-comments/past-issues/volume-12—2006/volume-12—issue-8/north-koreas-nuclear-test.

19. "North Korean Leader Said to Have Promised No More Nuclear Test," *Yonhap News*, October 20, 2006.

20. Hecker, *Report on North Korean Nuclear Program*, 3.

21. Kang and Hayes, *Technical Analysis of the DPRK Nuclear Test*.

22. Statement of the DPRK Korean People's Army General Staff Spokesman, KCNA, December 2, 1998.

23. For a detailed and helpful overview, see James Martin Center for Nonproliferation Studies, *CNS Special Report on North Korean Ballistic Missile Capabilities*, Monterey Institute for International Studies, March 22, 2006, http://cns.miis.edu/pubs/week/pdf/060321 .pdf.

24. B. B. Bell, testimony before the Senate Armed Services Committee, Washington, DC, March 7, 2006, http://armed-services.senate.gov/statemnt/2006/March/Bell%2003-07-06.pdf.

25. International Institute for Strategic Studies, "North Korea's Missile Tests—Troubling Trajectories," *IISS Strategic Comments* 12, no. 6, July 2006.

26. See in particular Squassoni, *Weapons of Mass Destruction*, 10–11. Despite the study's title, the report discusses North Korea's missile transactions with both Pakistan and Iran.

27. The information in this paragraph draws substantially on Kensuke Ebata, "North Korea's Nuclear Weapon Test Prompts Concerns about Iranian Missile Development," *Sekai Shuho*, November 14, 2006, 48–49. The author thanks Alan Romberg for calling this article to his attention.

28. Glenn Kessler, "U.S. Open to Bilateral Talks on Ties with N. Korea: Envoy's Offer Linked to Shutdown of Nuclear Programs, as Pyongyang Had Vowed," *Washington Post*, January 18, 2007.

CHAPTER FOURTEEN

The Iranian Nuclear Program

Sharon Squassoni

Iran's nuclear program is the most serious challenge to the nuclear nonprolifera-tion regime since Iraq in 1991, measured not by how far Iran has progressed to-ward a nuclear weapons capability, but by the extent to which the circumstances and responses of the international community call into question basic premises of the regime. Iran, a member state of the Nuclear Nonproliferation Treaty (NPT), claims its nuclear program is legitimate and at times has agreed to transparency measures to support those claims. Although two decades of clandestine activities have formed a disturbing pattern of deception, the International Atomic Energy Agency (IAEA) chose not to find Iran in noncompliance with its safeguards agree-ment but rather asserted it could not ensure the absence of undeclared nuclear material or activities in Iran, leaving the IAEA Board of Governors to find Iran in noncompliance. This has been noted not just by Iran, but also by Russia and China, two key votes on the United Nations Security Council (UNSC). Coming on the heels of the intelligence debacle over Iraq's purported weapons of mass destruction capabilities in 2003, many states have argued to go slowly. In the meanwhile, Iran has continued to develop its uranium enrichment capabilities, which could be used either to enrich uranium for fuel or for nuclear weapons.

Iran's vast reserves of oil and natural gas provide it with leverage and cash sur-pluses that arguably have weakened the resolve of states to impose sanctions. Fur-ther, Iran's support of terrorism and international terrorist organizations has made it difficult for the United States to engage in direct diplomacy, while increasing the stakes. A. Q. Khan's nuclear black market assistance in developing the most sensitive nuclear technology—centrifuge uranium enrichment capabilities—has further reduced leverage in this case, if only because getting crucial informa-tion requires political capital the United States is either unwilling or unable to expend with Pakistan, a key ally in the global war on terrorism. Perhaps most im-portantly, Iran's acquisition of a centrifuge enrichment capability is what makes this situation stand apart from that of Iraq in 1991 or North Korea in 1994, and gives it particular urgency. The challenges of detecting clandestine centrifuge enrichment facilities or undeclared material at a declared enrichment site, either through intelligence or inspections, are formidable. They are so formidable, in fact, that the international community has demanded that Iran halt uranium enrichment (and plutonium reprocessing) activities, perhaps forever.

Herein lies the most serious challenge to the NPT and its member states. Iran has continued to defy UN Security Council resolutions (1737 and 1747) that require suspension of sensitive nuclear activities to build confidence in the peaceful uses of its nuclear program, arguing that it has a right under Article IV of the NPT to pursue peaceful nuclear activities. The issue is really Iran's lack of compliance with its NPT safeguards obligations, rather than its NPT rights. But as long as Iran's enrichment activities comply with IAEA safeguards requirements, there appear to be few levers to halt them. Short of war, the lack of effective mechanisms to enforce UNSC resolutions and automatic penalties for noncompliance, such as a freeze in nuclear activities, have allowed Iran to continue to develop its capabilities with few apparent obstacles.

Although further unilateral and multilateral sanctions may be imposed to ratchet up the pressure on Iran, and Iran could even begin to truly come back into compliance, the system still needs to be fixed. Otherwise, additional states may follow Iran's path.

Here the debate becomes murky. Is Iran exploiting a loophole in the NPT that needs to be or can be closed? Should all states have to justify their national nuclear energy decisions, and if so, what are the criteria? Is there a need for a separate organization outside the IAEA devoted to maintaining the effectiveness of the NPT? Finally, will it be possible to devise and implement a fair and principled approach to restrict the development of sensitive nuclear technologies such as enrichment and reprocessing?

Nuclear Origins

Iran's nuclear program is almost fifty years old, but its development has proceeded in fits and starts. Until 1974, virtually the only nuclear facility was a 5-megawatt thermal research reactor supplied by the United States, which was purchased in 1959 and became operational in 1967. Nonetheless, by the mid-1970s, the shah had sent thousands of students abroad to study nuclear physics in the United Kingdom, the United States, and India, had bought a 10 percent share in Eurodif's uranium enrichment concern in 1975, and had set up nuclear cooperation agreements with France and Germany. The goal of the Atomic Energy Organization of Iran (AEOI), established in 1974, reportedly was to construct twenty-three nuclear power reactors by the mid-1990s. The plan might have been regarded as grandiose but not necessarily as a "back door" to a nuclear weapons program, possibly because Iran did not then seek the technologies to enrich or reprocess its own fuel.[1] There were a few suspicions of a nuclear weapons program, but these abated in the decade between the Iranian 1979 revolution and the end of the Iran-Iraq war, as both brought a halt to nuclear activities. Iran's current plans—to construct seven nuclear power plants (1,000 megawatts each) by 2025—are still ambitious, particularly for a state with considerable oil and gas reserves.[2] Iran argues today, as it did in the 1970s, that nuclear power is necessary for rising domestic energy consumption, while oil and gas are needed to generate foreign currency. Few observers believe that such an ambitious program is necessary or economical for Iran. However, the combination of rising oil prices, concern about global climate change, and strong economic growth in states like China and India have contributed to renewed enthusiasm for nuclear energy worldwide. In such an atmosphere, it could become increasingly difficult to support nuclear power for some states but not for others.

When the shah fell from power in 1979, two reactors at Bushehr had been partially completed by Germany's Siemens Corporation. Not only did the revolution and war with Iraq in the 1980s sideline the nuclear program, but Iraqi bombing raids destroyed a significant portion of the nuclear site at Bushehr. When Iran sought to reestablish ties with European technology firms after the war, many suppliers became uneasy about cooperation. In 1991, the German government decided not to allow reactor exports to Iran. A deal for a research reactor from India was called off reportedly after the U.S. government pressured the Indian government not to proceed. By 1995, only Russia appeared willing to finish constructing one 1000-megawatt power reactor at the Bushehr site. Russian government officials repeatedly assured critics that they could minimize any proliferation risks.

The United States has led efforts to virtually embargo nuclear cooperation with Iran since the 1980s, with some success. In 1995, the United States persuaded Russia not to provide a centrifuge uranium enrichment plant, although not before Iran had already received Russian technical assistance in uranium milling, heavy water production, and heavy water research reactors.[3] In 1997, China agreed to undertake no new nuclear cooperation with Iran, but again, after Iran had already received assistance in uranium mining, laser enrichment, and in the construction of a uranium conversion facility.[4] In 1998, the United States persuaded Ukraine not to supply turbines for the Bushehr reactor. In 2000, Russia agreed not to supply laser technology for uranium enrichment; and in 2002, Russia agreed to take back spent fuel from the Bushehr reactor, eliminating an excuse for Iran to pursue reprocessing technologies (used to separate plutonium from spent fuel for potential use in a nuclear weapon). Unfortunately, it was too late to head off assistance from Pakistani scientist A. Q. Khan's nuclear black market network.[5]

Iranian officials have asserted repeatedly that Iran's nuclear program is strictly peaceful, stating in May 2003 that "we consider the acquiring, development and use of nuclear weapons inhuman, immoral, illegal and against our basic principles. They have no place in Iran's defense doctrine."[6] The Iranian government spokesman Gholam-Hossein Elham said in July 2006 that Iran's nuclear activities are for peaceful purposes, and that the Islamic republic will never produce weapons of mass destruction.[7] Iranian officials have also insisted on their right to develop peaceful uses of nuclear technology. Ali Khamenei, supreme leader of Iran, said in November 2004 that Iran would not "give up" its enrichment "at any price," and former president Khatami stated in March 2005 that ending Iran's uranium enrichment program is "completely unacceptable." In August 2006, President Ahmadinejad told the Iranian press that "peaceful nuclear energy is the right of the Iranian nation. The Iranian nation has chosen that based upon international regulations, it wants to use it, and no one can stop it."[8]

Uranium enrichment can be used for both peaceful (nuclear fuel) and military (nuclear weapons) purposes. At the heart of the debate lie two issues: doubt about Iran's intentions, magnified by revelations of almost two decades of clandestine activities, and questions about whether the international community can adequately verify the absence of enrichment for nuclear weapons or should further restrict access to sensitive nuclear technologies.

IAEA Inspections at Nuclear Sites from 2003 to 2007

U.S. officials had been concerned about Iran's nuclear ambitions for over a decade when the National Council of Resistance of Iran (NCR), a group designated as a foreign terrorist organization by the U.S. State Department, held a press conference in 2002, alleging that Iran had clandestine nuclear sites at Natanz for uranium enrichment and at Arak for heavy water production. The allegations helped trigger intensive inspections by the IAEA beginning in early 2003, which revealed significant undeclared Iranian efforts in uranium enrichment (including centrifuge, atomic vapor laser, and molecular laser isotope separation techniques) and in separation of plutonium as well as undeclared imported material.[9] By June 2003, Iran placed the following new facilities under safeguards: Jabr Ibn Hayan Multipurpose Laboratories (JHL), its fuel manufacturing plant (FMP), its pilot fuel enrichment plant (PFEP), its fuel enrichment plant, and the Iran Nuclear Research Reactor (IR-40). Iranian officials have delayed inspections, revised explanations for discrepancies, cleaned up facilities to erase traces of activities, shifted operations to other locations, and, in the case of Lavizan-Shian, razed a site.[10]

According to IAEA Director-General Mohamed ElBaradei, "Iran tried to cover up many of their activities, and they learned the hard way."[11] Only in January 2005 did Iranian officials share a copy of Pakistani scientist A. Q. Khan's 1987 offer of a centrifuge enrichment "starter kit."[12] In November 2005, Iran finally admitted that the Khan network supplied it with information on casting and machining uranium metal—two key processes for making nuclear weapons.[13]

Iran's enrichment-related activities have attracted the most public attention and speculation. Inspections revealed two enrichment plants at Natanz—a pilot-scale facility almost ready for operation and a commercial-scale plant under construction. The pilot FEP was designed to have one thousand centrifuges, while the commercial-scale FEP is planned to eventually hold fifty thousand centrifuges. Under its comprehensive safeguards agreement (CSA), Iran would not have been required to declare the plants until 180 days before they were ready to accept nuclear material.[14] In this respect, construction of the plants without declaring them to the IAEA was not technically a safeguards violation. However, those plants raised serious questions about Iran's intentions for several reasons. First, only eleven countries worldwide have full-scale enrichment capabilities, and second, Iran has no clear need for such enrichment capacity, nor does it have fuel fabrication facilities. Third, Iran built the commercial-scale plant partly underground. Moreover, the requirements of one low enriched uranium (LEU)–fueled reactor still under construction hardly justify the development of a full-fledged uranium enrichment plant. Estimates vary between five and twenty 1,000-megawatt reactors (according to the price of uranium) before indigenous uranium enrichment becomes cost-competitive with buying enriched uranium on the international market. In the words of one commentator, Iran's construction of an enrichment plant is akin to a new car owner's purchase of an oil refinery plant to supply gasoline.[15]

In particular, it appears likely that Iran has not told the full story about its acquisition of more sophisticated centrifuge technology and components.[16] Its reluctance to provide such information is critical for two reasons: Iran could be trying to hide a more advanced enrichment capability that could translate into less time to make a bomb; or it could be trying to shield suppliers that it would like to use in the future, perhaps unknown Khan network suppliers. Iran only admitted in October 2003 that it pursued a laser enrichment program beginning in the 1970s and in January 2004 that it possessed more advanced centrifuge designs (P-2). Iran initially insisted that it received no P-1 or P-2 components after 1995 but later admitted receiving a limited number of magnets for P-2 centrifuges in 2003. It took until November 2007 for Iran to admit it received about 150 magnets for P-2 centrifuges, because larger orders had been canceled by suppliers. As for actually assembling the P-2 centrifuges, NCR alleged in 2006 that Iran had assembled a small number of these more advanced centrifuges that could double Iran's enrichment capability, reducing the time needed to produce highly enriched uranium (HEU). In late 2007, Iran informed the IAEA it was performing mechanical tests of a new generation of centrifuges, despite telling the agency for years that it had been devoting little effort to research and development.[17]

Another issue that inspections have tried to resolve is whether the presence of HEU particles in Iran, discovered in environmental samples taken by IAEA inspectors, are attributable to Iranian enrichment efforts or to contamination from imported components. In 2003, the IAEA found HEU particles at the Natanz pilot plant, which Iranian officials asserted came from contamination found on foreign centrifuge assemblies. This was a first clue revealing the handiwork of the Pakistani A. Q. Khan network. Other particles of HEU were found elsewhere. Although Iran admitted to enriching uranium to just 1.2 percent, the particles sampled ranged from 36 percent to 70 percent U-235.[18] In October 2003, Iranian officials admitted they tested centrifuges at the Kalaye Electric Company using uranium hexafluoride (UF6) between 1998 and 2002. Under a CSA, the starting point of safeguards is when nuclear material is ready to be fabricated into fuel or to be enriched. Testing centrifuges with UF6 would constitute undeclared enrichment and therefore be considered a safeguards violation in many circumstances.

Of equal concern, although less noted in the press, are Iran's plutonium-related activities. In October 2003 Iran revealed that it had conducted plutonium reprocessing experiments in a hot cell at the Tehran Nuclear Research Center and estimated the amount separated as 200 micrograms. The IAEA calculated that more plutonium would have been produced (about one hundred grams), and Iran admitted in May 2004 that it understated the amount. Inspections also revealed that Iran experimented between 1989 and 1993 on irradiating bismuth, which can be used to produce polonium-210 for civilian purposes (for nuclear batteries) or in conjunction with beryllium to create a neutron initiator for a nuclear weapon. The plutonium-related activities are particularly important in the context of Iran's heavy water program, which includes heavy water production, a heavy water–moderated research reactor, and radioisotope production using hot cells. In 2003, Iran told the IAEA that it planned to export heavy water, then suggested that the heavy water would be used as a coolant and moderator for a planned IR-40 reactor for research and development, radioisotope production, and training. However, Iran's design information for the facility, which omitted necessary hot cell equipment for producing radioisotopes, conflicted with reports of Iran's efforts to import hot cell equipment. Construction of the IR-40 reactor has proceeded, despite the IAEA Board of Governors' continued calls for a halt.[19] The heavy water production plant has been operational since 2004, and in August 2006 Iranian officials announced they would double its production. Iranian officials predict that the IR-40 reactor will not be operational until 2011.[20] Such a reactor could be ideal for producing weapons-grade plutonium, in contrast with light water power reactors like Bushehr.

Negotiating with Iran

Since 2003, negotiations with Iran on its nuclear program have essentially proceeded on two levels—with IAEA inspectors and at the IAEA Board of Governors in Vienna, and with the European Union foreign ministers (known as the EU-3) of Germany, the United Kingdom, and France. In 2006, the EU-3 were joined by the United States, Russia, and China, after Iran's noncompliance was referred to the UNSC.

The IAEA secretariat concluded in November 2003 that Iran's reporting failures and efforts to conceal them led to "breaches" in Iraq's obligation to comply with provisions of its safeguards agreement.[21] The board of governors strongly deplored those breaches and failures but did not use the term "noncompliance" and did not report the finding to the UNSC. At that time, Iran took several corrective actions, including signing an Additional Protocol (AP) in December 2003 and delivering initial declarations under the protocol in May 2004. In addition, Iran voluntarily suspended its enrichment- and reprocessing-related activities after discussions with the EU-3 in October 2003.

Although it may seem odd that a separate track of negotiations was necessary to extract concessions from Iran, a similar approach was taken with North Korea in the early 1990s. Some may question whether the failure of the IAEA and board of governors to take decisive action early on, or whether Iran's strong aversion to being taken before the UNSC with the not-so-veiled threat of pulling out of the NPT, necessitated such an approach. On the positive side, the voluntary measures Iran undertook through the EU-3 negotiations allowed IAEA inspectors greater access than would otherwise be granted under Iran's CSA. If the second track of negotiations appears to have left Iran free to set the terms of engagement, it still achieved a temporary shutdown that might otherwise have been impossible to gain, while buying time to potentially change Iran's mind about nuclear weapons.

The course of negotiations between Iran and the EU-3 has not been easy. In 2004, Iran continued activities that called into question its October 2003 suspension, leading to an agreement signed in Paris in November 2004 that specified exactly what was entailed in the suspension. Nonetheless, barely four months later, Iran proposed running its pilot-scale enrichment facility, which EU-3 negotiators rejected. In April 2005, Iran said that unless negotiations progressed, it would start up its uranium conversion plant, which it did in August 2005.[22] Following Iranian president Ahmadinejad's inflammatory remarks at the September 2005 UN Summit, the IAEA board voted on Resolution GOV/2005/77, which found Iran in noncompliance with its safeguards agreement. Specifically, the board found that "Iran's many failures and breaches of its obligations to comply with its NPT Safeguards Agreement, as detailed in GOV/2003/75, constitute noncompliance in the context of Article XII.C of the Agency's Statute."

For several months thereafter, Iran provided limited details on outstanding issues and discussed with Russia its offer to enrich Iran's fuel on Russian soil as an alternative to Iranian indigenous production. In January 2006, Iran abandoned its voluntary suspension of enrichment-related activities negotiations, as well as the interim application of the AP, prompting an emergency IAEA Board of Governors meeting. An IAEA report prepared for the meeting linked, for the first time, a Khan network document in Iran's possession on uranium casting and machining to the fabrication of nuclear weapons components.[23] Iran asserts that the Khan network provided the document on its own initiative. Nonetheless, Article II of the NPT obligates Iran not to receive any assistance in the manufacture of nuclear explosives, so the question of whose initiative prompted transfer of the document is moot. In February 2006, the board of governors voted, but not by consensus, to report Iran to the UNSC (see GOV/2006/14). Barely a week later, President Ahmadinejad hinted in a speech that Iran would consider withdrawing from the NPT, should Iran be deprived of its rights.[24]

The UNSC moved slowly, issuing a presidential statement on March 29 that called on Iran to reinstate its suspension of enrichment and reprocessing, reconsider construction of its heavy water reactor, ratify and implement the AP, and implement transparency measures.[25] Iran continued its enrichment activities, while claiming it was cooperating with the IAEA.[26] Shortly before the IAEA was to report back to the UNSC, Ayatollah Ali Khamenei reportedly issued a statement suggesting that Iran would begin to export its nuclear technology.[27] Nuclear negotiator Ali Larijani warned that Iran would cut oil production if sanctions were imposed, and the Iranian Oil Ministry reportedly canceled a $1.2 billion contract with companies from France, Germany, and South Korea to build a petrochemical plant in Iran.[28] Nonetheless, the IAEA's April 28 report (GOV/2006/27) stated that it was "unable to make progress in its efforts to provide assurance about the absence of undeclared nuclear material and activities in Iran." Its June 2006 report (GOV/2006/38) reported even less progress, given a lack of new information.

On June 6, 2006, the five permanent members of the UNSC plus Germany (P-5 + 1) offered Iran a new negotiating proposal. This included incentives such as affirmation of Iran's inalienable right to peaceful nuclear energy, assistance in building state-of-the-art light water reactors, a peaceful nuclear cooperation agreement between the European Atomic Energy Community (EURATOM) and Iran, fuel supply guarantees, dismissing UNSC consideration of Iran's NPT noncompliance, World Trade Organization (WTO) membership, and an end to certain U.S. sanctions to allow Iran to purchase agriculture appliances and Boeing aircraft parts.[29] In return, Iran would suspend enrichment- and reprocessing-related activities, resume implementation of the AP, and fully cooperate with the IAEA. Iran's moratorium could be reviewed once several conditions had been met, including resolving all outstanding issues and restoring international confidence in the peaceful nature of Iran's nuclear program. The proposal also outlined several measures targeted at Iran's nuclear program should Iran not agree to cooperate: a ban on nuclear-related exports, freezing of assets, travel/visa bans, suspension of technical cooperation with the IAEA, a ban on investment in related entities, and a prohibition against Iranians studying abroad in nuclear and missile-related areas. Broader measures could include an arms embargo, no support for WTO membership, and a general freezing of assets of Iranian financial institutions. Several of these measures were later incorporated into UNSC Resolutions 1737 and 1747.

Iranian officials called the proposal "a good start" but deferred a response until August 2006, which was apparently too muted and slow for the P-5 + 1. On July 31, 2006, the UNSC passed Resolution 1696 under Article 40 of Chapter VII of the UN Charter, with Qatar voting against the resolution.[30] The resolution called on Iran to take the steps required by the board of governors in GOV/2006/14: (a) reestablish full suspension of enrichment-related and reprocessing activities, including research and development; (b) reconsider the construction of the IR-40 heavy water–moderated reactor; (c) ratify and implement the AP; (d) pending ratification, continue interim application of the AP; and (e) implement transparency measures that would include access to individuals, documents, dual-use equipment, and certain military-owned workshops. The resolution also separately demanded that Iran suspend all enrichment-related and reprocessing activities, to be verified by the IAEA, endorsed the P-5 + 1 proposal, and clearly stated the UNSC's intention, should Iran fail to comply with previous demands, to adopt sanctions under Article 41 of Chapter VII of the UN charter. Such sanctions would be legally binding.

The resolution defined August 31, 2006, as the deadline for compliance, but Iran continued all of its uranium-related activities, as well as construction of the heavy water research reactor. Iran repeatedly sought to return its case to the IAEA but offered the agency little information in return. After four months of hard bargaining among the P-5 + 1, the UNSC adopted Resolution 1737 on December 23, 2006, which called for all states to impose sanctions on Iran. These were primarily limited to transfers of any nuclear-related and dual-use items (with a noticeable exception for Russian equipment to Bushehr) and technical or financial assistance that could contribute to Iran's enrichment, reprocessing, or heavy water–related activities. The resolution also identified individuals and entities associated with Iran's nuclear and ballistic missile program and called on states to freeze the assets of those individuals and entities. Among other things, Resolution 1737 required Iran's suspension of enrichment and reprocessing activities as a prerequisite for negotiations and offered the termination of sanctions once Iran fully complied with both UNSC resolutions and the requirements of the IAEA Board of Governors.

In the months following UNSC Resolution 1737, Iran continued to comply with the most minimal of its safeguards obligations but failed to halt activities required under the resolution or to provide the IAEA with information necessary to close the file. UNSC Resolution 1747, adopted on March 24, 2007, expanded the list of entities and individuals involved in the ballistic missile program, particularly those in the Iran Revolutionary Guard Corps. The resolution prohibited Iranian military exports and called on all states to exercise vigilance and restraint in major arms sales to Iran. Further, it called on states and international financial institutions not to give new financial assistance, grants, or loans to Iran except for humanitarian or developmental purposes.

Such restrictions seemed to have little impact on Iran, although by August 2007, Iran had entered into an agreement with the IAEA for a workplan to resolve all outstanding issues.[31] This workplan, although heralded by some as significant progress, stretched out the compliance schedule to virtually seven or eight months, because Iran insisted on a sequential resolution of issues. Thus, it was no surprise by November 2007 that many issues remained to be resolved. In the meantime, it appeared that Iran had finally managed to install three thousand centrifuges at the commercial-scale enrichment plant and was preparing to test a new generation of centrifuge design.[32]

How Close to a Bomb Is Iran?

Iran is inching closer to being able to produce weapons-grade plutonium or HEU. Then Director of National Intelligence John Negroponte told the Senate Select Committee on Intelligence on February 2, 2006, that "we judge that Tehran probably does not yet have a nuclear weapon and probably has not yet produced or acquired the necessary fissile material. Nevertheless, the danger that it will acquire a nuclear weapon and the ability to integrate it with ballistic missiles Iran already possesses is a reason for immediate concern."[33] According to one report, the 2005 National Intelligence Estimate on Iran assessed that it would be 10 years before Iran has a bomb.[34]

Calculations of nuclear weapons production are generally keyed to estimates of fissile material production. Yet, such estimates rely heavily on assumptions. For example, one calculation is that a cascade of one thousand P-1 centrifuges could produce one bomb's worth of HEU in 2.7 years, and a cascade of three thousand P-1s could produce the same amount of HEU in 330 days.[35] However, such an estimate assumes that Iran has the requisite quantity and quality of uranium hexafluoride feedstock for the plants and the necessary engineering skills to keep such cascades operating with few mishaps and little downtime. In addition, such an estimate assumes dedicated production, rather than an attempt to divert material in a safeguarded plant. There are several indications that Iran has encountered various problems in the uranium conversion and enrichment processes thus far, which are difficult to factor into estimates.

Iran's pursuit of three different methods of enriching uranium and experimentation with separating plutonium suggest a steady accrual of expertise in weapons-relevant areas. If Iran received the same nuclear weapon design that A. Q. Khan gave Libya, the weaponization process could be shortened. There is little public information about whether the design was complete, and there is at least one suggestion that it might have been a nuclear weapons design by Khan, rather than the presumably workable design given to Pakistan by China in the 1980s. Nonetheless, the weaponization process is not considered to be the most significant hurdle in a nuclear weapons development program.

Some observers are concerned that Iran is hiding other undeclared enrichment facilities, perhaps in a clandestine, dedicated military program. Such covert production of fissile material could be very difficult to detect, as evidenced by difficulties encountered by U.S. intelligence capabilities in locating clandestine centrifuge facilities in North Korea. Given that other parts of Iran's fuel cycle are under inspection, escaping detection entirely would require hiding sources of uranium (either imports or mining and milling) and uranium conversion. For this reason, there has been considerable interest in Iran's activities at the Gchine Mine.

By the end of 2007, Iran managed to enrich uranium to about 4 percent of U-235 and had installed (if not fully operated) three thousand centrifuges at its FEP. In terms of estimating how close Iran is to a bomb, however, the critical milestones are whether Iran can operate its centrifuges on a sustained basis without failure, and whether it can operate more advanced designs.

No Smoking Gun

Iran has argued that the IAEA has not detected a diversion of nuclear material to nuclear weapons, which is the exclusive purpose of the application of IAEA safeguards, and therefore it is not technically in violation of its safeguards agreement or the NPT. This claim was even echoed by Chinese and Russian officials in the run-up to the UN's August 2006 deadline. The IAEA's November 2003 report stated that "to date, there is no evidence that the previously undeclared nuclear material and activities . . . were related to a nuclear weapon program." In its November 2004 (GOV/2004/83) report, and echoed in subsequent reports (GOV/2005/67, GOV/2006/15), the IAEA remarked that the agency was following up on open source information, but that "the focus of Agency Safeguards Agreements and Additional Protocols is nuclear material, and that, absent some nexus to nuclear material, the Agency's legal authority to pursue the verification of possible nuclear weapons related activity is limited."

The NPT itself is silent on procedures for determining noncompliance, but the IAEA statute and INCFIRC/153, the model CSA, provide two routes for finding a state in noncompliance with its obligations under the NPT. According to the IAEA statute, if inspectors find a state in noncompliance with its safeguards agreement, they report that to the director-general, who informs the board of governors. Alternatively, under the CSA, the board may determine that the inability to verify nondiversion can constitute noncompliance. Specifically, Paragraph 18 of the CSA gives the board of governors the ability to call on a state to take what it deems to be essential and urgent actions to ensure that material under safeguards is not diverted. If, however, the board finds that the IAEA is not able to verify that there has been no diversion of safeguarded nuclear material, then it may report noncompliance to the UNSC, after affording the state "every reasonable opportunity to furnish the board with any necessary reassurance" (Paragraph 19 of INFCIRC/153). The board is likely to consider several other factors in determining whether discrepancies rise to the threshold of noncompliance (which *must* be reported to the UNSC) or an inability to verify nondiversion (which *may* be reported to the UNSC): the quantity of material in question, the nature of activities, efforts to conceal, and the overall pattern of action of the state.[36]

In the case of Iran, the board invoked the Paragraph 18 provision in September 2003 when it decided that it was "essential and urgent in order to ensure IAEA verification of nondiversion of nuclear material that Iran remedy all failures identified by the Agency," which led to Iran's negotiations with the EU-3, the suspension, and signing an AP.[37] In September 2005, the director general did not declare Iran to be in noncompliance with its safeguards agreement, despite numerous discrepancies, but concluded in GOV/2005/67 that "the Agency is, however, still not in a position to conclude that there are no undeclared nuclear materials or activities in Iran." This opened the way for the board of governors to make a noncompliance finding.

A few factors have detracted from a "clean" or unassailable finding of noncompliance for Iran. First, the board of governors as a rule operates by consensus, but it was unable to achieve a consensus for either the September 2005 resolution that found Iran in noncompliance or the February 2006 resolution that referred the matter to the UNSC.[38] Second, the board's judgments (as opposed to technical findings by the IAEA), particularly with respect to the nature of activities, efforts to conceal, and overall pattern of action of the state, are necessarily subjective. The emergence of two other cases of undeclared activities—in South Korea and Egypt—in 2004, in which neither the IAEA secretariat nor the board made a finding of noncompliance, probably didn't help. In the course of submitting its initial declaration under an AP, South Korea uncovered information on unauthorized uranium enrichment experiments using laser isotope separation in 2000, as well as plutonium separation experiments conducted in the 1980s that were not reported at the time. The secretariat reported its findings to the board in November 2004, noting that the Republic of Korea had taken corrective actions, and the board expressed concern that South Korea had not reported these activities in accordance with its CSA, but welcomed its active cooperation.[39] In the case of Egypt, an IAEA inquiry prompted Egypt to acknowledge in December 2004 that it had conducted experiments between 1990 and 2003 involving irradiation of uranium and thorium. The agency found that Egypt had failed to provide a complete initial inventory and failed to report the experiments.

Clearly, a key consideration for the board of governors is whether a state takes corrective action, which Iran has been quite consciously careful to do. Yet, some of Iran's corrective actions, like the suspension of enrichment, were not required by its safeguards arrangement, and the perception that the September 2005 noncompliance finding is linked to the abandonment of the suspension is seen by some as supporting Iran's claim that it has gone beyond its obligations in attempting to prove its innocence. Finally, press reports have added confusion by quoting Director-General Mohamed ElBaradei as saying he has no evidence of nuclear weapons programs. While undoubtedly true, observers may erroneously conclude that the IAEA must find evidence of a nuclear weapons program before a state is determined to be in noncompliance.

Impact of Iran's Noncompliance on the NPT

When Iraq's clandestine nuclear weapons program was uncovered in 1991, the response of NPT member states was to strengthen nuclear safeguards, which ultimately resulted in the AP, and to strengthen nuclear export controls by developing a second list of dual-use technology restrictions to be implemented by the Nuclear Suppliers Group (NSG). Concerns about Iran's activities, coupled with revelations about the A. Q. Khan nuclear black market network, have provided impetus for long-dormant concepts for an international fuel cycle that limits access to technology by assuring fuel supplies and services. Although Iran has agreed to limitations imposed by Russia on the return of spent fuel from the Bushehr reactor, Iran has asserted repeatedly that it has an inalienable right to the peaceful uses of nuclear energy. To Iran, this apparently means an inalienable right to enrich uranium.

The immediate issue is whether Iran's noncompliance status justifies forcing Iran to forego enrichment and reprocessing activities, even if those are under safeguards. The NPT is silent on the consequences of noncompliance for the conduct of peaceful nuclear energy. According to Article XII.C of the IAEA statute, the only foreseen consequence is suspension or termination of assistance or the return of materials and equipment made available by the IAEA to the recipient state. The statute does not foresee requiring suspension of a state's nuclear activities, although this is clearly an option for the UNSC. This is undoubtedly one reason why Iran sought to keep the locus of action at the IAEA, rather than at the UNSC. In the case of Iraq in 1991, the UNSC imposed a ban on "nuclear activities of all kinds," with an exception for the use of isotopes in medical, agricultural, and industrial applications, until Iraq was fully compliant with UN resolutions and its safeguards agreement. UNSC Resolution 1696 "demanded, in this context, that Iran shall suspend all enrichment-related and reprocessing activities, including research and development." Pierre Goldschmidt, former deputy director-general of the IAEA for safeguards, has argued that the right of a state found in noncompliance to engage in sensitive nuclear fuel cycle–related activities should be automatically suspended for a period of ten years, subject to an extension by the UNSC.[40]

A more far-reaching issue is whether an inalienable right to the peaceful uses of nuclear energy extends to even the most sensitive kinds of nuclear technology. This debate has taken place on two levels: on whether Article IV of the NPT constitutes a loophole in the treaty that must be closed, as President Bush has suggested, and on practical measures to restrict the further spread of enrichment and reprocessing capabilities.[41]

Article IV of the NPT states, in part: "Nothing in this Treaty shall be interpreted as affecting the inalienable right of all the Parties to the Treaty to develop research, production and use of nuclear energy for peaceful purposes without discrimination and in conformity with articles I and II of the treaty."[42] Few U.S. officials have been willing to dispute that states have an inalienable right to the peaceful uses of nuclear energy but point instead to making the exercise of that right conditional on meeting NPT obligations. Negotiators of the NPT debated on how far such "rights" extended. For example, the Swedish representative to the Eighteen Nation Disarmament Conference, Ambassador Alva Myrdal, made numerous interventions at the start of NPT negotiations on the question of where international control in the nuclear fuel cycle would be most effective. She suggested that "to prohibit just the final act of 'manufacture' would seem to come late in these long chains of decisions. . . . Must not regulations about effective controls be linked with certain definitive and uncontestable steps, such as actual purchases of nuclear reactors, fuel elements, and so on from abroad, and/or the establishment within a country of such installations as plutonium separation plants and the like?" U.S. officials at the time held a different view, which prevailed. As the director of the Arms Control and Disarmament Agency told the Senate Foreign Relations Committee in 1968:

> It may be useful to point out, for illustrative purposes, several activities which the United States would not consider per se to be violations of the prohibitions in Article II. Neither uranium enrichment nor the stockpiling of fissionable material in connection with a peaceful program would violate Article II so long as these activities were safeguarded under Article III.[43]

From a more immediate and practical perspective, it is likely that members of the NPT will continue to struggle for several years with the basic issue of how to determine which states should be restricted in their development of nuclear technology. The case of Iran has revived decades-old concepts of multilateral management of the nuclear fuel cycle, but it is not clear that their application will prove any less daunting today than it did years ago. Although the Bush administration has shifted its approach from denying access to enrichment and reprocessing to schemes providing incentives to refrain from enrichment and reprocessing, it is no closer to achieving its policy objective of limiting the further spread of such technologies. In fact, its Global Nuclear Energy Partnership program seems to have perversely provided incentives for states such as Australia, Canada, Ukraine, and South Africa to pursue enrichment for themselves or for export.[44]

Strengthening Compliance

IAEA Director-General ElBaradei outlined a few measures in June 2005 for strengthening the nuclear nonproliferation regime: "universalizing IAEA authority under the additional protocol; tightening control and dissemination of sensitive nuclear fuel technology while ensuring fuel supply; enhancing mechanisms for dealing with noncompliance; and accelerating nuclear disarmament."[45] It is very likely that had Iran signed and implemented an AP in 1998, discrepancies could have come to light sooner. The two years of inspection in Iran (2003 to 2005) during which its AP was implemented on an interim basis have highlighted the usefulness of the protocol in gaining access to sites that previously would have been off-limits. Yet, as of November 2007, eighty-four additional protocols were in force and another thirty-two had been signed. In short, a little more than one third of NPT parties have APs in place. A decision by the NSG to establish the additional protocol as a condition of supply could help implementation tremendously, yet the NSG failed to make such a decision in May 2006. However, the NSG did establish a procedure to suspend nuclear transfers to countries in noncompliance with their safeguards agreements (by national decision) and to make effective export controls a criterion of supply for nuclear material, equipment, and technology.[46]

The case of Iran clearly demonstrates the need to enhance mechanisms for dealing with noncompliance, particularly in the UNSC. In remarks to the 2005 NPT Review Conference, IAEA Director-General ElBaradei stated that "both the NPT and the IAEA Statute make clear our reliance on the Security Council. Whether it is a case of noncompliance or of withdrawal from the NPT, the Council must consider promptly the implications for international peace and security, and take the appropriate measures." Iran has attempted for several years to keep the locus of negotiations in Vienna, rather than in New York, presumably because the IAEA is powerless to exact real costs for noncompliance. Although the UNSC adopted two resolutions in 2007 that imposed sanctions on and limited arms sales to and from Iran, Iran ignored the legally binding requirements to halt its sensitive nuclear activities. Iran has continued to exploit the divide in responsibilities between the IAEA and the UNSC.

One way of tying the responsibilities more closely together has been proposed by former Deputy Director-General of the IAEA for Safeguards Pierre Goldschmidt, who suggests using the authority of the UNSC to strengthen the IAEA's hand in responding to noncompliance. This could be done by making three steps automatic once a state is found in noncompliance: enhanced verification and inspection authority for the IAEA (particularly the ability to go anywhere at anytime); the conclusion of a different form of safeguards agreement (INFCIRC/66-type) within sixty days that would effectively circumscribe a state's freedom of action should it withdraw from the NPT; and a ten-year suspension of the state's right to engage in sensitive nuclear fuel cycle activities (such as enrichment and reprocessing), subject to extension by the UNSC.[47]

Conclusions

Iran has been piecing together critical components, material, technology, and skills for two decades that advance it toward a nuclear weapons capability. Should

Iran maintain a centrifuge uranium enrichment capability under safeguards in the future, the technical challenges of detecting diversion to military uses would be formidable. Bigger uncertainties, however, lie in determining Iran's intentions, perhaps because it is unclear itself on its course of action. Although the IAEA has made major strides in evaluating states' nuclear activities in a comprehensive way to connect the dots between capabilities and intentions, the circumstances of Iran's noncompliance present particular challenges to making such an evaluation. Specifically, the agency's ability to make such a comprehensive evaluation is limited as long as Iran is not implementing its AP commitments, which is why this is such a key step for Iran to take.

What's more, many have been reluctant to assume Iran has nuclear weapons intentions in the aftermath of the 2003 Iraq War and apprehensive about pushing Iran out of the NPT nest, particularly after North Korea left the treaty in 2003 with few visible consequences. Iran's oil wealth and support for international terrorism may also give some leaders pause in assessing effective options for bringing Iran back to the negotiating table.

The drama that has unfolded about Iran's nuclear program since 2003 highlights what we have always known about the nuclear nonproliferation regime but find difficult to acknowledge—it is at best a mechanism for buying time for political change and, at worst, subject to political pressures from many sides. Efforts in the last fifteen years to shore up the nuclear nonproliferation regime have sought to tighten loopholes, build up political consensus, and enhance technical capabilities to detect noncompliance. It may be more important than ever for the regime to develop principled approaches for the future, if Iran is to be the last state to take advantage of weaknesses in the NPT regime, rather than the first of several more.

Notes

1. Reports in the 1970s indicated that Iran sought laser enrichment technology in the United States and conducted reprocessing-related experiments. Intelligence reports suggested that the shah had a secret group to work on nuclear weapons. See Leonard S. Spector, *Nuclear Ambitions* (Boulder, CO: Westview Press, 1990), 204.

2. See the statement by Iran's former foreign minister Kamal Kharrazi at http://www.pbs.org/newshour/bb/middle_east/july-dec04/iran_9-27.html.

3. David A. Schwarzbach, *Iran's Nuclear Program: Energy or Weapons?* Natural Resources Defense Council, September 7, 1995, 10. The Natural Resources Defense Council obtained a copy of a protocol between Russia and Iran. See also International Institute for Strategic Studies, *Iran's Strategic Weapons Programmes: A Net Assessment* (London: Routledge, 2005), 33.

4. Reportedly, Iran finished constructing the uranium conversion facility with the help of Chinese blueprints.

5. Steve Coll, "The Atomic Emporium: Abdul Qadeer Khan and Iran's Race to Build the Bomb," *New Yorker*, August 7 and 14, 2006, 50ff.

6. G. Ali Khoshroo, deputy foreign minister for legal and international affairs, statement, second session of the PrepCom for the 2005 NPT review conference, April 29, 2003.

7. "Iran Seeks Cooperation within IAEA Framework," Mehr News Agency, Tehran, July 18, 2006.

8. Michael Slackman, "Iranian President Meets Press and Is Challenged," *New York Times*, August 30, 2006.

9. See International Institute for Strategic Studies, *Iran's Strategic Weapons Programmes*, for an excellent description of the information uncovered by inspections through 2005.

10. David Albright and Corey Hinderstein, "Iran: Countdown to Showdown," *Bulletin of Atomic Scientists* 60, no. 6 (November/December 2004): 67–72.

11. Dafna Linzer, "Iran Was Offered Nuclear Parts," *Washington Post*, February 27, 2005.

12. International Atomic Energy Agency, Implementation of the NPT Safeguards Agreement in the Islamic Republic of Iran: Report by the Director General, IAEA Board of Governors document GOV/2005/67, September 2, 2005.

13. International Atomic Energy Agency, *Developments in the Implementation of the NPT Safeguards Agreement in the Islamic Republic of Iran and Agency Verification of Iran's Suspension of Enrichment-related and Reprocessing Activities*, update brief, deputy director-general for safeguards, January 31, 2006.

14. According to Implementation of the NPT Safeguards Agreement in the Islamic Republic of Iran , GOV/2003/40, June 6, 2003, Iran's subsidiary arrangements contained standard text that required design information for new facilities to be provided to the IAEA no later than 180 days before the introduction of nuclear material.

15. Comment by Henry Sokolski, president of the Nonproliferation Policy Education Center. For a detailed assessment of the economics of Iran's energy options, see Thomas W. Wood, Matthew D. Milazzo, Barbara A. Reichmuth, and Jeff Bedell, *The Economics of Energy Independence for Iran*, Pacific Northwest National Laboratory and Los Alamos National Laboratory, April 2006.

16. The pilot-scale plant utilizes P-1 centrifuges, which have an approximate efficiency of 2 kilograms separative work units (SWU) per year. About 200 kilograms SWU is needed to produce 1 kilogram of highly enriched uranium; about 25 kilograms of HEU is needed for a nuclear weapon. P-2 centrifuges (so-designated by Pakistan as modifications of German-designed G-2 centrifuges) operate at 5 kilograms SWU per year. For a discussion of SWU focused on the problem in Iran see http://www.armscontrolwonk.com/1035/more-fun-with-swu. See also appendix A ("The Gas Centrifuge and Proliferation" by Marvin Miller) in Victor Gilinsky, Marvin Miller, and Harmon Hubbard, *A Fresh Examination Of The Proliferation Dangers Of Light Water Reactors*, Nonproliferation Policy Education Center Paper, October 22, 2004.

17. See International Atomic Energy Agency, Implementation of the NPT Safeguards Agreement and Relevant Provisions of Security Council Resolution 1737 (2006) and 1747 (2007) in the Islamic Republic of Iran: Report by the Director General, GOV/2007/58, November 15, 2007.

18. Low-enriched uranium used in light water reactor fuel, such as in the Bushehr reactor, typically has enrichments of between 3.5 and 5 percent U-235. High-enriched uranium (HEU) is defined as 20 percent or more U-235, but nuclear weapons typically require 90 percent or greater concentrations of U-235.

19. International Atomic Energy Agency, Implementation of the NPT Safeguards Agreement in the Islamic Republic of Iran: Report by the Director General, GOV/2006/15, February 27, 2005.

20. For analysis, see http://www.isis-online.org/publications/iran/arakconstruction.html.

21. International Atomic Energy Agency, Implementation of the NPT Safeguards Agreement in the Islamic Republic of Iran: *Report by the Director General*, GOV/2003/75, November 10, 2003.

22. International Atomic Energy Agency, *Communication Dated 1 August 2005 Received from the Permanent Mission of the Islamic Republic of Iran to the Agency*, INFCIRC/648, August 1, 2005.

23. See International Atomic Energy Agency, *Developments in the Implementation of the NPT Safeguards Agreement in the Islamic Republic of Iran and Agency Verification of Iran's Suspension of Enrichment-Related and Reprocessing Activities.*

24. Nazila Fathi, "Bracing for Penalties, Iran Threatens to Withdraw from Nuclear Treaty," *New York Times*, February 12, 2006.

25. See http://www.un.org/News/Press/docs/2006/sc8679.doc.htm for full text.

26. "EU says Iran Nuclear Announcement 'Regrettable,'" *Reuters*, April 12, 2006.

27. Molly Moore, "Iran Raises Stakes in Nuclear Dispute," *Washington Post*, April 26, 2006.

28. Ibid.

29. ABC News released some details in Luis Martinez, "Nuclear 'Carrots and Sticks' for Iran: Proposal Offers Rewards, Punishment to Convince Iran to Dump Enrichment Program," June 6, 2006.

30. Chapter VII of the UN Charter covers actions with respect to threats to the peace, breaches of the peace, and acts of aggression. Article 40 states: "In order to prevent an aggravation of the situation, the Security Council may, before making the recommendations or deciding upon the measures provided for in Article 39, call upon the parties concerned to comply with such provisional measures as it deems necessary or desirable." Article 41 states: "The Security Council may decide what measures not involving the use of armed force are to be employed to give effect to its decisions, and it may call upon the Members of the United Nations to apply such measures. These may include complete or partial interruption of economic relations and of rail, sea, air, postal, telegraphic, radio, and other means of communication, and the severance of diplomatic relations." Finally, if measures under Article 41 are insufficient, Article 42 of Chapter VII of the charter authorizes the use of force. Several

states, including China and Russia, have sought to avoid this kind of escalation and therefore have advocated leaving the locus of action to Vienna and with the IAEA.

31. This workplan is described in International Atomic Energy Agency, Implementation of the NPT Safeguards Agreement in the Islamic Republic of Iran, GOV/2007/48, August 30, 2007, also issued as INFCIRC/711.

32. See International Atomic Energy Agency, Implementation of the NPT Safeguards Agreement and Relevant Provisions of Security Council Resolution 1737 (2006) and 1747 (2007) in the Islamic Republic of Iran, GOV/2007/58, November 15, 2007.

33. John Negroponte, "Worldwide Threat Briefing," testimony before the Senate Select Committee on Intelligence, February 2, 2006.

34. Dafna Linzer, "Iran Is Judged 10 Years from Nuclear Bomb," *Washington Post*, August 2, 2005.

35. Iran claims, according to testimony before Congress by Undersecretary of State Robert Joseph, that its P-2 centrifuges can enrich uranium four times faster than its P-1s. Other estimates, however, suggest that the P-2 would only double or triple the separative work unit (SWU) capacity. The estimate used in this text is from International Institute for Strategic Studies, *Iran's Strategic Weapons Programmes*, 54. That figure reflects low tails assay (meaning less U-235 in the waste stream) and assumes that the plant is configured for maximum HEU production, for which the PFEP is not presently configured. See the International Institute for Strategic Studies Iran report for a clear explanation of all the variables.

36. Mark W. Goodman, Alex R. Burkart, and J. Christian Kessler, "Overview of the Nuclear Nonproliferation Regime," paper presented at IAEA international training course on implementation of state systems of accounting and control of nuclear material, May 1, 2005, 22.

37. International Atomic Energy Agency, Implementation of the NPT Safeguards Agreement in the Islamic Republic of Iran: Report by the Director General, GOV/2003/69, September 12, 2003.

38. In the September 2005 vote, Venezuela voted against the resolution, while twelve countries abstained.

39. International Atomic Energy Agency, Implementation of the NPT Safeguards Agreement in the Islamic Republic of Iran: Report by the Director General, GOV/2004/84, November 11, 2004.

40. Pierre Goldschmidt, *The Urgent Need to Strengthen the Nuclear Non-Proliferation Regime*, policy outlook, Carnegie Endowment for International Peace, Non-Proliferation Project, January 2006.

41. In a speech at the National Defense University on February 11, 2004, President Bush stated: "The Nuclear Non-Proliferation Treaty was designed more than 30 years ago to prevent the spread of nuclear weapons beyond those states which already possessed them. Under this treaty, nuclear states agreed to help non-nuclear states develop peaceful atomic energy if they renounced the pursuit of nuclear weapons. But the treaty has a loophole which has been exploited by nations such as North Korea and Iran. These regimes are allowed to produce nuclear material that can be used to build bombs under the cover of civilian nuclear programs. So today, as a fourth step, I propose a way to close the loophole. The world must

create a safe, orderly system to field civilian nuclear plants without adding to the danger of weapons proliferation. The world's leading nuclear exporters should ensure that states have reliable access at reasonable cost to fuel for civilian reactors, so long as those states renounce enrichment and reprocessing. Enrichment and reprocessing are not necessary for nations seeking to harness nuclear energy for peaceful purposes." http://www.whitehouse.gov/news/releases/2004/02/20040211-4.html.

42. Article I of the NPT states the NWS's obligation not to provide nuclear weapons–related assistance, and Article II of the NPT states the NNWS's obligation not to receive such assistance.

43. William C. Foster, extension of remarks in response to question regarding nuclear explosive devices, Testimony before the Senate Committee on Foreign Relations, 90th Cong., 2nd sess., Executive H, Treaty on the Nonproliferation of Nuclear Weapons, July 10, 11, 12, 17, 1968, 39.

44. Reportedly, South Africa is also considering reviving its enrichment program. See "Argentina, South Africa Studying Revival of Enrichment Programs," *Nucleonics Week* 47, no. 35 (August 31, 2006).

45. IAEA director general Dr. Mohamed ElBaradei, introductory statement to the IAEA Board of Governors, June 14, 2005.

46. Nuclear Suppliers Group, "The NSG — Strengthening the Nuclear Non-Proliferation Regime," plenary meeting statement, Oslo, Norway, June 23–24, 2005.

47. Goldschmidt, *Urgent Need to Strengthen the Nuclear Non-Proliferation Regime.*

CHAPTER FIFTEEN

U.S.-Russia Cooperative Nonproliferation

Elizabeth Turpen and Brian Finlay

In the fifteen years since inception, the cooperative nonproliferation programs (CNP) at the U.S. Departments of Defense (DoD), Energy (DoE), and State have proven an unparalleled national security success.[1] These efforts have achieved numerous quantifiable disarmament goals and myriad less tangible accomplishments in stemming the potential threats of the Cold War legacy. More than 6,800 former Soviet nuclear warheads have been deactivated. Over 600 intercontinental ballistic missiles that once pointed at the United States and 150 strategic bombers that once prowled the skies preparing to drop their nuclear ordnance have been destroyed.[2] Russian and other former Soviet facilities storing approximately 267 metric tons of fissile material have received either comprehensive or rapid security upgrades, and as of June 2006, 276 metric tons of highly enriched uranium (HEU) from dismantled nuclear weapons has been blended down to non-weapons-usable low-enriched uranium (LEU).[3] Innovative new partnerships developed to promote peaceful joint U.S.-Russian research at forty-nine former biological weapons facilities are ensuring the nonproliferation of potentially nefarious knowledge to terrorists and rogue regimes.

Though poorly understood, almost as significant as the hard security dividends on these investments have been the immeasurable soft security "spin-off" benefits. For instance, programs designed to mothball former weapons facilities in the former Soviet Union (FSU) have spawned both new foreign and locally owned and operated companies. In turn, business management, marketing, and finance skills once anathema to the state-run economies of the region have been transferred from the U.S. private sector to its FSU counterparts. Innovative research partnerships between the scientific communities of erstwhile adversaries have generated new products from immune-boosting pharmaceuticals to new landmine detection technologies. A new and heretofore absent understanding of quality control, cost accounting, and financial auditing has been fostered in the close working relationships with U.S. private sector entities. Regional economic growth has promoted stability in potentially volatile countries and turned predominant models of development and democracy building on their head. The comprehensive list of successes is overwhelming in its breadth of accomplishment and impressive in its depth of engagement, particularly considering the minimal investments made and the only intermittent high-level political attention devoted to these efforts.

With both tangible "hard" and "soft" security benefits to these efforts, it is not surprising to have witnessed the adoption of Cooperative Threat Reduction (CTR)–type programs by multiple U.S. government agencies to address a wide range of weapons, materials, and knowledge proliferation concerns. Equally unsurprising has been the rush to embrace the programs' utility across the political spectrum. In what has been perhaps the most revisited quote of the 2004 U.S. election campaign, President George W. Bush and Senator John Kerry agreed during the first presidential debate that the threat of a nuclear-armed terrorist is the greatest threat to the national security of the United States. In response, the Bush administration has requested and the U.S. Congress has appropriated more than $1 billion annually for the array of threat reduction and nonproliferation programs that now are spread across three main government departments—Energy, Defense, and State.[4]

As one observer stated concisely, the rationale for cooperative nonproliferation is simple: No nuclear material. No bomb. No nuclear terrorism.[5] The Nunn-Lugar threat reduction and nonproliferation programs remain the best and most cost-effective means of mitigating the threat of international terrorist groups acquiring weapons of mass destruction (WMD) capabilities. Yet, despite the strong and widespread efforts dedicated to urging the acceleration and expansion of these programs, the pace of securing materials and providing civilian opportunities for former weapons scientists, engineers, and technicians has never been commensurate with the threat. A systematic look at the history of these programs indicates that failure to provide both adequate resources and focused high-level support necessary to catalyze a fundamental transformation in the relationship between the United States and Russia has been bipartisan. According to the members of the 9/11 Commission, the U.S. government has failed to request the personnel and resources or to provide the domestic and international leadership requisite to secure all weapons-grade material within the shortest possible timeframe.[6] Based on one assessment, at current rates, efforts to secure Russian weapons-grade materials alone may not be completed until the year 2030.[7] Clearly, that timeline does not match the urgency of the threat.

Assessing America's Post–Cold War Threats

In December 1991, as the world celebrated the end of the Cold War, a less palpable but no less dangerous threat emerged in place of overt hostilities. For forty years, the Soviet Union safely maintained tens of thousands of nuclear weapons, experimented with hundreds of deadly pathogenic agents, and stockpiled tons of chemical weapons. Management of this massive weapons complex occurred within the context of a closed society with redundant security measures that prevented incursion by the outside world. The omnipresence of the KGB and the threat of harsh penalties made clandestine behavior among insiders unlikely.

But by the early 1990s, Russia and its former Soviet neighbors were left to deal with the legacy of a massive WMD complex with a vastly diminished resource base. Moscow's ability to exercise adequate command and control and prevent unauthorized access into its WMD complex became frequently challenged. Security measures designed to keep foreigners out were now inadequate as knowledge, materials, and weapons became instantly marketable products to terrorists and rogue states. As economic conditions throughout the FSU worsened in the early 1990s, stories of the personal hardships experienced by thousands of under- or unemployed WMD workers began surfacing. Desperate insiders, international criminals, and terrorists now had both the motivation and the wherewithal to steal or otherwise divert the necessary components for nuclear, biological, and chemical (NBC) weapons—or even the weapons themselves. The temptation to surreptitiously divert materials from within the weapons complexes for profit led to new fears of an incipient NBC black market in the FSU. Potential proliferators recognized that only a small amount of fissile material was required to build a viable nuclear device—an amount small enough to fit into a can of Coca-Cola. The strain placed on several fragile new governments of the FSU by virtue of their nuclear inheritance alone was overwhelming. Of the approximately twenty incidents involving weapons-grade uranium and plutonium catalogued by the illicit trafficking database of the International Atomic Energy Agency(IAEA) from May 1993 to July 2001, more than half occurred in former Warsaw Pact countries such as Russia, Georgia, Lithuania, Bulgaria, and the Czech Republic.[8]

Despite the obvious dangers, weapons-usable materials are sometimes protected with little more than a chain-link fence and a padlock. Even where rudimentary security measures are in place, the ease of circumvention has led to widespread diversion of sensitive materials. In addition, approximately 130,000 to 150,000 scientists, engineers, and technicians in the FSU were thought to possess the knowledge to contribute to the design and construction of an indigenous nuclear device.[9] They lacked suitable employment, and evidence of their migration to so-called rogue states became a significant global proliferation concern.

Also at issue is the enduring threat from the massive Soviet biological weapons complex.[10] Often referred to as the "poor man's atomic bomb," biological agents are comparatively easy to obtain as they occur in nature, where they are readily accessible to determined proliferators. Over the course of decades, the Soviet Union weaponized thousands of tons of viruses, toxins, and bacteria including anthrax, smallpox, botulinum toxin, and the plague. With the disintegration of the USSR and its massive weapons program, the expertise and technology needed to manufacture these weapons became much more readily available. Today, the remnants of the once sixty-thousand employee–strong Soviet biological weapons complex continue to pose serious proliferation challenges. Astonishingly, an accurate accounting of the astronomically large community throughout the FSU that was once responsible for researching and manufacturing inventive new ways to kill using biological pathogens has never been undertaken, leaving to question how much expertise has already proliferated out of the region. According to an account by the former director of the Soviet biological weapons complex, recruiters from North Korea, Iran, Iraq, and elsewhere flooded the FSU to lure away leading researchers with promises of a return to the affluent lifestyles of the past.[11]

Such state-based threats are compounded by the rise of global terrorism and a widening diffusion of illicit technologies. While the nuclear secret was closely held throughout the Cold War, the technology and know-how for weapons development today are readily available to any determined buyer. Pakistani scientist A. Q. Khan's black market network in nuclear technologies spanned the globe and provided one-stop shopping for an as yet unknown number of customers. The terrorist attacks against the United States on September 11, 2001, demonstrated the urgent need to prevent the even greater tragedies that nuclear, biological, or chemical terrorism could yield. Osama bin Laden has declared the acquisition of WMD a "religious duty," and in November 2001, an al Qaeda spokesman boasted that the terrorist group had acquired Russian "briefcase" nuclear weapons on the black market.[12] The confluence of deteriorating economic conditions, lax security standards, and the rise of global terrorism led many to conclude that the age of relative stability, fostered earlier by the superpower standoff, had ended and that a new era of proliferation in which possession of WMD by countries in conflict-prone regions around the world was not only possible but probable.

Responding to Global Threats: Cooperative Nonproliferation as the First Line of Defense

In August 1991, Soviet hardliners, dissatisfied with the reforms of the Gorbachev government, launched a coup attempt while the president vacationed on the

Black Sea. For three days, the world watched and contemplated the implications of a breakdown in the custody and control of the world's largest arsenal of atomic weapons. Although ultimately unsuccessful in overthrowing the government, the coup attempt awakened the international community to the growing fissures within the Soviet empire and the potentially catastrophic consequences of a failure of command and control. Concluding that the traditional tools of defense and arms control remained necessary but ultimately insufficient instruments to stem the potential leakage of weapons, materials, technology, and expertise from the FSU, Senators Sam Nunn (D-GA) and Richard Lugar (R-IN) authored the Soviet Nuclear Threat Reduction Act of 1991 (Title 2, Public Law 102-228). Developed as an emergency response to the impending collapse of the Soviet Union that officially occurred only weeks later, this act gave rise to a bilateral government effort called the CTR program. Known colloquially as the Nunn-Lugar program, its mission would gradually evolve from an emergency effort led by the DoD to secure and destroy excess Soviet nuclear weapons to a broader, multidepartment attempt to keep WMD, the materials to build them, and the talent behind the massive Soviet arsenal out of the hands of hostile states and terrorist organizations.

When Senators Nunn and Lugar first envisaged the CTR program, the primary focus was on securing and destroying nuclear weapons and their delivery vehicles in the territories of the FSU. The enacted provisions authorized a program in the Soviet successor states designed to "(1) destroy nuclear weapons, chemical weapons, and other weapons, (2) transport, store, disable, and safeguard weapons in connection with their destruction, and (3) establish verifiable safeguards against the proliferation of such weapons."[13] Thus, beginning in 1991 the United States and Russia launched a multilateral initiative to cooperatively denuclearize Belarus, Kazakhstan, and Ukraine and to disassemble strategic warheads deemed excess to Russian security and slated for destruction under existing bilateral treaties. Lacking a separate appropriation, initial funding for CTR was diverted from other DoD projects. This disjointed effort made overarching CTR policy and budgetary decisions nearly impossible, as almost all funding came on an ad hoc basis. Lacking a line item within the budget also set up an internal competition for dollars within the DoD that would hobble the reputation, implementation, and effectiveness of the program from the start. Furthermore, due to the need to negotiate several umbrella agreements with FSU states, lingering Cold War hostility and mistrust, a lack of coordination within the U.S. government, and continued Russian secrecy about the FSU's weapons programs, bilateral CTR collaboration proved arduous.[14] Regardless, the dividends of this laborious new cooperation soon became evident. Cold War hardware representing decades of military investments was isolated, secured, and eliminated for a fraction of earlier investments. As the need for a more organized, long-term effort became apparent in 1993—two fiscal years into the effort—CTR was granted its own line in the DoD budget. With a dedicated CTR budget, the DoD was able to take a more streamlined and focused approach to program implementation.

Early success brought other members of Congress to the conclusion that existing efforts to manage the full spectrum of threats arising from the collapse of the Soviet Union were far too narrow. For cooperative nonproliferation efforts to succeed in the long run, a broader concept of the threat posed by all manner of Soviet WMD was needed. In 1992, the Freedom Support Act (Public Law 102-511) helped to expand the traditional rubric of arms control by promoting new efforts to "prevent [the] diversion of weapons-related scientific expertise of the former Soviet Union to terrorist groups or third countries."[15] While the Freedom Support Act described the threat of WMD terrorism, the link between counterterrorism and the CTR programs did not become explicit until later in the 1990s.

The sea change for CTR occurred with the passage of the National Defense Authorization Act for fiscal year 1997 (Title 14, Public Law 104-201), which finally brought the terrorist threat to the forefront of CTR planning by spotlighting domestic preparedness and a greater concentration on WMD material security.[16] Title 14 of that law, known as the "Nunn-Lugar-Domenici Act," greatly expanded the scope of cooperative nonproliferation programs. Fissile material remained an open target for terrorists interested in acquiring WMD without going to the trouble of stealing a nuclear weapon or acquiring first-hand bioweapons expertise. To counter this threat, the act strengthened the role of the DoE in nonproliferation efforts by adopting programs such as material protection, control, and accounting (MPC&A), which has become a central thrust of the DoE's nonproliferation agenda. Additionally, the legislation prompted the development of new efforts to address the long-overlooked threats posed by chemical and biological weapons (CBW). The focus on terrorism and materials was further reinforced by the bipartisan Baker-Cutler Task Force, which, in early 2001, declared the theft of WMD materials from Russia and their use in the United States as "the most urgent unmet national security threat to the United States."[17]

The view of the contemporary threat posed by nuclear, biological, and chemical material and weapons has been expanded beyond both the weapons complex and the FSU. CNP specialists now see nuclear material, specifically HEU in research reactors, as a proliferation threat that must be dealt with under CNP initiatives.[18] Similarly, young scientists the world over with modern laboratory skills and access to biological materials who harbor strong financial ambitions pose a potential new source of proliferation concern. In light of these evolving threats and perceptions, new programs at the DoE and State Department have been actively expanding their reach to non-FSU states, and Congress enacted the

Nunn-Lugar Expansion Act in the National Defense Authorization Act for fiscal year 2004 (Section 1308, Public Law 108-136) to permit the DoD's programs to address concerns beyond the borders of the FSU.[19]

Assessing Existing Programming

Over fifteen years, the CNP programs have evolved into a broad spectrum of preventive efforts to deny terrorists and rogue states access to weapons, the materials to assemble them, and the know-how to build them. Below is a summary of existing U.S. government efforts.

The Department of Defense

Today, the DoD operates a wide spectrum of CTR programs to assist FSU states to dismantle WMD and their infrastructure, to consolidate and secure WMD and related technology, to promote transparency and a positive security culture, and to support military-to-military cooperation to advance U.S. nonproliferation objectives. Among this array of programs, the DoD oversees the destruction of strategic weapons delivery systems, provides safety and security enhancements at warhead storage sites, and is building a nerve agent destruction facility. The department also consolidates, secures, and eliminates dangerous pathogen stocks, destroys biological weapons infrastructure, and redirects bioweapons experts into sustainable, civilian employment.

As the pioneer of CNP, the DoD deserves much credit for both its ingenuity and commitment to these programs. Program managers have been responsive to changing security challenges at both the strategic and tactical program implementation levels. Over time, managers have shifted from activities focused on the acquisition of critical equipment provided to host states in need to a more nuanced set of programs designed to dismantle legacy facilities and provide new or upgraded infrastructure to host states. More recently, large-scale construction and dismantlement activities have given way to more systematic efforts to achieve long-term program sustainability through extensive training focused on capacity building within the host nations. An ability to adapt to changing circumstances has been critical to the success of CNP efforts. The Pentagon also deserves credit for implementing new training initiatives for both incoming and existing project managers. Recognizing that on-the-job training meant an overextended "downtime" between personnel shifts, the DoD instituted new training programs for its personnel that provide the benefit of uniform standards and increased efficiency.

Yet another innovation in recent years has been the establishment of CTR directorate "field offices" in several capital cities throughout the FSU including Moscow, Kiev, Tbilisi, and Tashkent. The advent of field representation not only enhances oversight capacity but the foreign nationals hired to staff these offices help the DoD to better navigate the opaque legal and bureaucratic structures in each country, promoting program longevity and continuity.

The Department of Energy

As noted, realizing that CTR could benefit from additional expertise, and that an expanded mission was ultimately critical to manage the broad panoply of challenges emanating from the states of the FSU, the DoE and the State Department were directed to launch coordinated nonproliferation programs of their own. The logical expansion of nonproliferation efforts to other departments increased the variety and scope of CNP assistance that the United States was able to offer. The DoE, with long-standing expertise in U.S. nuclear weapons management and domestic materials control, logically assumed an enhanced role under new bilateral efforts with the states of the FSU. Today, the DoE operates a wide array of cooperative nonproliferation subprograms, including efforts that aim to consolidate, secure, and eliminate nuclear warheads and dangerous material, shut down plutonium-producing nuclear reactors, and assist Russia in fulfilling its agreement with the United States to turn thirty-four metric tons of excess plutonium into mixed oxide fuel to be burned in light water nuclear reactors. The DoE is also responsible for a variety of programs that engage the resident human capacity within the former WMD infrastructure of the Soviet Union, enhance global export controls and safeguards, and monitor the HEU purchase agreement that will ultimately eliminate five hundred metric tons of weapons-usable uranium.

As noted above, the threat posed by excess weapons and materials, while awesome in its scope, was dwarfed in its complexity by the problem of technology transfer through under- or unemployed FSU weapons experts. The plight of the former Soviet weapons community was indicative of the widespread inability of Russia and the other FSU states to support the massive Soviet weapons complex that they inherited. Tens of thousands of highly trained scientists, engineers, and technicians lost their jobs or went months without a paycheck. All told, it was estimated that the Soviets had employed some 50,000–60,000 highly specialized nuclear experts and an additional 65,000 specialists within a vast biological warfare complex.[20] All were capable of spreading critical components of sensitive information to hostile groups and states. Given the poor economic performance of Russia and other FSU states, many scientists who could not find jobs elsewhere faced a choice: literally go hungry, or sell their expertise to the highest bidder. The DoE acted innovatively through the mid-1990s with "scientist redirect" programming aimed at enhancing U.S. national security by engaging FSU scientists, engineers, and technicians currently or formerly involved with WMD in peaceful and sustainable commercial pursuits.[21]

One particular example of the DoE's ingenuity in addressing the so-called brain drain threat is the Initiatives for Proliferation Prevention program (IPP). Under this initiative, former Soviet WMD scientists are paired with American firms through the United States Industry Coalition (USIC). This nonprofit association serves as the commercial backbone of the DoE redirect efforts and represents an important innovation in how nonproliferation objectives are achieved. By linking FSU scientists with industry partners, the IPP—which the DoE realigned to its Office of Nonproliferation and International Security (NIS) for fiscal year 2007—attempts to establish commercially viable opportunities that will lead to sustainable employment.[22] For example, a group of Russian scientists have joined with Halliburton to create a more environmentally friendly way of removing abandoned offshore oil structures.[23] A small California-based biotech company is using former biological weapons (BW) researchers to develop and field test a novel drug for tuberculosis.[24]

The Department of State

From the outset, the Department of State has been a critical player in the CNP arena through its role in negotiating the implementing agreements that have allowed programs to operate. As CNP programming has expanded, the State Department role has grown accordingly, particularly regarding efforts to meet the brain-drain challenge. In 1992, the department helped pioneer the International Science and Technology Center (ISTC) in Moscow and in 1993 the Science and Technology Center in Ukraine (STCU) in Kiev to provide short-term research grants to former weapons scientists. In 2005, the ISTC paid out $43.9 million worth of grants to 24,984 former Soviet weapons personnel and leveraged $21.5 million from its private sector partners for new project funding. From inception to the present, the ISTC has distributed over $200 million to prevent the proliferation of weapons expertise.[25]

The State Department also helped establish the nonprofit U.S. Civilian Research and Development Foundation (CRDF), another government-supported redirect effort that aims to strengthen the Eurasian science industry and move it away from weapons research.[26] The foundation, which opened in 1996, has reached over 6,600 specialists in its Cooperative Grants Program, which "offers an avenue into new research directions and collaborative opportunities for both U.S. and Eurasian scientists and engineers."[27] CRDF has now expanded its work to the often overlooked Baltic countries, as well as outside of the FSU with projects in Iraq and the Middle East, increasing the pool of scientific personnel that can benefit from the redirection programs.[28] In Ukraine alone, CRDF has awarded 517 grants, committed more than $10.5 million, and helped redirect 674 weapons specialists.[29] The breadth of CRDF programming has expanded considerably, and today the organization, inter alia, promotes industry partnerships and science education and has developed a series of sustainable national research institutions across the FSU. The ingenuity that CRDF staff has applied to its mission has been facilitated by enviable flexibility the organization has been granted in pursuing its mandate—particularly when compared with similar "in-house" government efforts. This freedom of movement has made CRDF one of the most efficient and successful organizations operating at the seams of U.S. CNP efforts.

Along with the STCU, the Bio-Chem Redirect Program at the Department of State works to find sources of peaceful research for former CBW scientists. The program sponsors peaceful collaborative research between former CBW scientists from the FSU and American scientists at the U.S. Departments of Health and Human Services (HHS) and Agriculture (USDA) and at the Environmental Protection Agency (EPA). The Bio-Chem Redirect Program was designed to circumvent the institutional limitations within the Department of State emanating from that agency's inability to directly contract with outside entities.

The BioIndustry Initiative (BII) at the Department of State aims to convert bioweapons facilities into commercial biotech enterprises. The BII was created by Congress after September 11, 2001, in an attempt to engage the private sector and provide effective new models of sustainability. Its mandate is focused solely on biological threats, and it works to transition large-scale FSU biological weapons production facilities, their technology, and associated expertise to commercial uses. It also seeks to partner U.S. and former Soviet CBW scientists to develop and accelerate the production of vaccines for infectious diseases that affect the FSU and the world. The central priority of BII is the long-term transformation of existing facilities into viable research and production institutions. The program will eventually assist in the conversion of 30 percent of Russia's former bioweapons infrastructure.[30] BII seeks to engage specific institutes and assess their core capabilities as well as the appropriate domestic and international market, and it then pairs Russian laboratories with American researchers in both academic and industrial sectors. It is anticipated that in 2009 major commercial reconfiguration projects such as the dismantlement of BW production buildings and the development of an animal feed mill at a former production facility in Georgia will come to fruition, thus testing the viability of the BII model.[31]

The Overarching Challenges to the Cooperative Nonproliferation Agenda

While countless studies and assessments of CNP programs continue to call for an enhanced resource base, accelerated implementation will more likely be fostered by tactical-level actions: expanded sales and marketing both at the political and program levels, promotion of mutually trusting relationships, bureaucratic disentanglement, and enhanced strategic planning.

Sales and Marketing

Despite its undisputed national security benefits, the CTR program faces considerable political and bureaucratic challenges before its mission in the FSU is complete. If organizational capacity matters in government, what drives the bureaucracy is sustained, high-level political attention, and what feeds it is budgetary prioritization. An ongoing challenge for both government officials and their private sector counterparts has been the miniscule proportion of the DoD budget that CTR programming occupies within the broad defense budget. With annual nonemergency appropriations of about $400 million, CTR represents just 0.08 percent of Pentagon spending.[32] State Department spending is equally paltry. These minimalist budgets, irrespective of whether or not they are scaled to address the threat, in turn feed the cycle of reduced political attention. Indeed, with the exception of the vociferous debate heard at their inception, these efforts seldom receive high-level attention within the Pentagon or at Foggy Bottom. Without such support, responsibility for promoting these programs within government and championing them with host-country counterparts falls to committed but politically less potent civil servants or to their private-sector contractors. In short, sustained political attention remains one of the most significant ongoing challenges to cooperative nonproliferation activities at the Departments of Defense and State.

Such is not the case at the Department of Energy. Currently, the lion's share of U.S. government-wide CNP-related programs—and the largest budgets—are administered by the National Nuclear Security Administration (NNSA) and encompass a broad spectrum of FSU and non-FSU focused activities. Unlike CTR's experience at DoD, the overall size of nonproliferation activities as a percentage of the total DoE/NNSA budget has conferred a particular structural advantage to this agency's efforts. Nonproliferation funding for international programs accounts for about 9 percent of NNSA's annual outlays.[33] Also unlike DoD, program managers at NNSA enjoy the sustained involvement of senior DoE/NNSA leadership, including intermittent attention from the secretary of energy, in providing political muscle to move the agenda forward with the FSU leadership. Unlike their counterparts at the Pentagon, successive secretaries of energy from Hazel O'Leary (1993–97) through Sam Bodman (2005–present) have generally displayed sustained personal interest in the success of nonproliferation activities at NNSA. This high-level attention also translates into advocacy for NNSA programming up through and including Cabinet-level advocacy within the U.S. government. Of course, this comparatively large percentage for nonproliferation in the NNSA's budget must still be viewed within the context of competing for means and attention vis-à-vis the U.S. nuclear weapons programs encompassed in the same agency's mission and budget.

Mutual Trust

Coming on the heels of the Cold War, threat reduction was touted as a concrete example of the new, peaceful relationship burgeoning between former adversaries. Given the level of deep cooperation necessary, successful implementation of the CNP agenda has always been predicated on the principle of trust among all parties. More often than not, this confidence is fostered and driven by personal relationships between American program managers and their post-Soviet counterparts. In the main, when program implementation has relied on this tactical level engagement between mutually respectful parties, CNP has flourished. Despite monumental successes over the course of the last fifteen years, the DoD programs, particularly those with Russia, continue to be dogged by a strategic level legacy of mutual suspicion. This mistrust is exacerbated by a lack of continuity in the persons representing the U.S. government in DoD-directed efforts. A handful of government officials at the Pentagon have been present since the advent of these programs and have therefore built the trust necessary to move the programs forward. However, the nature of government personnel rotation is compounded by DoD's piecemeal contracting of implementation to actors in the private sector. This results in the near continuous rotation among the actors involved in the day-to-day implementation of U.S. efforts on the ground. When this occurs, strategic level suspicions are translated to, and can derail, tactical level program implementation. In short, without continuity in program management, trust cannot be built and sustained, and the threat reduction agenda suffers.

The DoE's nonproliferation programs have a special tool to build trust that is not available to the other U.S. departments. Whereas program direction and oversight are performed by DoE/NNSA headquarters, the National Laboratories continue to play a key role in nonproliferation activities. In many instances, due to lower turnover than is typical at the agencies or a rotating pool of company contractors, laboratory personnel provide continuity as interlocutors for their FSU counterparts and act as the "glue" among disparate activities across the spectrum of programs. In general, the long-term relationship and trust building between U.S. laboratory personnel and their FSU counterparts is largely undervalued, particularly by Capitol Hill. Because of their critical role, decreasing the funding and therefore the prioritization of science-to-science efforts in the mix of nonproliferation programs is short-sighted, as these activities often provide the necessary foundation of trust that supports the broader panoply of nonproliferation programming. Although some DoE/NNSA program implementation is contracted directly to a handful of businesses involved in these efforts, more frequently the National Laboratories are responsible for contracting the business counterparts responsible for achieving CNP program objectives.

The Turf Wars

Serious bureaucratic impediments arise as a result of the bifurcation of roles and responsibilities between departments. For instance, the DoD, charged with articulating the policy objectives for CTR efforts in the states of the FSU, is not responsible for generating an overarching strategic plan for each country, leaving nonproliferation efforts occasionally at odds with other foreign policy objectives. By linking seemingly discrete elements of U.S. foreign policy, impediments to CTR implementation emerge. For instance, the political focus on human rights in several of the host countries complicates or hinders efficient implementation of DoD's CTR programs.[34] Moreover, the lack of an overarching strategic plan offering a clear articulation of nonproliferation threats and objectives for each country is compounded by organizational structures within the DoD itself. A long chain of command separates those who make policy at the Pentagon and the myriad actors actually charged with achievement of those policy objectives. Policy is formulated at the level of the Office of the Under Secretary of Defense for Policy (OUSD[P]). These policies and articulated objectives are then funneled down through the Defense Threat Reduction Agency (DTRA) to the CTR directorate, where program managers must translate the vision into a contract, including a timetable for specific deliverables assumed to achieve the stated policy objective. DTRA contractors and their subcontractors in particular are often unclear as to where their activities fit into the broader U.S. government nonproliferation strategy. Nor are these implementing partners always clear as to how their discrete set of "deliverables" is assumed to achieve the articulated objectives. In addition, interactions with Capitol Hill audiences and the media on the part of the CTR directorate at the DTRA are strictly controlled by policymakers within OSD-P, hindering their ability to keep Congress informed regarding ongoing implementation issues and tout their success through proactive public affairs operations.

Although the DoE/NNSA has a comparable number of layers in the hierarchy between policymaking and on-the-ground program implementation, the connection between NNSA policy planning and nonproliferation program managers working to translate that policy into concrete plans for implementation is direct. Seldom do laboratory officials or any of the private sector contractors to NNSA experience CTR-like needs for greater clarity as to how their activities contributed to broad U.S. nonproliferation objectives. In addition, according to program managers at NNSA, interactions with offices on Capitol Hill, although not always positive, are frequent, and NNSA's public affairs office is proactive in its efforts to keep the media informed regarding program successes.

Program Integration and Sustainability

As the suite of U.S. government nonproliferation programs was being established throughout the 1990s, little thought was given to its eventual transition to self-sustaining efforts funded and undertaken by the host countries. The failure to develop full scope integration has led to current-day challenges in making such transitions. A telling example of the challenges program managers face as a result of these early choices is reflected in the Elimination of Weapons Grade Plutonium Production (EWGPP) program at DoE. Under this initiative, three plutonium-producing nuclear reactors at Seversk and Zheleznogorsk are to be shut down, eliminating a potentially dangerous terrorist source of nuclear weapons materials. But workforce redirect was not incorporated as part of the initial planning process for the EWGPP effort. This oversight leaves open the possibility that eventual shutdown of the plutonium-producing reactors may be delayed or even stopped entirely due to local concerns regarding the unemployment problems subsequent to reactor shutdown. Without an integrated strategy that addresses the consequences of U.S. program objectives in a more holistic manner, CNP program implementation is complicated, and sustainability will be virtually impossible.

In general, DoE/NNSA has been proactive as of late in working to incorporate practices that ensure sustainability in its program areas. This is particularly true of the MPC&A program. One weakness in this arena remains a lack of focus in leveraging synergies among different program areas in an effort to bolster sustainability. For example, as noted above, efforts to provide civilian employment for former weapons scientists and downsize the nuclear weapons complex have not been sufficiently integrated into broader U.S. nonproliferation efforts, including those at DoD and the State Department. The resident scientific talent in the region could be leveraged to provide the in-country expertise, including services or products, necessary to ensure sustainability after U.S. funding expires and initiatives are finalized. Examples of successful leveraging between program areas have generally occurred by happenstance rather than by design. Approaching the broad swath of U.S. government nonproliferation programming as different layers of an integrated preventive strategy might, again, offer different opportunities to leverage specific initiatives off of one another or provide more attractive incentives to achieve host-country participation.

Future Challenges

Despite the efforts of the United States, Russia, and, more recently, the rest of the international community, an enormous amount of work remains to be done before the WMD threat can be contained. As of the end of fiscal year 2005 only 77 percent of FSU buildings containing nuclear material had undergone some type of security upgrade, and only 64 percent of FSU warhead sites had completed their upgrades, leaving a large number of potential proliferation risks.[35] As of July 2006, DoD had deactivated only 52 percent of FSU warheads targeted by its dismantlement programs.[36]

Furthermore, only an estimated 35 percent of the population of excess weapons personnel targeted by DoE has been provided sustainable civilian work through Global Initiatives for Proliferation Prevention (GIPP) grants.[37] Thousands of scientists or workers with WMD expertise remain available to rogue states or terrorist groups looking to capitalize on weapons expertise. Even more disconcerting is a recent survey that found that approximately 20 percent of FSU weapons personnel would consider selling their expertise to a rogue state if the right offer were to be made.[38] Such a high percentage proves that the proliferation of expertise is a high-priority risk, yet it continues to be subordinated to other, politically popular programs that produce quicker, more quantifiable results — even if less enduring.

Much remains to be done to secure the WMD threat around the globe. Presidential support for cooperative nonproliferation has always been long on promise but short on delivery. Similarly, congressional support for CNP has fluctuated, hampering the efficiency and effectiveness of these critical national security programs. As a result, programs have languished due to lack of attention or from outright assaults by members of Congress who cannot see past the lack of near-term, readily quantifiable results in some program areas. If executive and congressional support for cooperative nonproliferation in the FSU wanes prior to completion of the necessary tasks and acquisition of assurances of continuing host-country support to sustain existing security controls and maintenance of systems, the global WMD proliferation threat will grow, and the consequences could prove catastrophic.

Accelerating Progress the Old-Fashioned Way

Although bigger budgets almost inevitably translate into greater wherewithal and accelerate program implementation, money is not the most efficacious fix for most of today's CNP limitations. Injecting more money into a bureaucracy ill equipped to handle it is as effective as filling the gas tank of a car with no engine. The first step to accelerated implementation of the CNP agenda is to repair damaged systems.

Matching Threats to Responses

The CNPs were conceived and launched in the early years following the unanticipated collapse of the Soviet Union. Despite radically different circumstances in Russia and the other FSU states today, there has not been a global reassessment of these programs' role and objectives to ensure efficiency and effectiveness. Not only does the U.S. government lack a hard-nosed current assessment of CNP program priorities based on new threats, but major new efforts in port security, interdiction, border security, and the like have come online since September 11, 2001. These new activities seek to address more diffuse and geographically dispersed proliferation concerns than the "traditional" CNP activities. In addition, some existing efforts under the "traditional" CNP umbrella, particularly those in science redirect, are being stretched to the limit by political pressures to apply these programs to regions outside the FSU.

In order to correct for this shortcoming, a National Security Council (NSC) designee should be appointed to spearhead an interagency process to reassess the global role of CNP efforts in today's context, including those that have arisen in the past few years. Such a close examination of the entire suite of programs across all relevant government agencies should strive to eliminate duplication, consolidate where necessary, and fill any gaps within the existing efforts. Not only do the changed circumstances in Russia and the region call for a reevaluation, but the role of CNP efforts beyond the FSU also needs scrutinizing in light of new opportunities, such as the Global Partnership Against the Spread of Weapons and Materials of Mass Destruction and the recently announced Global Initiative to Combat Nuclear Terrorism, and their utility in addressing other U.S. objectives, such as technical assistance to enhance the effectiveness of the Proliferation Security Initiative and support full implementation of UN Security Council Resolution 1540.

Promoting Continuity and Coherence

The Departments of Defense, Energy, and State all suffer under significant impediments resulting from unclear authorities between agencies or discontinuities in the interagency process. A definitive need exists for greater information sharing among agencies regarding their programs and activities in the field. This information deficit extends to the ongoing programs and activities of other countries participating in CNP efforts in the FSU.

The global reassessment of risks and objectives proposed above should be used to build a foundation for an ongoing process within the U.S. government to set priorities, ensure coherence, and streamline ongoing activities. Building this foundation and spearheading the process will require knowledgeable and active engagement by a senior NSC official. The NSC official would need to work hand in glove with the appropriate Office of Management and Budget (OMB), State, Energy, and Defense Department officials, and Capitol Hill to provide the assessment of and prepare the foundation for an ongoing interagency process to implement the findings of this assessment and to maintain coherence and efficiency in the U.S. government's CNP efforts as a whole.

In addition, we recommend the creation of an office at the State Department to serve as the U.S. government's "information clearinghouse" for all agencies' CNP-related activities as well as the focal point for timely information regarding global CNP programs and field activities. This office would be responsible for collection and dissemination of information regarding the status, site visits, and objectives of each program, including timely information regarding the programs and field activities of states in the Global Partnership Against the Spread of Weapons and Materials of Mass Destruction. The office would not have operational control over programs, but rather would serve as a node for ongoing communications and information sharing.

Informing Congress

A survey of CNP program implementation suggests that this suite of programs was never embraced at sufficiently high levels to become the "organizing principle" for a U.S. non- and counterproliferation strategy. Over the course of time, the collection of acronyms representing these efforts across multiple U.S. government agencies became relegated to a limited role of supply-side measures applicable to the FSU and, perhaps, other discrete scenarios. Given the programs' low-level status within agencies, mirrored by relatively meager funding allocations in the president's budget, the wherewithal of the legislative branch to further promote this approach remains limited. In addition, as outlined above, the complex, multijurisdictional, and preventive nature of funding allocated for CNP efforts stymies the intermittent efforts on Capitol Hill to generate greater support and assist in "organizing" the executive branch's efforts.

Officials at the operational level in all three agencies as well as some of their private sector counterparts are frustrated with "congressional oversight"—reporting requirements, nonsensical earmarks, lack of nuance in metrics for progress, and insufficient understanding of the programs. Although it is a universal truth that agencies will balk at congressional actions that limit their flexibility or mandate greater transparency, this example would appear to offer a potential solution that is not necessarily true or as applicable in other cases. In our assessment, the complexity of these programs, their wide distribution among different agencies, the limited agency personnel responsible for their execution, and the relatively small budgets afforded them all suggest that finding a more effective and less time-consuming means for informational exchanges between the agency actors and their congressional counterparts would be highly advantageous to both parties. Creating an informal convening mechanism within Congress that includes all relevant personal office and committee staff, with the potential for occasional participation of members, would not only enhance Congress's internal policy-making coherence on CNP efforts but would serve to bolster its knowledge base regarding the processes and larger prospects for these programs in meeting some of the non- and counterproliferation objectives of the United States.

In light of the obstacles internal to the legislative branch and the need for greater communication between agency officials and their congressional counterparts, we propose creation of a bicameral congressional task force whose objective is to regularly provide briefings from a broad array of the actors involved in actual implementation of CNP initiatives. This internal congressional mechanism would provide the necessary institutional counterpart to more coordinated interagency efforts outlined above. Members of Congress's sponsorship and a minimum of internal support could be bolstered by collaborating with a nonpartisan policy institute willing to facilitate the organization and content of the briefings, provide synopses of each meeting for internal use, and facilitate outreach beyond those in attendance, when necessary.

Managing Expectations, Promoting Buy-in, and Encouraging Sustainability

Host country buy-in is perhaps the single most important element to the long-term success of the CNP agenda. Although the United States is ultimately unable to control this, Washington is in a position to create fertile ground for agreement. Several interconnected efforts to promote an environment conducive to engagement include but are not limited to managing expectations in U.S. interactions with their FSU counterparts, seeding host country buy-in at the outset of any major program, and promoting sustainability after the conclusion of U.S. support for the efforts. Clarity regarding the U.S. commitment and objectives, in conjunction with meeting the host countries' needs or addressing any mismatch in threat perceptions, would go a long way in helping to build a foundation for program stability and long-term sustainability. At every stage of the process, joint planning should be undertaken. At the start of any program, the agency involved should build consensus with the respective host country regarding the threats and ensure host country support for the objectives and commitments to sustain the efforts after U.S. support ends. Ideally, every iteration of a program would include "training" elements for host country counterparts regarding U.S. processes and procedures.[39] Joint postprogram assessments to develop lessons learned would also serve as a needed feedback loop to enhance future program efforts.

The problem of unfulfilled expectations based on a glitch between agencies or congressional changes to a program's parameters or budgets could be mitigated by the proposed interagency and congressional task force structures and processes outlined above. Simultaneously, the aforementioned "training" for host country counterparts would entail honest depictions regarding potential program changes internal to each agency as well as the possibility of budgetary or other constraints being imposed by Congress. These mutually reinforcing processes would serve as a means to mitigate the enduring problem of unfulfilled expectations, which too frequently undermine host country support, impeding not only more immediate implementation objectives but also efforts to ensure sustainability.

Conclusion

What began as an emergency response to the collapse of a heavily armed WMD empire has spawned a panoply of effective programs not only to address Cold War legacies in the FSU but also to serve as tools in bolstering the efficacy of U.S. counterproliferation efforts (such as the Proliferation Security Initiative) and UN mandates designed to address the threat of nonstate actors (such as Resolution 1540). The first fifteen years of CNP efforts have proven an unparalleled disarmament and nonproliferation success when these achievements are viewed against the background of forty years of enmity between the United States and the Soviet Union and the relatively minimal monetary and political investments made to date. However, the enduring lack of high-level political commitment and the dispersion of programs across many agencies have given rise to formidable structural challenges within the departments implementing these efforts, as well as incoherence between them, despite their pursuit of similar objectives. The biggest challenge confronting CNP programs today is prioritizing these efforts within an entirely different context in order to ensure sustainability of U.S. efforts to date, while simultaneously enhancing U.S. capacity to apply some aspects of the tools available to address new challenges in preventing catastrophic terrorism. Meeting this challenge will require a clear-eyed global reassessment of U.S. priorities and commitments, establishment of an interagency process to provide greater continuity and coherence, creation of a congressional mechanism to mirror agency efforts and break down jurisdictional barriers, and a solid foundation for sustainability prior to program initiation in the next era of U.S. CNP efforts.

Notes

1. Throughout this chapter the term "cooperative nonproliferation" (CNP) will be used to refer to the entire suite of nonproliferation programs throughout U.S. federal agencies. Cooperative threat reduction (CTR) refers only to those programs managed by the Department of Defense (DoD). For a more comprehensive scorecard of nonproliferation successes, see http://www.stimson.org/ctr/?SN=CT20050804895.

2. Department of Defense, Defense Threat Reduction Agency, "CTR Scorecard: Strategic Offensive Arms Elimination," August 7, 2007, http://www.dtra.mil/oe/ctr/scorecard.cfm, accessed on August 15, 2006.

3. For metric tons secured see Matthew Bunn and Anthony Wier, *Securing the Bomb 2006: The New Global Imperatives* (Cambridge, MA: Belfer Center, Harvard University, 2006), 53. Figures on HEU blenddown can be found at U.S. Enrichment Corporation, *Megatons to Megawatts: Status Report*, June 28, 2006, http://www.usec.com/v2001_02/content/megatons/11k_insert.pdf, accessed August 15, 2006.

4. Starting with a budget at the DoD of just $25 million in fiscal year 1992, the programs today have grown into multiyear, multicountry efforts totaling approximately $1.3 billion in Russia, the former Soviet republics, and other nations of proliferation concern. The president's fiscal year 2007 request included about $372 million for the DoD's CTR program, $834 million for Department of Energy (DoE) nonproliferation programs, and $163 million for State Department nonproliferation programs.

5. Graham Allison, "How to Stop Nuclear Terror," *Foreign Affairs* 83, no. 1 (January/February 2004): 64–74.

6. 9/11 Public Discourse Project, "Final Report on 9/11 Commission Recommendations," December 5, 2005, http://www.9-11pdp.org/press/2005-12-05_report.pdf, accessed July 26, 2006.

7. Brian Finlay and Andrew Grotto, *The Race to Secure Russia's Loose Nukes: Progress since 9/11* (Washington, DC: Henry L. Stimson Center and the Center for American Progress, September 2005, 29, http://www.stimson.org/ctr/pdf/LooseNukes.pdf.

8. International Atomic Energy Agency, "List of Confirmed Incidents Involving HEU or Pu," *IAEA Illicit Trafficking Database*, 2003, 5, http://www.iaea.org/NewsCenter/Features/RadSources/PDF/itdb_31122003.pdf, accessed July 26, 2006.

9. United Kingdom Department of Trade and Industry, "Nonproliferation-Global Threat Reduction Program: Closed Nuclear Cities Partnership," http://www.berr.gov.uk/energy/non-proliferation/global-threat-reduction/portfolio/cncp/index.html, accessed April 30, 2008; Matthew Bunn, *"The Threat: The Threat in Russia and the Newly Independent States,"* in *Securing the Bomb* (Cambridge, MA: Belfer Center, Harvard University, 2002), http://www.nti.org/e_research/cnwm/threat/russia.asp, accessed July 26, 2006.

10. For a comprehensive overview of the former Soviet biological weapons complex see Amy E. Smithson, *Toxic Archipelago: Preventing Proliferation from the Former Soviet Chemical and Biological Weapons Complex*, report no. 32 (Washington, DC: Henry L. Stimson Center, December 1999), http://www.stimson.org/cbw/pdf/toxicarch.pdf.

11. Ken Alibek, *Biohazard* (New York: Random House, 1999), 270–71.

12. For a report on claims made by bin Laden's deputy, Ayman al-Zawahri, see "Journalist Says al-Qaeda Has Black Market Nuclear Bombs," *Sydney Morning Herald*, March 22, 2004, http://www.informationclearinghouse.info/article5915.htm, accessed July 26, 2006.

13. U.S. Congress, *Conventional Forces in Europe Treaty Implementation Act of 1991*, Public Law 102-228, title 2, section 211, January 1991, http://thomas.loc.gov/cgi-bin/bdquery/z?d102:h.r.03807, accessed July 26, 2006.

14. Amy F. Woolf, *Nonproliferation and Threat Reduction Assistance: U.S. Programs in the Former Soviet Union*, Congressional Research Service Report for Congress, April 6, 2006, 5, http://fpc.state.gov/documents/organization/66455.pdf, accessed July 26, 2006.

15. U.S. Congress, *Freedom for Russia and Emerging Eurasian Democracies and Open Markets Support Act*, Public Law 102-511, title 5, section 501, January 1992, http://thomas.loc.gov/cgi-bin/bdquery/z?d102:s.02532, accessed July 26, 2006.

16. U.S. Congress, *National Defense Authorization Act for Fiscal Year 1997*, January 2006, Public Law 104-201, title 14, section 1402, and title 15, section 1501 (January 2006), http://thomas.loc.gov/cgi-bin/bdquery/z?d104:h.r.03230, accessed July 26, 2006.

17. Secretary of Energy Advisory Board, A *Report Card on the Department of Energy's Nonproliferation Programs with Russia*, January 10 (Washington, DC: U.S. Department of Energy, 2001), iii, http://www.seab.energy.gov/publications/rusrpt.pdf, accessed July 26, 2006.

18. Philipp Bleek, *Global Cleanout of Civil Nuclear Material*, SGP Issue Brief 4, Strengthening the Global Partnership Project (Washington, DC: Center for Strategic and Interna-

tional Studies, 2005), http://www.sgpproject.org/publications/SGPIssueBrief/SGP%20Issue %20Brief%20Bleek.pdf, accessed July 26, 2006.

19. Sharon Squassoni, *Globalizing Cooperative Threat Reduction: A Survey of Options*, Congressional Research Service Report for Congress, July 2, 2004, http://www.fas.org/spp/ starwars/crs/RL32359.pdf, accessed July 26, 2006.

20. Smithson, *Toxic Archipelago*.

21. U.S. Industry Coalition, "GIPP Program: Accomplishments," http://www.usic.net/ GIPPprogram/index.cfm?cid=14.

22. United States Industry Coalition, "Reducing Proliferation Risks," IPP Program, http://www.usic.net/usic/test1.nsf/Links/Reducing%20Proliferation%20Risks, accessed July 26, 2006.

23. United States Industry Coalition, "Rarefaction Shock Wave (RSW) Cutter for Offshore Oil-Gas Platform Removal," July 2003, http://www.usic.net/userfiles/Halliburton.pdf.

24. United States Industry Coalition, "TB Peptides," April 2005, http://cisa1.lanl.gov/ Forms/Eposters/SciClone.pdf, accessed July 26, 2006.

25. International Science and Technology Center, Annual Report 2005 (Moscow: International Science and Technology Center, 2006): 1, http://istc.ru/ISTC/sc.nsf/AR-2005-en .pdf, accessed July 26, 2006.

26. U.S. Civilian Research and Development Foundation, "Overview: About CRDF," 2006, http://www.crdf.org/about/, accessed July 26, 2006.

27. U.S. Civilian Research and Development Foundation, "Our Key Focus Areas: Cooperative Research," 2006, http://www.crdf.org/focus/focus_show.htm?doc_id=290100, accessed July 26, 2006.

28. U.S. Civilian Research and Development Foundation, Annual Report 2004 (Arlington, VA: United States Civilian Research and Development Foundation, 2006), http://www .crdf.org/annualreport/2004_Annual_Report-Final.pdf.

29. U.S. Civilian Research and Development Foundation, "Looking Back, Moving Forward," September 1, 2005, http://www.crdf.org/newsletters/newsletters_show.htm?doc_id =309320.

30. Francis Record, "U.S. Nonproliferation Strategy: Policies and Technical Capabilities," testimony before the House International Relations Subcommittee on Oversight and Investigations, July 20, 2006, http://www.state.gov/t/isn/rls/rm/82125.htm.

31. As of May 2007 the Defense Threat Reduction Agency had completed tasks set forth under the Biological Weapons and Infrastructure Elimination (BWIE) aspect of this project. Currently, the State Department is in the process of building the grain mill facility at the site as a viable substitute for the vaccine production. This phase is projected to reach completion in 2009. See Statement of Lela Bekanidze, Head of the Department of Especially Dangerous Pathogens, National Center for Disease Control and Medical Statistics of Georgia at: http://www.bwpp.org/2007MSP/documents/20071211Georgia.pdf

32. The total amount appropriated for Defense Department spending in fiscal year 2006 was $70.2 billion; of that, $415 million (0.0837 percent) was allocated for CTR efforts. The fiscal year 2007 request included $439.5 billion for the Defense Department, with $372.2 million for CTR activities (0.0847 percent).

33. The amount appropriated for all of NNSA's activities in fiscal year 2006 was $9.1 billion, of which $823.3 million (9.04 percent) was designated for nonproliferation efforts. The fiscal year 2007 request for NNSA totaled $9.3 billion, with $834.4 million (8.97 percent) allocated to nonproliferation.

34. For example, in 1997, the United States suspended CTR funding to Belarus "as a result of the government of Belarus's worsening human rights record and anti-democratic behavior" (see http://minsk.usembassy.gov/policy19970701.html). Belarus has yet to be re-certified and has not received any CTR funding since 1997. Similarly, in 2003, the State Department decertified Uzbekistan for CTR assistance. However, the president waived the certification requirements, and assistance was allowed to continue (see http://hrw.org/english/docs/2003/12/31/uzbeki7024.htm). Finally, in 2004, Russia was decertified for CTR assistance because of the government's failure to "observe internationally recognized human rights" (see http://moscow.usembassy.gov/bilateral/bilateral.php?record_id=report_supporting_rights_2004). As with Uzbekistan, the president waived the certification requirements in order to allow assistance to continue.

35. U.S. Department of Energy, *FY 2007 Congressional Budget Request* (Washington, DC: U.S. Department of Energy, 2006): 514, http://www.cfo.doe.gov/budget/07budget/Start.htm.

36. Department of Defense, Defense Threat Reduction Agency, "CTR Scorecard: Strategic Offensive Arms Elimination."

37. In 2006, the Initiative for Proliferation Prevention was renamed the Global IPP. GIPP currently includes both IPP programs and the efforts under the Nuclear Cities Initiative at DoE (U.S. Department of Energy, *FY 2007 Congressional Budget Request*, 497).

38. Deborah Yarsike Ball and Theodore P. Gerber, *Will Russian Scientists Go Rogue? A Survey on the Threat and the Impact of Western Assistance*, Center for Strategic and International Studies, November 2004, http://www.csis.org/media/csis/pubs/pm_0357.pdf, accessed July 26, 2006.

39. The Department of Energy initiated a training program for host country personnel in order to clarify U.S. budget and contracting processes. Due to the perceived success of these training modules in helping to manage host country expectations and avoid misunderstanding in the ongoing efforts, the Defense Department has since started providing them in certain instances as well.

CHAPTER SIXTEEN

Russia's Nuclear Security Culture

Nathan E. Busch and James R. Holmes

Formidable technical barriers stand in the way of states and terrorist networks that aspire to build nuclear weapons. The "crossroads of radicalism and technology," as the 2002 U.S. *National Security Strategy* phrased it, is not so easy to traverse.[1] Producing plutonium and highly enriched uranium (HEU), the key ingredients of nuclear warheads, is especially difficult. Yet actors that bear the West ill will have simply turned elsewhere in pursuit of the ultimate weapon. Insider theft could help them surmount the technical barriers. With hundreds of tons of nuclear materials, an unwelcome holdover from the Soviet era, the Russian Federation is the most promising source of illicit fissile materials for al Qaeda and kindred groups.

The post–Cold War years have witnessed numerous thefts and attempted thefts from Russian nuclear facilities.[2] This points to an effort by al Qaeda and hostile regimes to gain entry to the Russian stockpile, with implications of enormous import for the United States and its friends.[3] To ward off this threat, the U.S. government has instituted an array of programs to help Moscow impose strict control on its warheads, nuclear materials, and expertise. Successive U.S. administrations have spent over $8.2 billion on these programs.[4] But most of this funding has gone into technical fixes such as installing or upgrading physical protection systems and material protection, control, and accounting systems (MPC&A) at Russian nuclear sites.

Although material upgrades are crucial and must continue, hardware is only as good as its operator. It has become abundantly clear that U.S. assistance programs have helped Russia modernize its security arrangements while neglecting the human element of security.[5] The United States, accordingly, must persevere with existing programs while making a new investment in transforming the professional culture at Russian nuclear sites. This will be money well spent, considering the stakes.

Can Material Solutions Ameliorate Cultural Problems?

The cultural challenge arises in large measure from the traumas Russia has undergone since the Soviet Union fell. Its faults notwithstanding, the regimented, security-obsessed Soviet regime held down the risk of insider theft or successful external attack on Russian nuclear installations. The Cold War conferred tremendous prestige on the nuclear sector, along with pay and benefits, reducing the incentive for nuclear personnel to divert or sell nuclear materials. But post-Soviet Russia has been reinventing itself as a more open society, with radically different values and priorities. The end of the Cold War inarguably benefited Russia, terminating the costly arms race with the West, but the attendant economic hardships denied the federal government tax revenues it needed to fund priorities such as nuclear security.

The post-Soviet political and economic transformations at once deflated morale among nuclear workers and deprived them of the generous pay and benefits to which they had grown accustomed. The recent rise in oil prices has replenished Moscow's coffers, allowing the government to fund priorities left wanting during the 1990s. Even so, many workers at Russian nuclear facilities still doubt the need to sink scarce resources into expensive security upgrades. They remain skeptical that stringent and expensive security procedures and accounting systems will help prevent theft by insiders—if indeed an insider threat exists. This lingering skepticism, combined with the lasting effects from the Soviet era, has created a professional culture that works against nuclear security.

We examine the roots of these attitudes and consider how the United States can help bolster the "security culture" at Russian nuclear sites. Only by adding a human dimension to its assistance efforts can the United States improve its own security against nuclear or radiological terrorism.

Definitions

"Security culture" has become a buzzword in nonproliferation and nuclear security circles. The concept has been featured in reports by the International Atomic Energy Agency (IAEA), the United Nations nuclear watchdog body.[6] But a consensus definition of the term has been slow in coming.[7] An early definition of "safeguards culture" captured some elements of nuclear security culture. Two specialists defined "safeguards culture" as a "pervasive, shared belief among political leaders, senior managers, and operating personnel that effective MPC&A is critically important, as manifested in decisions and actions, large and small."[8] The working IAEA definition of security culture is "that assembly of characteristics, attitudes and behaviors in individuals, organizations and institutions, which supports the objectives of nuclear security and ensures that it receives the attention warranted by its significance."[9]

We take these efforts at terminological clarity a step further, defining security culture as (a) the degree to which not only supervisors but also mid-level and junior personnel are aware of and committed to widely accepted norms, such as the tenets of nonproliferation and best practices; (b) the degree to which available security technology is put to use, maintained, and improved; and (c) the effectiveness with which security rules and procedures are implemented. A robust security culture exhibits the following traits: (a) clearly defined, widely promulgated, and strictly enforced standards; (b) workers who possess the know-how to use installed security equipment effectively; and (c) workers who understand why the technologies, rules, and procedures in place at their installations are necessary and perform their duties accordingly.[10] Clearly, then, security culture encompasses far more than technical proficiency.

Russians are intuitively aware of the cultural dimension of security and other human affairs. They commonly ascribe misfortunes, including incidents and mishaps in the nuclear sector, to the "human factor." While they recognize the importance of a skilled, motivated workforce in preventing nuclear incidents, many of them also seem resigned to the malaise that typified the early post–Cold War years. Russians point to several prerequisites, including decent, regularly paid wages and a stable working environment—things in short supply in 1990s Russia—for a healthy security culture.[11] Understanding how Russians perceive the human factor, and how the human factor relates to security culture, will help Western officials design programs that more effectively meet the Russian Federation's security needs. The human factor can, and must, be transformed from a liability into an asset to nuclear security culture.

Tenets of U.S. Security Culture

The United States, the world's first nuclear power, has amassed decades of experience in these matters and, though imperfect, provides a useful standard for comparison. How does the United States inculcate a security culture within its own nuclear sector? Researchers from the University of Georgia Center for International

Trade and Security (CITS) met with employees of the Westinghouse Savannah River Company who oversee security arrangements at the Department of Energy's (DoE) Savannah River Site (SRS) in South Carolina. While these individuals focused on security arrangements at SRS, similar programs are in place at all sensitive facilities in the U.S. nuclear complex. The following themes emerged:

Training for Security Executives and Managers. Because site managers and their senior staffs are crucial to the security culture at nuclear facilities, these supervisory personnel are enrolled in courses that train them to develop and manage security awareness programs. The Albuquerque National Nuclear Institute provides these seminars in Albuquerque and onsite at DoE facilities.

Establishing and Promulgating Security Procedures. Specific requirements for security awareness at DoE facilities are outlined in the DoE 470 series of regulations. All employees are expected to be conversant with these regulations, which are promulgated in hard copy and, in many cases, online.[12] Employees also undergo thorough briefings on security procedures, including (a) general employment training for all personnel who work at a facility; (b) comprehensive briefings and annual refresher training for all personnel granted access to classified information or special nuclear materials; and (c) termination briefings when employees relinquish their security clearances.

Personnel Reliability Program. The United States has enacted a personnel reliability program for employees in sensitive positions, such as those involving access to nuclear weapons, fissile materials, or classified material. The program requires extensive background investigations for employees who apply for security clearances, and it mandates annual in-house reviews of individuals granted clearances. These reviews consist of an interview, a urinalysis, psychological testing, and a credit check.[13]

Competitive Salaries and Benefits. An obvious but sometimes overlooked aspect of nuclear security in the United States is that employees of the nuclear complex are well paid and receive generous benefits packages. Unlike their counterparts in 1990s Russia, they have little incentive to run the risk of a jail term by selling classified information or materials. Incentives for whistle-blowing, including monetary rewards and anonymous hotlines, also check the temptation to sell or divert these materials.

Continuing Awareness Programs. Routine training takes place throughout the year. Follow-up training includes daily briefings on new security procedures or equipment introduced at the site and on any security breaches that may have occurred. At regular monthly meetings, groups and projects at SRS consider "security topics of the month," tailored to their particular activities. Finally, a "Security Meeting Guide" is published each month, complete with slides and talking points, to update employees on security-related events at the site.

A string of security breaches and espionage allegations has plagued Los Alamos National Laboratory and other DoE sites in recent years, showing that U.S. security culture is by no means perfect.[14] Still, security rules and regulations are in place and readily understood, and the personnel charged with nuclear security seem to be knowledgeable and committed to discharging their duties in accordance with established procedures. Despite its flaws, then, security culture in the United States provides a useful benchmark for the Russian Federation's own efforts.

Shortcomings of Russia's Current Approach to MPC&A Training

After the Cold War, the United States and Russia instituted collaborative programs to head off the danger of Russian "loose nukes."[15] In 1991, for instance, Congress approved funding for the Cooperative Threat Reduction (CTR) program, better known as the Nunn-Lugar program, after its primary cosponsors in the Senate. Since its inception the program has grown to encompass several projects, including some intended to help Russia improve its MPC&A infrastructure and procedures. U.S.-funded MPC&A upgrades range from the mundane, such as reinforced doors and bars across windows, to the highly sophisticated, such as precision measurement equipment that allows site personnel to take accurate inventories of fissile materials, confirming that not even a minute quantity of material has been removed.[16]

The MPC&A program made noteworthy progress after its inception, completing security upgrades for some 192 metric tons of fissile material by 2001 and working to improve the security of an additional 410 tons.[17] The Russian MPC&A program increasingly resembles that of the United States, largely because of the infusion of U.S. aid, but much remains to be done. A Harvard University study reported that as of the end of fiscal year 2002, "only about 37% of the potentially-vulnerable nuclear materials in Russia was protected by initial, 'rapid' upgrades, and less than one-sixth of Russia's stockpile of HEU had been destroyed."[18] Some 21 percent of the HEU Russia was believed to possess at the end of the Cold War has now been destroyed, primarily by "downblending" it to low-enriched uranium fuel for use in U.S. commercial reactors.[19]

To come to grips with this stubborn problem, Presidents George W. Bush and Vladimir Putin issued a joint communiqué in February 2005, following their summit at Bratislava, Slovakia. The two presidents vowed to continue efforts to improve nuclear security—including security culture—in both countries.[20] They reaffirmed their commitment to "a strong security culture" at the 2006 Group of Eight (G-8) summit in St. Petersburg, announcing the Global Initiative to Combat

Nuclear Terrorism.[21] It has become clear at the highest echelons of government that rehabilitating the human factor is central to MPC&A improvements.

Generational change has furnished Russia and the United States an opportunity to make good on the pronouncements of senior officials. Veterans of the Soviet nuclear complex are reaching retirement age. As early as 1994, foreseeing this changeover in personnel, the Russian Ministry of Atomic Energy (Minatom) initiated a U.S. and EU–backed effort to train the incoming generation in operational matters. One product of this effort was the Russian Methodological Training Center (RMTC), located at the Institute of Physics and Power Engineering in Obninsk, a city southeast of Moscow.

RMTC, which opened its doors in late 1998, boasts an impressive array of laboratories, state-of-the-art instruments, and computer-based classrooms. Its chief purpose is to train Russian specialists in MPC&A. The RMTC staff, numbering some 140 Russian, European, and American experts, also provides scientific and technical assistance to companies and facilities that develop MPC&A techniques and tests and evaluates methods and instrumentation for measuring the mass and content of nuclear materials.[22] The pioneering initiative embodied by RMTC represents a welcome step forward in the enterprise of safeguarding Russian nuclear materials and technology.

But culture is a stubborn thing, and the curriculum currently in place at RMTC displays little understanding of that basic fact, let alone any effort to instill the habits and attitudes that underwrite a vibrant security culture. RMTC offers a total of twenty-seven courses, divided into six series: (a) fundamentals of material control and accounting; (b) access control technology; (c) nondestructive testing techniques and instruments; (d) statistical methods and inventory control; (e) software engineering; and (f) MPC&A inspections.[23]

Conspicuously absent from the RMTC curriculum is any recognition that technical know-how imparted at the center serves any larger purpose. The courses do not portray MPC&A training as something that contributes to Russian or international security. Nor do they stress the perils that would accrue should nuclear materials fall into the hands of terrorist organizations or rogue regimes. And they make little effort to cultivate a professional ethos in which theft, diversion, or simple negligence is unthinkable.

As the various Bush/Putin statements attest, both the U.S. and Russian governments have come to recognize the dangers posed by a security culture that is indifferent to national and international security. To make good on their words, Washington and Moscow need to work together to foster a culture premised as much on ethics and esprit de corps as on technical prowess. At a minimum, that will involve reforming the training programs now in place. Russia bears primary responsibility for the reform effort, while the United States and other interested parties such as the G-8 should not skimp on new investments of their own.[24]

The Human-Factor-Centered Mindset and Its Consequences

Cultural transformation may be a bigger challenge than the Russian government and its partners understand. Security culture is a subset of Russian culture, which is still coming to grips with unhelpful habits and attitudes bequeathed to it by the Soviet experience. Those habits and attitudes work against efforts to nurture a robust security culture. The elements of security culture, as we have defined it, are a set of clear rules that are widely promulgated and strictly enforced, along with technically skilled workers who buy into the technologies, rules, and procedures in place at their installations. The security culture at U.S. DoE sites such as SRS fares reasonably well by these standards, but the Soviet Union was inhospitable to the qualities that make for robust security—particularly in its waning days.

Decades of arbitrary rule, for instance, taught Russians to mistrust or ignore written rules. Lax discipline and reluctance to follow written procedures arose not from a lack of procedures but from an overabundance of them. Like any overly bureaucratic, centralized political system, the Soviet Union proliferated countless laws, rules, and regulations. The Soviet legal order was bulky, complicated, contradictory, and mercurial—and therefore incomprehensible to the man on the street. It is often said that the severity of Soviet laws was equaled only by the selectiveness with which they were enforced. Both officials and ordinary citizens skirted the rules, both out of personal negligence and because vague, inconsistent procedures commanded scant respect among the populace.[25]

Cronyism flourished as a result. Characterized by the rule of law and safeguards for individual liberties, Western liberal democracies function more or less consistently, regardless of what political party happens to hold power at any given time. By contrast, Soviet governance vested tremendous authority in individual political leaders, affording the personal loyalties, beliefs, and preferences of these leaders an importance nearly unthinkable in the West. Because of this authoritarian reflex, top managers in Russia continue to enjoy far greater power and latitude to impose their will than their Western counterparts do. The prevailing lack of accountability only amplifies this tendency. Lower-level employees routinely flout inconvenient regulations, falling back on the old Russian saying, "I am just a small fish."[26]

The stark contradiction between the Soviet regime's utopian promises and the drab realities of everyday life infused Soviet society with apathy and cynicism. How?

First, the mismatch between theory and reality could not be openly attributed to flaws in the Soviet system. Shortcomings in the system were blamed on foreign conspiracies, individual mistakes, or the deeds of "enemies of the people." Scapegoating became a reflex. Second, the adversarial mindset produced by the system's economic failings channeled the resourcefulness and ingenuity of Soviet citizens into under-the-counter relationships of dubious legality.[27] They obtained the basics of life by gaming the system. "Central control over all political and economic aspects of society," wrote one analyst, "created an unmotivated, and often careless, workforce."[28] Far from commanding allegiance, the system became something to be beaten.

But there is a more utilitarian explanation for Russians' reliance on the human factor. The Soviet economy skewed heavily toward nonproductive sectors such as defense and space programs. As a result, the Soviet Union fell further and further behind the West in cutting-edge research and production, opening a technological gap that persists today.[29] Even the nation's impressive output of scientists and engineers yields few economic benefits. Thousands of highly educated Russians emigrated to the United States, Europe, and Israel amid the rampant unemployment of the 1990s. Predictably, Western information technology firms operating in Russia now complain about the makeup of the local talent pool. Graduates of Russian institutes and universities, they say, possess vast theoretical knowledge but lack the ability to adapt to and thrive in the nation's rapidly Westernizing work environment.[30]

Deficiencies in the human factor could have far-reaching consequences. Soviet engineers designed and built an impressive array of power plants, yet the world-class nuclear fuel cycle underpinning the Soviet nuclear complex coexisted with an obsolescent—by world standards—MPC&A system.[31] In the immediate post–Cold War years, Russian nuclear workers lacked the skills to operate sophisticated security equipment, treating U.S.-supplied hardware with suspicion and resisting expert help from the United States, which they still regarded as an adversary.[32]

These conditions were inimical to rigorous oversight over the nation's fissile-material stockpile. Indeed, evidence regularly surfaces indicating that nuclear personnel bypass regulations on the handling of radioactive materials and by-products. U.S. visitors report observing Russian guard forces making "exceptions" to security procedures in order to expedite distinguished guests' access to secure areas.[33] Even when modern surveillance and alarm systems have been installed at Russian facilities, they are often used improperly. At one facility, a new infrared intrusion detecting system was ineffective because the grass was not mowed. At another, staff members shut off the electrical power to reduce the facility's bills—rendering high-quality surveillance systems useless. Most troubling of all, numerous reports have documented guards shutting off security and monitoring systems out of annoyance at frequent false alarms or simply because they found the systems too burdensome for routine use.[34]

Reform Is Possible

What was done during the Soviet years can be undone given time, resources, and dedication on the part of the Russian political and nuclear leadership. Russia's decade-plus of political and economic reform has shown that, while inherited attitudes and habits of mind inhibit change, they are not fixed. Reform is gradually taking hold in traditional Russian industries such as agriculture, defense, and aerospace. The partial lifting of bureaucratic impediments to innovation has opened the way for an entirely new range of industries, including telecommunications, private security systems, personal computers, mobile telephones, and e-trade.

With this array of consumer-oriented goods and services — services that are largely of Western origin and that often enter the market by means of Western suppliers — has come substantial cultural change. A distinctive set of professional ethics, attitudes, and practices has accompanied these advanced technologies and products. Youthful Russians have been quick to embrace these standards, which bring concrete economic benefits. They are less burdened with the classic Soviet education and culture and have proved more receptive than their elders to new ways of doing business. Indeed, they look at the lethargic Soviet-era model of the human factor as an obstacle to be surmounted.

This transformation of Russian economic life is making its way throughout Russian society, though at a glacial pace in the public sector, where the benefits of change are not so obvious.[35] Since government plays an intimate role in the nuclear sector via its regulatory powers and state ownership, cultural change has been fairly slow to make inroads at Russian nuclear facilities. Although a modest number of university graduates have entered the nuclear industry, the older technical elite reared under the Soviet system still dominates senior management and sets policy.

Still, there are encouraging signs. Hiring in the nuclear establishment slowed to a trickle in the years immediately following the Soviet collapse, as talented youth sought more dependable, more lucrative posts elsewhere. A generation gap between aging managers and new recruits resulted. The upshot is that the younger generation, whose members began entering the nuclear complex in the late 1990s, is vaulting into middle management to replace retirees.[36] This youthful cohort will become increasingly influential as Soviet-era holdovers retire. If junior managers learn healthy attitudes and habits now, a new security culture could take root virtually overnight.[37] U.S.-Russian nuclear security programs must seize this opportunity, co-opting the next generation of senior leadership as it begins to ascend the ranks.

Realigning the Human Factor in the Nuclear Complex

Western donors cannot assume responsibility for enhancing the security culture within the Russian nuclear complex. Unless the Russian government grasps the challenge posed by the human factor and musters the determination to address this challenge, any Western efforts will yield limited results at best. Western experience and standards cannot be transposed wholesale to a Russia that is still undergoing rapid political and socioeconomic change and that remains suspicious of Western motives. Five principles should guide the strategy pursued by Moscow and its Western partners:

Get the Leaders on Board

The support of the nation's political leaders, top industry executives, and midlevel nuclear facility managers will be crucial to any effort to nurture a better security culture. Imposing direction on the bureaucracy, which will tend to pursue its own interests unless tamed by strong leadership, will likewise be essential to any reform. In particular, parochial interests and competition for scarce resources at Rosatom, the Russian Ministry of Atomic Energy, have tended to shunt nuclear security onto the back burner. The United States and the West should continue to engage Russia at the cabinet level or above in order to prevent bureaucratic politics from stymieing any new initiatives. If the West can enlist the support of the Russian prime minister, to whom Rosatom is directly responsible, its efforts will be that much more effective.[38]

Top Russian leaders also need to take a direct hand in the allocation of resources. They can do this by fixing priorities, promoting quality control, and tapping new funding sources. Given the magnitude of the challenge—at one time Russian MPC&A experts estimated that the agencies responsible for nuclear security needed thirty times their current funding to be effective—it behooves Moscow to husband available resources and seek out new ones.[39] Popular support will be a key ingredient in this effort. Senior officials, up to and including the president, must interject themselves into events related to fissile-material security and use their bully pulpit to muster public support for initiatives designed to bolster the human factor. There have been some halting steps in this direction—the Council of Ministers, or cabinet, discussed MPC&A issues on a couple of occasions in 2000, for instance—but much more needs to be done. The joint presidential statements at Bratislava and St. Petersburg came as welcome news, but only sustained, energetic presidential attention will bring about lasting improvement to the situation.

Get the Nuclear Managers—Especially the Younger Ones—on Board

Modifying the human factor will require implanting new standards within the management corps. Top- and midlevel nuclear managers must embrace new standards of personal responsibility, exemplified by professional pride, rigorous compliance with safety regulations, readiness to innovate, and determination to propagate the new ethic among their subordinates. One way to boost morale and performance would be to increase salaries by a sizable margin, relieving the financial hardships endured by even senior personnel in the nuclear sector. Yet, for political reasons, the West cannot simply underwrite the budgets for Russian nuclear facilities. Rather, the West should forge a regimen of intangible incentives and stimuli to improve the motivation of Russian managers.

Specifically, the United States and its partners should craft an interdisciplinary training package designed to effect a broad-based cultural transformation. The syllabus should not be confined to the technical dimensions of MPC&A, which are adequately covered in training courses at the RMTC and other sites. It should range as well across disciplines such as nonproliferation, threat analysis and risk management, leadership and management theory, organizational psychology, and defense conversion. It should include case studies recounting thefts, diversions, and smuggling of Russian nuclear materials. The syllabus should also acquaint trainees with American security culture: U.S.-Russian dialogue will prove elusive unless Russian nuclear personnel understand how the U.S. government coped with the issues now confronting Russia and unless they have some idea how Americans think about these matters. The RMTC would be an ideal venue to test out the new, expanded curriculum.[40]

Work on Threat Perceptions among the Rank and File

U.S. and Russian views of nuclear security diverge sharply on the matter of insider theft and diversion. Americans typically accord this dimension of nuclear security high priority. Steeped in the Cold War obsession with foreign espionage and attack, by contrast, Russians cite external attack as the chief menace to their security—this despite the fact that all known instances of nuclear theft from

Russian facilities have been inside jobs. The current managerial and administrative elite have been slow to adapt to new circumstances. Hence the training curriculum sketched above should include case studies demonstrating that internal security lapses endanger Russian radioactive materials far more than does the prospect of external sabotage or attack on a nuclear installation.

Western officials should accentuate the widely publicized incidents in which Russian military personnel supplied potential terrorists with weaponry and special equipment for financial gain. They should also remind Russian personnel of their nation's painful experience with terrorism. The string of terrorist attacks that rocked Russia in 2004, most notoriously the massacre at a school in Beslan, should supply ample proof that terrorists will strike with whatever weapon they can find.[41] Calling attention to egregious insider jobs and underscoring the likely impact of terrorist attacks carried out using nuclear or radiological weapons should help the United States and the West get their point across.

Make Written Rules and Procedures More User-Friendly

As noted previously, the Soviet approach to written instructions and regulations was dysfunctional. Covert noncompliance or even overt defiance of official policy resulted from this overly bureaucratic way of doing business. Russians' ingrained, reflexive resistance to written directives continues to beset the nuclear sector. Russian directives are far too long; unnecessary technical jargon pervades them, blurring their often-straightforward meaning; and they concentrate on technical minutiae at the expense of a broader perspective on the problems their readers are likely to encounter in the course of their duties. They provide little in the way of detailed algorithms to help nuclear personnel handle the chores associated with fissile-material security or with other everyday tasks.

The United States should encourage Russia to jettison its directives wholesale and issue a new set to replace them. The new instructions should incorporate U.S. and international best practices, suitably adapted to the realities of the Russian nuclear complex. To instill pride of ownership, the individuals who will implement these instructions should have a hand in developing them. Manuals and instructions should be short. They should be solution oriented rather than process oriented. They should lay out step-by-step operating procedures for routine tasks and problems. And they should be computer based, both to ease the process of tailoring them to different personnel with different levels of experience and to help diagnose and solve the problems that crop up at nuclear sites.

One or more facilities should be designated test beds, or "centers of excellence," for the new directives. These model facilities would test out the new manuals and refine them based on feedback from the managers and security personnel assigned to carry out their provisions. After this period of experimentation, the directives would then be gradually implemented throughout the nuclear complex, while the centers of excellence, having invigorated their security cultures, would provide a template for other facilities.

Improve Testing and Recruitment

A system of rigorous testing of personnel reliability should be devised for the Russian nuclear sector. No amount of training will bolster Russian security culture unless the individuals selected to work in the nuclear sector have the temperament for this demanding work. Personnel reliability screening should span a worker's career, starting with accession testing and continuing regularly until retirement. The tests should be adapted to each position. Periodic psychological screening and random urinalysis would also help guarantee personnel reliability. The United States should share the hardware and software needed to implement such programs. Top Russian military officers have showered praise on the U.S. DoD, which supplied the Strategic Rocket Forces with polygraphs, dramatically enhancing the reliability of nuclear-weapons personnel. This positive experience bears replicating throughout the nuclear complex.

Conclusions

To date the human factor has been an impediment to a vibrant security culture at Russian nuclear sites. It need not be that way, but only a true partnership between Moscow and its Western partners will bring about lasting improvement. The United States, the EU, and other stakeholders such as the G-8 should make every effort to rally the Russian political and nuclear leadership behind these goals, focusing especially on junior managers rather than incumbent Soviet-era managers. To the extent possible, they should reach out to rank-and-file workers through appropriate training programs. And they should furnish Russia the wherewithal to carry out these programs, commensurate with Moscow's growing resources. In the end, Moscow will bear most of the burden of remaking the nation's security culture. Russian leaders must summon up the resolve to work with the West to craft training and assistance programs that fit their nation's special circumstances while factoring in international best practices.

Transforming Russian security culture will not be quick or easy. If all the parties with a stake in Russian fissile-material security show the necessary determination, however, the nation's nuclear complex can be set on a path of steady improvement. Traditionally an impediment, the human factor can be turned to the advantage of Russian and global security.

Notes

1. White House, *The National Security Strategy of the United States of America* (Washington, D.C.: GPO, September 2002), v, 13–16. Interestingly, the "crossroads" formulation does not appear in the latest iteration of the National Security Strategy. White House, *The National Security Strategy of the United States of America* (Washington, D.C.: GPO, March 2006).

2. Estimates vary on how many thefts and attempted thefts have taken place at Russian facilities. Prime Minister Mikhail Kasayanov admitted in September 2000 that twenty-one attempts to steal registered nuclear materials had occurred between 1991 and 1999. Others may have gone undetected or unreported. U.S. intelligence agencies believe that undetected thefts from Russian facilities have indeed occurred, but they are uncertain about the extent or magnitude. See Vladimir Kucherenko, "Russian Nuclear Material Monitoring System 'Far From Ideal,'" *RANSAC Nuclear News*, October 4, 2000, 2 (originally published in Russian in *Rossiyskaya Gazeta*, September 29, 2000); U.S. National Intelligence Council, *Annual Report to Congress on the Safety and Security of Russian Nuclear Facilities and Military Forces*, December 2004, 7–8.

3. For summaries of the efforts by states and terrorist groups to acquire stolen fissile materials, see George J. Tenet, "The Worldwide Threat 2004: Challenges in a Changing Global Context," Testimony of Director of Central Intelligence George J. Tenet before the Senate Select Committee on Intelligence, 108th Cong., 2nd sess., February 24, 2004, https://www.cia .gov/news-information/speeches-testimony/2004/dci_speech_02142004.html, and George J. Tenet, "Worldwide Threat—Converging Dangers in a Post-9/11 World," Testimony of the Director of Central Intelligence before the Senate Select Committee on Intelligence, 107th Cong., 2nd sess., February 6, 2002, 2, https://www.cia.gov/news-information/speeches-testimony/ 2002/senate_select_hearing_03192002.html; Matthew Bunn, *The Next Wave: Urgently Needed New Steps to Control Warheads and Fissile Materials* (Washington, DC: Carnegie Endowment for International Peace, March 2000, 14–15, http://belfercenter.ksg.harvard .edu/files/fullnextwave.pdf; Osama bin Laden, *Messages to the World: The Statements of Osama bin Laden*, trans. and intro. Bruce Lawrence (London: Verso, 2005), 23–30, 65–94.

4. The figure is $8.218 billion in 2005 dollars. Some $13 billion has gone to threat-reduction efforts of all kinds, including chemical weapons elimination. See Matthew Bunn and Anthony Wier, *Securing the Bomb 2006: The New Global Imperatives* (Cambridge, MA: Belfer Center, Harvard University, July 2006), 108–19. See also Matthew Bunn, Anthony Wier, and John P. Holdren, *Controlling Nuclear Warheads and Materials: A Report Card and Action Plan* (Cambridge, MA: Belfer Center, Harvard University, March 2003), 46.

5. Although deficiencies in Russia's safeguards and security cultures have been slow to find their way into the literature on U.S.-Russia cooperative programs, a number of articles and

reports do mention it as a yet-unmet challenge. See Nathan Busch, "Risks of Nuclear Terror: Vulnerabilities of Thefts and Sabotage at Nuclear Weapons Facilities," *Contemporary Security Policy* 23, no. 3 (December 2002): 19–60; William C. Potter, "Outlook for the Adoption of a Safeguards Culture in the Former Soviet Union," *Journal of Nuclear Materials Management* 26 (Winter 1998): 22–34; James E. Doyle and Stephen V. Mladineo, "Assessing the Development of a Modern Safeguards Culture in the NIS," *Nonproliferation Review* 5, no. 2 (Winter 1998): 91–100; Carrie Smarto, "MPC&A Site Operations and Sustainability: A Policy Overview," paper presented at the 40th annual meeting of the Institute of Nuclear Material Management, July 27, 1999; Oleg Bukharin, Matthew Bunn, and Kenneth N. Luongo, *Renewing the Partnership: Recommendations for Accelerated Action to Secure Nuclear Material in the Former Soviet Union* (Washington DC: Russian American Nuclear Security Advisory Council, 2000), 27–44; Siegfried S. Hecker, "Thoughts about an Integrated Strategy for Nuclear Cooperation with Russia," *Nonproliferation Review* 8, no. 2 (Summer 2001): 7–8; William C. Potter and Fred L. Wehling, "Sustainability: A Vital Component of Nuclear Material Security in Russia," *Nonproliferation Review* 7, no. 1 (Spring 2000): 184–87.

6. See, for example, International Atomic Energy Agency, "Measures to Improve the Security of Nuclear Materials and Other Radioactive Materials," item 19 of agenda, GC(45)/RES/14, general conference, 45th regular session, September 14, 2001; Anita Nilsson, "IAEA Material Security Programme Overview," Symposium on International Safeguards, October 29–November 2, 2001, Vienna, Austria, http:// f40.iaea.org/worldatom/Press/Focus/Nuclear_Terrorism/nilsson.pdf.

7. For example, an October 2005 NATO Advanced Research Workshop on Nuclear Security Culture, which brought together experts from nearly thirty countries, adjourned from two days of intensive meetings without a common definition. See "UGA's Center for International Trade and Security to Host Major International Events in Moscow, Russia," School of Public and International Affairs, October 2005, http://www.uga.edu/spia/news/cits_russia.htm.

8. Doyle and Mladineo, "Assessing the Development of a Modern Safeguards Culture," 91.

9. Anita Nilsson, "The IAEA's Perspective on Security Culture," presentation at NATO Advanced Research Workshop, Moscow, October 24–25, 2005, reprinted in *Nuclear Security Culture: From National Best Practices to International Standards*, edited by Igor Khripunov et al. (Amsterdam: IOS Press, 2007), 14.

10. We derived this definition from Igor Khripunov et al., *Nuclear Security Culture: The Case of Russia* (Athens, GA: Center for International Trade and Security, 2004), in particular ch. 1, 5–17. See also Igor Khripunov, "Nuclear Security: Attitude Check," *Bulletin of the Atomic Scientists* 61, no. 1 (January/February 2005): 59–64.

11. Nathan Busch, Maria Katsva, Igor Khripunov, and Dmitriy Nikonov, *The Human Factor and Security Culture: Challenges to Safeguarding Fissile Materials in Russia* (Athens, GA: Center for International Trade and Security, 2002).

12. See, in particular, U.S., Department of Energy, *Safeguards and Security Program Planning and Management*, DoE M 470.4-1, reviewed August 2007, www.hss.energy.gov/SecPolicy/directives/M_470.4-1c1_Planning.pdf; U.S., Department of Energy, *Personnel Security Program Manual*, DoE M 472.1-1B, July 2001, http://www.fas.org/sgp/othergov/doe/

m4721-1b.pdf; U.S., Department of Energy, *Personnel Security Activities*, DoE O 472.1C, March 2003; U.S., Department of Energy, *Physical Protection Program*, DoE O 473.1, December 2002.

13. U.S. Congress, Commission on Protecting and Reducing Government Secrecy, "Personnel Security: Protection through Detection," ch. 4 in *Secrecy: Report of the Commission on Protecting and Reducing Government Secrecy*, Senate, S. doc. 105-2 (Washington, DC: Government Printing Office, 1997), http://www.fas.org/sgp/library/moynihan/chap4.html.

14. Retired Gen. Eugene Habiger, a former "security czar" for the Energy Department and currently a distinguished fellow at the Center for International Trade and Security, depicts "good security" at DoE sites as "20 percent equipment and 80 percent people." Some evidence suggests that the problem persists. See, for instance, Michael McManus, "Illegal Immigrants Worked at Nuclear Weapons Facility," CNN.com, June 21, 2005, http://www.cnn.com/2005/US/06/20/nuclear.security/. For a detailed report highlighting difficulties in management and coordination of nuclear security programs within the Department of Energy, see U.S. General Accounting Office, *Nuclear Security: NNSA Needs to Better Manage Its Safeguards and Security Program*, report to the chairman, Subcommittee on National Security, Emerging Threats, and International Relations, Committee on Government Reform, House of Representatives, GAO-03-471, May 2003.

15. Graham Allison, *Nuclear Terrorism: The Ultimate Preventable Catastrophe* (New York: Times Books, 2004).

16. For summaries of the CTR and MPC&A programs, see Jason D. Ellis and Todd E. Perry, "Nunn-Lugar's Unfinished Agenda," *Arms Control Today* 27, no. 7 (October 1997): 14–22; Kenneth N. Luongo and William E. Hoehn III, "Reform and Expansion of Cooperative Threat Reduction," *Arms Control Today* 33, no. 5 (June 2003): 11–13.

17. Jack Caravelli and Chris Behan, "Accomplishments and Challenges in the MPC&A Program," *Monitor: International Perspectives on Nonproliferation* 7, no. 2 (Spring 2001): 3. See also "Text: U.S., Russia to Step Up Efforts to Safeguard Nuclear Materials," *Washington File*, December 4, 2001.

18. Bunn, Wier, and Holdren, *Controlling Nuclear Warheads and Materials*, vii.

19. Bunn and Wier, *Securing the Bomb 2006*, 100.

20. U.S. White House, *Joint Statement: Bush, Putin Pledge Enhanced Nuclear Security Cooperation*, February 24, 2005, http://www.whitehouse.gov/news/releases/2005/02/20050224-8.html. Another effort in this area is the G-8 Global Partnership Against the Spread of Weapons and Materials of Mass Destruction, a venture launched at the G-8's Kananaskis Summit in 2002. Under the Global Partnership, the United States pledged $10 billion over the ensuing decade to bolster WMD security in Russia, while the remaining G-8 members vowed to match that total. *Statement by G8 Leaders: The G8 Global Partnership Against the Spread of Weapons and Materials of Mass Destruction*, Kananaskis, Canada, June 27, 2002, http://www.g7.utoronto.ca/summit/2002kananaskis/arms.html.

21. White House, "Fact Sheet: The Global Initiative to Combat Nuclear Terrorism," July 15, 2006, http://www.whitehouse.gov/news/releases/2006/07/20060715-3.html.

22. Russian Methodological Training Center, "Overview—RMTC History, Reality, and Future," 2004, http://www.rmtc.obninsk.ru/history_eng.html. See also Nuclear Threat Ini-

tiative, "Russian Methodological Training Center (RMTC)," October 26, 2001, http://www
.nti.org/db/nisprofs/russia/forasst/doe/rmtc.htm.

23. Russian Methodological Training Center, course catalog 2006, http://www.rmtc
.obninsk.ru/catalog_eng.html.

24. For a wealth of information about the G-8 and its role in international security, consult
the G-8 Information Centre Web site, http://www.g8.utoronto.ca/.

25. Khripunov et al., *Nuclear Security Culture*, 19–28, 51–62.

26. Ibid., 63–67.

27. Busch et al., *Human Factor and Security Culture*, 13–23.

28. Ajay Goyal, "Russia's Untapped Treasures," *Russian Journal*, n.d., http://norasco.com/
ajay_goyal_6.html.

29. A study by Harvard University's Center for International Development underscored
Russia's plight a decade after the Cold War. The center's Growth Competitiveness Index
ranked Russia sixty-third of seventy-five countries in 2001, down from fifty-fourth in 2000.
Russia ranked sixtieth on the technology component of the index, while the United States
ranked first. See http://www.cid.harvard.edu/cr/index.html for more details.

30. Ajay Goyal, "Intellectual Capital: IT or Not to IT, That Is Not a Question," *Russian
Journal*, October 11, 2001, http://russoft.org/docs/print.php?doc=787.

31. For a discussion of some of the deficiencies in Soviet MPC&A systems, see Nathan
Busch, "Russian Roulette: The Continuing Relevance of Russia to the Nuclear Proliferation
Debate," *Security Studies* 11, no. 3 (Spring 2002): 71–76.

32. Jessica E. Stern, "U.S. Assistance Programs for Improving MPC&A in the Former
Soviet Union," *Nonproliferation Review* 26, no. 7 (Winter 1996): 18.

33. Eugene E. Habiger, "A Unique Opportunity: Seize It," in Khripunov et al., *Nuclear
Security Culture: From National Best Practices to International Standards*, 11, presentation
at NATO Advanced Research Workshop, Moscow, October 24, 2005; U.S. General Accounting Office, *Nuclear Nonproliferation: Security of Russia's Nuclear Materials*, Report
to congressional requesters, GAO-01-312 (Washington DC: Government Printing Office,
February 2001).

34. These incidents are summarized in Busch, "Risks of Nuclear Terror," 19–60.

35. Igor Khripunov and Maria Katsva, "Russia's Nuclear Industry: The Next Generation,"
Bulletin of the Atomic Scientists 58, no. 2 (March/April 2002): 51–57.

36. Interview with Russian MPC&A expert, Center for International Trade and Security,
University of Georgia, Athens, February 2003.

37. Potter and Wehling, "Sustainability," 184–87.

38. Here it is worth noting that the Putin administration has embarked on an ambitious
effort to reorganize the Russian government. Whatever its virtues, the administrative reform
effort has left the Russian nuclear sector with tangled lines of authority and responsibility.
The Russian Ministry of Atomic Energy, formerly known as Minatom and now known as
Rosatom, was initially demoted to agency status and placed under the jurisdiction of the
Ministry of Industry and Energy. In an effort to clarify matters, Rosatom was subsequently
made directly accountable to the prime minister. Khripunov et al., *Nuclear Security Culture*,
41–49.

39. Russian MPC&A experts, interviews by Igor Khripunov, Nathan Busch, and James Holmes, Center for International Trade and Security, University of Georgia, Athens, November 2000.

40. Potter and Wehling, "Sustainability," 184–87. Potter and Wehling recommend a two-stage approach to training within the Russian nuclear community. They urge Moscow and its Western partners to add a two- to four-hour module surveying nonproliferation and safeguards to the curriculum at the RMTC and subsequently to devise an Internet-based course accessible to the Russian nuclear cities and other sites. Neither of these recommendations has yet been adopted.

41. James R. Holmes, Igor Khripunov, and Eugene Habiger, "Secure Russian Stockpile: Beslan Showed Intent of Chechen Radicals," *Defense News*, October 4, 2004, 29.

Bibliography

Government Documents and Primary Sources

Aspin, Les. "Counterproliferation Initiative." PDD/NSC 18, December 1993, http://www
.fas.org/irp/offdocs/pdd18.htm.

Atomic Energy Act of 1954. August 30, 1954, Public Law 83-703, 68 Stat. 919.

Biological and Toxin Weapons Convention. Fifth Review Conference of the States Parties
to the Convention on the Prohibition of the Development, Production and Stockpiling
of Bacteriological (Biological) Weapons and on Their Destruction. BWC/CONF.V/17,
final document, Geneva, 2002.

Conference on Disarmament. Letter dated January 31, 1992, from the representative of
the Russian Federation addressed to the president of the Conference on Disarmament,
transmitting the text of the statement made on January 29, 1992, by B. N. Yeltsin, the
president of the Russian Federation, on Russia's policy in the field of arms limitation
and reduction. Document CD/1123, January 31, 1992.

Council of the European Union. *The Basic Principles for an EU Strategy against
Proliferation of Weapons of Mass Destruction*. 10352/03, June 10, 2003, http://www
.sipri.org/contents/expcon/eu_wmd.html.

———. Action Plan for the Implementation of the Basic Principles. 10354/03, June 13,
2003, http://www.sipri.org/contents/expcon/eu_wmd.html.

———. *Fight against the Proliferation of Weapons of Mass Destruction: Mainstreaming
Non-Proliferation Policies into the EU's Wider Relations with Third Countries*. 14997/03,
November 19, 2003, http://www.sipri.org/contents/expcon/euwmdmainstreaming2003
.pdf.

———. *EU Strategy against the Proliferation of Weapons of Mass Destruction*. 15708/03,
December 12, 2003, http://www.consilium.europa.eu/cms3_fo/showPage.asp?id
=392&lang=EN&mode=g.

———. *Council Joint Action 2006/184/CFSP*. February 27, 2006, http://eur-lex.europa
.eu/LexUriServ/LexUriServ.do?uri=OJ:L:2006:065:0051:0055:EN:PDF.

———. *Six-Monthly Progress Report on the Implementation of the EU Strategy against the
Proliferation of Weapons of Mass Destruction*(2006/I). EU document 10527/06, June 14,
2006, http://register.consilium.europa.eu/pdf/en/06/st10/st10527.en06.pdf.

European Commission. "*Council Regulation (EC) No 1334/2000 of 22 June, 2000*."

———. "Cooperation Agreement between the European Community and the Islamic
Republic of Pakistan on Partnership and Development." April 22, 2004.

———. Proposal for a Council Decision on the Conclusion of a Euro-Mediterranean Association Agreement between the European Community and Its Member States of the One Part, and the Syrian Arab Republic, of the Other Part." COM 808/2004 final, December 17, 2004.

———. "Council Regulation (EC) No 648/2005 of 13 April, 2005."

———. "India-EU Strategic Partnership Joint Action Plan." September 7, 2005.

European Parliament. *Draft Regulation of the European Parliament and the Council Establishing an Instrument for Stability.* A6-0157/2006, May 24, 2006.

EU-3. Paris Agreement. November 15, 2004, reproduced as an IAEA document, INFCIRC/637, November 26, 2004.

G-8. *Statement by G-8 Leaders: The G-8 Global Partnership Against the Spread of Weapons and Materials of Mass Destruction.* Kananaskis, Canada, June 27, 2002, http://www.g7.utoronto.ca/summit/2002kananaskis/arms.html.

———. *Statement on Non-Proliferation.* St. Petersburg, July 16, 2006, http://en.g8russia.ru/docs/20.html.

India, Prime minister's office. *Statement of PM in Rajya Sabha on the India-US Nuclear Agreement.* August 17, 2006, http://pmindia.nic.in/parl/pcontent.asp?id=30.

Information Office of the State Council (China). *China's National Defense in 2004.* Beijing: Information Office of the State Council, December 2004.

International Atomic Energy Agency. *The Structure and Content of Agreements between the Agency and States Required in Connection with the Treaty on the Non-Proliferation of Nuclear Weapons.* INFCIRC/153, June 1972, http://www.iaea.org/Publications/Documents/Infcircs/Others/infcirc153.pdf.

———. *Convention on the Physical Protection of Nuclear Material.* Adopted October 26, 1979, http://www.iaea.org/Publications/Documents/Conventions/cppnm.html.

———. *Model Protocol Additional to the Agreement(s) between State(s) and the International Atomic Energy Agency for the Application of Safeguards.* INFCIRC/540, September 1997, http://www.iaea.org/Publications/Documents/Infcircs/1997/infcirc540c.pdf.

———. Model Protocol Additional to the Agreement(s) between State(s) and the International Atomic Energy Agency for the Application of Safeguards. INFCIRC/540 corrected, December 1998, http://www.iaea.org/Publications/Documents/Infcircs/1997/infcirc540.pdf.

———. "Measures to Improve the Security of Nuclear Materials and Other Radioactive Materials." Item 19 of agenda, GC(45)/RES/14, general conference, 45th regular session, September 14, 2001.

———. Implementation of the NPT Safeguards Agreement in the Islamic Republic of Iran: Report by the Director General. IAEA Board of Governors document GOV/2003/40, June 6, 2003.

———. "Categorization of Radiation Sources." TECDOC-1344, July 2003.

———. Implementation of the NPT Safeguards Agreement in the Islamic Republic of Iran: Report by the Director General. GOV/2003/69, September 12, 2003.

———. Implementation of the NPT Safeguards Agreement in the Islamic Republic of Iran. GOV/2003/75, November 10, 2003.

———. "List of Confirmed Incidents Involving HEU or Pu." *IAEA Illicit Trafficking Database,* 2003, http://www.iaea.org/NewsCenter/Features/RadSources/PDF/itdb_31122003.pdf.

———. Implementation of the NPT Safeguards Agreement in the Islamic Republic of Iran: Report by the Director General. GOV/2004/84, November 11, 2004.

———. Implementation of the NPT Safeguards Agreement in the Islamic Republic of Iran: Report by the Director General. IAEA Board of Governors document GOV/2004/83. November 29, 2004, http://www.iaea.org/Publications/Documents/Board/2004/gov2004-83.pdf.

———. Implementation of the NPT Safeguards Agreement in the Islamic Republic of Iran: Report by the Director General. GOV/2006/15, February 27, 2005.

———. *Communication Dated 1 August 2005 Received from the Permanent Mission of the Islamic Republic of Iran to the Agency.* INFCIRC/648. August 1, 2005.

———. Implementation of the NPT Safeguards Agreement in the Islamic Republic of Iran: Report by the Director General. IAEA Board of Governors document GOV/2005/67, September 2, 2005.

———. "Safeguards Statement for 2005, Background to Safeguards Statement and Executive Summary of the Safeguards Implementation Report for 2005." 2005, http://www.iaea.org/OurWork/SV/Safeguards/es2005.pdf.

———. *Developments in the Implementation of the NPT Safeguards Agreement in the Islamic Republic of Iran and Agency Verification of Iran's Suspension of Enrichment-Related and Reprocessing Activities.* Update brief, deputy director-general for safeguards, January 31, 2006.

———. Implementation of the NPT Safeguards Agreement in the Islamic Republic of Iran: Report by the Director General. IAEA Board of Governors document GOV/2007/48, August 30, 2007. Also issued as INFCIRC/711.

———. Implementation of the NPT Safeguards Agreement and Relevant Provisions of Security Council Resolution 1737 (2006) and 1747 (2007) in the Islamic Republic of Iran: Report by the Director General. IAEAGOV/2007/58, November 15, 2007.

———. "Strengthened Safeguards System: Status of Additional Protocols." March 5, 2008, http://www.iaea.org/OurWork/SV/Safeguards/sg_protocol.html.

———. "Department of Safeguards." N.d., http://www.iaea.org/OurWork/SV/Safeguards/index.html.

International Court of Justice. *Legality of the Threat or Use of Nuclear Weapons.* Advisory opinion, July 8, 1996.

International Maritime Organization. "Revised Treaties to Address Unlawful Acts at Sea Adopted at International Conference." Press release, Diplomatic Conference on the Revision of the SUA Treaties, October 10–14, 2005, http://www.imo.org/About/mainframe.asp?topic_id=1018&doc_id=5334.

International Science and Technology Center. Annual Report 2005, http://istc.ru/ISTC/sc.nsf/AR-2005-en.pdf.

North Atlantic Treaty Organization, standing group, von Kármán Committee. *Future Developments in Chemical Warfare.* Report of working group 10 on chemical, biological, and radiological defense, March 1961, as distributed to the U.K. Ministry of

Defence Advisory Council on Scientific Research and Technical Development, paper no. SAC 1928, February 11, 1969, National Archive, Kew, file WO195/16864.

Nuclear Nonproliferation Treaty. Chairman's working paper. NPT/CONF.2000/PC. III/29, May 14, 1999.

———. Chairman's revised working paper. NPT/CONF.2000/PC.III/58, May 20, 1999.

Organization for the Prohibition of Chemical Weapons. *Decision, Tenure Policy of the OPCW.* C-SS-2/Dec. 1, April 30, 2003.

People's Republic of China. Embassy. *Sino-U.S. Joint Statement on South Asia.* June 27, 1998, http://www.china-embassy.org/eng/zmgx/zysj/kldfh/t36228.htm.

———. Ministry of Foreign Affairs. *Missiles and Missile-Related Items and Technologies Export Control List.* August 22, 2002, http://cns.miis.edu/research/china/chiexp/miscon.htm.

———. Ministry of Foreign Affairs. *Regulations of the People's Republic of China on Export Control of Missiles and Missile-Related Items and Technologies.* August 22, 2002, http://tr.china-embassy.org/eng/xwdt/t161702.htm.

Preparatory Committee for the 2005 Review Conference of the Parties to the Treaty on the Non-Proliferation of Nuclear Weapons. *Overcoming the Institutional Deficit of the NPT.* Working paper submitted by Canada, NPT/CONF.2005/PC.III/WP.1, April 5, 2004, http://www.dfait.gc.ca/arms/2004npt5-en.asp.

———. *Withdrawal from the Treaty on the Non-Proliferation of Nuclear Weapons: European Union Common Approach.* Working paper submitted by Luxembourg on behalf of the European Union, NPT/CONF.2005/WP.32, May 10, 2005, http://www.un.org/events/npt2005/working%20papers.html.

Preparatory Committee for the 2010 Review Conference of the Parties to the Treaty on the Non-Proliferation of Nuclear Weapons. *Model Nuclear Weapons Convention.* Working paper submitted by Costa Rica, NPT/CONF.2010/PC.I/WP.17, May 1, 2007, http://www.un.org/NPT2010/offdocs_7_May_onward/NPT_CONF_2010_PC_1_WP_17_E.pdf.

Russian Methodological Training Center. "Overview—RMTC History, Reality, and Future." 2004, http://www.rmtc.obninsk.ru/history_eng.html.

United Kingdom. Department of Business Enterprise and Regulatory Reform. "Nonproliferation-Global Threat Reduction Program: Closed Nuclear Cities Partnership." N.d., http://www.berr.gov.uk/energy/non-proliferation/global-threat-reduction/portfolio/cncp/index.html.

———. Department of Trade and Industry. *Operation of the Chemical Weapons Act 1996: Annual Report 2004,* 26–28. July 2005, http://www.berr.gov.uk/files/file26554.pdf.

———. Department of Trade and Industry. "Nonproliferation–Global Threat Reduction Program: Closed Nuclear Cities Partnership." N.d., http://www.berr.gov.uk/energy/non-proliferation/global-threat-reduction/portfolio/cncp/index.html.

———. Secretary of State for Foreign and Commonwealth Affairs. *Strengthening the Biological and Toxin Weapons Convention: Countering the Threat from Biological Weapons.* Cm 5484, April 29, 2002, www.brad.ac.uk/acad/sbtwc/other/fcobw.pdf.

United Nations. *Chemical and Bacteriological (Biological) Weapons and the Effects of Their Possible Use.* Report of the secretary-general, 1969. New York: United Nations, 1969.

———. Address of the secretary-general to the UN General Assembly. September 23, 2003, http://www.un.org/webcast/ga/58/statements/sg2eng030923.htm.

———. *A More Secure World: Our Shared Responsibility*. Report of the High-level Panel on Threats, Challenges and Change (New York: United Nations, 2004).

———. "Secretary General Offers Global Strategy for Fighting Terrorism in Address to Madrid Summit." Press release SG/SM/9757, March 10, 2005, http://www.un.org/News/Press/docs/2005/sgsm9757.doc.htm.

———. *In Larger Freedom: Towards Development, Security and Human Rights for All*. Report of the secretary-general, March 21, 2005, section 3.

———. "United Nations General Assembly Adopts Global Counter-Terrorism Strategy." Plan of Action, Measures to Prevent and Combat Terrorism. September 8, 2006, http://www.un.org/terrorism/strategy-counter-terrorism.shtml#plan.

United Nations Security Council. Resolution 1540. S/RES/1540, April 28, 2004, http://www.un.org/Docs/sc/unsc_resolutions04.html.

———. *United Nations Monitoring, Verification and Inspection Commission*. UN Security Council document S/2006/420, June 21, 2006.

———. Resolution 1696. S/RES/1696/2006, July 31, 2006, http://www.un.org/Docs/sc/unsc_resolutions06.htm.

United States. Central Intelligence Agency. *Unclassified Report to Congress on the Acquisition of Technology Relating to Weapons of Mass Destruction and Advanced Conventional Munitions, 1 January through 30 June 2000*. February 2000, https://www.cia.gov/library/reports/archived-reports-1/jan_jun2000.htm.

———. Central Intelligence Agency. *Unclassified Report to Congress on the Acquisition of Technology Relating to Weapons of Mass Destruction and Advanced Conventional Munitions, 1 January through 30 June 2001*. January 2002, https://www.cia.gov/library/reports/archived-reports-1/jan_jun2001.htm.

———. Central Intelligence Agency. *Unclassified Report to Congress on the Acquisition of Technology Relating to Weapons of Mass Destruction and Advanced Conventional Munitions, 1 January through 30 June 2002*. April 2003, https://www.cia.gov/library/reports/archived-reports-1/jan_jun2002.html.

———. Central Intelligence Agency. *Unclassified Report to Congress on the Acquisition of Technology Relating to Weapons of Mass Destruction and Advanced Conventional Munitions, 1 January through 31 December 2004*. November 2004, http://www.dni.gov/reports/2004_unclass_report_to_NIC_DO_16Nov04.pdf.

———. Congress. *Conventional Forces in Europe Treaty Implementation Act of 1991*. Public Law 102-228, January 1991.

———. Congress. *Freedom for Russia and Emerging Eurasian Democracies and Open Markets Support Act*. Public Law 102-511, January 1992.

———. Congress. Testimony of Richard T. Cupitt before the United States Senate Committee on Governmental Affairs, Subcommittee on International Security, Proliferation, and Federal Services on Enhancing Export Controls to Combat Terrorism. November 7, 2001.

———. Congress. *National Defense Authorization Act for Fiscal Year 1997*. Public Law 104-201, January 2006.

————. Congress. Testimony of B. B. Bell before the Senate Armed Services Committee, March 7, 2006, http://armed-services.senate.gov/statemnt/2006/March/Bell%2003-07-06 .pdf.

————. Congress. *U.S. Additional Protocol Implementation Act.* Public Law 109-226, April 3, 2006.

————. Congress. Commission on Protecting and Reducing Government Secrecy. "Personnel Security: Protection through Detection." Ch. 4 in *Secrecy: Report of the Commission on Protecting and Reducing Government Secrecy.* Senate document 105-2 (Washington, DC: Government Printing Office, 1997), http://www.fas.org/sgp/ library/moynihan/chap4.html.

————. Department of Defense. *Nuclear Posture Review Report.* January 2002, www .defenselink.mil/news/Jan2002/d20020109npr.pdf.

————. Department of Defense. National Defense Strategy of the United States of America. March 2005, http://www.defenselink.mil/news/Mar2005/d20050318nds1.pdf.

————. Department of Defense. *Quadrennial Defense Review Report.* February 6, 2006, http://www.defenselink.mil/pubs/pdfs/QDR20060203.pdf.

————. Department of Defense, Defense Science Board Task Force on Globalization and Security. Final Report. Washington, DC: Office of the Under Secretary of Defense for Acquisition and Technology, December 1999, http://www.acq.osd.mil/dsb/reports/ globalization.pdf.

————. Department of Defense, Joint Chiefs of Staff. *National Military Strategy to Combat Weapons of Mass Destruction.* February 13, 2006, http://www.defenselink.mil/ pdf/NMS-CWMD2006.pdf.

————. Department of Defense, Office of the U.S. Undersecretary of Defense for Acquisition and Technology. *Final Report of the Defense Science Board Task Force on Globalization and Security.* December 1999.

————. Department of Defense, U.S. Army Chemical Center and School, Fort McClellan. "New Chemical Agents and Incapacitating Agents." Lesson plan LP6075, undated (ca. 1965).

————. Department of Defense, U.S. Strategic Command. *Deterrence Operations Joint Operating Concept.* Final draft, version 2.0, August 2006, http://www.dtic.mil/ futurejointwarfare/concepts/do_joc_v20.doc.

————. Department of Energy. Secretary of Energy Advisory Board. *A Report Card on the Department of Energy's Nonproliferation Programs with Russia.* (Washington, DC: U.S. Department of Energy, 2001). January 10, 2001, http://www.seab.energy.gov/ publications/rusrpt.pdf.

————. Department of Energy. *Personnel Security Program Manual.* DOE M 472.1-1B, July 2001, http://www.fas.org/sgp/othergov/doe/m4721-1b.pdf.

————. Department of Energy. *Physical Protection Program.* DOE O 473.1, December 2002.

————. Department of Energy. *Personnel Security Activities.* DOE O 472.1C, March 2003.

————. Department of Energy. *FY 2007 Congressional Budget Request.* Washington, DC: U.S. Department of Energy, 2006. http://www.cfo.doe.gov/budget/07budget/Start.htm.

————. Department of Energy. *Safeguards and Security Program Planning and Management.* DOE M 470.4-1, August 2007,http://www.pnl.gov/isrc/2006/pdf/DOEM4704.pdf.

————. Department of State. *Text: U.S.-China Joint Statement on South Asia.* June 27, 1998, http://www.fas.org/news/china/1998/sasia.htm.

————. Department of State. *Adherence to and Compliance with Arms Control, Nonproliferation and Disarmament Agreements and Commitments.* Washington, DC: U.S. Department of State, August 2005, http://www.state.gov/t/vci/rls/rpt/51977.htm.

————. Department of State. Office of the U.S. Secretary of State. *Patterns of Global Terrorism: 1990.* April 30, 1991, http://www.fas.org/irp/threat/terror_90/index.html.

————. General Accounting Office. *Defense Industry Consolidation: Competitive Effects of Mergers and Acquisitions.* Testimony before the Subcommittee on Acquisitions and Technology, Senate Armed Services Committee, GAO/T-NSIAD-98-112, March 4, 1998.

————. General Accounting Office. *Nuclear Nonproliferation: Security of Russia's Nuclear Materials.* Report to congressional requesters, GAO-01-312, February 2001.

————. General Accounting Office. *Nuclear Security: NNSA Needs to Better Manage Its Safeguards and Security Program.* Report to the chairman, Subcommittee on National Security, Emerging Threats, and International Relations, Committee on Government Reform, House of Representatives, GAO-03-471, May 2003.

————. National Intelligence Council. *Annual Report to Congress on the Safety and Security of Russian Nuclear Facilities and Military Forces.* Washington, D.C.: National Intelligence Council, December 2004, http://www.dni.gov/nic/special_russiannuke04 .html.

————. 9/11 Public Discourse Project. "Final Report on 9/11 Commission Recommendations." December 5, 2005, http://www.9-11pdp.org/press/2005-12-05_report.pdf.

————. Office of Technology Assessment. *Technologies Underlying Weapons of Mass Destruction.* OTA-BP-ISC-115, December 1993. Washington, DC: U.S. Government Printing Office, December 1993.

————. Office of Technology Assessment. *Export Controls and Nonproliferation Policy.* OTA-ISS-596, May 1994.

————. White House. "Counterproliferation Initiative." Presidential Decision Directive PDD/NSC 18, December 1993, Federation of American Scientists Website, http://www .fas.org/irp/offdocs/pdd18.htm.

————. White House. "Fact Sheet: Accomplishments of the U.S.-China Summit." October 30, 1997.

————. White House. *National Security Strategy of the United States of America.* Washington, DC: Government Printing Office, September 2002, http://www .whitehouse.gov/nsc/nss/2002.

————. White House. *National Strategy to Combat Weapons of Mass Destruction.* Washington, DC: Government Printing Office, December 2002, www.whitehouse .gov/news/releases/2002/12/WMDStrategy.pdf.

———. White House. "Fact Sheet: Proliferation Security Initiative: Statement of Interdiction Principles." September 4, 2003, http://www.whitehouse.gov/news/releases/2003/09/20030904-11.html.

———. White House. "President Announces New Measures to Counter the Threat of WMD." Speech at the National Defense University. February 11, 2004, http://www.whitehouse.gov/news/releases/2004/02/20040211-4.html.

———. White House. *Joint Statement: Bush, Putin Pledge Enhanced Nuclear Security Cooperation.* February 24, 2005, http://www.whitehouse.gov/news/releases/2005/02/20050224-8.html.

———. White House. "Joint Statement between President George W. Bush and Prime Minister Manmohan Singh." July 18, 2005, http://www.whitehouse.gov/news/releases/2005/07/20050718-6.html.

———. White House. *National Security Strategy of the United States of America* (Washington: Government Printing Office, March 2006), http://www.whitehouse.gov/nsc/nss/2006/nss2006.pdf.

———. White House. "President Delivers Commencement Address at the United States Military Academy at West Point." May 27, 2006, http://www.whitehouse.gov/news/releases/2006/05/20060527-1.html.

———. White House. "Fact Sheet: The Global Initiative to Combat Nuclear Terrorism." July 15, 2006, http://www.whitehouse.gov/news/releases/2006/07/20060715-3.html.

———. U.S.-China Economic and Security Review Commission. Testimony of Stephen G. Rademaker, assistant secretary of state for arms control, U.S. Department of State. March 10, 2005, http://www.uscc.gov/hearings/2005hearings/written_testimonies/05_03_10wrtr/rademaker_stephen_wrts.htm.

———. U.S. Civilian Research and Development Foundation. Annual Report 2004. Arlington, VA: U.S. Civilian Research and Development Foundation, 2006. http://www.crdf.org/annualreport/2004_Annual_Report-Final.pdf.

———. U.S. Civilian Research and Development Foundation. "Looking Back, Moving Forward." September 1, 2005, http://www.crdf.org/newsletters/newsletters_show.htm?doc_id=309320.

———. U.S. Civilian Research and Development Foundation. "Our Key Focus Areas: Cooperative Research." 2006, http://www.crdf.org/focus/focus_show.htm?doc_id=290100.

———. U.S. Civilian Research and Development Foundation. "Overview: About CRDF." 2006, http://www.crdf.org/about.

———. U.S. Enrichment Corporation. *Megatons to Megawatts: Status Report.* June 28, 2006, http://www.usec.com/v2001_02/content/megatons/11k_insert.pdf.

———. U.S. Industry Coalition. "Rarefaction Shock Wave (RSW) Cutter for Offshore Oil-Gas Platform Removal." July 2003, http://www.usic.net/userfiles/Halliburton.pdf.

———. U.S. Industry Coalition. "TB Peptides." April 2005, http://www.usic.net/userfiles/SciClone.pd.Weapons of Mass Destruction Commission. *Weapons of Terror: Freeing the World of Nuclear, Biological and Chemical Arms.* Final report. Stockholm, Sweden: Weapons of Mass Destruction Commission, June 1, 2006.

———. U.S. Industry Coalition. "GIPP Program: Accomplishments." 2007, http://www
.usic.net/GIPPprogram/index.cfm?cid=14.

———. U.S. Industry Coalition. "GIPP Program: Benefits." 2007, http://www.usic.net/
GIPPprogram/?cid=15.

World Health Organization. *Health Aspects of Chemical and Biological Weapons: Report of
a WHO Group of Consultants*. Geneva: World Health Organization, 1970.

———. *Public Health Response to Biological and Chemical Weapons: WHO Guidance*.
Geneva: World Health Organization, 2004.

Newspapers and Periodicals

BBC News (bbc.co.uk)
Boston Globe
Guardian
Global Security Newswire
Chosun Ilbo
CNN.com
Financial Times
Iran Focus
Jane's Defense Weekly
Japan Times
Mehr News Agency (Iran)
New York Times
NuclearFuel
People's Daily (China)
Reuters
Radio Free Europe (RFE/RL)
Times of India
Washington Post
Washington Times
U.S. News and World Report
Xinhua (China)
Yonhap News
Washington File

Journals, Books, Internet Resources

Acton, James, with Carter Newman. *IAEA Verification of Military Research and
Development*. Verification Matters, VERTIC Research Report no. 5, July 2006,
http://www.vertic.org/publications/VM5%20(2).pdf.

Ahlström, Christer. "The Proliferation Security Initiative: International Law Aspects of the Statement of Interdiction Principles." In *SIPRI Yearbook 2005: Armaments, Disarmament and International Security*, 741–65. Oxford: Oxford University Press, 2005.

Albright, David. *Preventing Illegal Exports: Learning from Case Studies*. Report, Institute for Science and International Security, April 6, 2001.

―――. Testimony before the House Committee on International Relations, Hearing on the U.S.-India "Global Partnership" and Its Impact on Non-Proliferation. October 26, 2005, http://www.isis-online.org/publications/southasia/abrighttestimonyoctober262005usindiadeal.pdf.

Albright, David, and Paul Brannan. *The North Korean Plutonium Stock Mid-2006*. Institute for Science and International Security, June 26, 2006, http://www.isis-online.org/publications/dprk/dprkplutonium.pdf.

Albright, David, and Holly Higgins. "A Bomb for the Ummah." *Bulletin of the Atomic Scientists 59, no. 2 (March/April 2003)*: 49–55.

Albright, David, and Corey Hinderstein. *Documents Indicate A. Q. Khan Offered Nuclear Weapon Designs to Iraq in 1990: Did He Approach Other Countries?* Institute for Science and International Security, February 4, 2004, http://www.isis-online.org/publications/southasia/khan_memo.html.

―――. "Iran: Countdown to Showdown." *Bulletin of Atomic Scientists* 60, no. 6 (November/December 2004): 67–72.

―――. "Unraveling the A. Q. Khan and Future Proliferation Networks." *Washington Quarterly* 28, no. 2 (Spring 2005): 111–28.

―――. "The A. Q. Khan Illicit Nuclear Trade Network and Implications for Nonproliferation Efforts." *Strategic Insights* 5, no. 6 (July 2006), http://www.ccc.nps.navy.mil/si/2006/Jul/albrightJul06.pdf.

Albright, David, and Kimberly Kramer. "Fissile Material Stockpiles Still Growing." *Bulletin of the Atomic Scientists* 60, no. 6 (November/December 2004): 14–16.

Alibek, Ken. *Biohazard*. New York: Random House, 1999.

Aliboni, Roberto. "The Non-Proliferation Clause in a Preventive Perspective." *Conflict in Focus* 1, no. 4 (December 2004): 2–3.

Allison, Graham. "How to Stop Nuclear Terror." *Foreign Affairs* 83, no. 1 (January/February 2004): 64–74.

―――. *Nuclear Terrorism: The Ultimate Preventable Catastrophe*. New York: Times Books, 2004.

Ansari, Massoud. "Daddy's Girl." *New Republic*, March 27, 2004, 12–13.

Arend, Anthony Clark. "International Law and the Preemptive Use of Military Force." *Washington Quarterly* 26, no. 2 (Spring 2003): 89–103.

Arend, Anthony, and Robert J. Beck. *International Law and the Use of Force: Beyond the UN Charter Paradigm*. London: Routledge, 1993.

"Argentina, South Africa Studying Revival of Enrichment Programs." *Nucleonics Week*, August 31, 2006.

Bailey, Kathleen. "Nonproliferation Export Controls: Problems and Alternatives." In *Proliferation and Export Controls*, edited by Kathleen Bailey and Robert Rudney, 49–57. Lanham, MD: University Press of America; Fairfax, VA: National Institute for Public Policy, 1993.

Bailey, Kathleen, and Robert Rudney, eds. *Proliferation and Export Controls*. Lanham, MD: University Press of America, 1993.

Ball, Deborah Yarsike, and Theodore P. Gerber. *Will Russian Scientists Go Rogue? A Survey on the Threat and the Impact of Western Assistance*. Center for Strategic and International Studies, November 2004, http://www.csis.org/media/csis/pubs/pm_0357 .pdf.

Barasch, Guy E. *Light Flash Produced by an Atmospheric Nuclear Explosion*. Los Alamos Scientific Laboratory, November 1979, http://www.gwu.edu/~nsarchiv/NSAEBB/ NSAEBB190/02.pdf.

Baute, Jacques. "Timeline Iraq: Challenges and Lessons Learned from Nuclear Inspections." *IAEA Bulletin* 46, no. 1 (June 2004): 64–68, http://www.iaea.org/ Publications/Magazines/Bulletin/Bull461/article21.pdf.

Baylis, John, and Robert O'Neill, eds. *Alternative Nuclear Futures: The Role of Nuclear Weapons in the Post–Cold War World*. Oxford: Oxford University Press, 2000.

Beck, Michael D. "Reforming the Multilateral Export Control Regimes." *Nonproliferation Review* 7, no. 2 (Summer 2000): 91–101.

———. "The Promise and Limits of the PSI." *Monitor* 10, no. 1 (Spring 2004): 12–16.

Beck, Michael D., et al., eds. *To Supply or To Deny: Comparing Nonproliferation Export Controls in Five Key Countries*. The Hague: Kluwer Law International, 2003.

Becker, Una, Harald Müller, and Carmen Wunderlich. "While Waiting for the Protocol: An Interim Compliance Mechanism for the Biological Weapons Convention." *Nonproliferation Review* 12, no. 3 (November 2005): 541–72.

Ben-David, Alon. "Hizbullah Hits Israel's INS Hanit with Anti-Ship Missile." *Jane's Defence Weekly*, July 18, 2006.

Bernauer, Thomas. *The Projected Chemical Weapons Convention: A Guide to the Negotiations in the Conference on Disarmament*. New York: United Nations, 1990.

Bertsch, Gary K. *East-West Strategic Trade, COCOM and the Atlantic Alliance*. Atlantic Papers no. 49. Paris: Atlantic Institute for International Affairs, 1983.

Bertsch, Gary K., Seema Gahlaut, and Anupam Srivastava. "U.S.-India Relations in the Coming Decades." In *India's New Dynamics in Foreign Policy*, edited by Subrata K. Mitra and Bernd Rill, 107–27, Studies and Comments 4, Hanns Siedel Foundation, 2006.

Bertsch, Gary K., and Suzette Grillot, eds. *Arms on the Market: Reducing the Risk of Proliferation in the Former Soviet Union*. New York: Routledge, 1998.

Betts, Richard K. "Universal Deterrence or Conceptual Collapse? Liberal Pessimism and Utopian Realism." In *The Coming Crisis: Nuclear Proliferation, U.S. Interests, and World Order*, edited by Victor A. Utgoff, 51–85. Cambridge, MA: MIT Press, 2000.

Bhutto, Benazir. "Musharraf Knew about A. Q. Khan's 'Private' Proliferation." *New Perspectives Quarterly* 21, no. 2 (2004): 39–43.

Bin, Li. "Comments on the Chinese Regulation on Missile Technology Export Control."
    August 26, 2002, http://learn.tsinghua.edu.cn/homepage/S00313/eexctl.htm.
Blackford, Jacob. "Asher Karni Case Shows Weakness in Nuclear Export Controls."
    Institute for Science and International Security, September 8, 2004, http://www
    .isis-online.org/publications/southafrica/asherkarni.html.
Blank, Stephen. "Russo-Iranian Proliferation: Once More around the Mulberry Bush."
    Monitor 7, no. 1 (Winter 2001): 10–14.
Bleek, Philipp. *Global Cleanout of Civil Nuclear Material.* SGP Issue Brief 4,
    Strengthening the Global Partnership Project. Washington, DC: Center for Strategic
    and International Studies, 2005. September 2005, http://www.sgpproject.org/
    publications/SGPIssueBrief/SGP%20Issue%20Brief%20Bleek.pdf.
Boese, Wade. "The Proliferation Security Initiative: An Interview with John Bolton." *Arms
    Control Today* 33, no. 10 (December 2003): 37.
———. "Security Council Unanimously Adopts Resolution on Denying Terrorists
    WMD." *Arms Control Today* 34, no. 4 (May 2004): 34.
———. "Implications of UN Security Council Resolution 1540." Presentation to
    the Institute of Nuclear Materials Management panel discussion, March 15, 2005,
    http://www.armscontrol.org/events/20050315_1540.asp.
Bowen, Wyn Q. "Brazil's Accession to the MTCR." *Nonproliferation Review* 3, no. 3
    (Spring/Summer 1996): 86–91.
———. "The United Kingdom and Nuclear Deterrence." *Adelphi Papers* 46, no. 380
    (May 2006): 7–10.
Bowett, Derek. *Self-Defence in International Law.* Manchester, UK: Manchester University
    Press, 1958.
Braun, Chaim, and Christopher F. Chyba. "Proliferation Rings: New Challenges to the
    Nuclear Nonproliferation Regime." *International Security* 29, no. 2 (Fall 2004): 5–49.
Brownlie, Ian. *International Law and the Use of Force by States.* Oxford: Clarendon Press,
    1963.
———. *Principles of Public International Law.* 6th ed. Oxford: Oxford University Press,
    2003.
Bukharin, Oleg, Matthew Bunn, and Kenneth N. Luongo. *Renewing the Partnership:
    Recommendations for Accelerated Action to Secure Nuclear Material in the Former
    Soviet Union.* Washington DC: Russian American Nuclear Security Advisory Council,
    2000.
Bundy, McGeorge, William J. Crowe Jr., and Sidney D. Drell. "Reducing Nuclear
    Danger." *Foreign Affairs* 72, no. 2 (Spring 1993): 141–55.
Bunn, George, and John B. Rhinelander. "NPT Withdrawal: Time for the Security
    Council to Step In." *Arms Control Today* 35, no. 4 (May 2005): 17–21.
Bunn, George, and Roland M. Timerbaev. "Security Assurances to Non-Nuclear-Weapon
    States." *Nonproliferation Review* 1, no. 1 (Fall 1993): 11–20.
———. "Security Assurances to Non-Nuclear-Weapon States: Possible Options for
    Change." Programme for Promoting Nuclear Non-Proliferation (PPNN) Issue Review
    no. 7, (September 1996). Mountbatten Centre for International Studies.

Bunn, George, Charles N. van Doren, and David Fischer. "Options and Opportunities: The NPT Extension Conference of 1995." Programme for Promoting Nuclear Non-Proliferation study 2, 1991. Mountbatten Centre for International Studies.

Bunn, Matthew. *The Next Wave: Urgently Needed New Steps to Control Warheads and Fissile Materials.* Washington, DC: Carnegie Endowment for International Peace; Cambridge, MA: Harvard Project on Managing the Atom, 2000. http://belfercenter.ksg.harvard.edu/files/fullnextwave.pdf.

———. *Key Issues: The Threat in Russia and the Newly Independent States.* Harvard Project on Managing the Atom, Belfer Center, and Nuclear Threat Initiative (NTI). Updated October 2, 2006, http://www.nti.org/e_research/cnwm/threat/russia.asp.

Bunn, Matthew, and Anthony Wier. *Securing the Bomb 2006: The New Global Imperatives.* Cambridge, MA: Belfer Center, Harvard University, July 2006.

Bunn, Matthew, Anthony Wier, and John P. Holdren. *Controlling Nuclear Warheads and Materials: A Report Card and Action Plan.* Cambridge, MA: Belfer Center, Harvard University, March 2003.

Burr, William, and Jeffrey T. Richelson. "Whether to 'Strangle the Baby in the Cradle': The United States and the Chinese Nuclear Program, 1960–64." *International Security* 25, no. 3 (Winter 2000/2001): 54–99.

Busch, Nathan. "Russian Roulette: The Continuing Relevance of Russia to the Nuclear Proliferation Debate." *Security Studies* 11, no. 3 (Spring 2002): 44–90.

———. "Risks of Nuclear Terror: Vulnerabilities of Thefts and Sabotage at Nuclear Weapons Facilities." *Contemporary Security Policy 23, no. 3 (December 2002): 19–60.*

———. *No End in Sight: The Continuing Menace of Nuclear Proliferation.* Lexington: University of Kentucky Press, 2004.

Busch, Nathan, Maria Katsva, Igor Khripunov, and Dmitriy Nikonov. *The Human Factor and Security Culture: Challenges to Safeguarding Fissile Materials in Russia.* Athens, GA: Center for International Trade and Security, November 2002.

Butler, Kenley, Sammy Salama, and Leonard S. Spector. "Where's the Justice?" Bulletin of Atomic Scientists 62, no. 6 (November/December 2006): 25–34, 62–63.

Byers, Michael. "Preemptive Self-Defense: Hegemony, Equality and Strategies of Legal Change." *Journal of Political Philosophy* 11, no. 2 (June 2003): 171–90.

Byman, Daniel. "Measuring the War on Terrorism: A First Appraisal." *Current History* 101, no. 659 (December 2003): 411–16.

Cameron, Gavin. "Multitrack Microproliferation: Lessons from Aum Shinrikyo and Al Qaeda." *Studies in Conflict and Terrorism* 22, no. 4 (October/December 1999): 277–309.

Carasales, Julio. "The Argentine-Brazilian Nuclear Rapprochement." *Nonproliferation Review* 2, no. 3 (Spring/Summer 1995): 39–48.

Caravelli, Jack, and Chris Behan. "Accomplishments and Challenges in the MPC&A Program." *Monitor: International Perspectives on Nonproliferation* 7, no. 2 (Spring 2001): 3–5.

Carter, Ashton B. "Three Crises with North Korea." Prepared testimony before the Senate Foreign Relations Committee, February 4, 2003.

Center for Contemporary Conflict. "Asymmetric Conflict in South Asia: The Cause and Consequences of the 1999 Limited War in Kargil." Conference report, Monterey, CA, May 29–June 1, 2002, http://www.ccc.nps.navy.mil/events/recent/may02Kargil_rpt .asp.

Center for Global Security Research (CGSR). Lawrence Livermore Laboratory. "'Whither Deterrence?' Final Report of the 2001 Futures Project." May 2002.

Center for International Trade and Security. "UGA's Center for International Trade and Security to Host Major International Events in Moscow, Russia." October 2005, http://www.uga.edu/spia/news/cits_russia.htm.

———. *Strengthening Multilateral Export Controls: A Nonproliferation Priority*. CITS report, September 2002.

Center for Strategic and International Studies. *Technology and Security in the 21st Century: U.S. Military Export Control Reform*. Washington, DC: CSIS, May 2001.

Cerny, Philip G. "Globalization and the Changing Logic of Collective Action." *International Organization* 49, no. 4 (Autumn 1995): 595–625.

Chang, Stephanie, and Alan Pearson. *Federal Funding for Biological Weapons Prevention and Defense, Fiscal Years 2001 to 2007*. Washington, D.C.: Center for Arms Control and Non-Proliferation, June 21, 2006, http://www.armscontrolcenter.org/assets/pdfs/fy2007_ bwbudget.pdf.

Cirincione, Joseph, Jon B. Wolfsthal, and Miriam Rajkumar. *Deadly Arsenals: Tracking Weapons of Mass Destruction*. Washington, DC: Carnegie Endowment for International Peace, June 2002.

Clary, Chris. "Dr. Khan's Nuclear Walmart." *Disarmament Diplomacy* 8, no. 76 (March/ April 2004), http://www.acronym.org.uk/dd/dd76/76cc.htm.

Coll, Steve. "The Atomic Emporium: Abdul Qadeer Khan and Iran's Race to Build the Bomb." *New Yorker*, August 7 and 14, 2006, 50–63.

Craft, Cassady. "New Challenges in Multilateral Efforts to Control the Conventional Weapons Trade." *Monitor* 8, no. 2 (Spring 2002): 15–19.

———. *Challenges of UNSCR 1540: Questions about International Export Controls*. Center for International Trade and Security Issue Brief, October 20, 2004.

Craft, Cassady, and Suzette Grillot. "Transparency and the Effectiveness of Multilateral Nonproliferation Export Control Regimes: Can Wassenaar Work?" *Southeastern Political Review* 27, no. 2 (June 1999): 279–302.

Croddy, Eric, with Clarisa Perez-Armendariz and John Hart. *Chemical and Biological Warfare: A Comprehensive Survey for the Concerned Citizen*. New York: Copernicus Books, 2002.

Cupitt, Richard T. *Reluctant Champions: Truman, Eisenhower, Bush, and Clinton: U.S. Presidential Policy and Strategic Export Controls*. New York: Routledge, 2000.

Cupitt, Richard, and Suzette Grillot. "COCOM Is Dead, Long Live COCOM: Persistence and Change in Multilateral Security Institutions." *British Journal of Political Science* 27, no. 3 (July 1997): 361–89.

Cupitt, Richard, and Igor Khripunov. "New Strategies for the Nuclear Supplier Group (NSG)." *Comparative Strategy* 16, no. 3 (July/September 1997): 305–15.

Dahlitz, Julie. *Nuclear Arms Control with Effective International Agreements*. London: Allen and Unwin, 1983.

Daly, Sara, John Parachini, and William Rosenau. *Aum Shinrikyo, Al Qaeda, and the Kinshasa Reactor: Implications of Three Case Studies for Combating Nuclear Terrorism*. Documented briefing. Santa Monica, CA: RAND, Project Air Force, 2005.

Dando, Malcolm, Graham Pearson, and Bohumir Kriz. *Scientific and Technical Means of Distinguishing between Natural and Other Outbreaks of Disease*. Dordrecht: Kluwer, 2001.

Davis, Paul K., and Brian Michael Jenkins. *Deterrence and Influence in Counterterrorism: A Component in the War on Al Qaeda*. MR–1619. Santa Monica, CA: RAND, National Defense Research Institute, 2002.

Defense Threat Reduction Agency. "CTR Scorecard: Strategic Offensive Arms Elimination." Updated August 7, 2007, http://www.dtra.mil/oe/ctr/scorecard.cfm.

Dershowitz, Alan M. *Preemption: A Knife That Cuts Both Ways*. New York: W. W. Norton, 2006.

Dhanapala, Jayantha, ed. *Regional Approaches to Disarmament: Security and Stability*. Aldershot, U.K.: Dartmouth, 1993.

Dinstein, Yoram. *War, Aggression and Self-Defence*. 3rd ed. Cambridge: Cambridge University Press, 2001.

Doolin, Joel A. "The Proliferation Security Initiative Cornerstone of a New International Norm." *Naval War College Review* 59, no. 2 (Spring 2006): 29–57.

Doyle, James E., and Stephen V. Mladineo. "Assessing the Development of a Modern Safeguards Culture in the NIS." *Nonproliferation Review* 5, no. 2 (Winter 1998): 91–100.

Drezner, Daniel W. "Globalization and Policy Convergence." *International Studies Review* 3, no. 1 (Spring 2001): 53–78.

———. "Globalization's Last Hurrah?" *Foreign Policy*, no. 128 (January/February 2002): 38–51.

Dunn, Lewis, and Herman Kahn. *Trends in Nuclear Proliferation, 1975–1995*. Prepared for U.S. Arms Control and Disarmament Agency by the Hudson Institute, May 15, 1976, http://stinet.dtic.mil/oai/oai?verb=getRecord&metadataPrefix=html&identifier=ADB011707.

Ebata, Kensuke. "North Korea's Nuclear Weapon Test Prompts Concerns about Iranian Missile Development." *Sekai Shuho*, November 14, 2006, 48–49.

ElBaradei, Mohamed. Prepared speech at the Carnegie Endowment for International Peace Nonproliferation Conference. June 21, 2004.

———. Introductory statement to the IAEA board of governors. June 14, 2005.

———. "Nuclear Non-Proliferation and Arms Control: Are We Making Progress?" Statement presented at the 2005 Carnegie International Nonproliferation Conference, November 7, 2005, http://www.carnegieendowment.org/static/npp/2005conference/2005_conference.htm.

Eldridge, John. "Terrorist WMD: Threats and Responses." *Jane's International Defence Review*, September 1, 2005.

Ellis, Jason D., and Todd E. Perry. "Nunn-Lugar's Unfinished Agenda." *Arms Control Today* 27, no. 7 (October 1997): 14–22.

Errera, Philippe. "The E3/EU-Iran Negotiations and Prospects for Resolving the Iranian Nuclear Issue: A European Perspective." Tehran, March 5–6, 2006, http://www.globalsecurity.org/wmd/library/report/2005/errera.htm.

"Ever More Perilous Isolation." *Economist*, May 27, 2003.

Falk, Richard A. "What Future for the UN Charter System of War Prevention?" *American Journal of International Law* 97, no. 3 (July 2003): 590–98.

Fedchenko, Vitaly. "Appendix 13.C: Multilateral Control of the Nuclear Fuel Cycle." In *SIPRI Yearbook 2006: Armaments, Disarmament and International Security*, 686–705. Oxford: Oxford University Press, 2006.

Ferguson, Charles D. *Preventing Catastrophic Nuclear Terrorism*. Council Special Report no. 11, Council on Foreign Relations, March 2006.

Ferguson, Charles D., and William C. Potter, with Amy Sands, Leonard S. Spector, and Fred L. Wehling. *The Four Faces of Nuclear Terrorism*. New York: Routledge, 2005.

Findlay, Trevor. "A Standing United Nations Verification Body: Necessary and Feasible." Weapons of Mass Destruction Commission paper no. 40. December 2005, http://www.wmdcommission.org/sida.asp?id=7.

Finlay, Brian, and Andrew Grotto. *The Race to Secure Russia's Loose Nukes: Progress since 9/11*. Washington, D.C.: Henry L. Stimson Center and the Center for American Progress, September 2005, http://www.stimson.org/ctr/pdf/LooseNukes.pdf.

Fischer, David. *History of the International Atomic Energy Agency: The First Forty Years*. Vienna: International Atomic Energy Agency, 1997.

Fischer, David, and Harald Müller. "The Fourth Review of the Non-Proliferation Treaty." In *SIPRI Yearbook 1991: World Armaments and Disarmament*, 555–84. Oxford: Oxford University Press, 1991.

Fischer, David, and Peter Szasz, eds. *Safeguarding the Atom: A Critical Appraisal*. London: Taylor and Francis, 1985.

Fitzpatrick, Mark, ed. *Nuclear Black Markets: Pakistan, A. Q. Khan and the Rise of Proliferation Networks*. London: International Institute for Strategic Studies, 2007.

Forsberg, Randall, et al. *Nonproliferation Primer: Preventing the Spread of Nuclear, Chemical and Biological Weapons*. Cambridge, MA: MIT Press, 1995.

Foster, William C. Testimony before the Senate Committee on Foreign Relations, 90th Cong., 2nd sess., Executive H, Treaty on the Nonproliferation of Nuclear Weapons, July 10, 11, 12, 17, 1968.

Frieman, Wendy. *China, Arms Control, and Nonproliferation*. London: RoutledgeCurzon, 2004.

Fukuyama, Francis. "The End of History?" *National Interest* 16 (Summer 1989): 3–18.

Gahlaut, Seema. "Reducing Nuclear Dangers in South Asia: A Review of Russian Perspectives." *Monitor* (special issue) 7, no. 3 (Fall 2001).

———. "Plugging the Proliferation Loopholes in Pakistan and Beyond." *Defense News*, March 22, 2004, 53.

————. "Misfiring at the India Nuclear Deal." *ForeignPolicy.com*, March 2006, http://www.foreignpolicy.com/story/cms.php?story_id=3404b.

————. "A Critical Look at the Opposition to the U.S.-India Agreement." In *Nuclear Cooperation with India: New Challenges, New Opportunities*, edited by Wade L. Huntley and Karthika Sasikumar, Simons Centre for Disarmament and Non-Proliferation Research, Vancouver, BC, Canada, March 2006, 18–22, http://www.lulu .com/items/volume_15/243095. pdf.

————. *Indian Export Control Policy: Political Commitment, Institutional Capacity, and Nonproliferation Record*. CITS Issue Brief, May 2006, http://www.uga.edu/cits/ documents/pdf/Briefs/Indian%20XC%20Brief%20Final.pdf.

————. *UNSC Resolution 1540: A Principled Necessity*. CITS Issue Brief, August 2006, http://www.uga.edu/cits/documents/pdf/Briefs/CITSbrief_004_1540_gahlaut _082006.pdf.

————. "India and the Nonproliferation Regime." In *India's New Dynamics in Foreign Policy*, edited by Subrata K. Mitra and Bernd Rill, 93–106, Studies and Comments 4. Germany: Hanns Siedel Foundation, 2006.

Gahlaut, Seema, and Anupam Srivastava. *Export Control Developments in India: Update 2005I*. CITS report for Carnegie Corporation of New York, July 2005, http://www.uga .edu/cits/documents/pdf/EXEC%20SUMMARY%2020050616.pdf.

Garwin, Richard, and Frank N. von Hippel. "A Technical Analysis: Deconstructing North Korea's October 9 Nuclear Test." *Arms Control Today* 36, no. 9 (November 2006): 14–16.

Geissler, Erhard, ed. *Biological and Toxin Weapons Today*. Oxford: Oxford University Press, 1986.

Gilinsky, Victor, Marvin Miller, and Harmon Hubbard. *A Fresh Examination of the Proliferation Dangers of Light Water Reactors*. Nonproliferation Policy Education Center paper, October 22, 2004.

Gill, Bates. *Chinese Arms Transfers: Purposes, Patterns, and Prospects in the New World Order*. Westport, CT: Praeger, 1992.

————. "Two Steps Forward, One Step Back: The Dynamics of Chinese Nonproliferation and Arms Control Policy-Making in an Era of Reform." In *The Making of Chinese Foreign and Security Policy in an Era of Reform*, edited by David M. Lampton, 257–88. Stanford, CA: Stanford University Press, 2001.

————. "The Growing Challenge of Proliferation in Asia." In *Strategic Asia 2003–04: Fragility and Crisis*, edited by Richard Ellings et al., 365–97. Seattle: National Bureau of Asian Research, 2003.

————. *Rising Star: China's New Security Diplomacy and Its Implications for the United States*. Washington, DC: Brookings Institution Press, 2007.

Gill, Bates, and Andrew Thompson. "A Test for Beijing: China and the North Korean Nuclear Quandary." *Arms Control Today* 33, no. 4 (May 2003): 12–14.

Goldblat, Jozef. "Appendix 20A: Final Declaration of the Third Review Conference." In *SIPRI Yearbook 1986: World Armaments and Disarmament*, 481–94. Oxford: Oxford University Press, 1986.

———. "The Third Review of the NPT Treaty." In *SIPRI Yearbook 1986: World Armaments and Disarmament*, 469–80. Oxford: Oxford University Press, 1986.

———. *Twenty Years of the Non-Proliferation Treaty: Implementation and Prospects*. Oslo: International Peace Research Institute (PRIO), 1990.

———. *Arms Control: A Guide on Negotiations and Agreements*. London: Sage; published for International Peace Research Institute, 1994.

———. *The Nuclear Non-Proliferation Regime: Assessment and Prospects*. The Hague: Martinus Nijhoff, 1997.

———. *Arms Control: The New Guide to Negotiations and Agreements*. 2nd ed. London: Sage, 2002.

Goldschmidt, Pierre. *The Urgent Need to Strengthen the Nuclear Non-Proliferation Regime*. Policy outlook, Carnegie Endowment for International Peace, Non-Proliferation Project, January 2006.

Goldstein, Avery. *Rising to the Challenge: China's Grand Strategy and International Security*. Stanford, CA: Stanford University Press, 2005.

Goodman, Mark W., Alex R. Burkart, and J. Christian Kessler. "Overview of the Nuclear Nonproliferation Regime." Paper presented at IAEA International Training Course on Implementation of State Systems of Accounting and Control of Nuclear Material, May 1, 2005.

Goyal, Ajay. "Intellectual Capital: IT or Not to IT, That Is Not a Question." *Russian Journal*, October 11, 2001, http://russoft.org/docs/print.php?doc=787.

———. "Russia's Untapped Treasures." *Russian Journal*, n.d., http://norasco.com/ajay_goyal_6.html.

Grant, Rebecca. "Osirak and Beyond." *Air Force Magazine* 85, no. 8 (August 2002): 74–78.

Gray, Christine. *International Law and the Use of Force*. Oxford: Oxford University Press, 2000.

Gribkov, Anatoli I., and William Y. Smith. *Operation ANADYR: U.S. and Soviet Generals Recount the Cuban Missile Crisis*. Chicago: Edition Q, 1994.

Gualtieri, David S. "The System of Non-Proliferation Export Controls." In *Commitment and Compliance: The Role of Non-Binding Norms in the International Legal System*, edited by Dinah Shelton, 467–86. Oxford: Oxford University Press, 2000.

Guthrie, Richard, John Hart, and Frida Kuhlau. "Chemical and Biological Warfare Developments and Arms Control." In *SIPRI Yearbook 2006: Armaments, Disarmament and International Security*, 715–16. Oxford: Oxford University Press, 2006.

Habiger, Eugene E. "A Unique Opportunity: Seize It." In *Nuclear Security Culture: From National Best Practices to International Standards*, edited by Igor Khripunov et al., 9–11. Amsterdam: IOS Press, 2007. Originally presented at NATO Advanced Research Workshop, Moscow, October 24, 2005.

Hart, John. "The ALSOS Mission, 1943–1945: A Secret U.S. Scientific Intelligence Unit." *International Journal of Intelligence and CounterIntelligence* 18, no. 3 (Fall 2005): 508–37.

Hart, John, and Shannon N. Kile. "Libya's Renunciation of NBC Weapons and Longer-Range Missile Programmes." In *SIPRI Yearbook 2005: Armaments, Disarmament and International Security*, 629–48. Oxford: Oxford University Press, 2005.

Hayes, Peter. *The Stalker State: North Korean Proliferation and the End of American Nuclear Hegemony.* Nautilus Institute Policy Forum Online 06-82A. October 4, 2006, www.nautilus.org/fora/security/0682Hayes.html.

Hecker, Siegfried S. "Thoughts about an Integrated Strategy for Nuclear Cooperation with Russia." *Nonproliferation Review* 8, no. 2 (Summer 2001): 1–24.

———. "Visit to the Yongbyon Scientific Research Center in North Korea." Testimony before the Senate Foreign Relations Committee, Washington, DC, January 21, 2004, http://www.fas.org/irp/congress/2004_hr/012104hecker.pdf.

———. *Report on North Korean Nuclear Program.* Center for International Security and Cooperation, Stanford University, Stanford, CA, November 15, 2006.

Henkin, Louis, et al. *International Law: Cases and Materials.* 2nd ed. St. Paul, MN: West, 1987.

Henry L. Stimson Center. *Study Group on Enhancing Multilateral Export Controls for U.S. National Security: Final Report.* Washington, DC, April 2001.

Hersh, Seymour M. "The Cold Test." *New Yorker,* January 27, 2003, 42.

———. "The Deal." *New Yorker,* March 8, 2004, 32–37, http://www.newyorker.com/archive/2004/03/08/040308fa_fact.

———. "The Iran Plans: Would President Bush Go to War to Stop Tehran from Getting the Bomb?" *New Yorker,* April 17, 2006, 30–31, http://www.newyorker.com/archive/2006/04/17/060417fa_fact.

Hibbs, Mark. "The Unmaking of a Nuclear Smuggler." *Bulletin of the Atomic Scientists* 62, no. 6 (November/December 2006): 35–41, 63.

Hinsley, F. H. *Power and the Pursuit of Peace.* Cambridge: Cambridge University Press, 1963.

Hirsch, Michael. "The Great Technology Giveaway." *Foreign Affairs* 77, no. 5 (September/October 1998): 2–9.

Hoelscher, Christopher, and Hans-Michael Wolffgang. "The Wassenaar Arrangement between International Trade, Nonproliferation, and Export Controls." *Journal of World Trade* 32, no. 1 (February 1998): 45–63.

Holmes, James R., Igor Khripunov, and Eugene Habiger. "Secure Russian Stockpile: Beslan Showed Intent of Chechen Radicals." *Defense News,* October 4, 2004, 29.

Holmes, James R., and Andrew C. Winner. "WMD: Interdicting the Gravest Danger." *U.S. Naval Institute Proceedings* 131, no. 2 (February 2005): 72–75.

Holmes, James R., Toshi Yoshihara, and Andrew C. Winner. "Maritime Counterproliferation with Chinese Characteristics." *Defense and Security Analysis* 22, no. 1 (March 2006): 5–21.

Howlett, Darryl, and John Simpson. "Nuclear Non-Proliferation: How to Ensure an Effective Compliance Mechanism." Ch. 1 in *Effective Non-Proliferation: The European Union and the 2005 NPT Review Conference,* 11–19. Chaillot Papers, no. 77, European Union Institute for Security Studies. April 2005, http://www.iss.europa.eu/index.php?id=143.

Hughes, Christopher W., and Richard Devetak, eds. *Globalization of Political Violence.* London: Routledge, 2007.

Institute of Medicine and National Research Council and the Committee on Advances
    in Technology and the Prevention of Their Application to Next Generation Biowarfare
    Threats. Stanley M. Lemon and David A. Relman, cochairs. *Globalization, Biosecurity,
    and the Future of the Life Sciences.* Washington, DC: National Academies Press,
    2006.

International Institute for Strategic Studies. *North Korea's Weapons Programmes: A Net
    Assessment.* International Institute for Strategic Studies, January 21, 2004, http://www
    .iiss.org/publications/strategic-dossiers/north-korean-dossier.

———. *Iran's Strategic Weapons Programmes: A Net Assessment.* London: Routledge,
    2005.

———. "North Korea's Missile Tests—Troubling Trajectories." *IISS Strategic Comments*
    12, no. 6 (July 2006).

———. "North Korea's Nuclear Test: Continuing Reverberations." *IISS Strategic
    Comments* 12, no. 8 (October 2006).

Isla, Nicolas. *Transparency in Past Offensive Biological Weapon Programmes: An Analysis of
    Confidence Building Measure Form F 1992–2003.* Hamburg Centre for Biological Arms
    Control occasional paper no. 1, June 2006, www.biological-arms-control.org/download/
    FormF_1992-2003.pdf.

James Martin Center for Nonproliferation Studies. *China's Missile Exports and Assistance
    to Pakistan.* Monterey Institute for International Studies. July 2000, http://cns.miis.edu/
    research/india/china/mpakpos.htm#Background.

———. *CNS Special Report on North Korean Ballistic Missile Capabilities.* Monterey
    Institute for International Studies. March 22, 2006, http://cns.miis.edu/pubs/week/
    pdf/060321.pdf.

Jasani, Bhupendra ed. *Peaceful and Non-Peaceful Uses of Outer Space: Problems of
    Definition for the Prevention of an Arms Race.* New York: Taylor and Francis, 1991.

Jenkins, Brian Michael. "The Future Course of International Terrorism." *Futurist* 21, no.
    4 (July/August 1987): 8–13.

Jentleson, Bruce W., and Christopher A. Whytock. "Who 'Won' Libya? The Force-
    Diplomacy Debate and Its Implications for Theory and Policy." *International Security*
    30, no. 3 (Winter 2005/6): 47–86.

Johnson, Nick. "War on Terrorism Poses New Challenges for Technology Exports."
    Aerospace Daily, January 2, 2002.

Johnson, Rebecca. "The 2000 NPT Review Conference: A Delicate, Hard-Won
    Compromise." *Disarmament Diplomacy*, no. 46 (May 2000): 2–21. http://www
    .acronym.org.uk/dd/dd46/46npt.htm.

———. "The NPT PrepCom: Papering over the Cracks?" *Disarmament Diplomacy*, no.
    64 (May/June 2002). http://www.acronym.org.uk/dd/dd64/64npt.htm.

———. "Report on the 2004 NPT PrepCom." *Disarmament Diplomacy*, no. 77 (May/
    June 2004). http://www.acronym.org.uk/dd/dd77/77npt.htm.

———. "Politics and Protection: Why the 2005 NPT Review Conference Failed."
    Disarmament Diplomacy, no. 80 (Autumn 2005). http://www.acronym.org.uk/dd/
    dd80/80npt.htm.

Jones, Scott. *The Evolution of the Ukrainian Export Control System: State Building and International Cooperation*. Aldershot, UK: Ashgate, 2002.

———. "EU Enlargement: Implications for EU and Multilateral Export Controls." *Nonproliferation Review* 10, no. 2 (Summer 2003): 80–89.

Joseph, Jofi. "The Proliferation Security Initiative: Can Interdiction Stop Proliferation?" *Arms Control Today* 34, no. 5 (June 2004): 6–13.

Joseph, Robert G. "Combating Weapons of Mass Destruction (WMD): Effective Multilateralism." Prepared remarks to the Lawrence Livermore National Laboratory Conference on WMD Latency, Livermore, California, January 20, 2006 (remarks as prepared, delivered by Ambassador Donald Mahley), http://www.state.gov/t/us/rm/60218.htm.

———. "Broadening and Deepening Our Proliferation Security Initiative Cooperation." Remarks in Warsaw, Poland, June 23, 2006, http://www.state.gov/t/us/rm/68269.htm.

Joyner, Daniel H. "The Nuclear Suppliers Group: History and Functioning." *International Trade Law and Regulation* 10, no. 3 (2005): 33–42.

———. "The Proliferation Security Initiative: Nonproliferation, Counterproliferation and International Law." *Yale Journal of International Law* 30, no. 2 (Summer 2005): 507–48.

———. *United Nations Security Council Resolution 1540: A Legal Travesty?* CITS Issue Brief, August 2006, http://www.uga.edu/cits/documents/pdf/Briefs/CITSbrief_003_1540_Joyner_082006.pdf.

———, ed. *Non-Proliferation Export Controls: Origins, Challenges, and Proposals for Strengthening*. Aldershot, UK: Ashgate, 2006.

———. *International Law and the Proliferation of Weapons of Mass Destruction*. Oxford: Oxford University Press, 2008.

———. *Jus ad Bellum in the Age of WMD Proliferation*. Forthcoming.

Kaldor, Mary. *New and Old Wars: Organized Violence in a Global Era*. Cambridge, U.K.: Polity, 1999.

Kang, Jungmin, and Peter Hayes. *Technical Analysis of the DPRK Nuclear Test*. Nautilus Institute Policy Forum Online 06-89A, October 20, 2006, http://www.nautilus.org/fora/security/0689HayesKang.html.

Kapur, S. Paul. "India and Pakistan's Unstable Peace: Why Nuclear South Asia Is Not Like Cold War Europe." *International Security* 30, no. 2 (Fall 2005): 127–52.

Karp, Aaron. *Ballistic Missile Proliferation: The Politics and Technics*. Oxford: Oxford University Press, 1996.

Kaysen, Carl, Robert S. McNamara, and George W. Rathjens. "Nuclear Weapons after the Cold War." *Foreign Affairs* 70, no. 4 (Fall 1991): 95–110.

Kearney, A. T. "Globalization's Last Hurrah." *Foreign Policy*, no. 128 (January/February 2002): 38–51.

Keller, William W., and Janne E. Nolan. "The Arms Trade: Business as Usual?" *Foreign Policy*, no. 109 (Winter 1997/98): 113–25.

———. "Proliferation of Advanced Weaponry: Threat to Stability." In *The Global Century: Globalization and National Security*, edited by Richard L. Kugler and Ellen L. Frost. Washington DC: NDU Press, 2001.

Kelly, David. "The Trilateral Agreement: Lessons for Biological Weapons Verification." In *Verification Yearbook 2002*, edited by Trevor Findlay and Oliver Meier, 93–109. London: VERTIC, 2002.

Kelsen, Hans. *Principles of International Law.* 2nd ed. Revised and edited by Robert W. Tucker. New York: Holt, Rinehart, and Winston, 1966.

Kemp, Geoffrey. "America and Iran: Road Maps and Realism." Washington, DC: Nixon Center, 1998. http://www.nixoncenter.org/publications/monographs/iran.htm.

———. "Iranian Nuclear Weapons and U.S. Policy." Program brief 6, no. 2, Nixon Center. January 2000, http://www.nixoncenter.org/publications/Program%20Briefs/vol6no2iran.htm.

Kerr, Paul. "Efforts to Strengthen IAEA Safeguards Advance." *Arms Control Today* 36, no. 6 (July/August 2006): 46.

Khan, F. Hassan. "Nuclear Proliferation Motivations: Lessons from Pakistan." *Nonproliferation Review* 13, no. 3 (November 2006): 501–17.

Khoshroo, G. Ali. Statement. Second session of the PrepCom for the 2005 NPT Review Conference, April 29, 2003.

Khripunov, Igor, et al. *Nuclear Security Culture: The Case of Russia.* Athens, GA: Center for International Trade and Security, December 2004.

———. "Nuclear Security: Attitude Check." *Bulletin of the Atomic Scientists* 61, no. 1 (January/February 2005): 59–64.

Khripunov, Igor, and Maria Katsva. "Russia's Nuclear Industry: The Next Generation." *Bulletin of the Atomic Scientists* 58, no. 2 (March/April 2002): 51–57.

Khripunov, Igor, et al., eds. *Nuclear Security Culture: From National Best Practices to International Standards.* Amsterdam: IOS Press, 2007.

Kokoski, Richard. *Technology and the Proliferation of Nuclear Weapons.* Oxford: Oxford University Press, 1995.

Krasner, Stephen D., ed. *International Regimes.* Ithaca, NY: Cornell University Press, 1983.

Krass, Allan S. *Verification: How Much Is Enough?* London: Taylor and Francis, 1985.

Krutzsch, Walter, and Ralf Trapp. *A Commentary on the Chemical Weapons Convention.* Dordrecht: Martinus Nijhoff, 1994.

Kucherenko, Vladimir. "Russian Nuclear Material Monitoring System 'Far from Ideal.'" Trans. Rossiyskaya Gazeta. *RANSAC Nuclear News*, October 4, 2000. Originally published in Russian in *Rossiyskaya Gazeta*, September 29, 2000.

Laden, Osama bin. *Messages to the World: The Statements of Osama bin Laden.* Trans. and intro. Bruce Lawrence. London: Verso, 2005.

Leitenberg, Milton. *The Problem of Biological Weapons.* Stockholm: Swedish National Defense College, 2004.

———. *Assessing the Biological Weapons and Bioterrorism Threat.* Strategic Studies Institute Monograph. Carlisle Barracks, PA: U.S. Army War College, December 2005.

Levi, Michael A. *On Nuclear Terrorism.* Cambridge, MA: Harvard University Press, 2007.

Libicki, Martin. "Rethinking War: The Mouse's New Roar." *Foreign Policy*, no. 117 (Winter 1999/2000): 30–43.

Littlewood, Jez. *The Biological Weapons Convention: A Failed Revolution*. Aldershot, UK: Ashgate, 2005.

Litwak, Robert S. "The New Calculus of Pre-emption." *Survival* 44, no. 4 (Winter 2002): 53–79.

Lopez, George A., and David Cortright. "Containing Iraq: Sanctions Worked." *Foreign Affairs* 83, no. 4 (July/August 2004): 90–103.

Luongo, Kenneth N., and William E. Hoehn III. "Reform and Expansion of Cooperative Threat Reduction." *Arms Control Today* 33, no. 5 (June 2003): 11–13.

MacFarlane, Allison. "All Weapons of Mass Destruction Are Not Equal." Audit of the Conventional Wisdom Series, MIT Center for International Studies, July 2005.

Marin, M. A. "The Evolution and Present Status of the Laws of War." *Académie de Droit International: Receuil des Cours* 92, no. 2 (1957): 633–749.

Mastanduno, Michael. *Economic Containment: CoCom and the Politics of East-West Trade*. Ithaca, NY: Cornell University Press, 1992.

Mathews, Robert J. "The Development of the Australia Group Export Control Lists of Biological Pathogens, Toxins and Dual-Use Equipment." *CBW Conventions Bulletin* 66 (December 2004): 1–4.

Mazari, Shireen M. *The Kargil Conflict 1999: Separating Fact from Fiction*. Islamabad, Pakistan: Institute of Strategic Studies, 2003.

McCloud, Kimberly, and Matthew Osborne. "WMD Terrorism and Usama bin Laden." CNS Reports, James Martin Center for Nonproliferation Studies, Monterey Institute for International Studies. November 20, 2001, http://cns.miis.edu/pubs/reports/binladen.htm.

McDougal, Myres S., and Florentino P. Feliciano. *Law and Minimum World Public Order: The Legal Regulation and International Coercion*. New Haven, CT: Yale University Press, 1961.

McGoldrick, Fred, Harold Bengelsdorf, and Lawrence Scheinman. "The U.S.-India Nuclear Deal: Taking Stock." *Arms Control Today* 35, no. 8 (October 2005): 6–12.

Medeiros, Evan S. *Reluctant Restraint: The Evolution of China's Nonproliferation Policies and Practices, 1980–2004*. Stanford, CA: Stanford University Press, 2007.

Medeiros, Evan S., and Bates Gill. *Chinese Arms Exports: Policy, Players and Process*. Carlisle Barracks, PA: Strategic Studies Institute, U.S. Army War College, August 2000.

Meselson, Matthew. "Averting the Hostile Exploitation of Biotechnology." *CBW Conventions Bulletin* 48 (June 2000): 16–19.

Meselson, Matthew, and Julian Robinson. "A Draft Convention to Prohibit Biological and Chemical Weapons under International Law." In *Treaty Enforcement and International Cooperation in Criminal Matters*, edited by Rodrigo Yepes-Enriquez and Lisa Tabassi, 457–69. The Hague: TMC Asser, 2002.

Milhollin, Gary. *Licensing Mass Destruction: U.S. Exports to Iraq, 1985–1990*. Wisconsin Project on Nuclear Arms Control report, June 1991.

———. "Can Sanctions Stop The Bomb?" Keynote address delivered at the Conference on Economic Sanctions and International Relations, Fourth Freedom Forum and the

Joan B. Kroc Institute for International Peace Studies, Notre Dame University, April 3, 1993.

Mingquan, Zhu. "The Evolution of China's Nuclear Nonproliferation Policy." *Nonproliferation Review* 4, no. 2 (Winter 1997): 40–48.

Mistry, Dinshaw. "Ballistic Missile Proliferation and the MTCR: A Ten-Year Review." Paper presented at the International Studies Association annual meeting, March 19–23, 1998.

Moodie, Michael. "The Challenges of Chemical, Biological and Nuclear Weapons Enabling Technology." In *The Transfer of Sensitive Technology and the Future of the Control Regimes*, edited by Péricles Alves Gasprani and Kerstin Hoffman, 65–68. Geneva: UNIDIR, 1997.

Morel, Benoit. "How Effective Is the Australia Group?" In *Proliferation and Export Controls*, edited by Kathleen Bailey and Robert Rudney, 57–68. Lanham, MD: University Press of America; Fairfax, VA: National Institute for Public Policy, 1993.

Mullen, Mike. Remarks at the U.S. Naval War College, Newport, RI. August 31, 2005, http://www.navy.mil/navydata/cno/speeches/mullen050831.txt.

Musharraf, Pervez. *In the Line of Fire: A Memoir*. New York: Simon and Schuster, 2006.

Nadelmann, Ethan A. "Global Prohibition Regimes: The Evolution of Norms in International Society." *International Organization* 44, no. 4 (Autumn 1990): 479–526.

Negroponte, John. "Worldwide Threat Briefing." Testimony before the Senate Select Committee on Intelligence, February 2, 2006.

———. "Threat Assessment of the Director of National Intelligence for the Senate Armed Services Committee." February 28, 2006, http://www.dni.gov/testimonies/20060228_testimony.htm.

Newberg, Paula. "Pakistan: The Eye of a Coming Storm?" *YaleGlobal*, February 28, 2007, http://yaleglobal.yale.edu/display.article?id=8838.

Newman, Richard J. "The Qadhafi Question." *U.S. News and World Report*, April 15, 1996, 15.

"News Chronology: February–May 1996." March 22, 1996, entry. *CBW Conventions Bulletin* 32 (June 1996): 27.

"News Chronology: November 1996 through February 1997." November 25, 1996, entry. *CBW Conventions Bulletin* 35 (March 1997): 24.

"News Chronology: May through August 1997." May 6, 1997, entry. *CBW Conventions Bulletin* 37 (September 1997): 16.

"News Chronology: November 2003 through January 2004." January 6, 2004, entry. *CBW Conventions Bulletin* 63 (2004): 37.

Nielsen, Jenny, and John Simpson. "The NPT Withdrawal Clause and Its Negotiating History." Mountbatten Centre for International Studies, NPT Issue Review, July 2004, http://www.mcis.soton.ac.uk/Site_Files/pdf/withdrawal_clause_NPT_nielsen&simpson_2004.pdf.

Nilsson, Anita. "IAEA Material Security Programme Overview." Paper presented at Symposium on International Safeguards, October 29–November 2, 2001, Vienna, Austria.

————. "The IAEA's Perspective on Security Culture." In *Nuclear Security Culture: From National Best Practices to International Standards*, edited by Igor Khripunov et al., 13–14. Amsterdam: IOS Press, 2007.

Nuclear Suppliers Group. "The NSG—Strengthening the Nuclear Non-Proliferation Regime." Plenary meeting statement, Oslo, Norway, June 23–24, 2005.

Nuclear Threat Initiative. "Russian Methodological Training Center (RMTC)." October 26, 2001, http://www.nti.org/db/nisprofs/russia/forasst/doe/rmtc.htm.

Oehler, Gordon. Statement at the hearing of the Senate Foreign Relations Committee on Proliferation of Chinese Missiles. June 11, 1998.

Ogilvie-White, Tanya, and John Simpson. "The NPT and Its 2003 PrepCom Session: A Regime in Need of Intensive Care." *Nonproliferation Review* 10, no. 1 (Spring 2003): 40–58.

Oostuizen, Gabriel, and Elizabeth Wilmshurst. *Terrorism and Weapons of Mass Destruction: United Nations Security Council Resolution 1540*. Chatham House Briefing Paper 04/01, September 2004.

Ordover, Janusz, and Linda Goldberg, eds. *Export Controls and Nonproliferation Policy*. Office of Technology Assessment, 1994.

"Pakistan's Quest for UF6 Sensors Underlines Limits of NSG Controls." *NuclearFuel*, March 28, 2005.

Pande, Savita. "The Challenge of Nuclear Export Controls." *Strategic Analysis* 23, no. 4 (July 1999): 575–99.

Pearson, Alan M., Marie Isabelle Chevrier, and Mark Wheelis, eds. *Incapacitating Biochemical Weapons: Promise or Peril?* Lanham, MD: Lexington Books, 2007.

Pearson, Graham. *The UNSCOM Saga: Chemical and Biological Weapons Non-Proliferation*. London: Macmillan, 1999.

————. *The Search for Iraq's Weapons of Mass Destruction: Inspection, Verification and Non-Proliferation*. Basingstoke, UK: Palgrave Macmillan, 2005.

————. "Report from Geneva: The Preparatory Committee for the Sixth BWC Review Conference." *CBW Conventions Bulletin* 71 (May 2006): 6–15.

Pikayev, Alexander. "Strategic Dimensions of the Russo-Iranian Partnership." *Monitor* 7, no. 1 (Winter 2001): 7–10.

Pilat, Joseph, ed. *Atoms for Peace: A Future after Fifty Years?* Baltimore: Johns Hopkins University Press, 2007.

Pollack, Jonathan D. "North Korea's Nuclear Weapons Program to 2015: Three Scenarios." *Asia Policy* 2, no. 3 (January 2007): 105–23.

Porth, Jacquelyn S. "Bush Urges All Nations to Halt Illicit WMD Proliferation Trade." June 23, 2006, http://www.america.gov/st/washfile-english/2006/June/20060623165009sjhtrop0.1716577.html.

————. "Weapons Proliferation Initiative Seeking More Partners." June 23, 2006, http://www.america.gov/st/washfile-english/2006/June/20060623193821sjhtrop0.3565332.html.

Post, Jerrold M. "Prospects for Nuclear Terrorism: Psychological Motivations and Constraints." In *Preventing Nuclear Terrorism: The Report and Papers of the International*

Task Force on Prevention of Nuclear Terrorism, edited by Yonah Alexander and Paul A. Leventhal, 91–103. Lexington, MA: Lexington Books, 1987.

Potter, William C. "Outlook for the Adoption of a Safeguards Culture in the Former Soviet Union." *Journal of Nuclear Materials Management* 26 (Winter 1998): 22–34.

Potter, William C., and Fred L. Wehling. "Sustainability: A Vital Component of Nuclear Material Security in Russia." *Nonproliferation Review* 7, no. 1 (Spring 2000): 184–87.

Powell, Bill, and Tim McGirk. "The Man Who Sold the Bomb." *Time,* February 14, 2005, 22–30, http://www.time.com/time/magazine/article/0,9171,1025082-2,00.html.

"Progress in The Hague." *CBW Conventions Bulletin* 67 (March 2005): 6–11.

Rademaker, Stephen G. "The Proliferation Security Initiative (PSI): A Record of Success." Testimony before the House International Relations Committee, Subcommittee on International Terrorism and Nonproliferation, Washington, DC. June 9, 2005, http://www.state.gov/t/ac/rls/rm/47715.htm.

Ramachandran, R. "India and the U.S.: Cooperation and Hurdles." *Frontline* 23, no. 15 (July 29–August 11, 2006), http://www.flonnet.com/fl2315/stories/20060811003211200 .htm.

Raman, B. *Madrid Impressions 1: Pakistan, The Nuclear Walmart.* South Asia Analysis Group Paper no. 1303, March 25, 2005, http://www.saag.org/%5Cpapers14 %5Cpaper1303.html.

Rauf, Tariq. "The April 1998 NPT PrepCom." *Nonproliferation Review* 5, no. 2 (Winter 1998): 121–31.

———. "Successes of the Nuclear Non-Proliferation Regime: Curbing the Spread of Nuclear Weapons." Discussion at Vienna International Centre, October 8, 1999.

———. "An Unequivocal Success? Implications of the NPT Review Conference." *Arms Control Today* 30, no. 6 (July/August 2000): 9–16.

Rauf, Tariq, and John Simpson. "The 1999 NPT PrepCom." *Nonproliferation Review* 6, no. 2 (Winter 1999): 118–33.

Record, Francis. "U.S. Nonproliferation Strategy: Policies and Technical Capabilities." Testimony before the Bureau of International Security and Nonproliferation, House International Relations Committee, Subcommittee on Oversight and Investigations, July 20, 2006, http://www.state.gov/t/isn/rls/rm/82125.htm.

Rice, Condoleezza. "Remarks on the Second Anniversary of the Proliferation Security Initiative." May 31, 2005, http://www.state.gov/secretary/rm/2005/46951.htm.

Riedel, Bruce. *American Diplomacy and the 1999 Kargil Summit at Blair House.* Center for the Advanced Study of India Policy Paper, 2002, http://www.ccc.nps.navy.mil/ research/kargil/reidel.pdf.

Rifaat, Ahmed. *International Aggression: A Study of the Legal Concept.* Stockholm: Almquist and Wiksell, 1979.

Rioux, Jean-François, ed. *Limiting the Proliferation of Weapons: The Role of Supply-Side Strategies.* Ottawa: Carleton University Press, 1992.

Ritter, Scott. *Iraq Confidential.* New York: Nation Books, 2005.

Rivasseau, François. Statement. Third session of the Preparatory Committee for the 2005 Review Conference of the Parties to the Treaty on the Non-Proliferation of Nuclear Weapons, cluster I, New York, April 29, 2004.

Roberts, Brad. "Export Controls and Biological Weapons: New Roles, New Challenges." *Critical Review in Microbiology* 24, no. 3 (Fall 1998): 235–54.

Robinson, Julian Perry. *The Rise of CB Weapons.* Stockholm: SIPRI, 1971.

———. *CB Weapons Today.* Stockholm: SIPRI, 1973.

———. "The Impact of Pugwash on the Debates over Chemical and Biological Weapons." In *Scientific Cooperation, State Conflict: The Roles of Scientists in Mitigating International Discord,* edited by Allison L. C. de Cerreño and Alexander Keynan, 224–52. New York: New York Academy of Sciences, 1998.

———. "The General Purpose Criterion and the New Utility of Toxicants as Weapons." Paper presented at the 15th workshop of the Pugwash Study Group on Implementation of the CBW Conventions, Oegstgeest, the Netherlands, June 23–24, 2001.

———. "Disabling Chemical Weapons: A Documented Chronology of Events." Paper for private distribution, Harvard-Sussex Program, November 1, 2003.

Roffey, Roger. "Biological Weapons and Potential Indicators of Offensive Biological Weapon Activities." In *SIPRI Yearbook 2004: Armaments, Disarmament and International Security,* 557–71. Oxford: Oxford University Press, 2004.

Rosand, Eric. "The Security Council as 'Global Legislator': *Ultra Vires* or Ultra Innovative?" *Fordham International Law Journal* 28, no. 3 (2005): 542–90.

Rosecrance, Richard N. *Action and Reaction in World Politics.* Boston: Little, Brown, 1963.

Rosenne, Shabtai. *The Law and Practice of the International Court.* 2nd ed. Dordrecht: Martinus Nijhoff, 1985.

Sagan, Scott. "Why Do States Build Nuclear Weapons? Three Models in Search of a Bomb." *International Security* 21, no. 3 (Winter 1996/97): 54–86.

Sagan, Scott, and Kenneth N. Waltz, eds. *The Spread of Nuclear Weapons: A Debate Renewed.* 2nd ed. New York: W. W. Norton, 2003.

Salander, Henrik. "On the 2002 NPT Preparatory Committee." Interview conducted by William Potter, Mary Beth Nikitin, and Tariq Rauf. *Nonproliferation Review* 9, no. 2 (Summer 2002): 1–14, http://cns.miis.edu/pubs/npr/vol09/92/92sala.pdf.

Sam Nunn Bank of America Policy Forum. *Executive Summary: Globalization, Technology Trade and American Leadership: A New Strategy for the 21st Century.* Athens: University of Georgia, March 2000.

Sanders, Ben, and George Bunn. "A New View of Review." Programme for Promoting Nuclear Non-Proliferation (PPNN). Issue Review no. 6, September 1996.

Saunders, Phillip C. *Preliminary Analysis of Chinese Missile Technology Export Control List.* James Martin Center for Nonproliferation Studies, Monterey Institute of International Studies, September 6, 2002, http://cns.miis.edu/cns/projects/eanp/pubs/prc_msl.pdf.

Scheur, Michael. *Imperial Hubris: Why the West Is Losing the War on Terror.* Washington, DC: Brassey's, 2004.

Schmidt, Fritz. "The Zangger Committee: Its History and Future Role." *Nonproliferation Review* 2, no. 3 (Fall 1994): 38–44.

———. "NPT Export Controls and the Zangger Committee." *Nonproliferation Review* 7, no. 3 (Fall/Winter 2000): 136–45.

Schneider, Barry R. *Future War and Counterproliferation: U.S. Military Responses to NBC Proliferation Threats.* Westport, CT: Praeger, 1999.

Schwarzbach, David A. *Iran's Nuclear Program: Energy or Weapons?* Natural Resources Defense Council, September 7, 1995.

Shaker, Mohamed I. *The Nuclear Non-Proliferation Treaty: Origin and Implementation, 1959–1969.* Vol. 1. London: Oceana, 1980.

Shono, Naomi. *The Legacy of Hiroshima: Its Past, Our Future.* Tokyo: Kosei, 1986.

Shuford, J. L. "President's Forum: Creating a Thousand-Ship Navy." *Naval War College Review* 59, no. 3 (Summer 2006): 17–21.

Shulman, Mark R. *The Proliferation Security Initiative as a New Paradigm for Peace and Security.* Carlisle Barracks, PA: Strategic Studies Institute, U.S. Army War College, April 2006.

Simma, Bruno, ed. *The Charter of the United Nations.* 2nd ed. Oxford: Oxford University Press, 2002.

Simpson, John. "The 1990 Review Conference of the Nuclear Non-Proliferation Treaty: Pointer to the Future or Diplomatic Accident." *Round Table,* no. 318 (April 1991): 139–54.

———. "The Nuclear Non-Proliferation Regime after the NPT Review and Extension Conference." In *SIPRI Yearbook 1996: Armaments, Disarmament, and International Security,* 561–89. Oxford: Oxford University Press, 1996.

———. "The Consequences of the 1997 PrepCom and Their Implications for the Review Process." In *South East Asia: Regional Security and Nuclear Non-Proliferation.* Southampton, UK: Mountbatten Centre for International Studies, Programme for Promoting Nuclear Non-Proliferation, 1997.

———. "The 2000 NPT Review Conference." In *SIPRI Yearbook 2001: Armaments, Disarmament and International Security,* 487–502. Oxford: Oxford University Press, 2001.

———. "The Nuclear Landscape in 2004: Past, Present and Future." Weapons of Mass Destruction Commission paper no. 3, 2004, http://www.wmdcommission.org/files/No3.pdf.

Simpson, John, and Darryl Howlett, eds. *The Future of Nuclear Non-Proliferation: Issues at the 1995 NPT Review and Extension Conference.* Programme for Promoting Nuclear Non-Proliferation study 6. Southampton, UK: Mountbatten Centre for International Studies, University of Southampton, 1995.

———. *The Future of the Non-Proliferation Treaty* (New York: St. Martin's Press, 1995).

Simpson, John, and Jenny Nielsen. *The NPT and Nuclear Sharing.* Southampton, UK: Mountbatten Centre for International Studies. N.d., http://www.mcis.soton.ac.uk.

———. "Fiddling While Rome Burns? The 2004 Session of the PrepCom for the 2005 Review Conference." *Nonproliferation Review* 11, no. 2 (Summer 2004): 1–26.

———. "The 2005 NPT Review Conference: Mission Impossible?" *Nonproliferation Review* 12, no. 2 (Summer 2005): 271–301.

Sims, Nicholas. *The Diplomacy of Biological Disarmament: Vicissitudes of a Treaty in Force, 1975–1985.* Basingstoke, UK: Macmillan, 1988.

Sinha, Samrat. *Major Terrorist Attacks in India (2000–2006).* Institute of Peace and Conflict Studies special report 27, New Delhi. July 2006, http://www.ipcs.org/IPCS-Special-Report-27.pdf.

Sirohi, Seema. "Hyphen Begone!" *Outlook*, March 2, 2004, http://www.hvk.org/articles/0304/48.html.

Smarto, Carrie. "MPC&A Site Operations and Sustainability: A Policy Overview." Paper presented at the 40th annual meeting of the Institute of Nuclear Material Management, July 27, 1999.

Smith, Derek D. *Deterring America: Rogue States and Weapons of Mass Destruction*. New York: Cambridge University Press, 2006.

Smith, Ron, and Bernard Udis. "New Challenges to Arms Export Control: Whither Wassenaar?" *Nonproliferation Review* 8, no. 2 (Summer 2001): 81–92.

Smithson, Amy E. "Separating Fact from Fiction: The Australia Group and the Chemical Weapons Convention." Occasional paper no. 34, Henry L. Stimson Center, March 1997.

———. *Toxic Archipelago: Preventing Proliferation from the Former Soviet Chemical and Biological Weapons Complex*. Report no. 32, Henry L. Stimson Center, December 1999, http://www.stimson.org/cbw/pdf/toxicarch.pdf.

Snyder, Glenn H. "The Balance of Power and the Balance of Terror." In *The Balance of Power*, edited by Paul Seabury, 198–99. San Francisco: Chandler, 1965.

Solana, Javier. *A Secure Europe in a Better World*. December 12, 2003, http://ue.eu.int/uedocs/cmsUpload/78367.pdf.

Soltanieh, A. A. "Statement by the Resident Representative of the Islamic Republic of Iran to the IAEA." Vienna, February 2, 2006, http://www.iaea.org/NewsCenter/Focus/IaeaIran/index.shtml.

Spear, Joanna. "The Emergence of a European 'Strategic Personality.'" *Arms Control Today* 33, no. 9 (November 2003): 13–18.

Spector, Leonard S. *Nuclear Ambitions*. Boulder, CO: Westview Press, 1990.

———. "Repentant Nuclear Proliferants." *Foreign Policy*, no. 88 (Fall 1992): 21–37.

Speier, Richard. "A Nuclear Nonproliferation Treaty for Missiles?" In *Fighting Proliferation: New Concerns for the Nineties*, edited by Henry Sokolski. Maxwell Air Force Base, AL: Air University Press, 1996.

———. "Can the Missile Technology Control Regime Be Repaired?" In *Repairing the Regime: Preventing the Spread of Weapons of Mass Destruction*, edited by Joseph Cirincione and Kathleen Newland, 205–16. New York: Routledge and the Carnegie Endowment for International Peace, 2000.

———. *How Effective Is the MTCR?* Proliferation Brief 4, no. 7, Carnegie Endowment for International Peace, April 12, 2001, http://www.carnegieendowment.org/publications/index.cfm?fa=view&id=672&prog=zgp&proj=znpp.

Squassoni, Sharon. *Weapons of Mass Destruction: Trade between North Korea and Pakistan*. Congressional Research Service Report for Congress, March 11, 2004, http://fpc.state.gov/documents/organization/30781.pdf.

———. *Globalizing Cooperative Threat Reduction: A Survey of Options*. Congressional Research Service Report for Congress, July 2, 2004, http://www.fas.org/spp/starwars/crs/RL32359.pdf.

Srivastava, Anupam, and Seema Gahlaut. "Curbing Proliferation from Emerging Suppliers: Export Controls in India and Pakistan." *Arms Control Today* 33, no. 7 (September 2003): 12–16.

———. "The New Energy in the US-India Relationship." *Defense and Security Analyses* 22, no. 4 (December 2006): 353–72.

Stern, Jessica E. "U.S. Assistance Programs for Improving MPC&A in the Former Soviet Union." *Nonproliferation Review* 26, no. 7 (Winter 1996): 17–32.

Strulak, Tadeusz. "The Nuclear Suppliers Group," *Nonproliferation Review* 1, no. 1 (Fall 1993): 2–10.

Stützle, Walther, Bhupendra Jasani, and Regina Cowen, eds. *The ABM Treaty: To Defend or Not to Defend?* Oxford: Oxford University Press, 1987.

Suzuki, Motoshi. "Economic Interdependence, Relative Gains, and International Cooperation: The Case of Monetary Policy Coordination." *International Studies Quarterly* 38, no. 3 (September 1994): 475–98.

Swibel, Mathew. "Trading with the Enemy." *Forbes*, April 12, 2004, 86–93, http://www.forbes.com/free_forbes/2004/0412/086.html.

Tajvidi, Ali. "'Rogue State' versus 'The Great Arrogance.'" *CSD Bulletin* 5, no. 1 (Autumn 1997): 7. http://www.wmin.ac.uk/sshl/page-114.

Talbott, Strobe. *Engaging India: Diplomacy, Democracy, and the Bomb.* Washington, DC: Brookings Institution Press, 2004.

Talmon, Stefan. "The Security Council as World Legislature." *American Journal of International Law* 99, no. 1 (January 2005): 175–93.

Tellis, Ashley. *Atoms for War? U.S.-Indian Civilian Nuclear Cooperation and India's Nuclear Arsenal.* Carnegie Endowment Report, June 2006.

Tellis, Ashley J., C. Christine Fair, and Jamison Jo Medby. *Limited Conflicts under the Nuclear Umbrella: Indian and Pakistani Lessons from the Kargil Crisis.* Santa Monica, CA: RAND, 2001.

Tenet, George J. "Worldwide Threat—Converging Dangers in a Post-9/11 World." Testimony of the Director of Central Intelligence before the Senate Select Committee on Intelligence, 107th Cong., 2nd sess., February 6, 2002, https://www.cia.gov/news-information/speeches-testimony/2002/senate_select_hearing_03192002.html.

———. "The Worldwide Threat in 2003: Evolving Dangers in a Complex World." Testimony before the Senate Select Committee on Intelligence, February 11, 2003, https://www.cia.gov/news-information/speeches-testimony/2003/dci_speech_02112003.html.

———. "The Worldwide Threat 2004: Challenges in a Changing Global Context." Testimony of Director of Central Intelligence George J. Tenet before the Senate Select Committee on Intelligence, February 24, 2004, https://www.cia.gov/news-information/speeches-testimony/2004/dci_speech_02142004.html .

Trevan, Tim. *Saddam's Secrets: The Hunt for Iraq's Hidden Weapons.* London: HarperCollins, 1999.

Tucker, Jonathan B. "Case Studies of Bioterrorism." Presentation to class in the Johns Hopkins University's Homeland Security Certificate Program, September 29, 2005.

———. *War of Nerves: Chemical Warfare from World War I to al Qaeda.* New York: Pantheon, 2006.

Utgoff, Victor, ed. *The Coming Crisis: Nuclear Proliferation, U.S. Interests, and World Order.* BCSIA Studies in International Security. Cambridge, MA: MIT Press, 2000.

Waltz, Kenneth N. "More May Be Better." In *The Spread of Nuclear Weapons: A Debate Renewed*, edited by Scott Sagan and Kenneth N. Waltz, 3–45. New York: W. W. Norton, 2003.

Webster, Daniel. *The Papers of Daniel Webster: Diplomatic Papers. Vol. 1, 1841–1843.* Edited by Kenneth E. Shewmaker. Hanover, NH: University Press of New England, 1983.

Weinberger, Sharon. "Export Control Changes Will Address Old Issues, New Threats, Says DOD Official," *Aerospace Daily*, March 22, 2002.

Winner, Andrew C. "The Proliferation Security Initiative: The New Face of Interdiction." *Washington Quarterly* 28, no. 2 (Spring 2005): 129–43.

Wisconsin Project on Nuclear Arms Control. "Pakistan: U.S. Approves Most Nuclear-Related Exports." *Risk Report* 1, no. 6 (July/August 1995), http://www.wisconsinproject .org/countries/pakistan/usapproves.htm.

———. "Pakistan: Nuclear Helpers." N.d., http://www.wisconsinproject.org/countries/ pakistan/nukehelpers.htm.

Wood, Thomas W., Matthew D. Milazzo, Barbara A. Reichmuth, and Jeff Bedell. "The Economics of Energy Independence for Iran." Paper issued by Pacific Northwest National Laboratory and Los Alamos National Laboratory, April 2006.

Woolf, Amy F. *Nonproliferation and Threat Reduction Assistance: U.S. Programs in the Former Soviet Union.* Congressional Research Service Report for Congress, updated April 6, 2006, http://fpc.state.gov/documents/organization/66455.pdf.

Wulf, Norman A. "Observations from the 2000 NPT Review Conference." *Arms Control Today* 30, no. 9 (November 2000): 3–9.

Yuan, Jing-dong, Phillip C. Saunders, and Stephanie Lieggi. "Recent Developments in China's Export Controls: New Regulations and New Challenges." *Nonproliferation Review* 9, no. 3 (Fall/Winter 2002): 153–67.

Zanders, Jean Pascal, Melissa Hersh, Jacqueline Simon, and Maria Wahlberg. "Chemical and Biological Weapon Developments and Arms Control." *SIPRI Yearbook 2001: Armaments, Disarmament and International Security.* Oxford: Oxford University Press, 2001.

Zilinskas, Raymond. "Cuban Allegations of Biological Warfare by the United States: Assessing the Evidence." *Critical Reviews in Microbiology* 25, no. 3 (1999): 173–228.

Zvedre, Yevgeny. "The U.S.-Russian Nonproliferation Dialogue: The Iranian Factor and Export Control Cooperation." *Yaderny Kontrol Digest* 5, no. 3 (Summer 2000).

Contributor Biographies

Dr. Ian Anthony is a project leader and research coordinator at the Stockholm International Peace Research Institute. He is the project leader for SIPRI's Non-proliferation and Export Control Project and the Internet Database on European Export Controls Project. He has authored and edited numerous books and SIPRI studies, including *Reforming Nuclear Export Controls: The Future of the Nuclear Suppliers Group* (2007); *A Future Arms Control Agenda: Proceedings of Nobel Symposium 118, 1999* (2001); and *Russia and the Arms Trade* (1998).

Dr. Michael D. Beck is Associate Director of the International Center for Democratic Governance (ICDG) at the Carl Vinson Institute of Government at the University of Georgia (UGA). Prior to joining ICDG he served as executive director of UGA's Center for International Trade and Security. His research focuses on illicit weapons trade and international efforts to control such trade. He is coauthor of *To Supply or to Deny: Comparing Nonproliferation Export Controls in Five Key Countries* (2003).

M. Elaine Bunn is a senior research fellow at the Institute for National Strategic Studies (INSS) at the National Defense University and director of INSS's Future Strategic Concepts Program. Before joining INSS, she held a number of policy management and analysis positions in the Office of the Secretary of Defense, including principal director of nuclear forces and missile defense policy. Her awards include the Defense Medal for Distinguished Civilian Service and the Medal for Meritorious Civilian Service.

Dr. Nathan E. Busch is Associate Professor of Government at Christopher Newport University, where he teaches courses in international relations, U.S. foreign policy, and WMD proliferation. He is author of *No End in Sight: The Continuing Menace of Nuclear Proliferation* (2004).

Vitaly Fedchenko is a researcher at the Stockholm International Peace Research Institute (SIPRI). His research focuses on EU cooperative threat reduction programs, energy security, and nonproliferation. He is coauthor of *Reforming Nuclear Export Controls: The Future of the Nuclear Suppliers Group* (2007).

Dr. Charles D. Ferguson is a fellow in the science and technology program at the Council on Foreign Relations. He is also an adjunct assistant professor in the School of Foreign Service at Georgetown University and an adjunct lecturer at Johns Hopkins University. He has authored and coauthored numerous publications on nuclear safety and WMD terrorism, including *The Four Faces of Nuclear Terrorism* (2005); *Commercial Radioactive Sources: Surveying the Security Risks*; and the Council on Foreign Relations special report *Preventing Catastrophic Nuclear Terrorism*.

Brian Finlay is a senior associate at the Henry L. Stimson Center and currently serves as codirector of the Cooperative Threat Reduction Project. He is the author of numerous publications on national security issues, including *Securing Russia's Loose Nukes: Progress since 9-11*, and is coeditor of *Ultimate Security: Combating Weapons of Mass Destruction* (2003).

Dr. Seema Gahlaut is the director of training and outreach at the Center for International Trade and Security and adjunct faculty at the School of Public and International Affairs at the University of Georgia. Dr. Gahlaut is the coeditor of *Engaging India: U.S. Strategic Relations with the World's Largest Democracy* (1999).

Dr. Bates Gill is the director of the Stockholm International Peace Research Institute and a specialist in East Asian foreign policy and politics. Prior to his position at SIPRI, he was Freeman Chair in China Studies at the Center for Strategic and International Studies. Dr. Gill is author of numerous books and articles, including, most recently, *Rising Star: China's New Security Diplomacy* (2007) and *Contrasting Visions: United States, China, and World Order* (2006).

John Hart is the head of the Chemical and Biological Warfare Programme (Non-proliferation and Export Control Project) at the Stockholm International Peace Research Institute. He has authored and contributed to numerous publications, including *The Historical Dictionary of Nuclear, Biological and Chemical Warfare* (2007) and *Deadly Cultures: Biological Weapons since 1945* (2006).

Dr. James R. Holmes is an associate professor at the Naval War College and specializes in U.S. national security strategy, homeland security, nuclear nonproliferation, and maritime strategy. He is author or coauthor of numerous books and articles, including *Theodore Roosevelt and World Order: Police Power in International Relations* (2005) and *Asia Looks Seaward: Power and Maritime Strategy* (2007).

Dr. Scott A. Jones is a senior research associate at the Center for International Trade and Security at the University of Georgia and director of the Center's Export Control Programs. He has published widely on export control issues, authoring *The Evolution of the Ukrainian Export Control System: State Building and International Cooperation* (2002) and coediting *To Supply or To Deny: Nonproliferation Export Controls in Five Key Countries* (2003) and *Crossroads and Conflict: Security and Foreign Policy in the Caucasus and Central Asia* (1999).

Daniel H. Joyner is Associate Professor of Law at the University of Alabama School of Law. He is the editor of *Non-Proliferation Export Controls: Origins, Challenges and Proposals for Strengthening* (2006) and the author of *International Law and the Proliferation of Weapons of Mass Destruction* (2008).

Dr. Joseph F. Pilat is a Senior Advisor in the National Security Office at the Los Alamos National Laboratory. He has written numerous articles and opinion pieces for U.S. and European scholarly journals and newspapers and is the author or editor of many books, including *Ecological Politics: The Rise of the Green Movement* (1980); *1995: A New Beginning for the NPT?* (1995); and, most recently, *Atoms for Peace: A Future after Fifty Years?* (2007).

Dr. Jonathan D. Pollack is Professor of Asian and Pacific Studies and a former chairman of the Strategic Research Department at the U.S. Naval War College, where he also directs the college's Asia-Pacific Studies Group. Prior to this he served as Senior Advisor for International Policy at the RAND Corporation. He is author and editor of numerous books and RAND studies, including *Korea: The East Asian Pivot* (2006) and *Strategic Surprise? U.S.-China Relations in the Early Twenty-first Century* (2004).

Dr. Mitchell B. Reiss is director of the Wendy and Emery Reves Center for International Studies and vice provost for international affairs at the College of William and Mary. He has served in numerous positions in the U.S. government, including as director of policy planning at the U.S. State Department (2003–4) and member of the National Security Council at the White House. He is author of *Bridled Ambition: Why Countries Constrain Their Nuclear Capabilities* (1995) and *Without the Bomb: The Politics of Nuclear Non-Proliferation* (1988). He has contributed to nine other volumes and written over fifty articles on international security and arms control issues.

Dr. Julian Perry Robinson is the director of the Sussex end of the Harvard-Sussex Program on Chemical and Biological Warfare Armament and Arms Limitation, and since 1988 he has been coediting the *CBW Conventions Bulletin*. Since 1967, he has published or presented some 420 papers and monographs, including much of the six-volume SIPRI study *The Problem of Chemical and Biological Warfare* (1971–76); *NATO Chemical Weapons Policy and Posture* (1986); and *The Problem of Chemical-Weapon Proliferation in the 1990s* (1991).

Dr. John Simpson is director of the Mountbatten Centre for International Studies at the University of Southampton. He is an expert of international standing on the evolution of the Nuclear Nonproliferation Treaty (NPT) and other international mechanisms to prevent nuclear proliferation. He has authored and edited numerous books including, most recently, *Deterrence and the New Security Environment* (2006). He was awarded the OBE (Order of the British Empire) in 1999 for services to nuclear nonproliferation.

Sharon Squassoni is a senior associate in the Nonproliferation program at the Carnegie Endowment for International Peace and has been analyzing nonproliferation, arms control, and national security issues for two decades. Prior to her position at Carnegie, she was a specialist in national defense issues with the Congressional Research Service. She has contributed to journals, magazines, and books on nuclear proliferation and defense.

Dr. Elizabeth Turpen is a senior associate and codirector of the Security for a New Century and Cooperative Threat Reduction projects at the Henry L. Stimson Center. Prior to her position at the Stimson Center, she worked as a legislative aid for Senator Pete V. Domenici (R-NM) on defense, nonproliferation, and foreign affairs. She is coauthor of *Policy Matters: Educating Congress on Peace and Security* (2004).

Dr. Andrew C. Winner is Professor of Strategic Studies in the Strategic Research Department at the Naval War College, Newport, Rhode Island. His areas of focus are South Asia, nonproliferation, maritime strategy, the Middle East, and U.S. national security strategy. In addition to academic and consulting positions, he served over a decade in the U.S. Department of State's Bureau of Political-Military Affairs.

Index

Books in the series

Studies in Security and International Affairs

From Superpower to Besieged Global Power: Restoring World Order after the Failure of the Bush Doctrine
Edward A. Kolodziej and Roger E. Kanet, eds.

Combating Weapons of Mass Destruction: The Future of International Nonproliferation Policy
Nathan E. Busch and Daniel H. Joyner, eds.

Nonproliferation Norms: Why States Choose Nuclear Restraint
Maria Rost Rublee

LaVergne, TN USA
23 June 2010
187172LV00003B/2/P